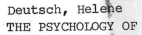

The Psychology of Women

VOLUME ONE

The Psychology
of Women

A PSYCHOANALYTIC INTERPRETATION

By

HELENE DEUTSCH, M.D.

Associate Psychiatrist, Massachusetts General Hospital
Lecturer, Boston Psychoanalytic Institute

Foreword by

STANLEY COBB, M.D.

Bullard Professor of Neuropathology
Harvard University

VOLUME ONE

GRUNE & STRATTON

NEW YORK

1944

First printing, April 1944
Second printing, May 1944
Third printing, August 1944
Fourth printing, December 1944
Fifth printing, January 1945
Sixth printing, April 1945
Seventh printing, September 1945
Eighth printing, July 1946
Ninth printing, June 1947
Tenth printing, October 1948
Eleventh printing, April 1950
Twelfth printing, October 1950
Thirteenth printing, January 1954
Fourteenth printing, October 1958
Fifteenth printing, May 1962
Sixteenth printing, February 1965
Seventeenth printing, September 1967
Eighteenth printing, August 1971

GRUNE & STRATTON, INC.
757 Third Avenue, New York, New York 10017

Library of Congress Catalog Card Number   44-5287
International Standard Book Number   0-8089-0115-X

Printed in the United States of America (U-B)

Contents

Foreward

THE study of psychology takes many forms. This is legitimate and necessary because human psychology is the study of man's behavior, motives, and feelings, i. e., the study of his most complex neurophysiological mechanisms. Some investigators experiment on animals and apply the general conclusions more or less reasonably to similar phenomena in man (Cannon, Pavlov, Lashley); others construct tests to be used on man, to measure roughly certain forms of human behavior, and by great numbers of observations learn what is the "norm" and and what is "abnormal" response (Binet, Rorschach, Murray, McKinley). Recently analysis of mental abilities by batteries of performance tests, mathematically analyzed, has given "factor analysis" an important place in human psychology (Spearman, Thurstone). Many other methods might be mentioned, most of them aimed at general conceptions. The clinical approach is at the other end of the scale, for it is primarily concerned with the individual, and unique. From these observations, generalizations can eventually be drawn, but it takes longer to accumulate valid data. Nevertheless the great value of such a clinical method as psychoanalysis is that it attacks directly the question one wishes so much to answer: Why do people act that way? The crying need of our generation is for insight into the human nature, the behavior of man.

What French calls "the clinical approach to the dynamics of behavior" is as old as the art of writing, but Freud made it a medical discipline. In so far as it is disciplined, in so far as it makes careful observations, and tests and retests theories, it is already a science. One need not bother with the intellectual snobs who would keep the term "science" for laboratory "gadgeteering." First approximations, if honest, are just as "scientific" as final determination. On the other hand, the clinical psychiatrist has no right to say, as some do, that nothing can ever be learned about the mind by anatomical, chemical, and physiological methods. Much has been learned in these ways, and there is more to come. The clinical approach, however, remains for the physician the most direct and rewarding method.

Anyone reading this book will realize that Helene Deutsch has great knowledge of what women do and great insight into why they do it. Her data are the hundreds of cases she has seen; her approach is intuitive (which to me merely means that she has seen so much that she recognizes situations via mental short-cuts). Her postulates are those of Freud, some of which she has modified.

Here is a book based on experience, the experience of "feeling as one's own" the emotions of a great number of girls and women. In her role as counsellor for many girls in difficulties, as psychoanalyst for a great many women suffering from neurosis, and as hospital psychiatrist, Dr. Deutsch has had an extraordinary clinical opportunity to observe the behavior of women of all ages and sorts. Trained by Freud and working closely with him for years, she speaks the psychoanalytical language; but with her, understanding always comes first, with interpretation and theory following in secondary roles.

She understands and vividly reports how adolescent girls act, and this throws light on some of the troubles the police are now having with "wayward schoolgirls." The developmental treatment of the subject emphasizes how the adult attributes of femininity may be logical consequences of early reactions. The role of emotion is most important; women seem to put more emotion into their life interests than men, hence their ability to observe and remember minutiae is greater. From this may arise intuition, "the most striking characteristic of woman." These are just a few of the stimulating ideas I get from the book. There are, of course, points of philosophy and methodology incompatible with my own way of thinking, but they are details. The book is a real contribution, a great storehouse of information about feminine psychology. It is important to all of us, whether we happen to be parents, teachers, authors, or psychiatrists.

STANLEY COBB

Boston, February, 1944

Preface

From the beginning of my psychoanalytic work, my investigations have been centered on the problems of feminine psychology. Earlier results of these studies were published in a book entitled *Psychoanalysis of the Sexual Functions of Women*.[1] The purpose of this book was to present a systematic picture of female instinctual development and its relation to the reproductive function. I was fully aware that the empiric data of this publication were insufficient and intended to supply further material in a subsequent publication. Since then I have continued to make observations and to gather material and have from time to time presented the results of these observations in various publications. I feel that it is now necessary to restate my previous views in the light of this long experience, to reassert those which have stood the test of later investigations, and to correct or discard those which have proved inadequate.

Many ideas expressed in my previous book have been taken up by other authors and supplemented and enriched by new observations. The work which I am now presenting will supplement the previous one not only with my own experiences, but also with contributions made by other writers, above all by Freud in his later publications concerning the psychology of women.

Several of the problems of femininity discussed here have given rise to lively debate. These differences of opinion were often based on misunderstanding and vagueness of definition, as for example in relation to the psychologic concepts of "active-masculine" and "passive-feminine." These concepts were directly applied to the energy of the sexual instincts and this led to a confusion of psychologic and biologic phenomena.

[1] Deutsch, H.: Psychoanalyse der weiblichen Sexualfunktionen. Vienna: Internat. Psychoanal. Verlag, 1925.

ix

The criticism and insistence that these spheres should not be confused is fully justified.

On the other hand, there is an increasingly strong tendency to explain the differentiated psychologic behavior of the sexes on the basis of educational and cultural factors and to reduce the part played by biologic and anatomic factors to a minimum. Psychoanalysis has never denied that the social milieu is of the utmost importance, that it both creates problems and determines how they are to be solved. The final chapter of the present book deals with this question and discusses the psychoanalytic conception of feminine psychology in the light of social conditions.

Although psychoanalytic psychology was originally built upon the theory of the instincts, its foundations have been greatly broadened. The instinct of self-preservation, the instinct of aggression, and the death instinct have been differentiated from the sexual instincts, and psychoanalytic research is turning with increasing interest to the psychology of the ego. In this book the psychoanalytic theory of the instincts is used to illuminate the biologic background from which the psychologic personality of woman emerges. While the social milieu on the one hand, and the biologic factors on the other, have determining importance in relation to the psychologic manifestations, emphasis is placed here on the individual emotional experiences and the conflicts connected with them. They cannot be reduced to either the biologic or the sociologic influences, although there is a constant interplay between these factors.

The purpose of this book is to explain the normal psychic life of women and their normal conflicts. We know that degree of psychic health is not determined by the absence of conflicts, but by the adequacy of the methods used to solve and master them. Pathology reveals the normal conflicts and helps us to understand normal processes in the light of morbid ones. Most psychoanalytic contributions to normal psychology have been made through the medium of pathology. For the study of feminine psychology, neurotic behavior is particularly rich in implications. For this reason, case histories of neuroses are frequently cited here as evidence: the phenomena they portray, although not "normal," often represent only a distortion or quantitative intensification of the "normal," and thus can provide a kind of macroscopic insight into things that psychoanalysis deals with microscopically.

Psychoanalysis has often been reproached for using only a relatively small number of technical terms to describe the extreme complexity of psychic life, and for always reducing the most varied manifestations to a unique dynamic process. The kind of evidence with which its theories are supported has been characterized as lacking in objectivity.

The first reproach originates from a misconception of the task that psychoanalysis set for itself at the beginning. This task was to trace psychologic manifestations back to their source, to discover the interconnection of all psychic phenomena, and to reveal their common origin in definite instinctual tendencies. But such an effort at simplification and generalization is not peculiar to psychoanalysis. It is the fundamental goal of all scientific research, and in psychoanalysis it represents the sum of insights gained empirically.

The second reproach—that psychoanalysis cannot support its theories with direct objective data, as experimental sciences can—is perfectly in order. Yet, despite this defect, psychoanalysis has been able to explore a dark region of the soul that has always been—and probably will always remain—inaccessible to more objective study. Today, however, it is possible for psychoanalysis to surmount this shortcoming to some degree. Because of the biologic character of the psychoanalytic theory of the instincts, its application to somatic processes is proving increasingly fruitful, and discoveries relating to the interdependence of organic and psychic factors have changed our conception of both, pointing to the presence of a common denominator. The relatively objective procedures employed in the study of somatic problems increases the possibility of also achieving greater objectivity in the analysis of psychologic factors.

The material used in this book is not restricted to my personal observations in the course of psychoanalytic therapy. It is taken from case and life histories recorded by other observers—physicians and social workers—not prejudiced in favor of any psychologic theory. Routine hospital records proved a particularly valuable source of information. It goes without saying that I used these when I considered them to be reliable and when I could check them through personal contact with the patients involved. Another part of my material is taken from the files of various social agencies.

This attempt at objectivity will not convince the prejudiced. As Freud[2] somewhat humorously says: "Throughout the ages, the problem of woman has puzzled people of every kind—you too will have pondered over this question in so far as you are men. From the women among you that is not to be expected, for you are the riddle yourselves." However, woman's desire to solve the riddle of her own ego, her introspective contemplation of her own psyche, her capacity for identification with other women, are positive factors that can abundantly compensate for a feminine observer's lesser degree of objectivity.

Very often instructive data for this book have been found in creative literature, which is less objective than clinical observation but all the more true because more inspired. After all, the ultimate goal of all research is not objectivity, but truth.

Because of the widely varied sources of the material and the continual necessity of deviating from the chronologic order of exposition, the individual chapters of the present book are perhaps less integrated than would be desirable. While the main theme and the sequence of the chapters were established

[2] FREUD, S.: Introductory lectures on psychoanalysis. Transl. by Joan Rivière. London: Allen & Unwin, 1929. P. 154.

from the outset, each chapter took on a life of its own in the course of the work. This repeatedly made it necessary to introduce considerations of a general nature in order to explain and round out a special subject. I hope that the material as a whole and the conception of the different problems involved have thus been unified, despite the repetition and overlapping unavoidable in such a procedure.

No special chapter has been devoted to the childhood of girls. In order to clarify the relationship between the psychology of the adult woman and that of the little girl, it seemed preferable to go back to the childhood phase in contextual relation with the special problems of adults.

A few words may be necessary to explain the organization of my material. I am dealing with three distinct although related themes. The first concerns the exposition of the psychologic life of woman, starting with the young girl's psychologic development into womanhood, a process that is physiologically completed with the onset of menstruation. In the course of this process the foundations of the feminine personality are laid: what I call "the feminine core" is definitely formed. The analysis of this feminine core is comprised in my second theme. A special chapter is devoted to each of the three essential traits of femininity—narcissism, passivity, and masochism, and the exposition of narcissism is combined with a description of the principal types of feminine women. But observation reveals the existence of types of women and modes of feminine behavior that seem to be at variance with our concept of femininity. My third theme is the analysis of this non-feminine aspect of femininity. Here I attempt to locate the feminine core beneath the surface even where psychologic or sexual behavior seems to contradict it or when social pressure compels women to assume "masculine" functions. The last three chapters deal with this problem.

Because of the abundance of the material, it seemed impossible to deal with the central problem of femininity—

motherhood—within the confines of one volume. Therefore the fundamental duality of womanhood was formally divided: the individual development and personality of woman is discussed in the first volume, and her role as servant of the species will be the subject of the second volume.

As the exposition of the psychologic life of woman in her reproductive function requires constant reference to the fundamental traits of femininity and to the psychologic development of girlhood, as defined in this study, the two parts are continuous. However, each of the two volumes, within the scope of its subject, is complete in itself.

I wish to acknowledge my gratitude to Mr. Norbert Guterman for his assistance in the editorial preparation of the book.

I am indebted to the publishers of the *Psychoanalytic Quarterly* for permission to quote two cases from my paper "On Female Homosexuality" (vol. 1, 1932).

HELENE DEUTSCH

Boston, January, 1944

CHAPTER ONE

Prepuberty

THE basic tenets of psychoanalysis were expounded by Sigmund Freud in his *Three Contributions to the Theory of Sex*.[1] From comprehensive and far reaching clinical observations of adult neurotics over a long period of time, he deduced the laws of sexual development in the child. Later, analysts of children working in various countries largely confirmed his findings by direct observations and gave us an insight into child psychology that goes far beyond Freud's original framework.

Freud's theory that the first phases of the child's development, the so-called pregenital, that is, the "oral" and "anal" phases, are the same in boys and girls, must be modified as a result of subsequent investigation. For while these phases give both sexes the same type of instinctual gratification, and the organic sources of the instincts as well as the person at the center of the instinct-gratifying environment, the mother, are the same for boys and girls, the objective observer can clearly distinguish sex differences despite these apparent identities.[2] The climax of this differentiation is reached in the so-called "phallic" phase. During this phase, the anatomic difference between the sexes, although previously noticed by the child, assumes a special significance. The little boy's pride in his male organ, his fears concerning it, the comparisons he makes between him-

---

[1] FREUD, S.: Three contributions to the theory of sex. New York: Nerv. & Ment. Dis. Pub. Co., 1910.

[2] I am aware of the controversy and confusion regarding the terms "instinctual" and "sexual," but retain them until a better terminology is convincingly established. Here the terms are used to denote the extragenital pleasure functions of the infant, which merge and interact with the alimentary, excretory, and other biologic functions. Such use of the word "instinctual" should not be interpreted as a denial of the existence and importance of other instincts.

self and other boys and girls, are his main interest. Parallel
processes take place in the little girl, but in her psychic life
pride is replaced by envy, and fear of loss by complicated emotional reactions connected with nonpossession. In both sexes
the emotional reactions relating to the genitals are usually
summed up in the term "castration complex."

The interest in the previously unexplored field of infantile
sexuality as discovered by Freud is now gradually giving place
to an interest in the development of the child's ego, and here
too there is a justifiable tendency to stress the difference between the sexes. At present, scientific interest in child psychology is focused on the methods of adjustment to reality and
the development of emotions and intelligence. Psychoanalysis
must be credited with having made a significant contribution
in this field too, through its discovery that important elements
in the psychologic development that seem to have nothing to
do with the sexual drives, can in the last analysis be traced to
them. Thus, the child's sexual curiosity, which, as we know,
reaches its greatest intensity during the "phallic" phase and is
manifested first of all in his preoccupation with the anatomic
difference between the sexes, contributes to the development of
a more general curiosity. This interest, sexual in its beginning,
continues in the sublimations of the so-called latency period.
Many social and intellectual forces of the maturing human being
develop out of the instincts of childhood; the process of adjustment to reality grows more and more active and reaches its
apex at the end of the latency period, in prepuberty.

We know that the child's freedom from sexual drives during the latency period is only relative; on the other hand,
there is no doubt that, conversely, the infantile phase preceding
it is not taken up exclusively with sexual development, and that
active adjustment to the environment, the drive to conquer it,
and many forces other than the sexual ones, are present in
the human child from the very beginning. During the latency
period, the child's interest in sexual matters largely subsides,
but does not disappear altogether. All the inner dynamics, all

the drives in this period of weakened sexual urges, can be used for the unhampered development of the ego. Training and education strengthen the ego in its struggle for liberation from infantile instinctual forces and further its adaptation to reality and its socialization. Within the framework of the family, the infantile ties are now freed from the dross of sexuality. Tenderness takes the place of erotic needs, activity that of infantile aggression, etc.

Psychoanalysis is par excellence an evolutionary theory, and even when it speaks of "thrusts" in the process of development, it refers to more or less revolutionary intensifications of evolutionary processes. Thus, when we call puberty a psychologic revolution, we are quite well aware that it is only a thrust forward from the previous evolutionary stages. It has become a cliché in psychoanalytic parlance to define puberty as a "new edition of the infantile period." But we have not paid sufficient attention to the preparatory activity upon which puberty completely depends, the prerevolutionary mood, so to speak, that prevails in the psyche during the period immediately preceding puberty, that is, in prepuberty.

I must confess that my information about these processes does not always have the full authority of direct personal observation. My sources are, first, women whom I have observed in the course of psychoanalytic treatment and whose behavior can be understood only as a direct continuation of prepuberty, and, second, many young girls of college age who have consulted a psychoanalyst about difficulties experienced in adapting themselves to their milieu, which requires them to be "free" and "modern." As a rule it is a conscious conflict, a feeling of helplessness, that induces them to consult a psychiatrist; but often they seek help as a result of anxiety states and inability to do their work. In the short psychotherapy I apply in such cases, I try first of all to obtain detailed information about the patient's puberty and prepuberty. Third there are direct clinical observations and a large number of records and case histories of young girls who have become psychically ill or presented educational difficulties during prepuberty. Often pathologic manifestations have given me an insight into normal processes. Fourth, and this is a far from negligible source, there are works of literature in which artistic intuition, often with striking clarity, has confirmed what we have painstakingly reconstructed by means of objective observations.

I define prepuberty as that last stage of the latency period in which certain harbingers of future sexual drives may be discerned, but which in the main is the period of greatest freedom from infantile sexuality. It is a phase in which sexual instincts are at their weakest and the development of the ego most intense. This definition is not entirely in accord with that given by other authors, for whom prepuberty is characterized by the intensified sexual needs that mark the onset of puberty. For the purposes of my exposition it has seemed preferable to consider this rise of sexuality as belonging to the subsequent phase of early puberty. I call prepuberty prerevolutionary because, as I shall demonstrate, the very forces that are summoned to combat the sexual drives in puberty are prepared in prepuberty, the period of greatest freedom from sexual urges. In this the human psyche is a wise government, forging its weapons before the aggressor appears.

It is difficult to state the exact age at which prepuberty, as I conceive it, occurs. The transition stages between the different phases are fluid, and attempts to construct and define a period of development too precisely lead to the error of drawing too sharp lines. However, so far no way has been found for eliminating this defect in method. I would suggest that we limit prepuberty to the years between the ages of 10 and 12, not forgetting the fact that its manifestations continue far into puberty, and, exactly as is the case with puberty itself, may even persist until the age of the climacterium. In varying degrees we all carry our infantilism, our prepuberty, and our puberty with us right into old age.

Much the easiest way to proceed would be to take as our starting point the physiologic developments, which throughout this phase of life are particularly important in determining psychologic developments, and to make the appearance of menstruation the boundary line between prepuberty and puberty. But our observation seems to show that although menstruation is the key to the struggles of puberty and has great significance in the young girl's psychology, we cannot draw an absolute parallel between physical and psychologic events. There are girls who menstruate before they reach psychologic puberty and others who enter upon psychologic puberty before the corresponding physical signs make their appearance. Similarly as regards the climacterium: there are tired old women who still menstruate and women who remain vigorous and youthful even after the physical climacterium has occurred.

In view of our conception of prepuberty, what do we consider typical of the girl in this phase? We all assume, as does Freud, that the young girl's development into womanhood is inaugurated by a sudden increase of passivity. In 1925,[3] I expressed the view that a "thrust of activity" precedes this increase of passivity. In my opinion, this thrust of activity is the principal characteristic of prepuberty. In this respect boys and girls are still the same, since in the boy also the last phase of the latency period is characterized by an intensification of activity. But the form and content of this activity are clearly differentiated in girls and boys, and give the prepuberty of girls a very specific character. I believe that the thrust of activity represents not an increase of aggression but rather an intensive process of *adaptation to reality* and of mastery of the environment made possible by the development of the ego. That this activity contains certain dangers for the future sexual development of the girl, i.e., for her future passivity, cannot be denied.

The intensified activity characteristic of prepuberty serves to mobilize the child's intellectual and artistic talents and his or her aspirations, affective hopes, new identification tendencies, etc. Its source lies in the inherent drive of the ego toward

[3] Op. cit.

growth and independence. From earliest infancy there exists
in all normal individuals an urge to grow up and achieve something. This drive is particularly strong in prepuberty, when
the young girl of 11 lives in a world situated between the past
and the future, between childhood and adulthood. A further
loosening of the affective ties of childhood and an increased
sense of responsibility and independence are also to be noted at
this period. The renunciation of infantile fantasy life is of the
greatest importance for the growing girl. This is principally
accomplished through the search for new object relationships,
that is, new objects to love, to hate, and with which to be
identified. The need to be recognized as an adult is great at
this time and the battle for such recognition is all the more acute
and painful because the young person in her insecurity and need
for protection has an unconscious desire to remain a child.

Thus the young girl launches an offensive against the environment, and her principal weapon is the effort to become adjusted
to it. This involves a "turn toward reality" that is another
characteristic of prepuberty, closely connected with the thrust
of activity.

A certain degree of ego strength must be attained before the
offensive can begin, but it is also true that activity and the
effort to master the environment serve to build up an ego
strength that brings the child closer to adulthood. There is a
physical analogy to this reciprocal psychologic relation: muscular activity implies possession of a certain degree of strength and
muscular development, but at the same time it increases
strength and furthers growth.

This offensive of prepuberty avails itself of various means;
these vary according to the child's milieu, education, and,
above all, psychologic history. The expressions of this turn
toward reality naturally have an individual character. The
events of early childhood, environmental influences, particular
talents—in other words, all the elements of the girl's disposition
and constitution—give this development its individual content.
Its form is determined by the cultural and social milieu.

In discussing personality formation in prepuberty, we shall turn our attention again and again to the problem of identification. The weaker the child's ego, the more it resorts to identification with adults in its adjustment to the adult world. This process is now more complicated than before. We often make the mistake of assuming that identification with the mother makes for "femininity" in the child's personality, and identification with the father for 'masculinity." We tend to forget that in the wide range of child-parent relationships developed in the course of childhood there is no one single consolidated idea of the mother or the father. There is a beloved mother, and a hated mother; a sublime ideal mother and a disreputable sexual one; a mother who has castrated the father and another who has been castrated by him; one who bears children and one who kills them; one who nourishes them, another who poisons them; there is the rival, and the personification of security and protection. Similarly, there are many different fathers creating a host of possibilities for identification. The choice of identification objects in prepuberty depends largely upon these earlier developments. The way in which the child resolved its conflicting feelings of ambivalence in earlier periods is also important. Much depends on whether identification with the loved objects is possible or whether the intensity of the child's own aggressive and intensive guilt feelings drives him or her to identification with a malign, punitive, suffering, or even dead object.

Each of these possibilities becomes stronger in this period of active searching for methods of strengthening the ego and influences the character of the child's prepuberty. Simultaneously, the tendency to abandon earlier identifications becomes noticeable. The young girl begins to be extremely critical of her parents and particularly of her mother; she develops a very realistic approach to the outside world, gives up her infantile overestimation of her parents, and frequently makes energetic attempts to be different from her mother. This critical depreciation is not consistently carried out. On the contrary, the young girl who is sharply critical of everything at home often tries to make it appear in school that her parents are extremely important and noble people. She often tells completely false stories glorifying them, stories that nobody believes, in order to negate her tendency to belittle them.

This is the form that the so-called "family romance"[4] assumes in prepuberty. In her urge to independence the young girl tries to rid herself of all the old traces of identification; not being ready for independence, however, she makes compromises. She may, for instance, place a friend's family in the position of her own, bringing home tales of how wonderful everything is in her friend's house, despite the fact that the standard of living there is far inferior to that in her own home. Or she may develop a passionate love for a woman teacher who suggests an ego ideal and to whom she ascribes all the qualities she feels to be lacking in her mother. Such a relation clearly indicates unconscious dependence on the mother, and we often wonder why the latter, who is sometimes a much finer person than the adored teacher, should be displaced by her. The obvious answer is that the relationship to the mother is extremely ambivalent and that it seems emotionally more "economical" to resolve this conflict of ambivalence by creating a split between the mother and the teacher. Love for the teacher is also a compromise formation that makes it possible to avoid the danger of infantile dependence on the mother. But the longing for the mother is expressed in the outer world in relation to this new object.

In the prepuberty of girls, attachment to the mother represents a greater danger than attachment to the father. The mother is a greater obstacle to the girl's desire to grow up, and we know that the condition of "psychic infantilism" found in many adult women represents the outcome of an unresolved attachment to the mother during prepuberty. Nevertheless,

[4] The term "family romance" is applied to a common psychoanalytically disclosed childhood fantasy: the child fancies that his parents are not his real progenitors; his real parents are famous and powerful, and his birth is shrouded in mystery.

the displacement of the old objects of identification is in itself a certain step forward and sometimes creates new social and ideologic values. The new object of identification may actually prove to be the representative of a more progressive, more ideal world. But, interestingly enough, in other instances the object selected is a sexually disreputable person. On closer examination, even this choice, directed either toward the mother's opposite or toward an unconscious image of the mother conceived as predominantly sexual, betrays the girl's dependence.

Naturally, relations with brothers and sisters play an important role in the struggle to achieve adulthood. During the period of her increased activity, a young girl who has grown up with a brother may strive to appear not only grown-up, but also boyish. The girl's sister, especially if she is only a little older but old enough to be obviously ahead in the race for adulthood, becomes an object either of hateful envy or, more rarely, an ideal figure. More often, a friend of the sister, the sister of a friend, or an older schoolmate will be selected as the ideal object. Because such an identification can be achieved quickly by the girl, this choice expresses the sense of the real that is characteristic of girls in prepuberty.

Such a relationship to an older girl is often dangerous, since the older one may entice the younger into actions for which she is not yet ripe. We shall return to this later in our discussion.

Along with these most important objects of identification, there are many other temporary figures, such as characters found in books, films, or plays. These various identifications, which later in puberty can be explained as defense mechanisms,[5] and which one meets in schizoid personalities as expressions of a pathologic emotional condition,[6] prove on closer inspection to have a completely specific character in prepuberty. They remind us strongly of the play of small children, and seem to be an "acting out" of those transitory, conscious wishes that express

[5] FREUD, A.: The ego and the mechanisms of defense. London: Hogarth, 1937.

[6] DEUTSCH, H.: Some forms of emotional disturbance and their relationship to schizophrenia. Psychoanalyt. Quart., vol. 11, 1942.

the idea, "That's what I want to be like." It is noteworthy
that this acting out has a concrete and real character, quite
different from fantasying.

An inner urge forces the young girl in prepuberty to act. She
must turn toward reality, and her tendency to take everything
most realistically at this period can readily be observed.
Phrases, symbols, etc., are endowed with full reality value, and
this, combined with the tendency to experience things directly,
makes her acting out quite bizarre. Let us consider, for
example, the behavior of a certain 12-year-old girl who was
preparing for her first formal dance. She was tormented by
anxieties and feelings of inferiority, and above all feared that
she would not look sufficiently grown-up. She had her hair
done elaborately so as to make herself look older, and the hair-
dresser prophesied that she would surely turn all the boys'
heads. For hours in front of her mirror she practiced the gestures of a *femme fatale*, but when evening came she refused to
go to the party. She was overwhelmed by a panic fear of
"turning all the boys' heads" and did not wish to take upon her
conscience the terrible state she would precipitate in them.
"After all I cannot marry all the boys who fall in love with me,
so what will the poor fellows do?" she exclaimed in despera-
tion.

The fantasy that she had borrowed from an outside source
had immediately been endowed with reality and given a
practical application, in the negative form of a refusal to act.

Because of the limitations of her own tiny personality, the
young girl resorts to all kinds of methods to give content and
purpose to her activities. For instance, she works out a detailed plan of living that she follows strictly for a short time,
and then replaces it with another. She tries to pattern her
existence after that of characters in books or in real life. Sometimes she even utilizes newspaper advertisements. Having
used some widely advertised cosmetic, she naïvely experiences
all the satisfactions of an enchantingly beautiful woman.

Fascinating examples of such identifications in a 12-year-old girl are to be found in Sally Benson's *Junior Miss*.[7] No clinical or statistical studies can tell us as much about the psychology of prepuberty as do the little episodes in Judy's life as described by this sensitive and talented author. Young Judy even makes her own person an object of identification whenever by so doing she can play a dramatically attractive role. For instance, after having seen a play in which the heroine is a self-sacrificing daughter, she plays the role of a young girl who loves her daddy more than she cares for anything else in the world, and is quite disillusioned by her father's prosaic response. A younger child would have drawn her father into the play; a girl in puberty would fill her inner life with fantasies relating to this situation. But Judy, who is in prepuberty, "play acts." A little later, as puberty approaches, this form of play acting is replaced by the desire to become an actress.

Another form of the young girl's play acting is continual meddling in the affairs of grown-up people. Full of intense curiosity, she notices everything, makes her own interpretations, elaborates what she sees with her usually not overrich imagination, and takes upon herself an active role as either a helper or a disturber. For the most part she identifies herself with persons madly in love, or with the suffering, persecuted people of some drama, set not in any fantastic world but in humdrum reality. Her activities are often hypomanic in character and are a perfect nuisance to everyone around her, particularly when they are accompanied by any considerable measure of aggressive tendencies.

An important role is also played by *secrecy*, the counterpart of curiosity in prepuberty. The 12-year-old is always sensing that others have secrets; she wants to know what is going on in everyone else's life, but at the same time surrounds her own person with secrecy. For this she needs a partner, and most often she finds one in a girl of her own age or in a group of girl friends. The urge to have secrets is usually directed

[7] BENSON, S.: Junior miss. New York: Random House, 1941.

against the grownups, above all against the mother or her substitute. Revenge for the mother's having secrets that she keeps from the child—that old reproach—now, at the age of increased activity, takes the form of having secrets of one's own. The reproach, "Why didn't she tell me that?" formerly referred not to the concealing of the event, but to the mysterious event itself. In prepuberty the affective reaction is transferred from the event to the secrecy about it. A typical example is the situation connected with the birth of a little brother or sister: it is not the birth that becomes the reason for conscious reproach of the mother, but the concealment of the fact of pregnancy. The fact that the mother, as is often the case, really spoke many times of the coming birth, is ignored or repressed. Exactly the same thing takes place later with regard to menstruation.

The need to have secrets is often expressed in a paradoxic manner. The young girl confides to everyone under seal of secrecy. "You are the only person to whom I am telling this. Swear that you won't repeat it to anyone," she says—and then proceeds to tell her secret to the very next person.

The need to have secrets and to reveal them leads to invention of lies when real events are lacking. A harmless kind of pseudology thus arises—less rich in fantasy, however, and less developed than the pseudology of adolescence. A not inconsiderable number of adult women retain this compulsion to confide secrets to all sorts of people.

Now let us turn to the question of what happens to the young girl's affective life during this period. The flight from childhood marked an energetic attempt to weaken the old affective ties, especially to escape the tender or critical protection of the mother. We know what difficulties the mother encounters when she tries to explain to her daughter that she is ready to help her to achieve successful adulthood (even when the attempt is sincere). Adulthood achieved with the mother's help is not attractive. There is no doubt that despite strenuous efforts to loosen the fetters of childhood dependency, many of the young girl's emotional ties to the family persist. Such emotions are often transferred to persons who are direct successors to or substitutes for the family members (for instance, teachers). The girl's deep and consciously felt love turns toward another girl, either an older girl representing her ego ideal, or a girl like herself with whom she giggles and titters, with whom she locks herself up in her room, to whom she confides her secrets, and with whom she experiences the harmless sexual gratification typical of this age.

The choice of this object is of the greatest importance, for it is an alter ego, an extension of the girl's own ego, identical with her in respect to age, interests, and desires. At this period, when the ego is not yet capable of creating a new emotional relationship with the surrounding world and is too weak to feel independent, the young girl runs the danger of diffusing herself in numerous identifications. During prepuberty these identifications for some time have a rather playful, imitative character. As the girl grows older their importance in the formation of her personality increases. As a rule, identification gradually assumes a more fixed form and attaches itself to definitely valuable objects. But varying identifications may continue to exist and in some cases lead to a far reaching impoverishment of the girl's personality.

There are various ways of avoiding self-diffusion in identifications. The easiest device of the young girl in prepuberty is to attach herself directly to another girl in order to feel more secure. Despite her noisy self-assurance, she is aware of her inadequacy and needs someone as insignificant as herself in order to feel stronger, doubled as it were. She wants someone who not only shares with her the pleasure and burdens of secrecy and curiosity, but who also resembles her and who, like herself, is undergoing the suffering of feeling insignificant. She can endure the burden of secrecy, the feeling that the surrounding world is hostile, and the torments of guilt, with greater ease because she endures them with another.

This relationship is "monogamous." Faithfulness and

exclusiveness are demanded of the friend and, above all, complete partnership in common secrets. The partners must tell each other everything and exclude all others, particularly the grownups, from their confidences. The momentous discoveries they impart to each other relate chiefly to the sexual sphere. Just as the phallic phase of childhood was taken up with the interest in anatomic differences, so prepuberty concentrates on physiologic processes. It is no longer the problem of genital differences that fascinates girls in this stage, for they already know about these differences and more or less accept them. Absorption in the functions of the sexual organs and their size, in the inside of their own bodies, in the development of their breasts, etc., now replaces their old interest in the difference between boys and girls.

In this realm they tell each other truths and falsehoods, and together they examine the world from the point of view of sexual events. One of them may even attempt to experience something in order to have a secret to tell. When they are separated they write each other all matter of important information or each keeps a diary for the other. In this special secrecy everything assumes a sexual character. Harmless words like "that," "this," "make," etc., acquire a double meaning.

Hug-Hellmuth's self-portrayal in *A Young Girl's Diary*[8] seems to offer a perfect example of such behavior in prepuberty. After the death of its author, academic psychologists branded it as a falsification, offering as proof the fact that it did not conform to the character of young girls as observed by them. In one respect they were right: the life of the young girl includes not only what was expressed in the diary but also school, sports, musical interests, family events, etc. However, a diary is the expression of that part of a girl's inner life that she shares only with her best friend or with a selected group of friends. The value of the Hug-Hellmuth publication

[8] Hug-Hellmuth, H.: Tagebuch eines halbwüchsigen Mädchens (ed. 2). Vienna: 1921. A young girl's diary. New York: Seltzer, 1921.

is that it gives us an insight into areas of the young girl's life that she would ordinarily hide from a psychologist or any other authoritative grownup. Secrecy is an essential element of the young girl's pleasure in sexual investigations and discussions. Professional people who for therapeutic reasons wish to get close to such girls repeatedly find that it is only with greatest difficulty that they can obtain a true picture of the child's secret life. These children display particularly stubborn resistance to motherly women. It is possible to achieve an intimate relationship with them only if one can assume the role of a "girl friend."

For my own part I completely concede the authenticity of Hug-Hellmuth's diary. It is so absolutely true to life that I feel that only a young girl could have had the experiences described in it and written about them in such fashion.

Let us return to our two-girl friendship. We have endowed sexual investigations and the keeping of common secrets with the significance of sexual gratification. Actually they are the only form of such gratification at this age. Expression of intense tenderness between girls is not found at this time, and mutual masturbation almost never occurs under normal circumstances. Moreover, it is rare to find any direct, conscious masturbatory activity. We have seen that the fantasy life of the girl in prepuberty, in contrast to that of puberty, has a more extroverted character and tends in the direction of play acting. The problem of pregnancy, for example, plays an important role in both these periods. The young girl in puberty represses her pregnancy fantasies and suffers from anxieties and symptoms relating to them. But in prepuberty she shuts herself up in a room with her friend and both of them stuff little pillows under their dresses and play at being pregnant. Similarly with respect to prostitution fantasies: the younger girls are very much occupied with this subject, tell tales about it, use their mothers' powder, paste red paper on their cheeks, redden their lips with candies, and act out their prostitution fantasies together, whereas in puberty girls with the same fantasies become extremely ascetic or develop symptoms of agoraphobia.

Naturally, their physiologic investigations are centered around the sexual act, pregnancy, and childbirth. They elaborate many theories about the "how" and the "what" of these things, but here too they use material taken from reality. They are particularly prone to pick up any suggestion that the whole business is due to a brutal act on the part of the man and that the unfortunate woman suffers great pain and distress. It is interesting to note that in every phase of life feminine masochism finds some form of expression.

The friendship between the two girls always has a more or less mutually complementary form, that is to say, one girl is the more active and the other the more passive. This relation can be of various intensities: the passivity of one partner may be only subtly indicated or may take the form of absolute subjection to the other.

As puberty approaches, these relations assume a more sadomasochistic character. They can have a great and even harmful effect, particularly on the masochistic partner. Sometimes young girls suffer from inhibitions in study or work, as a result of which they suddenly or gradually become incapable of doing anything that requires exercise of will and endurance of any discomfort. The explanation of these difficulties is to be found in the girl's absorption in fantasies. I recently had an opportunity to observe a young girl who stubbornly refused to do anything. She gave up every activity she undertook as soon as she found that it involved the slightest discomfort. I discovered that she was masochistically subjected to a sadistic girl of her own age and that she had become unable to endure discomfort unless it was accompanied by rewards in the form of masochistic pleasure. Such a sadomasochistic relation can continue into puberty and exert a determining influence on subsequent heterosexuality.

The relation between the two girls evolves in different ways. It is dissolved, or the objects change, or, much less frequently, it leads to a sublimated friendship that may continue throughout life. Sometimes one of the two girls develops sexually more quickly than the other. Out of jealousy or identification, the more immature one tries for her part also to take the heterosexual path the other has followed, although she lacks the necessary psychologic preparation or has only a sham preparation. She easily falls into confusion, and this may have unfortunate results, the nature of which will depend upon the girl's social milieu. Many acts of gangsterism, prostitution, or criminality in very young girls are the consequence of a violent interruption of prepuberty, with its harmless homosexual attachments, in favor of a heterosexuality for which they are not yet really ready. In my opinion the real dangers of this period of life lie in any anachronistic behavior. Either the young girl is retarded in her psychologic growth by the excessive solicitude of the persons around her or by her own excessively infantile emotional ties, sense of guilt, and fears; or, conversely, premature experiences produce disturbances in the development of her whole personality, perhaps even neurotic difficulties.

The relation to the other sex in this period is normally non-sexual in both boys and girls. In the eyes of the boy, who is extraordinarily proud of his manliness, friendship with girls amounts to a devaluation of his manliness (this is in contrast to the attitude in late puberty). The girl adopts an "I don't care" attitude, but at bottom she believes in the superiority of the boy. This is especially true in groups that value achievements in the field of sports. A strongly active girl engages in competition and becomes a tomboy, especially if she finds that her girl friends have ambitions in the same direction. What often brings boys and girls together in quiet corners at this age is curiosity rather than sexual attraction. Even when there are concrete sexual activities in relations between girls and boys, curiosity plays the main role.

Tomboyishness, which so frequently manifests itself during the activity phase, is not only normal but also often more desirable from the point of view of psychologic health than a passive girlish attitude and withdrawal into domesticity. More than at other periods of childhood, individually varying dispositions now become noticeable. Some girls develop feminine charm, show a growing interest in feminine pursuits, sometimes even simulate stupidity in order to be treated more tenderly. Others display more active boyish traits from the outset. The influences of the milieu and the attitudes of parents and brothers and sisters probably play a large part in determining the character of the girl; but every manifestation of a boyish attitude in prepuberty undoubtedly represents a strengthening of the previously existing desire to be a boy. If this desire is not accompanied by reactions like feelings of inferiority, depression, etc., it should not cause concern.

As puberty approaches and the young girl experiences the first symptoms of sexual anxiety or some love disappointment, this tomboyishness is often used as a weapon, as a protection against femininity, particularly if her fantasies have a masochistic character. Such an anxiety can drive the girl into passivity and domesticity or into masculinity and homosexuality. But these processes take place much more often during puberty.

In my description of the development characteristic of prepuberty, I have several times referred to its "offensive." It is clear that the motive force in this phase is the inherent urge of the ego to grow up and achieve things.

On the road to this goal the maturing girl must liberate herself from her former dependences. The first prerevolutionary storms take place within the modest framework of her home environment. For the most part, adaptation to the school milieu proceeds well for a long time. The difference in behavior at school and at home is often striking: we are all familiar with the type of child who is completely out of hand at home but a model of good behavior at school. The converse, good behavior at home and trouble making in school, is less frequent. The transfer of the conflict from home to school is mostly bound

up with complicated emotional processes. Playing hooky
in order to be outside during school hours and fear of school
on one hand, and the desire to remain at home on the other,
usually prelude graver neurotic symptoms. Here we are concerned with the simple, "normal" mode of development of the
young girl's ego toward increasing independence. But even
the most normal preadolescents have their difficulties. The
simplest expressions of these are disobedience, defiant rebellion
against educational measures, and rejection of previously accepted discipline. These are sometimes accompanied by extremely aggressive acts. Occasionally the educational achievements of early childhood that have long since become habits,
begin to regress, and bodily cleanliness, regularity of the excretory functions, in short, the "somatic order" represented by
the mother or her substitute, is rebelliously thrown overboard.
This expresses principally a protest against hitherto existing
dependence, aggression against educational influences, and,
paradoxically, ever more intense longing on the part of the
child for her own childishness. On the one hand, the child
energetically resists her childishness; on the other, she is trying
to reach it again by detours. Moved by this longing, she is
inclined once more to leave to her mother the care of her body.
The intensification of many oral tendencies, above all gluttony,
serves as an aggressive gratification of the appetite, which is
increased by the processes of growth. In all these functions
the girl struggles against the "interference" of the mother; she
senses in every one of the latter's gestures an attack on her
adulthood—the mother is the embodiment of the strongest tie
with the past.

The struggle for independence in this period strongly reminds
us of the processes that take place approximately between
the ages of 1½ and 3 years, in the course of what we call the
pre-oedipal phase of childhood. In order to take his first
steps in the outside world, the little child after the utter dependence of his babyhood, must also disengage himself from his
mother who carried and later fed him. He no longer wants

the mother's guiding hand and yet clamors anxiously for one finger if she removes her hand during his attempt to walk. He becomes enraged when he is not given his spoon to handle independently. Very similar is the behavior of the girl in prepuberty: full of hatred and rage, she wants to tear herself away from her mother's influence, although at the same time she frequently betrays an intensified, anxious urge to remain under the maternal protection.

A corresponding process takes place in the mother: in both the stages we are comparing, she wants to keep the child under her protection and yet she knows that she must lessen and in the end desist from this protection. How often are the young girl's fears of the dangers threatening her in the outside world intensified by similar fears on the part of her mother! In many a girl this fear becomes a conviction that the moment she is separated from her mother something "terrible" will happen either to her or to her mother. We are familiar with this fear in pathologic cases, but relatively normal girls often display it in a milder form. Prepuberty repeats the pre-oedipal phase not only in the struggle for liberation from the mother that is the central point of the girl's psychologic life at this time. It repeats this phase in other respects too. Again the father, loved or rejected, remains in the background as a powerful or a weak figure; normally he does not exert any considerable influence on the child's psychologic development in this period of life.

Freud raised the problem regarding the manner in which the girl's love object changes from mother, hitherto the only object of her attachment, to father. Numerous attempts to explain this, on the part of Freud and other authors, have been based on the assumption that this change is accomplished during childhood, but, according to my view, it is never completely achieved. In all the phases of woman's development and experience, the great part played in her psychologic life by her attachment to her mother can be clearly observed. Many events in that life are manifestations of attempts to detach herself, attempts made in thrusts, and the woman's psychologic equilibrium and eventual fate often depend on the success or failure of these attempts.

Prepuberty is marked by a particularly vigorous thrust in this direction, and that is why this phase of growth is so important in determining the character of the girl's puberty and her subsequent development. A prepuberal attempt at liberation from the mother that has failed or was too weak can inhibit future psychologic growth and leave a definitely infantile imprint on the woman's entire personality. In such girls puberty lacks its normal revolutionary impetus and intensified urge to independence. Their relations to persons of both sexes express dependence and a need for support. Friendship and love are replaced by passive clinging and a querulous demand for love that is difficult to gratify. If after prepuberty such infantile girls achieve a more active behavior, it is characterized by the play attitude that we have seen to be typical of prepuberty with its play acting. Such girls renounce all purposeful aspirations the moment they encounter difficulties, they belittle everything they do, etc. They frequently achieve good results in intellectual and artistic fields, but usually these are not expressions of their own personalities and are completely dependent upon outside influences. Such women fall in love often and ardently, but even this emotional activity is largely limited to fantasy and retains a playful character. Without a considerable amount of tenderness and motherly protection—a function in some cases taken over by the husband—they find life unbearable. They are usually inaccessible to psychoanalytic treatment, because they cannot endure the renunciations involved in analysis. The emotions mobilized by the analysis are immediately brought into play and the mother transference is endowed with a real and hostile character. When they are stricken with neurosis, their symptoms are usually manifestations of the abnormally intensified relation to the mother that was reactivated in prepuberty. Thus for instance various alimentary disturbances, from mild upsets to anorexia nervosa (rejection of food up to the point of total abstinence), may represent a pathologically intensified struggle between the extremely infantile tie to the mother and unsuccessful attempts at liberation.

Many cases occur in which prepuberty has apparently been normal, but a provocative situation during puberty or some later stage brings pathologic reactions to the fore. For instance, an attempt to reduce that begins with oral renunciations may sometimes produce a reaction that leads to obsessive eating. This is combated with the greatest energy, and all the deep-rooted longing for the mother is mobilized in this fight. This longing can assume an extraordinarily infantile form and, if it is accompanied by infantile aggression against the mother, the ardently desired food becomes poison, and the longing can develop into a psychosis.

In all these cases it is found that, although the alimentary neurosis (or psychosis) manifested itself at a later age (frequently toward the end of adolescence), the normal attempt to loosen the tie with the mother encountered difficulties as early as in prepuberty. Neurotic illness did not occur at that time, but it is clear from later developments that the "prepuberal offensive" was either too passive or too aggressive with regard to the mother.

In our discussion of prepuberty we have confined ourselves to relatively normal states, but we often find neurotic difficulties during this phase too. These either are continuations of neuroses that existed during childhood or they arise under the influence of traumatic experiences, such as the birth of a new brother or sister, separation of the parents, death, etc. Most frequently the disturbances consist in anxiety states and typical feelings of inferiority. Girls in this condition do not feel equal to the task of adulthood; but if they are admitted to a favorable group or make new friends, their feelings of inferiority disappear. Behind such feelings deeper motives can usually be discovered, as for instance feelings of guilt that may mark the beginning of neurotic complications.

My use of the term "offensive" in this discussion is deliberate. I wish to emphasize that certain developments of the ego are valuable because in an emergency they can serve as mechanisms of defense against dangers arising from sexual urges. I do not believe, however, that such defense mechanisms are created exclusively under the pressure of instinctual dangers, as weapons against them. In my view these mechanisms begin to develop before puberty, as offensive weapons for the conquest of reality. In fact, any element of personality can become a defense mechanism: intelligence as well as stupidity, flight into reality as well as flight from reality. Aggressiveness can be a defense against passivity and vice versa, while masculinity can be a defense against feminine masochism; the urge to be an adult is used as a defense against the dangers of childhood, the flight into childhood can signify a defense against adulthood, etc.

Similarly, great inventions in chemistry and physics are often used as weapons in war, although their primary purpose is not military. They still have a value when the war is over, and they can then serve better purposes. This is true also of certain important ego functions: they are products of normal development and can be used as defense mechanisms in dangerous situations; but they perform their most valuable services in "peacetime"—that is, when used directly for conquering the environment.

CHAPTER TWO

Early Puberty

URING prepuberty, with its intensified activity, the young girl's ego attempts to break the fetters of childhood dependency. This attitude continues for many years beyond prepuberty, up to adolescence. The girl's struggle against her home milieu, still a primitive struggle in prepuberty, is the expression of her growing need to oppose her own ego as an independent personality to the personalities around her. Her consciousness of herself as ego grows increasingly stronger and is the prelude to various events that later, in adolescence, become more complicated and interesting. Very often we fail to realize that the youthful mischievousness we find so negative stems from positive forces of growth. The girl whose self-confidence is maturing naturally feels for some time that her surroundings are obstructive and hostile. In order to further the development of her own personality, she must resort to methods that are not progressive and mature in themselves but that nevertheless aim at progress and maturity. In her deepest being the young girl, during prepuberty and for a long period during puberty, remains completely childish; she is frightened by her own increased self-confidence and her new responsibilities. Between these two elements—heightened self-confidence on the one hand and growing perception of her own weakness on the other—she tries to build a bridge. The numerous imitations, identifications, devaluations, and revaluations that we have noted above serve this purpose. All of them stem from the need to fill the growing gap between her greater self-reliance and the ever greater demands that reality makes upon her. The very fact that the youthful soul feels insecure strengthens its active aspiration to master its insecurity. Later, during adolescence, it will find better means for achieving this aim.

As we follow the development of girls from prepuberty to adolescence, we can observe, in the period directly following prepuberty, certain peculiarities that justify us in giving it the special name of "early puberty." The lines separating this phase from thepreceding and the followingphases—prepuberty, and adolescence or advanced puberty—are fluid. The transition from prepuberty via puberty to adolescence takes place gradually through the organic and psychic development of the young girl. The most important organic achievement of puberty is sexual maturation. The biologic factor strongly influences the relation of the girl to her own body, and the tendency to neglect personal appearance that is so typical of prepuberty, is reversed in a most striking manner: the girl begins to devote great care to her body; she uses creams, powder, and rouge no longer just to imitate the grownups but rather to gratify her own very real vanity and need to be beautiful. Dresses, jewelry, and fashionable accessories become so important that the young girl is often led to commit unsocial acts in order to procure money for these things.

During the entire latency period the girl's interest in the sexual organs recedes into the background. During prepuberty her intense curiosity about sexual processes in general directs her interest toward her own body. The wish to be a grownup and to be considered as such steers her attention toward growth and other somatic processes. As a result of this wish, the little girl between 10 and 12 years of age welcomes the first signs of breast development, stuffs out her blouse, and makes exaggerated reports to her friends about her progress. Thus, she often seems more mature and more feminine than her older, already menstruating sister, who is so full of the anxiety and shame mobilized by the rise of sexual excitation that she is not a bit proud of her maturity, is even ashamed of it, and tries to conceal it by such means as very tight brassieres and other appropriate articles of clothing.

It is understandable that the girl who during prepuberty behaved in a tomboyish way should at first react negatively to the developing secondary sex characteristics that give her body a feminine appearance. The redistribution of the fat deposits, the growing roundness of her hips, the budding of her breasts, etc., fill her with vexation and shame. But sometimes a boyish girl suddenly gives up her earlier attitude and contemplates her new femininity with interest and joy. Conversely, there are girls who during prepuberty behave rather passively and femininely without displaying any tendency toward tomboyishness and who, with the progress of puberty and the feminization of their bodies, develop a more masculine attitude. Finally, there are girls whose development follows a straight line from childhood through puberty to adulthood; of such girls their families say, "She has always been a little woman."

One would expect the activity of the biologic, above all of the hormonal forces in puberty to exert a decisive influence on the psychologic factors, and this is largely the case. However, this activity does not always prove strong enough to master the psychologic complications and to steer the process of maturation in a straight line toward femininity.

The girl's interest in her genitals, which has long remained in the background, is now activated by renewed masturbation and even more by menstruation. The psychologic effects of learning through experience that the organ bleeds and causes discomfort and frustration are extremely strong and varied (see chap. IV). Here we limit our discussion to pointing out that the role of the female genital organ for the girl is completely different from that of the penis for the boy. For him, the genital organ is an old acquaintance with which he has always been familiar because of its double function. Unlike the girl, the boy can become interested in the growth and intensified sexual functioning of his genitals at an early date and be very proud of them.

But the young girl's diversified behavior during puberty depends on still other factors. Her disposition, the vicissitudes of her childhood, the influences of her environment, the cultural milieu, her intelligence and natural gifts, her methods of overcoming anxiety—all these create individual variations in the girl's personality at this period. It is nevertheless possible to distinguish certain general traits; and several types of behavior even at this time reveal the personality trend that will later characterize the mature woman.

We defined the prepuberal phase as homosexual, because the love object is of the same sex. This choice is expressed in two forms: one consists in strong attachment to the mother, in inner and outer conflict with her, in the girl's wish to liberate herself from her mother, and in the tendency to transfer her feeling for the mother to another, ideal woman who acts as a substitute for the mother. The other form is the less conflict-ridden relation with a friend. The girl to girl relation that begins during pre-puberty passes through various vicissitudes in early puberty, and these likewise are strongly influenced by the milieu. Often this personal relation ends when the two girls leave the group to which they have belonged—for instance, when they change schools; and at this point the fact that the girls come from different social strata may be of great importance. If the relation has been close, it may continue despite the change of schools, or the separation may be accompanied by more or less intense bereavement reactions. But usually the change of milieu brings new interests with it, and the last traces of pre-puberal friendships disappear. Such an outcome should be considered desirable; another and relatively favorable possibility is that of continuation of the relation in a sublimated friendship that does not interfere with further development.

As we have shown above, the sexual content of the relation with a person of the same sex during prepuberty consists exclusively in the exchange of secrets and in sexual curiosity.

Friendship between girls is of the greatest importance. Identification with a similar being can strengthen the young girl's consciousness that she is an independent ego. Such friendships are a source of warm emotional experiences and by relieving guilt feelings they create a certain freedom in areas of behavior that are still strongly subject to inhibitions. When

the common activity of the two girls goes beyond the limits of
the permissible, we often hear accusations on the part of the
girls' families, in which there is question of who was the "seduced" and who the "seducer." Such accusations are usually
reciprocal, so that one is confronted with two victims and two
seducers, and as a rule it is impossible to discover the part
played by each girl   All the accusations have a foundation of
truth, for each of the girls would in most instances have renounced the forbidden activity had she not been encouraged
by the other.

In spite of certain dangers, the positive aspects of such friendships are paramount, and lack of them is a serious loss in this
period of life. The typical trauma of prepuberty and the
period immediately following is the loss of the friend through
separation or through her unfaithfulness in favor of another
girl or of a boy. The deserted girl normally turns to another
friend. Sometimes she returns to the dependence upon her
mother that she has only recently given up. Such a return
may occasion many inhibitions in her development; it can delay
or completely prevent her psychic maturation.

Severe anxiety states and neurotic difficulties are not infrequent in early puberty; on several occasions I have observed
onsets of psychosis in girls who had lost their friends and could
not find compensation in their mothers. In two of these cases
the mothers had been dead for a long time, and the mourning
process that had been postponed set in only after the friends
had also been lost, in both cases as a result of infidelity. This
led to the gravest anxiety states and to symptoms that indicated
extensive infantile regression. These girls had to be fed like
babies, urinated and moved their bowels in their clothes, talked
baby talk, clung to their nurses, etc.

Franz Werfel, in his novel *The Song of Bernadette*,[1] has presented a beautiful description and an interesting solution of
such a conflict. Fifteen-year-old Bernadette, who is an
asthmatic, inhibited, and introverted girl, goes out to gather

[1] WERFEL, F.: The song of Bernadette. New York: Viking, 1942.

wood with her sister Marie and her friend Jeanne. Their home
is cold and miserable, the children are hungry, and the sickly
Bernadette has to implore her mother for permission to go out.
The mother finally agrees, but warns her not to do anything
that might cause her to catch cold. The three girls reach a
brook that separates them from a rich fall of wood. Jeanne,
who is energetic and full of vitality, wades through the icy
water, and Marie follows her. Bernadette remains on the
hither side of the river, deserted by both her sister and her
friend. Upon seeing Marie's bared legs, Bernadette is overwhelmed by a sudden feeling of revulsion; this is peculiar,
because she sleeps in the same bed with her sister. Jeanne,
who is the overactive, aggressive type of girl, makes fun of the
weak Bernadette and calls out to her: "The devil take you!"

Bernadette experiences a flood of emotional reactions so
violent that she can hardly master them. She replies to
Jeanne's curse by saying: "You are no longer my friend."

She reacts to Marie's leaving her by devaluating her sisterly
love through a feeling of aversion that it is not our task to
analyze here. Bernadette has no way of asserting her will and
overcoming her physical weakness, because to wade across the
cold river would mean to disobey her mother and later to be
reprimanded and perhaps even beaten by her. Her feeling of
guilt for not doing her duty and helping to gather the wood—
"she is the oldest and should not shirk"—is in conflict with her
obedience to her mother's orders.

Bernadette has a strong tendency to self-accusation and she
can hardly bear the tension of this insoluble conflict. She expresses her helplessness symbolically, as it were, when she
removes one stocking but does not remove the other. Then
she resorts to a method that she has probably often used before,
whenever reality has become unbearable: she turns away from
reality and abandons herself to a fantasy, which she experiences
this time with hallucinatory intensity. The river Gave is no
longer a river but a dirty, noisy, and dangerous road; the whole
picture is one of dreadful imminent peril in which Jeanne's

curse—"The devil take you!"—is fulfilled. It is not our purpose here to analyze these symbols, but the real content of
images such as a wide, dirty, dangerous road is well known to
us from the anxieties of pubescent girls. Then Bernadette
emerges from the devil's power and has the great experience
that determines her future: in the dark grotto of Massabielle,
"the lady" appears to her. Here is the fulfillment of her need
to love a woman who can replace both her lost friend and her
mother, the latter being unsuitable as a love object because she
is a source of punishments and prohibitions.

Bernadette does not turn her longing and love toward the
woman of her hallucination in religious ecstasy, as one might
think. Actually she conceives her quite realistically, simply
as "the lady," an earthly being with whom she will from now on
enter into an ardent love relation. Bernadette's relation with
her lady differs from the usual young girl's love for an idealized
women only in that the lady is a product of fantasy. This
difference is diminished by the fact, mentioned above, that in
the case of other girls too the loved woman often has no actual
objective reality value, for they know her very little, sometimes
only from a picture or casual personal impression. Subjectively, however, the role of such an ideal is all the more important. As with Bernadette, it is a substitute for the lacking or
lost friend, and often a compromise solution between the longing for the mother and the defense against an attachment to
the latter that cannot be gratified or is dangerous. The lady's
love frees little Bernadette from her feelings of guilt. Later
the lady, by such modest means as nodding, smiling, or making
little gestures of displeasure, points out ways in which Bernadette can remain free of guilt feelings, thus satisfying a need
that she shares with many young girls. The realistic character
of Bernadette's fantasy love, humanly true and not super-
humanly divine, is the most fascinating element in Franz
Werfel's heroine.

We know that the friendship of children of the same sex involves many dangers. One is mutual seduction into imper-

missible acts as a result of release from guilt feelings; another is eventual fixation of homosexual tendencies and the influence that these may exert later on the course of psychosexual development during adolescence.

We have mentioned before that the friendship of two girls often continues in a typical fashion after the appearance of the first heterosexual tendencies in early puberty. A triangular situation arises, lending to this phase a bisexual character. The young girl still wavers between homosexual and heterosexual objects, and her turn toward heterosexuality is accomplished only gradually. This triangular constellation may be inaugurated in prepuberty, as in the common love of two girls for their teacher or leader. The first groping excursions in the direction of heterosexuality are playfully undertaken in common. The girls take pleasure in experiences that they can exchange with each other. As they grow older, various complications take place within the triangle. The more mature of the two girls begins to be more serious about the partner of the other sex, and the more passive or younger girl assumes the role of sympathetic matchmaker and helper. This often occurs in a triangle in which a brother of one of the girls occupies one angle. A good example can be found in Tolstoy's *War and Peace*.[2] Natasha strives to win the love of her brother Nicholas for her friend Sonya:

> "You know, Sonya is my dearest friend. *Such* a friend that I burned my arm for her sake. Look here." She pulled up her muslin sleeve and showed him a red scar on her long, delicate arm. "I burned this to prove my love for her. I just heated a ruler in the fire and pressed it there. . . . We are such friends, such friends. . . . And she loves me and you like that."

Natasha loves her brother very much and obviously yields him to her friend with mixed feelings. As the third partner in their love relation, she can retain both her friend and her brother and can solve the conflict better by sharing their happi-

[2] TOLSTOY, L.: War and peace. Transl. by Louise and Aylmer Maude. New York: Simon & Schuster, 1942.

ness than by a painful renunciation.   The masochistic element
may well be noted here.

Further development toward heterosexuality in early puberty will depend upon the successtul overcoming of bisexuality
in the triangular situation.   The biologic and psychic developments in this period of life display far reaching parallelism.
But the processes do not unfold according to a prearranged
schedule.   The phases become mixed, and the intensification
of sexual tendencies occasioned by biologic growth may under
certain circumstances manifest itself in a regressive torm.

If the prepuberty phase repeats the pre-oedipal intantile
period, the triangular situation of early puberty repeats a
phase that occurs in childhood between the pre-oedipal and
oedipal periods.   At that time the little girl gradually turns
trom her almost exclusive attachment to her mother toward her
father, wavers between the two, and wants to have them both,
until finally she turns toward her father with greater intensity,
although still not exclusively.   In early puberty this bisexual
triangle recurs, and if regressive forces succeed in asserting
themselves, the young girl finds herself in a situation similar
to that of the bisexual period of early childhood.   At that time
the triangle was tormed by the parents and child; now the
objects are different but similar difficulties and problems arise.

The Child,[3] a masterful short story by Karin Michaelis, is
an example of a poet's intuitive insight into the psychologic
processes of young girls. Andrea, the "child" who is loved by
everyone, is on her deathbed.   She is 16 years old, actually a
grown-up girl.   But in her psychologic development she is still
a child, with all the struggles and conflicts of a pubescent girl.
Andrea's parents have for a long time been estranged; they are
enemies living under one roof, and they know that "Andrea
seems to see into our very thoughts."   For the sake of the sick
child, the two parents go hand in hand into her room, and
Andrea smiles.   "You come in so nicely, you two," she says.

[3] MICHAELIS, K.: Das Kind. Transl. from the Danish by M. Mann. Berlin: Axel
Juncker.

She has little parties with them, and they pretend not to hate each other for the sake of their sick and dying daughter. "What will you do when you are alone? . . . If only I knew that you would be happy with each other . . . if only you wanted to kiss each other every morning, and you both slept in here and thought of me. . . . If only I knew that, I would not be in the least afraid of . . ." Andrea's last wish on her deathbed is that her parents should be reconciled; it is as though she was giving her life to unite them by her death.

Experience teaches us how often and how intensely even healthy children are dominated by the idea that their parents do not love each other and that they will eventually separate. This idea may be a product of fantasy or stem from direct observation. The little girl would gladly remain with her father, but her sense of guilt usually induces her to decide in favor of her mother. Thus the sense of guilt often creates pressure in the direction of homosexual or at least bisexual behavior, for the normally developed girl naturally wishes to give her love to her father, but feels obliged to show loving faithfulness to her mother.

The sick Andrea is blissful in the arms of her father: "Kiss me, Daddy, my magnificent, splendid father, put your hand on my forehead, then we will be silent together." In the face of imminent blindness, she says: "Father, if I really become blind, it won't matter much . . . couldn't we both do with one pair of eyes?" But then her deep longing for her mother expresses itself: "Mother, you're not so far away; if only I make myself quite small and thin, can I come to you?"

The mother takes her in her arms, as when she was a baby at the breast, and Andrea presses close against her. Thus little endrea dies, and the last moments of her life are spent in an Affort to obtain a promise from her parents that after her death, and because of it, they will find each other again and remain together.

Later the mother discovers Andrea's diary, in which the child confesses her great love for her father; she would rather renounce heaven, she writes, than her father. "But mother is pious and she should go to heaven. .... When I put my hand on Father's forehead, I can feel that we belong together as closely as a pair of eyes. He has exactly the same likes and dislikes as I have and, just like me, he won't eat peas and meat soup." She confesses that she has listened at night and knows that her parents sleep apart. "Father could be a little in love with Mother, she is certainly very much in love with him, but I can't stand the fact that she always questions me about what we talked about when we went walking together. . . ." Andrea suspected her father of having a mistress and went through all the torments of jealousy. She experienced triumphant joy upon learning that her suspicions were unjustified. But she refused carnations from her father "unless he bought flowers for Mother too." In another diary entry she writes: "If only I could live one day with Father and the other with Mother, for each separately is so lovely! It's only when they are together that I am quite miserable and chilly."

As Andrea grew older, the triangle reappeared in a different form; instead of her father, her love object was now his brother: "I could not possibly touch another man, perhaps Uncle Steffen, but then he is father's brother." This love matured and promised her real happiness, when the shadow of her consuming passion for the girl Josse fell over it, and the triangle Andrea-mother-father was repeated in a new form. Her diary records:

No one can get the better of Josse, she is incredibly strong, yesterday she bit me in the neck because I said I loved Uncle Steffen as much as her. Josse hates Uncle Steffen, she wants him to be dead; it's a pity they can't love each other as I love them. . . . All men love Josse, old ones and young ones, they don't want to live without her, they want to lie like dust at her feet. . . . Now we've made a bet—for Steffen's heart. This was a betrayal on my part. She is to go to him and bring him my greetings and I must not tell him of our bet. We talked so much about him, and it was night and the moon was shining, and then I moved over to Josse because I was so scared. We said so many good things about him. Then she said: "He is not like the others, I want to have him." Now he really ought to love her. Josse says she knows she will win. I dreamed that she bit my heart because I loved him better. The blood ran out. Father Mother, Uncle Steffen and Josse—I shall die.

If Andrea had remained alive she might have become involved in triangular situations again and again. As a result of her deep wish to have her father for herself, combined with her childish love for her mother, she separated her parents in her fantasy in order later to reconcile them by her suffering and death.

When she repeated the triangle in her relation with Josse and Steffen, her love for the girl was more violent, and heavily tinged with the masochistic desire for suffering; and this time instead of renouncing her father's carnations for the sake of her mother, she must give up the heart of the man she loves to her hated and passionately loved "friend." This is a poetic representation of the bisexual wavering of puberty in its character of a repetition of the old relation to the parents. Andrea dies amidst a tragic complication of her triangular problems. It is interesting to note that the intuitive Mme. Michaelis called her book *The Child*. Because of her sickness and proximity to death, Andrea certainly was more childish than girls usually are at her age; hence the repetition of the triangular situation of her childhood has a more naïve, childish, regressive character, and is acted out very strongly and directly in her relation to her parents. Normally this repetition in early puberty is less direct and less intense, especially if the young girl has reached her sixteenth year of age.

Many tasks confront the young girl in puberty. In addition to the still uncompleted task of resolving her ties with her family, she must free herself from too strong ties with other girls and break up the new triangular situation in favor of the male. In contrast to the circumstances of prepuberty, when all these emotional relations were present, though in a less intense form, the situation in early puberty is much sharper and surrounded by numerous dangers. The sexual urges are strengthened but they still lack a direct goal. As a result, all the relations are subject to the danger of sexualization. The atmosphere of the home is much more pregnant with conflicts than during prepuberty, the period of naïve protests and relations with girl friends; the love for an older woman becomes disquieting because of the sexual danger, and numerous internal and external difficulties obstruct progress toward heterosexuality. In addition to the numerous individual defense mechanisms formed previously,[4] puberty puts in operation methods that have a more general character and that are of the greatest importance.

The ever more oppressive and unbearable situation in the parental home creates in the child the need to be free and to belong to a group different from the family. This can come about through the child's joining a group composed of members of one sex or of both. In the lower social strata, under the influence of youthful adventurousness, such a group can often assume the form of a disorderly or even criminal gang. Yet it also can perform important functions of social adjustment and facilitate solution of the individual problems of youth by a collectivist ideology. However, there is always the danger that individual characteristics and emotional developments will come off badly in this process. It is interesting to note that in such groups the behavior of the girl is markedly different from that of the boy. The boy, from earliest puberty, tries to form prerevolutionary or revolutionary communities pitted against the power of the grownups who, in his view, enslave him. At first aggressive unions are formed against the "tyrannic" teacher, and the weapon of petty mischievous attacks is used to annoy and anger him. Later, political and ideologic groups are formed. The young girl, unless she has an ambition to vie with the boys, displays a much stronger inclination to form particular friendships and triangles within the group. Thus she partly avoids the danger of having her individual qualities and emotional growth frustrated.

[4] BLOS, P.: The adolescent personality. Appleton-Century, 1941.

One of the less commendable methods of breaking the tie with the parental home, and one that is frequently used in puberty, is actual flight. Such flights often end in return and reconciliation; sometimes, however, as we shall see in one case, they lead to tragedy. This flight from home is resorted to most often when the girl's relation with her friend has been disturbed or when her attempt to join a group has failed. From the material at our disposal it seems that heterosexual eroticism rarely provides an immediate motive for flight in early puberty. Sometimes one gets the impression that such a motive is present, especially if the flight is accompanied by heterosexual actions. Actually, such actions are induced by the girl's general sexual disquiet, usually without the presence of a real heterosexual impulse. *This is characteristic of early puberty.*

Neurotic illness is a more complicated solution. In favorable cases this may appear as a temporary disturbance of puberty, in less favorable cases it may represent a malady protracted for many years.

Clinical observations will reveal to us the traumatic liabilities of puberty, and will serve for objective illustration of the theoretic assumptions of psychoanalysis.

The following case histories were recorded as objectively as possible by physicians and social workers—that is, they were not selected, prepared, or arranged for purposes of psychoanalytic interpretation. Except for some degree of condensation, they follow almost literally the wording of the records. Some modifications have been made for the sake of concealing the identities of the patients and from other considerations of discretion, but nothing essential has been changed.

Case History of Evelyn

Evelyn is a 14-year-old girl who was referred to the clinic by the social service department of a Boston hospital. She had been running away from home and had stayed away nights on a number of occasions. The following history was obtained by the social worker in the case.

Evelyn is the fourth of seven children, and the mother is expecting another baby soon. She has three older sisters, younger twin brothers, and a younger sister. The parents are of middle-class Scotch origin, and it is obvious that they are struggling financially. The mother, who seems to dominate in the family, appears careworn and much older than she actually is; she has a shrewd intelligence, is energetic, and evidently has some ambitions for her children, for she wants them all to complete high school training. She is very strict but encourages them to bring their friends home and to dance and play cards; there are a number of boy friends coming to the house. Apparently the mother is tolerant as long as she can observe what is going on; however, she seems to be easily excitable and at times quite irritable. She is very secretive with the children as far as sex problems are concerned. She has never given them any sex information and has forbidden infantile masturbation. Nor has she told them that she is going to have another child. She obviously resents her frequent pregnancies and woman's lot in life; at the same time she seems to get considerable satisfaction from having children.

The father looks very young and immature. The mother treats him almost like one of the children. He seems quiet and much less excitable than she; however, once aroused, he becomes furious and it takes him a long time to get over his angry feelings. Evelyn seems to have been his favorite until the twins were born (Evelyn was 7 years old at the time). Until then he spoiled her and "gave her everything she wanted."

According to the mother, Evelyn was not a planned baby. Both parents would have welcomed a boy and were disappointed when this fourth girl arrived. She was a healthy, attractive baby. Her physical development was normal. At the age of 10 she fell downstairs, injured her arm, and had to have prolonged treatment. At that time she appears to have developed an anxiety state; for a week she screamed and cried whenever the mother left the house, and subsequently she often cried "to get her own way." Apart from this, however, she was a good-natured, likable, somewhat docile child. At the age of 12 she began to menstruate and shortly thereafter developed her present difficulties. She took to leaving home and staying away overnight. The mother does not know why. The first time she did it the police found her and brought her back. Since then there have been numerous similar escapades; the mother cannot remember when each of them happened. Once Evelyn was gone for three days. They looked all over for her and finally found her hidden in the attic. She had been without food all that time.

She then behaved normally from the fall of 1941 till August, 1942. At that time the mother was away with the younger children, having left Evelyn with the father. One night the young girl came home very late.

On that occasion the father hit her—for the first time. Afterward, the mother learned that she had been out dancing with some sailors. (Subsequent venereal tests were negative.) After the mother returned, Evelyn went away for three or four days.

The mother does not know where the girl goes—or what she does during these periods, but thinks that she usually stays by herself. She either returns home or is found wandering in the streets or at a friend's. She seems to have a compulsion to leave the house even when tired, for she comes home thoroughly exhausted and sleeps heavily. Shortly before the time of this history, Evelyn stole for the first time. She took $10 from a friend of her mother's who lives upstairs. She spent part of it, lost part of it, and brought back a few dollars. She cried and said she did not know why she had taken the money. She just saw it lying there and took it, and then did not know what to do with it. There has been no recurrence of stealing.

Coincident with the development of these difficulties, there has been an increasing lack of interest and a slump in the girl's school work. The mother has no explanation for all this. At times she feels that Evelyn's early illnesses are the cause of her present behavior: "It's affecting her now that she is fourteen."

On another occasion she expressed the opinion that the family's removal from their previous neighborhood, and the ensuing illnesses of the other children, who thus required her attention, as well as the coming of the twins, may have been contributing factors. At other times she expressed bewilderment and asked for help in understanding Evelyn.

The mother says that Evelyn is not lazy, but helpful in the house when she wants to be. She shows a special interest in cooking and took a great deal of responsibility when one of the twins was in her charge. She goes to church but is not bound up with any activities there. She likes movies and "love story magazines," seems to have a number of friends of both sexes, and is lively in a group. At one period, when she was between 3 and 5 years of age, she had nightmares; she would wake up screaming, dreaming of snakes, fire engines, and deformed people. She always preferred her father, but he could not quiet her at such times, while the mother could. The mother thinks that Evelyn is not really interested in boy friends. There are a number of nice boys who call her up, but she won't go out with them because she thinks they are too tame. The mother says that she cannot understand how Evelyn has escaped having sex experience, going around with sailors as she does. She thinks that Evelyn has got sex information from other children and through reading. Evelyn formerly had a lot of friends but the *mother forbade her to associate* with her group, as they "are the kind who sit in doorways and smoke." Evelyn formerly shared a bedroom with Mary, but *since Mary has a boy friend, Evelyn wants a place for herself, so the mother has fixed up a bedroom for her in the attic.*

The mother describes Anna, her oldest child, as quick-tempered and nervous; Mary is her favorite, and everybody likes this girl. Lucy is more like Evelyn: she is secretive, keeps to herself, and from time to time runs away and stays with her aunt and uncle. She says that Evelyn and Lucy are both trials to her because they are so secretive. The father is now very angry with Evelyn; he has turned against her completely and won't even talk to her. He is withholding her allowance and feels that they should be very strict with her. The mother shows great resentment against Evelyn and feels that she must give the father full control now and let him handle the situation, because she does not know how to do it herself. With marked feeling she said that Evelyn seems to have changed overnight from a nice, docile child into a grown-up person who is interested in boys and make-up. She has no use for her. Like the father, she intensely dislikes her using so much lipstick. The father told her that she looks like a tramp. She says that they have tried everything they can think of and have done their best according to their lights, but there is something there they know nothing about.

In these interviews with the parents it is evident that they want to do their best, but that they are overwhelmed by the ambivalence of their feelings toward Evelyn. Sometimes they have quite a good understanding of her, and try to be kind and tolerant, at other times they feel they should be severe and discipline her. Sometimes it seems that Evelyn is beginning to adjust at home, but she suddenly runs away just before something nice that was planned for her by her parents—a party or movie, for example—can be carried out.

DOCTOR'S INTERVIEWS

Evelyn is an attractive, red-haired girl who, despite her earrings, necklace, and heavy make-up, gives an impression of sturdiness and tomboyishness. She is sullen, wary, and very tense, but talks easily and willingly. She describes people vividly and makes objective evaluations of them that are astonishingly mature and well thought out. Although apprehensive and resentful, she displays wit and an appreciation of dramatic values. She says that she came to the clinic because she had run away and it was suggested that she be brought there. Her mother thought that she might have to go to jail or to a reform school.

Evelyn is the fourth of five girls and has twin brothers, George and Bill, aged 7. Anna, the oldest, is 20. Lucy, aged 16, is the favorite of her uncle and aunt; she moved to their home and did not even return to visit until her mother told her that she could not stay there unless she came to see her parents once a week. "Don't you think that's kind of funny?" Evelyn said. "She just moved right out."

Mary, aged 17, is Evelyn's favorite, and up until the last year, when Mary acquired a boy friend, they were very close friends. Tom visits Mary or takes her out almost every evening, and Evelyn and Mary did not go out together even on Halloween, as they had planned. Louise is 4 years old and very pretty but terribly spoiled; she is in Anna's special charge. George is the twin whom Evelyn took care of from the time he was a baby, and he liked her best. Now he is a tough little boy and doesn't seem to like her any more. Bill, who was Mary's particular charge, is a very sweet and clever little boy. Evelyn spoke of how considerate he is: when she had a headache recently, Bill said he was sorry and asked her why she did not go to bed. She added: "Catch George saying anything like that. He wouldn't care if you had ten headaches."

Evelyn said that her father works for Montgomery Ward and Company, that he is 39 years old and a very nice-looking man. "He's red-haired like me", she said. "Louise, George, and I take after him in looks. The others are dark, like mother. He always gave us everything. He wasn't like other fathers. He never beat us. But lately he is more strict. Maybe he is older and wiser now."

Her mother is a quiet, jolly woman when she is happy. "But sometimes she can holler and argue all the time. Nothing I do suits her and she's awfully mad at me now."

When asked what particularly had upset her mother, Evelyn said that she thought it was probably the gang. She and her mother had always got along fine until two years before, when the family moved from North Cambridge to South Boston. Evelyn missed her old friends but finally met a group of boys and girls about two years older than herself. The girls wore slacks and had a great deal of fun: "We can do everything the boys can do. Jane is one of the leaders. She's a crippled girl and she thinks she's pretty tough, but she is not so awfully tough. I can fight, too, even if I am little."

She said that this group gathered at various homes, went to movies and parties together, went roller skating, etc. She didn't think it was much fun to pair off and she liked doing things in the gang. Sometimes they rang fire alarms—"Don't tell my mother; she doesn't know that"—but did nothing worse. One of the boys she liked especially had gone into the navy the week before. She didn't unsually go out with boys alone, although her mother was willing to let her, because she liked the gang better. Two boys come to see her, and her mother can't understand why she doesn't go out with them. She explained: "If she knew them the way I do, she wouldn't want me to go."

Evelyn said that she was in the second year of high school, that she was particularly interested in cooking, and that after she graduated she wanted to go to trade school to take a course in catering. She said spontaneously: "I want to earn my own living. I am not going to get married and have children. I am going to get things for myself and have them as I like them."

In another interview the girl began to talk rapidly about an argument she had had with her mother that morning. She said that her mother had kept her in all the weekend and that she had refused to do her work that morning. She said: "I think she hates me, and I hate her, too." She said the children at school think that it is bad to dislike one's mother, but she added: "I am not the only one. All of us plan to get away. We can't wait."

She said that the four girls had plans for having an apartment together, and added that Lucy had not left home for nothing. She continued to express great resentment toward her mother, told of frequent beatings, said that of late her father had been stricter and that she could not wait until she was 16, when she would be able to go to work and leave home. She said that one day her mother threw a shoe at her; the heel struck her temple and she was knocked out. She said that her mother was very quick-tempered and did things without thinking, but sometimes she did the wrong thing when she had plenty of time to think it over.

She then talked again about her gang and particularly about Helen Green, a 21-year-old sailor's wife with whom she had gone out only a couple of times.

By the end of the interview she was again friendly and appeared relieved to have talked as freely about her mother as she had.

Another day Evelyn came to the clinic fifteen minutes late. She apologized and said frankly that she had overslept. She said that her family had taken her allowance of 50 cents a week away from her and had kept her in. She said that the only thing that had saved her from being bored to death was that three boys came to visit her. She said: "My father scowls at me now. All I want to do is to get out of there. I can't wait until I am sixteen."

She said that she had had a card from her sailor friend, but he never gave his address; he moved around so much that she guessed that he couldn't be reached. She is sorry, because she would like to write to him. She then added: "My mother doesn't trust me, you know. She never did. I don't blame her, but if she knew how the gang trusted me, she would be surprised. They used to earn money doing little things, and they gave it to me to keep. I always wondered what my mother would say if she found the money."

At the next interview, Evelyn was untidy: two of the buttons on her blouse were missing, there was a large spot on her skirt, her hair looked uncombed. She wore no make-up. She apologized for the way she looked, saying that her mother would not let her wear make-up any more and she knew she looked like a ghost.

When the physical examinations were given to her, she cooperated well and was interested in the different tests. She is decidedly left-handed, although she writes with her right hand, and she is definitely right-eyed. When asked about her menstrual periods, she remarked that she had not known anything about menstruation when her periods began, but that she had gone to ask Anna, who told her that all girls had it and that bad blood had to go somewhere. Evelyn then laughed and said: "The doctor has since told me what it is all about, so I know now that Anna didn't have the right idea."

Evelyn was taking her psychologic tests and was quite interested in them and pleased that she had done well. Her school course was mentioned, since the psychologic tests indicated that she could do more academic work than is required in the commercial course. She says frankly that she knows that she cooks well, and that some work involving cooking would probably be best for her, but she is not going to learn catering, "no matter what anyone says." The question of whether she might not be able to take some other work that would utilize her interest in cooking was brought up, and she was greatly interested and said that she would like to find out something more about courses in nutrition or dietetics.

Evelyn then began to speak spontaneously about her mother, expressing considerable resentment of the fact, which she had just learned, that her mother was going to have another baby. She said: "She did not tell me, of course. She told Lucy and Mary."

Evelyn said that Anna had told them all several weeks ago that she knew her mother was going to have a baby, but they did not believe it. Evelyn commented: "I think seven is enough, don't you? But if we are going to have a baby, I hope it's a girl." She then went on to speak of how grouchy her mother was, commenting: "Of course she doesn't feel well now, and she is more nervous because of the baby, but she was always grouchy. She and Anna fight something terrible. I don't get along with Anna myself, but I hate the way my mother treats her. The other day Anna got up late, so my mother scolded her and Anna answered her back, and my mother, who had been cutting bread, took the knife and struck Anna with it in the shoulder. It drew blood in three places. She has a terrible temper."

Evelyn then complained about her mother's close supervision and distrust of her. She asked the physician if she did not think that it was all right to have a little privacy about one's own things. Without waiting for an answer, she went on to say that Lucy would not allow her mother to go through her pocketbook and that the mother was a little scared of Lucy. Evelyn said that some day they were all going to gang up on the mother, that she might be murdered some day. She then said that she was never going to get married. She asked the physician whether she was married. When told she was not, Evelyn commented: "Well, you get along all right, don't you?"

Two weeks later Evelyn completed her psychologic tests. She was obviously fatigued and somewhat discouraged about her efforts. She said that the only new thing that had happened at home was that her father and mother had had a row on the previous night. Her father came home late for supper and her mother chided him, telling him to get his own meal. He lost his temper, and, among other things, shouted to his wife that she let Evelyn go out and stay out, so why should she yell at him. Evelyn commented: "He is like a kid. Imagine him saying a thing like that. Can you beat it! My mother runs the roost in our house, but my father lets her."

She spoke contemptuously about this incident but at the same time appeared worried about it. She did not mention the new baby except when commenting on the mother's irritability. In this connection she said that the mother was always telling the girls to be more considerate of her in view of her condition. Evelyn remarked: "She is never considerate of anybody, anyway. Why should we be considerate of her?"

Evelyn was worried about her Italian course. She was not getting along well with the teacher who, she felt, was unjust to her, and her inclination was to drop the course. She had been talking with her sophomore sponsor, but they could not find another course she could take that would give her five points. The physician suggested that Evelyn might find considerable satisfaction in studying her Italian a little harder, mastering it, and thus making a better impression on the teacher, to which Evelyn made no comment.

At the next interview, a week later, Evelyn was more composed and talked in a more mature manner than ever before. Her clothes were untidy and her face and neck not quite clean. She wore pearl earrings and a large necklace. She spoke spontaneously about the new baby, saying she could hardly wait for it to be born. She had been shopping with her mother and was delighted to pick out baby clothes. She thinks it is a good thing that she is interested in the baby, because no one else in the family really is. Her mother is divided in the things she says about the baby. The father thinks it is a nuisance and the other girls also think another baby will be a bother. She can see why her mother is not entirely enthusiastic, because she was very ill during her last two pregnancies and a small baby will greatly increase her household burdens. She also sees some reason for her father's attitude, because he has a hard time supporting seven children. She hopes that the baby is a boy, because otherwise it will have a hard time in their household.

Evelyn then turned to the subject of Helen Green, the 21-year-old married girl, with whom on several occasions she had gone to a place of ill repute. This place seems very intriguing and mysterious to young people because it is frequented by prostitutes and soldiers. Evelyn said that she had been curious about the place and was greatly disappointed to find that it did not look very wicked. Helen had given Evelyn her birth certificate so that the young girl could avoid the curfew restriction. She and Helen went into one of the grills, and there were soldiers and sailors and all kinds of women there, but the place did not look very different from any other grill. "Of course," she added, "there were lots of those cheap women around. Gee, the way they pile on the make-up. It's not hard to spot them a mile off."

She smiled and agreed when the physician pointed out that the opposition that mothers have to their daughters' using too much make-up is connected with this very fact. She then went on to talk about Helen Green's appearance, of how she was never quite clean, of how there was always a button or two missing from her dress, and of how she put on powder and perfume instead of bathing. Helen Green is married to a sailor who is at sea, but she goes out with many men, and Evelyn expressed definite disapproval of this behavior. She said that she thought that Helen had no business getting married if she was going to carry on like that. Anna has a new boy friend who is a sergeant in the army. He is a big cowboy from Oklahoma, stationed at P— camp, and he came to Boston on his furlough to spend the time with Anna. Evelyn's mother asked him to supper one night and they all enjoyed having him. Evelyn describes him as a tall, rather shy, very nice young man, the kind she would like to marry if she ever married. She observed that he was not "smooth," but would make a very good husband, and with someone like that a woman could have peace and quiet in her home. She declared that she was determined to have such a home whether or not she married. She did not want quarrels and yelling, because she had had enough of that. She had decided to continue with her Italian, although she still was not getting along with her teacher.

Some days later Evelyn ran away from home at night and came to the clinic early the next morning. She said little except that she would not go home and that she was hungry. She appeared exhausted, was sullen, very tense, and rather uncommunicative, and kept saying that she would not go home. She said that nothing had happened to make her run away; on the preceding day she had played hooky and spent the day with her friend Rose. She left Rose's house at 11 o'clock at night and suddenly decided she could not return to her own home. She sat on Rose's front porch all night and came to the clinic in the morning because she did not know what else to do. Arrangements were made for her to go temporarily to a foster home, and Evelyn said that she would like to do that.

Five days later Evelyn came in, still sullen and a little reticent. She said that the only thing she was certain of was that she could not go home. She asked whether we could not find her a permanent foster home. The physician talked with her about some of the difficulties she would have in adjusting herself to a foster home, but she repeated that she would have to try it, since she could not go back to her own family. She finally burst out: "They do not want me there. The other night when they thought I was asleep, I overheard my father and mother talking about me. My mother asked him why he did not give me back my allowance, and he shouted that he would not give me my allowance nor anything else ever again."

Two days later Evelyn made up her own mind that she would not miss any further school work. She had lost her way the day before and had not arrived at the foster home in which she had been placed until 6 o'clock. She had little to say about this home except that she was a little lonely there. She said that on the previous night when Kate Smith began to sing "White Christmas" she got homesick and had to run upstairs to cry. She said very seriously that she felt that she could not go to her own home, but that she was unhappy being away. She observed that it must be her own fault, because her sisters live through the same things she does and they manage to stand it better. She does not know why she feels the way she does about home and about her mother. One thing that makes her very angry is that her mother goes through her pocketbook. "She should talk about secrets!" she said. "She is the one that has secrets! We did not even know her age until two years ago."

That day she appeared no longer sullen but friendly and earnest in her attitude. She talked willingly with her physician about the necessity of learning more about herself, so that she could find out what forces inside her made her react as she did. And when the physician suggested that she could not always run away from things, she smiled and said that she knew that.

Ten days later Evelyn was subdued and very serious. She said that she did not want to stay any longer in the foster home, although the presence of a new girl there had helped her a little. She still believed that she should stay away from home, but she missed the kids and the fun. She talked at considerable length about how hard it would be for her away from home, but kept repeating that she did not see how she could do anything about it.

Five days later Evelyn was still more discouraged and subdued, admitting readily that she was lonesome, unhappy about the holidays, but still determined not to go home. To take up her spare time she is writing the story of her life. She plans to tell the truth for the most part, but to touch it up a little so that it will be more interesting. Maybe she will be able to sell it to a magazine. She laughed as she said this and added that she had started the biography with a statement that she was born during the first year of the great depression, although she was actually born the year before. "But," she argued, "you have to make things interesting if you want to sell them."

The physician suggested that she adhere to the truth as much as possible, because writing such a story might help her a great deal in solving her problems. She said that she realized this and that she remembered one thing that she had not thought of in years. When she was 6 years old, her mother had lost her pocketbook. The family was discussing the loss one day when her uncle was there. His behavior struck Evelyn as funny, and she giggled.

He quickly turned upon her and said: "You are the one who stole the pocketbook."

The mother promptly took up this accusation and would not listen to the girl's denials. Bitterly, Evelyn observed: "Even then, you see, she was against me."

Evelyn had not been regular in her school attendance since she had gone to the foster home. She said that she knew this was not good, but several things she needed for her classes were in her own house. Her family had not brought these things to her, and she did not want to explain to the teachers that she was not living at home. She is concerned about her future and asked the physician if she thought she would ever amount to anything. The importance of her school work for her future plans was discussed, and she maintained that she not only wanted to finish high school but also to take further work in some branch of nutrition science.

The physician asked her whether she would like to go home for Christmas and she said in a surprised tone of voice, "Oh, yes. If they want me. It's up to them to decide."

Ten days later Evelyn came to the clinic very gaily. She appeared happy and self-confident. She said that she had gone home Christmas Eve and was still there. She was going to stay home until New Year's anyway, possibly for good. Everyone there was so nice to her that she felt like visiting royalty, but she did not know how long it would last. She and Lucy had quarreled a little bit, but it did not mean anything. She said that it was good to be home and that she had never realized before how much she liked her home. She said that she felt so sorry for Elizabeth (the 16-year-old girl at the foster home) because Elizabeth has no home and no family.

Evelyn thinks that the main trouble with her is that she has done things for which she is not yet really old enough. The summer before, when her mother was away on vacation, she started going out with older boys and girls. She sees now that this was a mistake, but she is bored with younger boys and girls. In many ways she is much older than her 14 years. Most of her recent battles with her mother grew out of her going out with older boys, because her mother did not know that she could take care of herself. As she thinks it over now, Evelyn realizes that her mother was right to worry about a 14-year-old girl, but when her mother told her not to go out she went anyway. Another thing that made Evelyn feel older than 14 was that she and her three sisters were always lumped together. She liked housework and did a great deal of it when she was only a little child. She took almost complete care of George, one of the twins, and she has always had more responsibility than most girls of her age. Evelyn cannot or will not say why she thinks that acting older than her age was a mistake, but concluded: "I was wrong in a lot of things."

She then began to speak of her mother, saying that while her mother still did not feel well, she was not as grouchy as she had been. They had bought more clothes for the baby together, and Evelyn said with a grin and a little wriggle of her body: "I just can't wait for that baby."

Except for occasional mild cramps Evelyn has never had any trouble during her menstrual periods and is not bothered by them. She had picked up a considerable amount of information about sex at school, but until she talked with Dr. T., she did not know the "straight facts." She grinned and told of going at once to her sisters and telling them all that Dr. T. had told her. She commented: "I was the first to know it straight. Just as I am always the first in everything."

She said that her mother had never mentioned sex matters to her and she thinks this was a mistake. As a matter of fact, Evelyn has always been able to take care of herself, but if this had not been the case, her mother would have been to blame had anything evil happened to her because of her ignorance. She thinks that parents should tell children about sex as soon as they begin to ask questions, but comments: "I do not know how I would do it if I had to do it, though. I can see why mother thought it was too hard."

One week later Evelyn appeared happy and contented about her decision to stay at home. She talked quite sensibly about her parents' current attitude and said that she knew that the family would not keep on treating her so well, but they had missed her just as she had missed them, and she thought that in the future things would go more smoothly.

The story of her life was finished, but she had decided that it was not good enough to be published. She did not know quite what to do with it and thought she would tear it up. She neither agreed nor disagreed with the physician's casual suggestion that she bring it to her to read. Her main interest now is the new baby and she told again how everyone has decided that it will be a boy and its name is to be Andrew. She does not know what will happen if it is a girl. She does not like the name Andrew, but it is a Scotch name and both the parents are Scotch. She said that she enjoyed reading anything about Scotland and that she would like to go there some day.

She likes writing very much and her teacher frequently reads her compositions to the class. The teacher scolds Evelyn because her spelling and punctuation are poor, but she likes her ideas. That day Evelyn was worried about Elizabeth and seemed relieved to hear that Elizabeth was still in the foster home and apparently behaving quite well.

A week later Evelyn presented a neater appearance than usual. Her make-up was carefully put on. She looked clean and was wearing an attractive sweater and skirt. Things are going fairly well at home. Her mother was sick Thursday and Evelyn stayed home from school to help her. The mother asked the other girls to stay, but each one refused in turn, giving some flimsy excuse. The satisfaction Evelyn obviously gets from being the dependable one in the family was discussed, and it was observed that she has always been the one who did things for the mother. She is very much excited about the baby. Her mother has promised her that she can take complete charge of the child, and she wants to bring it up her way or not at all. The twins and Louise are spoiled brats, and she won't have anything like that with her baby. She told her mother that she wanted to have the final word on anything relating to the baby and her mother agreed. She is looking up girls' names and hopes the baby is a girl. She likes girls better and thinks a boy would be spoiled by the whole family.

Evelyn has never mentioned taking $10 from her mother's friend, although several opportunities have been made for her to bring up the subject. When asked about it directly she became quite distressed. She wriggled in her chair, seemed ashamed, and was very reluctant to discuss it. Finally she said: "I guess maybe everybody has something he is ashamed to remember."

She said that she had not planned to do it, but she saw the money on the friend's dresser. She was upset about something, so she took the money and went out to have a good time trying to forget everything. She went to the movies, bought a few little things for herself, and came home in a taxi. She lost some of it. She does not know why she did such a thing, and no one else could understand it either. She paid back all the money to the woman. "The worst of it was," she said, "that it was somebody I loved very much."

When asked if the woman behaved differently toward her, Evelyn replied: "Oh, no, but I feel different about her."

The physician pointed out that this episode was part of her whole problem and may have been similar in origin to much of her impulsive running away. After considerable reassurance, she gradually appeared more comfortable, but was subdued during the rest of the interview.

One week later Evelyn, who had been coming late to the clinic and had discussed this question with her physician, came on time. Again she looked neat, her make-up was subdued, and her clothing was clean. Her mother had been feeling rather miserable but not sick enough to go to the doctor. Evelyn expressed concern about her and said that her mother would not stay in bed if she were not really sick. The question of Evelyn's supervision of the new baby was brought up and discussed at some length. Evelyn agreed that she probably would not be allowed to take complete charge of the baby and that she would not be able to decide really important matters, but she wants to take care of it, and she thinks that if she pays considerable attention to it, she can keep it from becoming quite spoiled. She thinks that she is so much interested in this baby because she likes babies in general, and also because she would like the feeling of having something of her own. She knows that this baby won't be quite that, but it will be more her own than anything or anyone she has right now.

Evelyn inquired about Elizabeth, having learned that the latter had run away and been sent to Lancaster. She is unhappy and concerned about her and says that she hates to think of her in a reform school. She thinks that if she had stayed at the foster home, Elizabeth would have had a girl friend and would not have run away, at least not for a long time; but she is not really blaming herself, because she knows that she cannot live just to take care of Elizabeth. She thinks that Elizabeth would not have run away if she had been in a different place where there was more to do, and where the foster mother was more congenial. However, she does not think that Elizabeth would have stayed very long even in a very nice foster home. Elizabeth talked about wanting a home and a few years earlier she probably did want one; but now she likes excitement, and a quiet life in a nice home would bore her to death. Evelyn agrees that Elizabeth is too young to be entirely on her own and adds: "And not smart enough, either."

She does not think that Elizabeth is really boy crazy, but that she likes boys. Boys can take her dancing and to the movies and provide some of the excitement she craves. She is a little different from Evelyn in her attitude toward boys. Evelyn says: "I can take them or leave them."

Evelyn then asked some rather searching questions about the law in regard to young girls, also about reform schools and foster homes. She wanted to know about the authority and responsibility of a place like the clinic in such a case as Elizabeth's. She asked, too, who chose the people who were to act as foster parents, and said that it was very difficult to find the right people for a certain girl or boy she was interested in. She declared that when she grew up, she was going to try to do something to help the work of such a clinic.

Since Evelyn went to the foster home she has apologized for her former behavior and has gradually come to regard the physician casually. She made teasing inquiries about an army air force package of matches that she saw on the physician's desk, and apparently feels comfortable and secure in the relationship she has established with her.

Here the interviews were interrupted because Evelyn ran away and during the succeeding weeks it was impossible to find out her whereabouts.

Evelyn began to menstruate at the age of 12, apparently before she had reached a maturity adequate for the psychologic assimilation of this physiologic event. We do not know exactly what her direct reactions to this sign of growth were, but we know that she began to behave abnormally soon afterward. The fact that a physiologic event was such a strong provocation points to the existence of a disposition to neurotic behavior stemming from other sources. What was Evelyn's emotional situation before she began to menstruate? We can find an answer to this question by examining her life history.

She is a fourth daughter, and her domestic situation was such that an object for the typical prepuberty attachment to another girl was present in the home. As Evelyn herself says, there was a kind of little "gang" in her home, a small revolutionary group united by their common hatred of their mother. It is immaterial for our purposes to determine how much this situation existed in Evelyn's fantasy and how much in reality. At any rate, the girls had secrets among themselves of the typical character described above (chap. 1); they displayed sexual curiosity and at the same time resented the secrets of their mother. In Evelyn's case the situation was particularly clear-cut, because her mother actually does surround herself with an atmosphere of secrecy. She is extraordinarily prudish sexually and in this way strengthens the need for secrecy in her young daughters. Evelyn is the youngest in the foursome, and for this reason has a particularly strong need to be "grown-up." Her joyful remark to the physician who enlightened her on sex matters is very characteristic: "My sisters do not know about all that; I will be the first in this as in everything else."

The desire to be the first to have experiences involves great dangers for Evelyn and for girls like her: it may lead them to actions that arise not from genuine sexual need, but from the urge to show the grownups that they, too, are grown up. The inner tension that pushes children to fatal adventures often derives from the desire to be grown up rather than from a strong sexual urge.

Evelyn's relation to her sister Mary was a clear example of the two-girl situation and obviously played a part typical of the prepuberty period in Evelyn's emotional life. In the course of this relation Evelyn experienced a trauma. Her sister-friend acquired a boy friend who is in the navy, and Evelyn complained that instead of the triangular situation she unconsciously expected, a completely new regrouping took place.

Mary spent her evenings with her boy friend, while Evelyn exiled herself to solitude and no longer wanted to share her bedroom with her sister. This trauma recurred in a somewhat less intense form in her relation with the oldest sister, who also has a boy friend. Of the group of four sisters, only 16-year-old Lucy suffers from the same difficulties as Evelyn and experiences similar emotions. She cannot bear her parental home and from time to time runs away to her uncle and aunt. This is a mild form of flight that falls far short of Evelyn's in emotional level. But, as Evelyn says, Lucy gets "everything she wants" at her uncle and aunt's—a remark that betrays the fact that Evelyn had no refuge where she could have her wishes fulfilled.

It is perfectly clear that Evelyn has run away from home in order to find a substitute in the outside world for her destroyed relation with her sister friend. She has become attached to Helen, the 21-year-old wife of a sailor, with whom she has the important satisfaction of being treated by a girl seven years older than herself as an equal, a grownup. Helen expresses this attitude by lending the 14-year-old Evelyn her own birth certificate to protect her from the curfew imposed on the young, thus making it possible for her to go out at night. In addition, Helen, just like Evelyn's sisters, has a boy friend, also in the navy; true, she is married to him, but since her husband is at sea, her situation is similar to that of the lonely Evelyn, and thus she can offer her better conditions of friendship than her sisters. Apparently Evelyn has skipped the triangular situation that she did not succeed in establishing with her sister, and has herself found a boy friend in the navy. He is a real character, but one so pale that he resembles a fantasy product. Evelyn really did meet him, but immediately afterward he went to sea, like Helen's husband, and his whereabouts is unknown. The fantasy is as pale as reality in this case, because at bottom Evelyn has not the slightest interest in men. All she wants is to be a grownup and to have what her deserting sister has. The war makes the choice of a fantasy object easy for her, because all the men involved in the relationships of those around her are soldiers and sailors. Helen, as a sisterly figure and object of identification, is very dangerous: Evelyn is not yet ready to have a man independently. According to her development, she should play the part of the third partner, and her premature independence cannot give her any emotional gratification.

The dangers into which Evelyn is plunged are extremely typical for the young who have not yet reached adolescence. The situation described here has, moreover, become a specific war problem. The combined effects of the emotional disturbance characteristic of this age period and the overstimulation of imagination connected with the war are turning the formerly sporadic and more or less morbid cases of running away into a mass problem. The majority of the young girls encountered in parks or dubious hotels as soldiers' sweethearts, or caught outdoors after the curfew, are by no means "precociously mature"; they play and act as young people of their age have always done, only the reality of the war has given their behavior a more dangerous form. The older girl, that is, the older sister or friend who now hastily marries the formerly platonic boy friend or becomes pregnant as a result of intercourse with him, has actually become precociously mature; in doing this she leaves her younger companion or sister in the lurch, as Evelyn's sister has done, and the younger girl, left alone and unsatisfied, is seized by an urge for identification that moves her to sham-sexual actions. As a result of their weakened self-control and psychologic instability, immature girls are exposed to serious personal dangers and as a mass phenomenon create an almost insoluble social problem.

Thus, in her imitation of Helen, several of Evelyn's fantasies have become enhanced as a result of her feeling of solitude. The prostitution fantasy, to which we shall return later, has taken a form in her that is found in girls between the periods of prepuberty and puberty. It is still a play without content, deriving from curiosity and a desire for secrecy, but it is no longer confined to playing with a friend, as is the case with younger girls. Now it is actually played out in the street. This is obviously accompanied by more mature fantasy elements that are, however, not yet strong and dangerous enough to be successfully repressed by the girl. The most interesting thing here is that Evelyn denies that there is any danger in this situation, that she herself considers it a harmless game, because actually she does not feel any desire for sexual experiences.

This feeling represents the greatest danger of all for young girls: they have no sexual urge, they desire no sexual gratifications, and because of this absence of desire they feel secure. But the game itself is provocative, and although make-up and lipstick have no more significance for them than for the little girl playing in front of her mirror, the reactions of the outside world are more serious. The provocative behavior of the young girl often has a seductive effect, and the fact that she often exaggerates her age (as by means of Helen's birth certificate in Evelyn's case), frees the man from any scruples he might have concerning a juvenile. Gradually, as a result of the male's wooing, the girl's sexual excitability is mobilized too. At first this leads to seemingly harmless preludes, but later the young girl is no longer able to master her excitement and the game becomes all too serious before she realizes it. Often the first accidental experience gives rise to a number of others on the basis of the feeling that "now everything is lost anyhow." Frequently the girl's restless urge leads her to sexual crimes against herself; sexual experience takes the place of love, and its consequences—prostitution, syphilis, and illegitimate children—often constitute an irretrievable disaster.

Evelyn's abnormal situation is like a magnifying glass that can show us several other phenomena. We have assumed that her normal development was disturbed by the mortification she suffered in her friendship with her sister. It is known that such experiences have a traumatic effect only if they take place on soil prepared in advance. Evelyn's limit of tolerance had been reached with the appearance of menstruation; but other

factors explaining her pathologic behavior can be shown. Some
of these lie in her present situation, the unfavorable character of
which does not result only from the loss of her friend. We have
seen that substitute gratifications outside the home are extremely important for overcoming the psychologic difficulties
of the young. A comradely gang of girls and boys, in which
sex is much talked about but nothing is done about it, and common play acting in groups of a homogeneous cultural level,
create better opportunities than more individual ways of
gratifying psychologic urges.

Modern educational and social institutions try to create the
most favorable conditions for the formation of such groups.
To a runaway more normal than Evelyn—to a certain extent
the inclination to run away is typical of all young people—the
group supplies many gratifications. Evelyn has found this
solution for herself; she has even created a respected position
for herself in a group and enjoys in it the confidence that her
mother has refused her at home. She has been able to exchange
the unsatisfactory gang within her family for a better one in the
outside world. Here she has the opportunity of satisfying her
wish to be a leader and to "know" things ahead of the others.
Apparently it is also very important for her to be admitted as
a tomboy and an equal of the boys.

The need to be respected and to enjoy confidence is of extraordinary importance for Evelyn and for all girls of her age The
urge to independence is usually accompanied by a feeling of
insecurity. To create a sense of self-responsibility and self-
criticism, the approval of the outside world is at first urgently
needed. Evelyn's ambition to "be the first," to take over the
part of the leader, to feel important and fully recognized, is
generally characteristic of this phase of development. There
is no doubt that Evelyn's family situation has only intensified
this need in her. Her desire to be a boy is also fed by very
personal motives, but at her age it is so typical that in this
respect we can generalize her motives. Thus, her mother's

forbidding her to associate with the gang because it was not up
to her social standards deprived Evelyn of this favorable possibility for gratification and was for her a second trauma.

Every action that keeps the young from finding normal outlets provokes a reflex of the psychologic forces toward the past;
in other words, it intensifies the infantile feelings that are still so
strong in them. We have learned that during prepuberty and
puberty the young girl has an intense urge to free herself from
her mother's tutelage and that at the same time she still strongly
clings to her mother. The strong hate tendencies that such a
young girl displays in relation to her mother originate not so
much in the Oedipus situation as in her anger at the fact that
her mother prevents her from being a grownup. The old feeling of being utterly rejected and disdained is now connected
with a strong feeling of hatred and a wish for retaliation. This
hatred is then also used as a means to attain freedom. Evelyn,
whose thinking is strongly influenced by crime novels, says
without the slightest restraint that the gang at home, that is,
she and her sisters, are going to kill their mother.

Gradually other elements have probably entered into this
hatred. We have seen Evelyn's fury gain momentum as her
mother became pregnant, and from her utterances we can infer
that she takes her mother's sexuality very much amiss, that
she is jealous of the expected baby, and above all that this pregnancy has mobilized her own wish to have a baby. Perhaps
Evelyn ran away because she felt that she was not sufficiently
loved by her mother and wanted to take revenge on her; perhaps she did it also because she feared that she would realize
her hatred of her mother in murder.

Evelyn has given us an important hint as to what is going on
in her mind. She described the emotional processes in another
girl who is also of a runaway type; this description is a confession betraying her own emotions that she refuses to reveal
directly. Elizabeth, the other girl, says Evelyn, ran away
because she felt so deserted, empty, and bored; this feeling of
emptiness that must be overcome by action in order not to lead

to depression is so frequent among the young and so typical that we may well assume that Evelyn herself is suffering from such a state of emotional vacuum. The psychologic processes in a young person suffering from depression reflect a "provisional" situation such as occurs during a change of residence, when one has left the old apartment and not yet taken possession of the new. The "under way" period is marked by rich fantasies, extravagant infatuations, and various defense mechanisms not necessarily resulting in grave morbid symptoms. But we must not forget that Evelyn has behind her a heavily laden past. At home she has experienced a whole series of love disappointments: the favorite of her father, she was deserted by him upon the birth of a new child; her mother has never concealed from her that she came into the world undesired and that she was expected as a boy. We also know that a few years ago this girl experienced anxiety states during which she obviously suffered gravely each time she was separated from her mother. But Evelyn overcame all this normally until she had to cope with the sensitivity of pubescence, and external interference began to prevent the normal solutions she desired.

Then, too, there are probably motives—we have not, however, learned them directly from her—that created in her the need to drive herself from her home in order to become a freezing and starving Cinderella. She passed several night on the steps of a strange house in just such a miserable state. This behavior perhaps expressed a strong feeling of guilt that was the consequence of her aggressions against her mother, and perhaps this was strengthened by elements arising from other sources. On the basis of our knowledge of this age period, we may safely conjecture something of this kind, even though Evelyn's case history does not give us any direct evidence of it. There is no young girl in whom menstruation does not arouse genital tension and a need to masturbate. From Evelyn's mother we learned that "such things" do not happen in her family, that they are "the dirtiest and most terrible things imaginable." Lucy did it once, but she was so energetically reprimanded that the misdemeanor was never repeated. Lucy is the sister who cannot stand her home and from time to time runs away to her uncle and aunt. We may suppose that the emptiness and solitude at home cannot sufficiently divert Evelyn's sexual tensions and that as a result her temptation to masturbate is increased. She prefers to fill out this emptiness by diversions outside her home and thus to avoid the forbidden act. She apparently thinks that she can control herself better in the outside world with its real dangers than when confronted with the dark forces at home.

As has been said, this very security involves the greatest danger for Evelyn and for girls like her. Early puberty is characterized by intensified psychologic excitability and an urge to motor discharge, but there is not yet at this time a conscious realization of sexual longings. Therefore this period is dangerous; the psychologic defense mechanisms that repress the sexual urge and can supervise it are not yet sufficiently formed, as they will be later during adolescence. Young girls of Evelyn's age often experience sexual situations that are for them only an insignificant, harmless game, because they feel sufficiently protected by their awareness of their own lack of sexual interest. In so far as such actions are carried out, they are principally motivated, as we have seen, by the desire to imitate older sisters or friends, the urge to be grown-up, the feeling of isolation, the wish to take revenge on the parents, etc. The atmosphere of the war particularly intensifies these manifestations of prepuberty and early puberty and makes them a focus of danger.

In cases such as Evelyn's, there are two possible solutions—individual treatment by an appropriate and trained person (the motherly approach will seldom prove sufficient, because the rejection of the mother is usually too strong at this stage; it is often possible to achieve better results by adopting a comradely attitude) or admission to a well organized group outside the family. By throwing light on the processes within the individual, psychoanalysis can distinguish the different types of difficulties and thus give the best suggestions both for individual treatment and for the formation of favorable groups.

We have used Evelyn as an illustration in our discussion of normal processes, although she cannot be regarded as normal. In her pathologic distortion she has shown us the norm as through a magnifying glass. The difference between normal and pathologic behavior is quantitative. In this sense the processes that have partly been found in the case history and partly been reconstructed can be regarded as typical of the phase of early puberty in girls.

CASE HISTORY OF NANCY

Nancy, a 13-year-old girl, was admitted to the hospital because of bizarre seizures apparently of psychogenic origin.

She had been perfectly well all her life until about five months before the onset of menstruation, when she began to complain a great deal of pains in her abdomen. These came on immediately after she took exercise; later, when she bagan to menstruate, the pains occurred immediately before the menses. She would not go to see any doctor, however, despite the insistence of her sister, who says that she has the same feelings about doctors that Nancy has. Some months before the time of this history the young girl began to have occasional frontal headaches accompanied by intensified abdominal pain. Her condition was diagnosed as appendicitis and an immediate operation was advised. Her recovery was uneventful.

When she was first brought to the hospital Nancy did not know whether or not she was to be operated on. She was told that the operation would not take place until the next morning, but she was operated on one and a half hours after admission. The patient was terrified on the operating table, for she was afraid of dying. But above all she was furious at having been betrayed, operated on "by surprise," without warning. She also expressed fears that "they would take out the wrong thing; the nurse would give the wrong instruments to the doctors, and they wouldn't notice it." After the operation she was angry at the nurses. She thought that she should have been examined more thoroughly before the operation. She still thought the nurses had given the wrong instruments to the doctor. She was also worried as to whether her whole appendix had been taken out—perhaps a part had been left in her that would cause an infection, or perhaps another organ had been taken out by mistake.

The patient was discharged and went to the home of her married sister Anna in S—— to convalesce. There she had the first of her seizures. She was sitting down at about 9.30 a.m., having had breakfast an hour before. She suddenly "got all hot," felt queer, and was very much upset. She was quite frightened, a little nauseated and unsteady afterward, and went to sleep for a few hours. There was no loss of consciousness on that occasion. Nancy is able to recall the exact time of this attack, because her brother-in-law had had to stay in bed for eleven days after an accident, and she can calculate it from that circumstance. When the next attack occurred she was all alone, taking care of her 1½-year-old niece. She does not remember what happened, but she had the same feeling as before. When she woke up, the whole family was there and she was sitting on the edge of a bed.

By and by her attacks became more violent and more frequent and she began to lose consciousness with them. There was no aura, according to her account, although the attacks often came just after she drank water. The family noted this fact and someone used to stand behind her whenever she drank a glass of water. After the loss of consciousness without warning, the patient says, she "gets wild and acts kind of crazy." She calls out to her brother Dick "in a funny way." She thinks that she has been so violent that she has even bruised various members of the family at times. She always has a severe frontal headache when she wakes up. She remembers that one night when she fell and her sister tried to catch her, her head hit her sister's foot. She also recalls that she fell out of bed on one occasion when she was in the hospital.

The family was very much afraid that she might injure herself while thrashing around, and both father and mother mention that they tried to restrain her by holding down her hands and her feet. The mother said it took both the father and the brother to hold the girl. On coming out of such a spell, Nancy seemed only partially conscious; she did not recognize the family, often acted very silly, and laughed and jumped around on the bed like an animal. Once she stood on the davenport, and banged an electric light suspended on a cord against the wall; another time she tried to overturn a pail of water; on several occasions she tore up pieces of paper and asked for matches. The family was terrified for fear that she would set fire to something. Twice she forgot what had been going on immediately before the attack. For example, her sister Anna and her husband were visiting, and Nancy had been out driving with them all morning. In the afternoon she had a spell and then spoke to them as if she were seeing them for the first time that day. Sometimes she would talk very angrily, saying that they had beaten her or that they wanted to get rid of her or that someone was trying to hurt her and that she wanted her own father and mother. On other occasions, she would, on recovering from her attack, hug and kiss her mother and father very demonstratively, which is not her usual habit. On one occasion she called her mother "a bathing beauty" and her father "an old bull."

The father, who is of Italian birth, is the dominant figure in the home. He disciplines the children by talking to them but has never punished them physically. They are afraid of him and obey him, however. They think that this is because he never gives in to them as the mother does.

The mother, also Italian, had a terrible temporal headache in the fourth or fifth month of her pregnancy with Nancy. She was admitted to the hospital at that time and for sixteen days had to be fed by rectum because of her frightful nausea and vomiting. From that time on she was not sick until five or six months before the time of this record. Then she began to have dizzy spells in which she would occasionally fall if there was no one at hand to catch her. She felt considerably better after she got glasses and had her teeth taken out. Her youngest child, George, was burned to death in a kitchen fire some years ago and for a time the mother was extremely nervous and very lonely. She cried a great deal, was sad and depressed, and had a poor appetite, although she was able to sleep fairly well. This lasted for about six or seven months. The priest thought that she might be happier if she had another little child to look after, so she adopted a boy.

There are four other children in the family besides Nancy; Anna, the eldest, is 11 years older than Nancy; Tom, the youngest, is 4 years old.

Anna, Nancy's favorite sister, is married and lives in a little town near by. Anna says that Nancy has always been a quiet child, obedient and helpful. She never had tantrums and was not impudent to her elders. She is therefore very much surprised at Nancy's present "fresh behavior" in the ward.

Anna and Nancy have always been very much attached to each other and during the first year of Anna's marriage Nancy visited her sister almost every day and lived with her during the summer vacation. Anna's baby was born almost two years before this account begins. Despite the fact that Nancy was visiting her almost every day, Anna does not believe that the girl knew there was going to be a baby. At that time Anna was making some baby clothes and Nancy asked her what they were for. Anna answered that she was planning to buy a baby. Nancy accepted this without comment. The baby was born prematurely at eight months, to everyone's surprise. Anna had gone to another town for a few days and the baby was born immediately upon her return. Nancy had not visited her for several days and was very much surprised when she found the baby. She has been very loving toward her little niece and has devoted a great deal of attention to her. While visiting her sister in S—— Nancy slept in the back room with the baby most of the time. The sister does not believe that Nancy has ever seen her husband making love to her.

Nancy has always liked J., her brother-in-law, and will do anything he tells her to do. She became very much excited and upset when he burned himself in the fireplace when she was visiting the couple after her operation. She wanted to wait on him hand and foot and spent hours playing cards with him; she likes to "fool" with him, wrestles with him, and teases him. It was at this time that she had the first of her attacks. The sister says that the young girl was sitting on a chair in the kitchen. Suddenly she complained of feeling dizzy and her body was flushed and perspiring. Anna made Nancy lie down for a while. During this period she was having great difficulty in sleeping at night and read a great deal. She used to fall asleep at about 4 or 4.30 a.m. and would wake up at about 10 a.m. After she returned home she began to have more violent seizures, but the sister did not see any of these until some months ago, when she came to visit her family. She and her husband took Nancy to church and then to a restaurant for a simple dinner. The younger sister enjoyed herself immensely, but when they returned home she took a drink of water, fell to the floor, and had a generalized convulsion, recovering consciousness in about ten minutes. She then greeted Anna and her husband very joyfully, asked when they had arrived, and said that she had been expecting them. She had total amnesia as far as the events of the day were concerned. This is the only severe attack that Anna ever observed.

Anna is a stepsister, a daughter of Nancy's mother by a previous marriage. She has never got along particularly well with her stepfather, who limited her activities and forbade her to go out when she was a young girl. She used to meet her present husband secretly during their engagement, and their marriage was kept secret for several months. Nancy was the only one who knew what was going on. When her father learned about it, there was a terrible scene. For a year afterward, Anna refused to speak to him. Nancy continued to visit her older sister secretly and Anna feels that she was carrying a large burden of family troubles at this time. In this period of great strain, Anna says, she herself suffered from spells similar to Nancy's as well as from markedly increased irritability, headaches, and dizziness. She even manifested semiviolent behavior. Since her pregnancy she has been having too frequent menstruations with a very profuse flow. She is again suffering from headaches and dizziness.

According to the parents and Anna, Nancy is a very honest, quiet, obedient, helpful, and religious child. She is somewhat shy and usually keeps to herself. She has always been finicky about food and seems not to like anything except candy, of which she eats a large quantity. Apart from that she has been a well behaved and healthy girl, with no history of tantrums, nail biting, nightmares, or enuresis, nor of fainting before the onset of the present trouble. She is sensible and careful, more reliable about errands than the other children. Whereas the siblings quarreled among themselves or with other children in the neighborhood, Nancy always walked by herself to avoid trouble. However, she seems to get along very well with her classmates at school, even though she seldom smiles or laughs. She has been very much interested in her little baby brother Tom and quite helpful with him. She is apparently a conscientious child.

The only unusual thing that the mother brought out in the history relates to the last four years. About four years ago an older sister, Clara, had her appendix removed. The accident in which little George died occurred at about the same period.

The mother says that Nancy very much liked the religious instruction at school; for example, she always insisted on repeating a prayer to the Mother of Sorrows. She says that the other children were encouraged to pattern themselves after her. The school in which Nancy was a model pupil is a convent school, much stricter than most. The children must wear long stockings and no ankle socks are allowed; they are also supposed to wear long sleeves. The building is for girls only.

The nun teacher described the child as a perfect lady, but says that when she got good marks, she slaved for them; she is not very able. Because the mother works out, the teacher is under the impression that Nancy does a great deal of work at home and comes to school tired. For a month before the operation, she said, Nancy was not well, complained of a pain in her side, and seemed to her to be "failing." The nun sent her home once, telling her to inform her mother that something was wrong with her.

Absolutely no information concerning sex has been given to the child by the parents. They know nothing of her sex interests or practices. When her first menses occurred, about a year ago, she was with her sister Anna. Anna attempted to explain something about this phenomenon to Nancy, told her it was a natural occurrence in girls of her age, and that it was nothing to be frightened about, but Nancy was very bashful and her sister soon dropped the subject. She is still shy about her periods and does not mention them to her mother.

EXCERPTS FROM DOCTOR'S CASE HISTORY

Nancy's behavior on the ward was at first antagonistic. She was flippant and forward in her remarks to the doctors and said things that were evidently intended to be embarrassing and shocking. She is preoccupied with her own thoughts, which, as her comments reveal, are fantasies about love affairs and babies.

She often complained that she still had abdominal pains. One morning she declared that she had swallowed a penny. Accordingly she was sent to the X-ray room for a flat plate of her abdomen, since there was considerable doubt as to whether she had actually swallowed the coin. That night she demanded to know what the X-rays showed. [She was evidently very much interested in the inside of her body; later, the treatment in the psychiatric clinic clarified the motives of this preoccupation.] One evening she asked to see me and came into the office about 9:30. This time her attitude was in striking contrast to what it had been previously. Her manner was quiet, friendly, warm, and quite natural, in direct contrast to the antagonistic, flippant, impudent attitude she had previously exhibited. She was much concerned over the possibility of being sent home and wanted to know what I would tell her father and mother. I assured her that she would not be sent home now that she had abdominal pain again. She was greatly relieved at this, because, as she says, there is no one at home to look after her, since her mother works, and she does not want to worry her father by being at home sick while the rest of the family is away. She said that since she was having pain she was going to stay up all night and that she was going to talk to me all night long. I let her talk on perfectly freely. She told me that she had had a great deal of experience, that she knew a lot of things that most girls of her age do not know. She did not divulge any of these experiences, but told me that she had been with her sister almost every day since her marriage. When questioned further about this, she explained that she used to visit Anna very frequently in the period before she had her baby. However, for several days before this event, she just did not feel like going over there. Then suddenly she had the feeling that something had happened to her sister and later she learned that the baby had been born. She also talked about her brother-in-law, who is "a good egg," as she put it.

She referred to various patients and was very critical and jealous of all of them. She said that "Miss F. was making a cat and then she acted out something that was disgusting." From further conversation it was apparent that the group had been talking about babies and that Miss F. pretended that she was having one. She thought that this was terrible and something that Miss F. should not have done.

She does not understand why people get married anyhow, she said. She referred to the photograph on my desk, and said, "You said that picture was taken five years ago. Have you been married that long?"

I explained to her that the picture had been taken that long ago, but that I had been married only about two and a half years and she said: "Then that explains it, because most people who have been married as much as two years have a baby."

She told me again that she intended to stay up all night and manifested considerable curiosity about where I sleep on my night on duty, saying that this is another reason why people should not marry doctors: they never spend any time at home. She suggested that I spend the night in the office with her and pointed out the couch where I could sleep. I assured her that I would much prefer my comfortable bed, whereupon she said that she might as well spend the night in the office whether I did or not, and fixed herself comfortably on the couch. I told her that I was going to bed and switched out the light when I left the room.

After I left her in the office that night, Nancy's behavior and dreams revealed that she had violent aggressive feelings toward me.

She made difficulties in the ward, continued to complain of headache and pain in her abdomen, and was irritable at times. She was extremely jealous of other patients, especially young girls, and it was evident that this jealousy and the feeling of being rejected by the doctor provoked immense anger and attacks. She confided to him alone the material that was given in her history: the secrecy surrounding Anna's marriage, and the fact that she was in on the secret and felt the responsibility heavily. She was willing to go to a foster home, but only to one where there would be no other children.

Throughout her stay at the hospital she expressed a great deal of antagonism toward the other patients and continued to make rather overt passes at me. She improved in regard to her attacks, admitted that she was putting on her pain, and that in reality she only wanted sympathy. After two months she was discharged and followed up by a woman psychiatrist in the outpatient department.

When Nancy left the hospital, she was placed in a foster home, with the consent of her mother. There was another girl of her age there, which was very desirable, for we all considered it important for her to have a companion of her own age. On her first day there she seemed dazed; the next morning she slept late and wanted to stay in bed. She was stubborn, and declared: "No one is going to boss me."

At the beginning she was very difficult to handle, complained that we had let her down by putting her in such a place, etc. She was very fussy about food and complained about a pain in her stomach. She was dramatic about her fear of the dogs, etc.

By and by she began to like the foster home and to enjoy the new school, especially the fact that there are both boys and girls there. The new girl friend, Louise, has introduced her to a boy, "Mr. Jones." Louise is very much interested in the opposite sex. A young man from across the street visits her regularly. Another eighteen-year-old boy comes to see her quite often. Apparently there is endless conversation between the two girls about these boys and the foster mother encourages them to talk. Nancy, who at first refused to make a garden, now thinks she would like one because maybe Mr. Jones will come over and help her. She is interested in her appearance, and wants to keep her clothes in order and be neat in her school work. The girls spend much time dressing their hair, at which Louise is an expert. Nancy's hair has been dressed with curlers. She is much freer, and interested in housework. At rare intervals she has an attack, in which the emotional provocation and the dramatic character of the spells are evident. She had a menstrual period and this time turned to the foster mother for instruction. She was very willing to receive information about child bearing and childbirth.

After some weeks Nancy was more contented in general and there was a tremendous change in her appearance. She was very well adjusted to the foster home and was eating everything. She worked well at school and in the garden.

A few more weeks passed and the foster parent again had troubles with Nancy. These arose in connection with her visits to her parents. She wanted to go home, said that there was nothing wrong with her, and was unhappy because she was not with her family. Louise and Nancy had dates with boys, which did not seem to work out well for Nancy. She developed increased jealousy and the feeling that she was being cheated by Louise. She continued the treatment under a woman psychiatrist that had been started during her stay in the hospital ward. From this source we were able to learn more about her case. The following is an excerpt from the clinic record.

REPORT OF OUTPATIENT DEPARTMENT

Nancy complains to her new doctor that the doctors in the ward treat her badly; they do not understand her, they laugh at her. Her feelings and her pride are hurt all the time, even by things that should not hurt at all. She cannot understand this and she cannot get over it. The reason why she sleeps so much is that she does not want her feelings to be hurt nor to hurt those of others. She is so depressed now, she would not care if she died: "I once yelled at night that I would kill somebody, my father, but I would not do it, I just haven't the courage, I want to be a reporter."

She confesses to the doctor that she was in love with Dr. M. She had a spell last week. Her mother had spells two years ago. Nancy witnessed the first one: "Something like mine . . . she must have been sleeping, then yelling —that sounds like mine. I used to be white in my spells, maybe Mother got her spells from worrying about me; Mother worried about my brother who died. I actually blamed myself for his death."

The brother, aged 4, had walked into the kitchen with one of Nancy's girl friends. The door of the stove was open, and Nancy shouted to her friend to warn her. The girl turned toward her and left the little boy, who ran into the flames. His clothes caught on fire and there was not much left of him, just a lot of burned flesh. He was taken to the hospital. Since then Nancy has dreamed of this incident and has been afraid of death. She spoke about her operation and still feels that she was cheated, that the nurses gave the wrong instruments to the doctor, etc.

Two days later Nancy seems more at ease, although when asked anything she dislikes, she looks like a furious animal, with her eyes staring and her lower teeth clenched tight over the upper, as if to bite. She has had no spells in this interval, but headaches all day long, every day, so that she saw double; she is less depressed, but still does not want to see people. This is one of the reasons why she prefers to stay in bed or to go back to bed whenever she gets up. Her feelings are hurt very often—as when the head nurse called her "Grandma" for not getting up [Nancy often looks like a very old woman]. So she did get up and felt worse. She had not vomited for six days, but she threw up her supper the night before. "Food does not look good to me," she said. Formerly she liked to eat.

As she lies in bed at night, she always reviews the happenings of the day. Every night she has to think over the question of the new doctor—whether she considers herself a friend of Dr. M. Nancy, with tremendous moral disgust, states that if the doctor thought she was in love with Dr. M. she was terribly mistaken: children cannot be in love. She never heard of such a thing. Anyhow, she does not like people. Why should she be in love? She does not even care about anybody.

About a month later Nancy is very suspicious. The new doctor keeps secrets; she always thinks over what the doctor says to find out what is behind it. She would like to have faith, but she never can believe what she is told without doubting. She has been fooled by people many times, so she is suspicious. People have made promises to her and have not kept them. For example, someone told her that she could go some place and that another person would be invited too; then she got suspicious. One girl invited four kids, but there was room only for three. Then she tells that the other three children did not want Nancy to come along. They wanted their own friends.

A week later Nancy is more cheerful, less tense, less shut in; she states on questioning that she is happier now. She tells about a dream that she had the night before. She was in bed at night. In the bed next to her was a little boy. Dr. M. came in; a nurse called him to come down and perform an operation to bring a baby into the world. She wondered what a baby looked like when it was just born; she asked Dr. M. whether she could see it. For a while he refused but finally he let her see it. The baby looked like a long, long piece of something, folded over like a blanket; the skin was funny, like a turtle's; between the folds was "all that is in you, all that terrible stuff, it turned my stomach." Therefore she went out of the room. The little boy ran out and Nancy came back to see what he had done. He had pulled at the baby's blanket and the whole thing had fallen to the floor. It all opened up, it was a flat piece and everything showed up, simply terrible things, all kinds of things were there. "I don't know what they were. I picked it up and put it in the blanket so that it looked all right. Dr. M. came in and took the thing out." Then Nancy woke up.

Nancy complains that her memory is so bad lately that she never knows what happened three days ago. She does not like to think of her dream, it was too ugly; she asks why she had it. She feels that she often knows in advance what will happen to her and to other people. The day before she had a feeling the world was going under—everything was far away. She felt as if she were dead (this happened when she saw another patient come out of Dr. M.'s office. Dr. M. had not talked with her). She then clutched another patient and asked for water. Both girls went for the water and on the way back Nancy fainted before reaching her bed; she cannot remember the fainting.

She has an outburst of hatred against women doctors. She had more fun with Dr. M. than she ever had in her life. But she doesn't like him the way the new doctor thinks; she wants to be in Dr. M.'s office all the time and see more of him than other patients do.

She is rather unwilling to associate with her dream; she tells spontaneously that she saw her niece before she was twelve days old. Nancy shuddered over the ugly appearance of the child ("like a stuffed rat"), not human at all; the skin was ugly, but unlike that of the baby in the dream, which had no arms, legs, nor head. Her brother Tom used to hold the niece, and this was funny, for the baby in its blankets was almost as big as he was. She expresses some disgust about diapers.

Ten days later Nancy is in a foster home. She comes to the clinic very angry and tense; she feels she has been cheated by being sent to the country. First she says that she was not told about it, then adds that she was asked whether she would like to try it. She won't stay—"If it goes on longer than a week from Sunday, something will happen."

She hints at suicide. The people in the home are lovely, the foster parents and Louise, the other girl. But it is too lonesome and she is afraid of the dogs and the horses; and the goats and chickens get under her skin. Then she suddenly looks sentimental and says that she always cries when she hears the song "O Mamma" over the radio. She is homesick for her mother. When she is at home she takes her mother for granted, but when she is away she longs for her; she had the same feeling when she was at her sister's. The last time she was there, "I took it all out on myself and cried when I was alone, and then the spells started and this feeling that I was going to die."

When she came home after three weeks, she felt "swell," even went to school for one week, but then "had spells and was unhappy again." Nancy always has the feeling that she is missing something and always holds the environment she happens to be in responsible for her unhappiness. She says that she fears her mother will have another stroke and die.

She talks spontaneously about her brother-in-law and his accident. She says that he and she were the patients in the house, both of them had had operations (the brother-in-law for verrucosis). She still worries about whether they took her whole appendix out; maybe they left a part of it in her—which will cause an infection—or perhaps they took out another organ by mistake. The nurses ridiculed her for such an idea, but anyway no one ever tells her the truth. Nancy can be made to realize that this is a recurrent theme in her thoughts and that she suspects people of keeping secrets from her all the time. She has had no spells since she has been in the foster home, but sometimes she feels that she is dying. She is less tense and softer.

A week later, Nancy is angry that she has had to wait, but she unbends quickly. She appears more mature, more at ease, more interested in the outside world. She tells the doctor that she is mad at her sister Emma, two years her junior. Emma tries to be "smart," picks on her, tickles her, takes things away from her. Emma always got more than Nancy; Nancy ever since childhood has wanted to tear Emma to pieces; she thought of twisting her around and smashing her on the floor. She had similar feelings toward her niece, although she loves this little baby more than anybody else on earth. Last summer Nancy was playing with her niece and suddenly she felt so mad that she could only think of killing her. Fortunately her sister came in just then. Nancy says that she never wants her sister to know that she has such thoughts. Shortly after this incident she went into the kitchen and hit the kitten, although the kitten had not done anything naughty. Nancy often feels full of hate toward babies, in spite of the fact that she is fond of them.

She tells spontaneously that she knew a long time in advance that her sister was going to have a baby, as she overheard her mother and Anna talking about it. Nancy then asked her sister whether this was true; the latter denied it, yet Nancy was convinced that her sister always told her the truth. However, two weeks before the birth of the child Anna told her about her pregnancy. Nancy is quite emotional as she tells this; she blushes, puts her hands to her face, then scratches her legs.

She asks whether the doctor has noticed her hair-do; she has had a haircut and pretends not to care whether anyone notices it, although she does care very much. She says that she wants to go to the ward and see the patients. The doctor does not mention her idea that Nancy also wants to see Dr. M. and show him her hair; Nancy says proudly that she will be 14 in two weeks.

A week later, Nancy says that she has a crush on a boy of 14 whom all the girls like; he rides on the same bus with her and Louise.

She has an outburst against her woman teacher because she has not given her a seat in the classroom; she says that her desk "is covered with other kids' books." In discussing this Nancy starts to excuse the teacher. She wants to be transferred to be in the same class as her boy friend. She only knows his last name, Smith. She thinks his first name is Dick; Louise has decided that. Louise "kids" Nancy and tells her that Dick belongs to her, Louise, and that she sees him all day long.

One week later, it is Nancy's birthday. She is happy and friendly and talks a lot about "Mr. Smith"; she has found out that his name is Arthur.

Two weeks later there had been no fainting fits and no seizures. She manifested a slight irritability and some aggressive impulses against kittens and other young animals, but she showed a good relationship toward the foster parents and toward other children. She is friendly and warm and displays a sense of humor; she can laugh at the things that formerly aroused her bitterness or rage. She will continue to come once a week for psychotherapy.

A week later, still no seizures. She felt some anxiety when she went swimming for the first time that week. She has a warm relationship to her environment and the doctor. Nancy notices the change in herself: "Fourteen makes quite a difference."

The doctor points out the change in her relationship to others. Nancy emphasizes that she never had anybody of her own age before. Her sister Anna is much older, Emma much younger; but seeing Louise, who is one year older, makes her enjoy life; she feels that the doctor understands what she means. She would like to stay at the foster home for the winter and catch up with her school work.

Some weeks later everything seems to be fine (she came in with Louise). She wants to be a reporter when she finishes school. She sleeps well, has no dreams, says they are going to let her go home in September, if she wants to (she is not sure). She seems to have no problems to discuss. She and Louise have had a "couple of dates"; she has been to a movie that day. When she leaves she says, "It's been lovely meeting you," in a quite conventional way. We spoke for only ten minutes (somewhat perfunctorily) as there semed little to say and things seemed to be going satisfactorily.

Three weeks later, she feels well; she will spend the winter at the foster home; she goes to see her parents over a long weekend. She has good relations all around. She is still "furious" sometimes but much less so: "I am too happy to be as mad as I used to be."

Some weeks later Nancy has had quite a disappointment: a group of boys had been coming to see her and Louise almost every evening. In the last few days they had said they were coming, and both girls got all dressed up, but no boys appeared. Afterward the boys said casually that they had had something else to do. Nancy feels that they were making fun of her and Louise.

One day Nancy's foster mother took her to a dance. There was a boy for Louise and a boy for another girl they had taken along, but none for Nancy, and she is somewhat resentful of this. She has had no seizures, no dizziness nor weak spells, and physically feels very well.

Two weeks later she is again full of hatred and resentment; she has been scolded at her foster home; she feels that the criticism was justified, but nobody has the right to tell her anything. She thinks her father has been offended by the hospital and she won't take that. One source of her discontent seems to be the fact that all her classmates are younger than she, as she is repeating the grade.

Two weeks later she talks in hints. There is something wrong inside her; she is doing something wrong to herself, but she will not talk about it. She is going to keep everything secret, for whenever she confides in her foster mother or the doctor or anybody else, they sooner or later betray her. There also is some secret between Louise and her. Louise gets all the blame, but that is not right. Only Nancy knows that Louise is really nice; Nancy feels she should be punished for certain things; but she is very sensitive if she is scolded for certain other things she does not feel guilty about. She talks a good deal about disappointment and what she received in return whenever she tried to be nice to someone, etc.

Louise might leave and Nancy thinks it will be dull without her.

A month later, Nancy is very much concerned about having lost Louise's confidence: "I was like a mother to her."

She looks pale and seems blue, although she tries to act like a person who knows how to get fun out of life. She says that she got detention in school several times for being noisy and antagonizing the teacher. She says she always used to be very well behaved till the other kids called her "stuck-up." Now she wants to show them that she can be just as mischievous as they are or even more so. Since she has changed her attitude, the kids are on her side; one teacher also accuses her of being flirtatious with the boys. Nancy finally breaks down, complains that Louise still keeps away from her, never confides in her any more, will hardly speak to her, and cares only for boys. She is very popular with them and they think that she is much prettier than Nancy. Nancy is now on good terms with the foster parents, whereas Louise is the bad girl in the house.

Three weeks later she is in good spirits. She expresses some resentment toward the foster mother and Louise, and some disappointment because there are no boys in her class in public school. There is some friction with her family, but she takes it all with a sense of humor and a certain insight into her part in the game.

In the interview it is clear that Nancy reacts with rage to every situation in which her confidence is abused, particularly if her new friend Louise is involved. At the same time she is extremely jealous of Louise in relation both to boys and to the foster mother. If she succeeds in triumphing over Louise (e.g., in her relation to the foster mother), she is contrite and full of guilt feelings.

Nancy has no fits any longer and is obviously improving. We are continuing the treatment with good results.

Although Nancy is one year younger than Evelyn, the psychologic picture she presents contains more elements of later puberty than Evelyn's. We nevertheless use her case to illustrate the processes of early puberty because much of her behavior still belongs to this phase of life. Compared with Evelyn, Nancy is much more sick in the clinical sense of the term. Neurologically there was evidence of cerebral disorder in the high voltage, slow waves of the electro-encephalogram, a few right-sided reflex changes at the end of an attack. The clinical record gave a description of a few of the attacks. However, the impression was that most of the attacks were hysterical. There was also an IQ of only 94.

Whether or not this patient is diagnosed as an epileptic case is not of importance for our considerations here. The dynamic pressure of psychologic conflicts can disturb an abnormal brain just as much or more than a normal brain, and can precipitate attacks with cerebral dysrhythmia, as well as without. Nancy's psychologic conflicts are a characteristic product of a puberty trauma.

When Nancy came to the hospital she frightened everyone by her appearance. On a small and undeveloped body sat the head of a mature and wicked woman. The suspicion arose at once that this child had lived through a great deal. She was extraordinarily defiant and absolutely unwilling to reveal anything about her mental state, and her attitude toward treatment was completely negative. What could be learned from her related directly to her operation for appendicitis. Her fits started after this operation; immediately before it she had violently resisted being anesthetized; she maintained that this surgical intervention had taken her by surprise, that she had been overpowered; and her anger was directed particularly against the nurse in charge of the physical preparations for the operation. She justified her excited behavior on the ground that she had not been told when the operation was to be performed; thus it was the element of surprise that aroused her anger and fear.

Otherwise, almost nothing could be learned from her about her personal life. It seems that she felt happiest in the home of her married sister. There she had lived before her operation and there she returned after it, in accordance with her wish. She also spoke several times of her little niece, born a short time before her operation, and gave the impression that she tenderly loved this baby.

It was obvious from the start that she had neither the wish to recover nor the slightest confidence in the medical treatment she was receiving. She fell in love with her physician and all her behavior in the hospital expressed her desire to be treated and loved by him as a grown-up woman. She had fits of anger and dreams that revealed strong aggressive tendencies in relation to this doctor. One could often clearly detect the connection between her frequent attacks and her fits of anger. These manifestations of her love were in harmony with her precocious facial expression rather than with her age. She was unashamedly aggressive, tried to remain alone in the room with Dr. M., assured him that she "knew everything," and attempted to seduce him by these assurances. She made a jealous scene about the doctor's wife, whose photograph she discovered on his desk. She asked him to spend the night with her on the couch, was jealous of his other patients, etc. And yet this love had a theatric quality throughout; moreover, one had the impression that she gave free play to her arts of seduction only because she was sure that the doctor would not be taken in by them. What seems genuine was her wish to be accepted by him as a grownup, her disappointed anger when he rejected her proposal, and her jealousy of his wife.

Nancy's history showed clearly—less in the sparse information she herself gave us, than in the data supplied by her family—that before the beginning of her illness she was in a situation typical of early puberty. A short stretch of her history reminds us of Evelyn's. Like Evelyn, she was in alliance with her older sister and fell into a triangular situation because her sister took a husband (just as Evelyn did when her sister took a lover). But while the cause of Evelyn's misfortune was perhaps the fact that her sister had driven her out of the triangle too soon, Nancy fell ill because she remained in the triangle too long.   With her sister she enjoyed a common erotic secret, which doubtless inflamed her imagination.   The love relation of her sister was carefully guarded from the rest of the family, and Nancy was the only one who knew about it. The whole period of preparations, the secret wedding, etc., gave Nancy the keen pleasure of being "in the know."   Later, after the marriage had ceased to be a secret, Nancy spent much of her time in the home of the newly wed couple.   We do not know much of her relations with her brother-in-law, except that they had playful scuffles during which he often overpowered her and threw her on the floor.   Her frequent visits to her sister certainly gave the young girl many opportunities to share, in her fantasy, the secret experiences of her sister and brother-in-law, and thus to continue the triangle in a less realistic form.

It seems, however, that the traumatic element must be sought elsewhere.   The sister became pregnant, and Nancy was no longer in the situation of sharing a secret.   Not recognized as a grownup, she was not initiated into the great new development in her sister's life.   She noticed the preparations for the birth of the baby and questioned her sister, who, however, failed to tell her that she was pregnant and said only that she intended to buy a baby.   To be thus thrust back into the role of a child from whom one has secrets and whom one deceives was unbearable for Nancy.   Probably her first reaction to this disappointment was violent anger against her sister and the expected baby.

The picture that unfolds now is already morbid in character and typical of a hysterical puberty neurosis.   In order correctly to understand pathologic behavior, we must realize what constitutes a normal development   Normally, the end of a triangular situation such as that in which Nancy found herself might be that Nancy, the third partner in the alliance, more or less consciously should fall in love with her sister's husband, then free herself from this love and turn to a new object.

Or, especially if the triangle was not constituted by an older sister and a brother-in-law, it might lead to a conscious or unconscious sharp rivalry, the outcome of which again would vary individually. The girl renounces the man, leaves him to her friend, and frees herself from the triangle with more or less effort; the scar of a disappointment will remain in her psyche and may affect her subsequent life. Or she triumphs over her friend by winning the man and renouncing the friend; even then the victorious rival may be left with a scar, caused this time by her sense of guilt in relation to her friend, and such a scar too may have painful effects in later life.

A frequent result of such a triangle is the impulse to repeat this incompletely solved situation later. There are women who can fall in love only with the husbands of their friends, in order to take them away or to renounce them; others must always have a woman friend in order to be satisfied in their relations with their husbands. Many a marriage is endured and maintained because whatever defects it has are compensated by the wife's relations with a woman friend.

But let us return to Nancy, whose history illustrates the development of pubescent girls. We must leave one question unanswered because our case history gives us no clue about it. Was Nancy unconsciously in love with her brother-in-law, and, if so, what was the character of this love? The supposition that such feelings existed seems justified by the fact that during her stay in the hospital Nancy displayed extraordinary readiness to bring about a triangular situation or, as we conjecture, to repeat it. To express her desire to be grown up, Nancy played at being in love with the doctor and being jealous of his wife. She also showed a lively curiosity about his eventual fatherhood. We have no doubt that this amorous game expressed a typical fantasy that was reinforced by her experiences in her sister's house.

But what put Nancy into a frenzy of rage and rekindled all her old aggressions and guilt feelings was her jealousy of her sister's child. She had been partly deprived of her gratification at being a grownup when she herself was treated like a little child, and later the love to which she had a claim was given to another child, the newborn baby. Jealousy was the source of her fury against this baby, and her fits were a manifestation of her aggression. At the same time they were a form of flight from this aggression, as well as a form of self-punishment. It is not without significance that Nancy suffered her first attack on the day her brother-in-law was burned as her own little brother had been burned several years earlier. She took particularly loving care of her brother-in-law and then collapsed in a fit. Later we learned from Nancy that whenever she took tender care of anyone she did it in order to mask her aggressiveness against that person. Her brother-in-law, just like the little niece, had deprived her of the love of her sister Anna; he was allied with Anna in the "secret" from which Nancy was excluded.

In the hospital it could be observed how jealous Nancy was of the other "children" in the department. She waged a most intense struggle for the gratification denied her and discharged her emotional reactions to these denials in violent attacks. From the data supplied by her mother it is clear that she was engaged in a constant competitive and jealous struggle with all her siblings.

Direct psychiatric observation during her treatment revealed that in the symptoms that constituted her puberty neurosis Nancy was really repeating childhood experiences. Her disappointment over her sister's failure to confide in her, combined with the increased vulnerability characteristic of puberty, had traumatic effects, so that Nancy, instead of developing normally, took a regressive step toward the past—that is to say, she endowed her current experiences with the emotional significance of events that had happened long before. She confessed to her physician that her little brother had been burned accidentally when she was 5 years old and that she was guilty of his death. She often had bloody dreams that reproduced this accident. Like every little girl, Nancy was jealous of her little brother and harbored death wishes against him, although certainly not in a conscious and consistent manner. The unexpected realization of these wishes through the sudden death of the child resulted in a severe shock and produced violent guilt feelings in her.

We can conjecture that Nancy was angry and disappointed when her mother, after the death of her little son, took another baby to care for, instead of giving all her love to Nancy. However, her behavior, as it was reported by her mother, seems to have been determined by her sense of guilt rather than by aggression and spite. She took loving care of the new baby. We do not know with certainty how Nancy, at the age of 5, reacted to her mother's new pregnancy; but our experience in similar cases leads us to surmise that she had a dark foreboding of it and reacted to it with mixed feelings, even though her reaction was not entirely conscious. Certainly many elements in Nancy's dizzy spells and seizures reminded us of the symptoms from which the mother had suffered during the pregnancy that followed her little boy's death. These symptoms of the mother were imitated indirectly through the intermediary of the sister who, after her own pregnancy, behaved very much like her mother and who thus showed Nancy her mother's symptoms in a new edition, so to speak. Nancy probably knew that while her mother was pregnant with her she had suffered from "dizzy spells, in which she would fall." A short time before the onset of her illness, Nancy witnessed her mother's spells, "something like mine." Nancy thought that her mother had these spells because she worried about her; Nancy has worried about the brother who died, and added: "I actually blamed myself for his death." These remarks make us suspect that by her fits Nancy hoped to arouse her mother's concern, so that her mother would love her as she loved her dead brother. Her constant self-accusations and her statement that she never could get rid of the memory of the fatal accident showed that since her fifth year this girl had been crushed by her guilt feelings. This created a definite disposition in her.   During the latency period such a disposition often manifests itself in the development of a personality with typical reaction formations.   She became a religious, overdocile child, as is clear from the evidence given by her teachers, the nuns.   It may be surmised that if her development had been undisturbed, she would have reacted to puberty by an intensification of this reaction formation, i.e., with still more marked religiosity and dutifulness.   But the events of her sister's life were such that they were bound to reopen her old wounds, expecially since they took place in the most vulnerable period of her puberty.

Nancy's traumatic experience was a blow against her triangular situation, against the sharing in the secret that gratified her, and against the wish to be treated as a grownup.   Again and again Nancy reiterated that she had been cheated, that false promises had been made to her, thereby arousing her fury, of which she was quite aware.   Moreover, we must consider Nancy's relation to her sister, despite their great difference in age, as a two-girl relation for a certain time. Because Anna's love relation was forbidden and had to be guarded as a "secret," the grown-up sister had played the role of a young girl to whom certain things are prohibited.   In her relation with her sister Nancy enjoyed various gratifications, one of which was for her of the greatest importance. Because she shared in the life of this grown-up sister who was limited in her freedom just as Nancy herself was, and because of Anna's confidence in her, Nancy could feel like a grownup in this relation and it helped to strengthen her consciousness of her ego.   As soon as this ego-strengthening position had to be given up, Nancy's identification with her sister assumed a regressive character, her adjustment to reality collapsed, and she fell sick.

Normally, Nancy would have had the opportunity of seeing the partial fulfillment of her pregnancy fantasies—these are always a component of the psychologic life of pubescent girls— in her sister's pregnancy.   In that case she might have reacted with minor pregnancy symptoms and then have awaited the birth of the child in tense expectation, just like her sister. Later she would have loved and cared for the baby with her. But the collapse of the triangle resulted in Nancy's first trauma; then came her sister's pregnancy, the birth of the child, jealousy and aggression in relation to this child, and reactive feelings of guilt. Her brother-in-law's accident, by its similarity with her little brother's accident, revived her memories of the latter, and thus added a new burden to her already great inner tension. Disappointed, angry, and guilty, she fell into a state in which, instead of letting her fantasy life develop into one of normal femininity, she entered a regressive path, i.e., she unconsciously identified herself with her pregnant sister and in her subsequent morbid actions reproduced several elements of her childhood relations with her mother.

She provoked an operation during which she had the opportunity to express her rage and fears. Her rage was discharged above all upon the nurse who assisted in the operation and was characteristically connected with the element of surprise. Thus she expressed her protest against the fact that things were held back from her, that secrets were kept from her. It is interesting to note that her sister too was surprised by the somewhat premature birth of her child.

Later we learned that Nancy had not adequately discharged her aggression and fear during the operation. Her attacks revealed a considerable amount of unspent rage. She also said that after her operation she developed a fear that she did not give up throughout her stay in the hospital, a fear that something had been left in her stomach that would later endanger her health.

This craving for operations in pubescent girls is well known; we know also that surgical intervention at this time later creates the wish for its repetition. To satisfy this need repeated operations are necessary and, typically enough, the appendix usually seems most suitable for the role of *agent provocateur*. Such operations gratify rape, pregnancy, and childbirth fantasies, and they are effective because they are real experiences in which anxiety can be discharged. Sometimes the operation achieves what is expected of it; often, however, it results only in increased psychologic tension that gives rise to the desire for repetition. If Nancy had not developed the fits that enabled her to discharge her emotions, she would probably have become a typical candidate for further operations.

The interpretation of the operation as a symbolic childbirth seems confirmed by Nancy's dreams ("to perform an operation, to bring a baby into the world"). In the "baby broken to pieces" the same destructive idea reappeared as in Nancy's tears after the operation. She was still full of these ideas during her stay in the hospital and the probable purpose of her assertion that she had swallowed a penny was to provoke the taking of an Xray of her abdomen. She felt that destruction threatened her own body as well as her sister's child, as she later confirmed directly. She confessed to the woman doctor that she hates her niece and has had completely conscious murderous impulses toward her. She herself was surprised by them because she loved the little girl "more than anyone on earth." She also accused herself of cruelty toward little animals and toward her younger sister, and of impulses of hatred toward babies, whom at the same time she loved, etc. Many things she said and did showed how much she was tormented by harrowing feelings of guilt. Her confessions often had the character of self-accusations that were in sharp contrast to her oft-repeated accusations against other people.

The seeming peculiarities in Nancy's behavior can easily be explained. The contradictions must be ascribed to the fact that her emotional reactions, detached from the awareness of time, took place simultaneously in different strata of her psychologic life. At first she wanted to share in events as a third partner, then she wanted to love and take care of a child like a sexually mature woman. This disappointed girl was exceedingly jealous of her sister's newborn baby. She killed it in her fantasy with the same cruelty she had harbored, when she was 5 years old, against her brother. In her unconscious she cut to pieces the body of her mother (or sister), while on the other hand she experienced the gratification of child-birth, the horror of being cut to pieces herself, and the threat of death in the operation on her own person. She was con-scious of her apprehension that her mother might die and of her fear for her sister's life; but the aggression concealed behind her fear remained unconscious and was discharged in her at-tacks.

Nancy's case history contains another element that typically follows an operation in puberty. The feeling that the ap-pendix has remained in the body, that something else ought to be cut out, that "something is wrong" inside, is characteristic of girls who think that their bodies have been damaged. The child that Nancy had "killed" was a boy, and it is natural to suppose that at that time physical sex differences played an important part in the development of her feeling of jealousy, and that the old reaction manifested itself again in the convic-tion that "something was wrong." Our case history does not unequivocally confirm this supposition, although it does permit us to construe several of Nancy's symptoms as repetitions of infantile experiences.

There is a strong suspicion that despite her pregnancy fantasies, Nancy's puberty orientation was in the direction of a relationship with her mother, later of a relation with her sister. She hated the little niece as she hated her little brother, because she herself wanted to be her mother's best-loved child. From the unsuccessful triangle the path leads back to the phase of childhood that, as we have seen, reappears in pre-puberty—that is to say, to the mother, with the whole hatred-love orientation of the girl who, while already struggling for liberation, remains connected with her mother by her old ties and guilt feelings.

The fact that Nancy also fell into the complications of the Oedipus situation and that many elements of her neurosis were connected with it, is not in contradiction with what we have just said. The triangular situation subsists, but at the same time we are confronted with the new edition of the Oedipus situation, in the relations that Nancy had with her brother-in-law, as we suppose, and that we can observe her having with the doctor. In the history of her childhood, her father remained a very shadowy figure.

Another typical process of puberty is illustrated in the following case.

Helen is a 15-year old girl, very pretty and very talented. Her parents have been separated for two years, and she lives with her mother and her sister Susie, who is three years older than she is. Her father and older brother have left the home. Susie has always been her father's favorite, while Helen had a very harmonious and tender relationship with her mother. The sister has always been a placid girl, as a result of her mildly obsessional tendencies, and inclined to perfectionism. She was a model pupil in school, while at college, where she was studying music, she was one of the outstanding students in the class. Helen has always been an unruly child, and Susie has been her model. The separation of the parents caused a certain regrouping among the children, because the extremely fair and understanding mother realized that she had to give more attention to Susie, who was now without her father. Helen did not display direct jealousy, and in the last few years before she sought treatment her relation to Susie actually deepened. She worshiped her sister, took her advice even more willingly than her mother's, and planned after finishing high school to go to the same college in which Susie was making such a fine name for herself.

Susie has had a boy friend for the past few years, with whom she shared her musical interests. They became engaged, and Helen, who was very fond of Bill, approved of this engagement. Then she began to show such changes in her personality that her mother realized that she needed psychiatric help. In the first place, without any apparent reason, she became very hostile toward Susie. Every time Susie was to come home from college to visit her family, Helen warned her mother with a mysterious smile that "evil things" would happen, but refused to divulge any details. She was not inclined to fall in love, and, in contrast to Susie, had always been a popular girl who liked to be surrounded by many worshipers, without showing preference for any one of them. Shortly before Susie's most recent visit home from college, Helen told her mother that she now had a boy friend. Her mother had the impression that Helen was not really interested in this boy, and that she had taken the first one who came along. After Susie's arrival there were two young couples in the home. Susie's behavior continued to be decorous, while Helen began to visit night clubs and bars with her boy friend. To all her mother's or sister's attempts to criticize her, Helen replied spitefully that they would do better to concern themselves with Susie's behavior. Helen let herself be caught, obviously deliberately, in very intimate situations with Ralph, and whenever her mother reproached her for this, she told her to watch Susie. But what particularly upset the mother was that Helen, who had always been extremely truthful, now began to lie. She lied to her mother without any reason whatsoever, knocked about more and more in night clubs, and compromised the reputation of a highly respectable family.

After treating Helen for a period of two weeks, I found that the separation of her parents and her mother's increased interest in Susie had aroused violent emotional reactions in Helen. But her jealousy of her older sister did not manifest itself as long as her love and admiration for the latter continued. One might even say that Helen combated her "spiteful feelings" by bestowing even more devotion upon Susie and elevating her to the position of the younger girl's ideal. Susie's engagement surely created for Helen a situation similar to that created for Evelyn by her sister's affection for her boy friend (see p. 40).

The difference between these two cases lies first of all in the fact that these two girls belonged to different social groups. Moreover, Helen's relation to Susie, who was her ideal, was on a higher level of development than that of Evelyn to Mary. Helen was not only, like Evelyn, deserted by her sister in favor of a boy, but the resultant situation produced a flaw in her ideal. If Helen saw Susie and Bill exchange one tender glance or one kiss, she immediately started constructing sexual fantasies of her own and projecting them on Susie. First, there was a period during which she was constantly obsessed by the thought, "What are they doing together?" and imagined the most ardent erotic situations; when she later saw them reserved and controlled, she thought contemptuously, "What an actress my sister is!" and pitied her poor mother, who was in her opinion being deceived by the supposedly virtuous

Susie. When she could no longer identify herself with Susie as an ideal figure, she began to identify herself with the Susie her fantasy had lowered to the status of a debauched liar. I was soon able to reassure the mother that nothing serious had actually taken place between Helen and her boy friend, that Helen had remained as chaste and truthful as before, and that it would be easy to reduce all this behavior to a temporary symptom. This promise was kept, and today Helen, who came fully to understand her own case, is an assistant counselor in a girl's camp under a leader whom she worships. She herself enjoys being an ideal figure in relation to the younger girls.

As a rule this kind of identification with an ideal model is a favorable contribution to psychologic development. Helen was quickly cured after she was given a new opportunity to make such an identification.

During puberty, identification is a complicated and individually varying process that makes a necessary and important contribution to the further elaboration and strengthening of the ego. It often rescues a still weak personality or leads to renunciation of personality. We have seen that Nancy fell neurotically ill because she had sexualized her identification with her older sister, and that Evelyn's wish to be grownup and experience the same things as her older sister brought her to an unfortunate pass. But even the most favorable kind of identification, an idealization that expresses the wish "to be as good as you are," can become dangerous. Helen's history is an excellent example of this type of development.

We know that the process of identification plays an important part in the relation of the child to his parents, and later in all his educational experiences. Observation of adults teaches us that we rarely meet personalities sufficiently strong and integrated not to make use of identifications with others. We do this in our thinking, acting, and creating, and people whose emotional life is disturbed identify themselves with others also in their emotions. Absolute originality is probably a quality peculiar to genius alone. Throughout puberty and adolescence identification plays such an important part that we shall have to return to this process again and again.

Like identification, the triangle of early puberty can survive for a long time. As an expression of bisexuality it can become the battleground of hetorosexual and homosexual conflicts, lend the distribution of ambivalent feelings (love and hatred) a definite form, and combine the masculine-active and feminine-passive impulses into a whole that is often extremely complicated.

We have examined the bisexual triangle in order to stress the progression in the development from homosexual friendship to hetorosexuality. But the triangle may also be arrested at an intermediary stage, and all three partners may be of the same sex. Love of two girls for the same woman (teacher, artist, etc.), with or without jealousy, is very frequent. Friendships in which two girls ally themselves against a third, but with changing roles, so that the persecuted third one is not always the same, are also typical. More normal and more progressive is the mixed triangle (like Natasha's); the masculine corner in such a triangle is often occupied by the brother of one of the girls.

The presence of a strongly bisexual tendency shortly before the conflicts of adolescence, that is, at its beginning, is less repressed in girls than in boys. In this period of their life girls are quite willing to stress their masculinity, while the boy is ashamed of his femininity and denies it. "Tomboy" is often a compliment, "sissy" always an insult. This bisexual phase affords us an opportunity to observe the two components—homosexuality and heterosexuality—before the synthesis has been accomplished in the process of maturation. The gradual disintegration of the homosexual component is more favorable for later development than its sudden interruption through disappointment. Similarly the girl's sexual development may take an unfavorable course if a strong heterosexual attack from outside prematurely drives her from homosexual friendship into heterosexuality. If the outcome is to be favorable, the development should be gradual.

If the young girl, as a result of her own inhibitions or external circumstances, is unable to objectivize her feelings toward both sexes, whether in direct relations or sublimations, her bisexual tendencies may remain locked up in her psyche without an object. Her problem is this dangerous case is not "Do I love men or women?" or "How will I manage these two emotional tendencies?" but "Am I a man or a woman?" Her psychologic indecision is expressed in a typical fantasy in which she plays alternately feminine and masculine parts. This fantasy has a predecessor in early childhood and is preserved for years in its original form or a modified one: "I once had a brother [often a twin brother]; I lost him, but I remember him very well." Girls often richly embroider this theme. The brother is endowed with all the qualities that the girl would like to have herself, or he is blamed for all the impulses repressed and rejected by the girl's ego. Referring to her childish misdemeanors she maintains that it was he who was so "wicked" and "dirty," not she. With many children this double assumes such a real character that they give him a name, have conversations with him, and in general behave as though he actually existed. Such fantasies often take on a pseudologic character and are communicated to others as truth. The fate of this lost brother is related to the listener, and it is often a tragic fate. One girl I know used to shed bitter tears as she described the premature death of this beloved brother who never existed. The feeling that such a brother did exist often assumes the character of a vague memory, and this is an interesting example of the girl's "inner perception" of her own masculinity.

A fantasy describing the young girl's own lost boyishness sometimes more consciously expresses wish fulfillment. The girl imagines that she is a boy or answers the question "Am

I a girl or boy?" in a manner that satisfies both tendencies. Waking or sleeping, she invents a more or less fantastic situation in which she sometimes figures as a boy and sometimes as a girl. Or she is more realistic and expresses her bisexual wish through simple disguises.

A classic illustration of this is the case of Betty, described by Peter Blos,[5] who in dreams by night was sometimes dressed as a boy and sometimes as a girl. There is scarcely a girl who has not had such fantasies for a shorter or longer period. They do not all admit having them as freely as Betty did, and are not as conscious of them as Betty was. The fact that Betty struggled so much against these fantasies, that she performed the most complicated bodily exercises in order to get rid of them and in order not to be disturbed by them in her sleep, is also very typical. From numerous girls with similar fantasies, I have learned that this effort really represented their struggle against masturbation. The fantasies constituted the content of their bisexual masturbatory activities; the exercises served both to gratify their desires and to combat them.

Returning to the three girls whose case histories we have discussed above, we can observe that two of them, Evelyn and Nancy, suffered trauma in the typical triangular situation; the traumatic experience led Evelyn to premature actions instead of to fantasies. Through her flight Evelyn tried to realize her prostitution fantasies without in fact having any real interest in sexual activity. Nancy reacted to the trauma by more complicated neurotic behavior. The unconscious pregnancy fantasy that is almost always present in puberty was strengthened in her and assumed a pathologic form as a result of events in her immediate surroundings. She experienced this fantasy in a regressive manner, that is, with a renewal of old vengeance-rage-anxiety and guilt feelings. Under pressure of these, she exhibited the symptoms of her illness, her attacks and other neurotic reactions. Helen's

[5] BLOS, P.: Op. cit.

trauma resulted from her depreciation of the object that she still urgently needed for purposes of identification. All three cases have given us an insight into the processes of puberty. The objection that these cases illustrate morbid rather than normal processes is not without justification. But we have tried to see the normal behind the morbid and to understand pathologic reactions as the typical result of certain caracteristic disturbances of the normal development of girls.

The successful treatment of young girls can be completed sooner if one keeps in mind the normal behavior typical of the patient's phase of development. If, for instance, it seems necessary to place a pubescent young girl in another milieu, our choice must not be guided exclusively by considerations of the cultural level, the favorable emotional atmosphere, and the presence of favorable influences, although these factors should of course be taken into account. In the main we should be guided by our knowledge that we are dealing with a traumatic disturbance or inhibition of definite developmental tendencies. Our therapeutic or pedagogic aim should be the ultimate correction of this disturbed development. In Nancy's case, the treatment consisted in the creation of a corrected triangle in which she had the opportunity to act like a normal growing girl. Our understanding of the typical puberty situation pointed the way: first a girl friend of the same age, then, with her, under equal conditions of rivalry, relations with boys, and gradual preparation for catching up with her delayed development. It turned out—and according to our experience this was to be expected—that Nancy reacted quite well to this situation, but that she later developed the tendency to reproduce her traumatic experience in a milder form, that is, to involve herself in violent rivalries that provoked great hatred in her. These struggles were carried on in two forms: jealousy of the friend as competitor for the love of the mother (foster mother), and a maturer form of competition in the relation of both girls with boys. She again felt that her friend had betrayed her and the original traumatic situation returned

in a weakened form.   By continued psychotherapeutic treatment it was possible to cure the child of this neurotic tendency
to repetition; she has been secure against further seizures since
she achieved a good relation with her woman doctor and since
she has been placed in a favorable milieu.

In the case of Evelyn, the treatment met with difficulties
from the outside and could not be completed.   From our
knowledge of her psychic situation, it would seem proper to
give her an opportunity of playing, in a more orderly gang,
the role that was once so satisfying to her and in which she was
disturbed by her mother.   At home she would have had an
opportunity to gratify her growing motherliness in her relation
to her mother's newborn baby, provided of course that her
psychiatrist had succeeded in weakening her feeling of guilt
A harmonious juxtaposition of tomboyishness in gang activities
and femininity at home can be very successful at Evelyn's age;
and a correct treatment could have achieved this goal.

Helen's difficulties, as we have seen, were easily solved
once her situation was understood.

The reader will note that I have drawn a boundary line
between early puberty and later puberty.   I assume that
marked bisexual tendencies are characteristic of the former,
and that strong heterosexual tendencies are characteristic
of the latter.   Infantile features persist in both phases; hence
early puberty can be considered the second edition of the
childhood phase, which is characterized by irresolution in the
choice of objects and by wavering in choice between mother
and father (or substitute persons).   Later puberty was named
by Freud[6] the second edition of the Oedipus situation, because
at this period the young girl's relations to boys still include
many old unsolved elements of the father tie.   The differentiation into two phases that I have attempted here seems
important to me.   Of course the various phases of development
cannot be sharply separated from one another, and processes
of early puberty may continue throughout the whole of puberty

[6] FREUD, S.: Op. cit.

and adolescence and even longer. The case of Nancy offers a particularly clear example of such a juxtaposition of two phases of development. The new phase attacked her, so to speak, before she had been able to bring the preceding one to relative completion.

Sometimes development proceeds slowly, step by step, through the gradual addition of new elements; at other times, the entire picture of one phase of development is strongly differentiated from that of the preceding one, while at the same time isolated elements of this earlier phase still manifest themselves. For instance, we have seen what an important part was played by the relation with the "other girl" in prepuberty. This relation assumes different aspects in accordance with the degree of psychologic development. Giggling and secrecy or the danger of sexual imitation, ideal formation or ardent homosexual passion, may all develop in the period of maturation that extends over several years from prepuberty to adulthood. Exactly the same is true of the heterosexuality of puberty, which should free itself from previous ties, but which may preserve them until well into adulthood.

The processes that take place in the stormy years from puberty to maturity are so rich in content, and are determined by so many factors, that it is difficult to speak of them as homogeneous. For the sake of simplification, we shall discuss the psychologic reactions to the biologic processes that reach their climax in menstruation separately from the processes of maturation of the ego. In the latter discussion it will hardly be possible to draw a clearly defined line between puberty, which is still strongly under the influence of the biologic onslaught, and adolescence. In our terminology, we shall ascribe to adolescence a slow and long elaboration of the process of maturation. In this period, the final foundations are laid for the future personality of the adult, and the fate of the mature woman is decided.

CHAPTER THREE

Puberty and Adolescence

I N THIS chapter we shall discuss the personality of the young girl during adolescence. The psychologic events that take place in this period are initiated during prepuberty and continue in early puberty; adolescence is the period of the decisive last battle fought before maturity. The ego must achieve independence, the old emotional ties must be cast off, and new ones created.

Biologic development brings in its train great qualitative and quantitative changes, in both the physiologic and psychologic spheres, and as a result of these changes the adolescent ego is confronted with new difficulties. The emotions, because of their close connection with the instinctual life, are more affected by the process of growth than any other part of the personality and therefore present us with the most interesting problems of adolescence.

The liberation of the growing child from infantile dependences proceeds along various paths, of which one, as said above, is the loosening of the old affective ties. The emotions are the manifestation of dynamic psychic energy and make use of various means of expression; they constitute the most elementary reaction of the individual to the outside world, from the wailing, weeping, or lusty shouting of the baby to the most complicated direct and indirect relations of the mature adult to exterior objects and to himself. For this reason, the loosening of emotional ties raises the question: What happens to the psychic energy in adolescence—what outlet do the emotions find to take the place of the old ties? In order to answer this question, we must to some extent anticipate.

In the process of loosening the old ties, identification plays an important part. Like the emotions, the identifications of the adolescent go through the phase of "severance actions" and must be discussed from this point of view.

In both cases, the means of liberation is sought in devaluation of previous objects, regardless of earlier relations. The shaping of the adolescent's own personality may be in large measure the product of his successful identification with his parents; but some part of him seeks new possibilities of identification, rejecting the parents as objects. The devaluation made in this connection is to some extent rationally justified even in prepuberty. An increasingly critical attitude and a greater adaptation to reality gradually bring about abandonment of the infantile overestimation of the parents, and the pendulum begins to swing in the opposite direction: the parents are now underestimated. We have observed the strong urge to manifold identifications characteristic of prepuberty. At that time these identifications have the rather primitive character of playful imitations; later, in early puberty, although still split by bisexuality, they are consolidated to some extent in the relation to the girl friend. Now, in adolescence, they achieve further unification or succumb to an abnormal fate.

The emotions also utilize the mechanism of devaluation to loosen the ties binding them to formerly loved objects and thus give a rational motive to the adolescent's newly arisen aggressive hate tendencies.

An interesting feature of this devaluation tendency, which deserves some emphasis, is that actually it is not quite as serious as it seems to be, for once the dangers of puberty are overcome, adolescents often resume loving the objects previously rejected, and may even be proud of their own similarity to them. But if the devaluation tendency is accompanied by a new and real motive, it can become a serious threat to the young girl's emotional life and the development of her ego ideal and exert an unfavorable influence on her subsequent destiny. During the attempt to rescue the ego ideal, the place of the parents is taken for a while by other persons who answer the requirements of the young better than the parents. Their ego ideal is molded and tested against their teachers, group leaders, etc.; a part of the love that until then was given to the parents is for a time transferred to these objects. As the adolescents grow more mature, however, these newer objects too are critically devaluated, and their place is taken by an abstract ego ideal, the realization of which is reserved for the future. The identifications with heroes, leaders, etc., made in a group or ideologic movement are valuable, but they cannot satisfy the need for a personal relation. Only such a relation, and not a substitute for it, can give the emotional life the character of a real object relation.

The processes described here are prepared in prepuberty and continued in early puberty. In discussing these phases we have emphasized the necessity of individual emotional relations. Naturally, the course of adolescence depends upon the preceding developments. For this reason it will be useful, before trying to answer our question as to the fate of the affective energy, to recall the process of maturation that was discussed in the chapter on prepuberty. We showed that the processes used in making the adjustment to reality in this period represent an offensive and have nothing or little to do with the defensive processes developed for the control of the sexual instincts. Maturation in prepuberty consists in an aggressive thrust of activity that gradually loses its original intensity. Part of this thrust disappears under pressure of more passive tendencies, while the rest is replaced by other methods of adjustment to reality. The passive tendencies are of the greatest importance for the further development of the girl toward femininity, with which we shall deal later.

There is no doubt that the rising sexual urge in adolescence provokes fears and mobilizes defensive forces that make several important contributions to the psychologic picture of this period of life. Anna Freud[1] has made an extensive study of these defense mechanisms. She considers the adolescent ego the center of defense against the dangers involved in the sexual

[1] Op. cit.

urges. We must add that in adolescence, just as in the previous phases, the ego manifests powerful developmental thrusts that do not depend directly and exclusively on sexual processes.

We shall now consider another problem that is of very great importance in the psychology of adolescence. It involves those emotional forces that are directed toward the young girl's own ego or that, even when directed toward other persons, have a certain specific character. Earlier in our study, when we discussed the young girl's relationship with her girl friend, we said that it was narcissistic, by which we meant that the ego draws advantages for itself from its love for the other. By a process of identification with the friend, the girl's weak ego extends its own limits and gains some self-confidence.

The increase of narcissistic forces in the ego seems to play an important part in the process of maturation. Intensification of narcissism is generally regarded as a negative symptom. We encounter it in pathologic cases and also know it as a dangerous enemy of positive emotional relations to objects in the outside world. Nunberg, who called attention to the double role of narcissism and analyzed both its negative and positive aspects, points out that "since narcissism is essential for life, one might assume that narcissism strengthens the ego."[2]

During adolescence narcissism is very active in both ways, but its positive aspect at this time is especially noteworthy. In the first place, it has a certain unifying force that prevents dissolution of the young girl's personality as a result of too many identifications. In the second place, by increasing her self-confidence, it contributes considerably to strengthening the youthful ego. However, it certainly also exerts a negative influence on the ego; and it is this double action that gives rise to the movement back and forth, the ebb and tide of overweening pride and contrition, in brief, the whole picturesque medley that is the psychologic pattern of adolescence.

The problem of the sources of narcissism brings us back to

[2] NUNBERG, H.: Ego strength and ego weakness. Am. Imago, vol. 3, no. 3, 1942.

the fate of the emotions, which in puberty normally turn away from childhood objects. We can now answer our question about these emotions: they are turned toward the ego itself, the affective energy puts itself at the disposal of the ego in the shape of "intensified narcissism" and supplies it with important additional strength. Thus the process of psychologic consolidation initiated during prepuberty in friendships with girls of the same age continues. From the girl friend, identification is transferred to persons on the model of whom the girl's own ego is formed; by and by identification with others grows weaker, and identification with one's own ego all the stronger. The formation of the personality makes important progress; the adolescent becomes aware of the "I am I."

Thus the emotional vacuum between a world that is disappearing and another that has not yet come into being is filled by the emotions now turned toward the own ego. As though spontaneously the girl who wondered "Whom shall I love now?" and "Who will love me?" takes her own person as her object; and this fact determines many of the psychologic manifestations of puberty. It leads first to greater self-confidence, to the "arrogant megalomania" of adolescence. But an excess of narcissism makes relations with other people difficult. The adolescent's narcissistic ego is extremely exacting and extremely sensitive to love frustrations; it is easily disappointed in its expectations of being loved and admired. Hence the adolescent's intolerance of any criticism, especially on the part of members of the family. In the emotional give and take a disturbance occurs through increase of the "give" and decrease of the "take." The result of this is the feeling, "Nobody loves me." The adolescent girl's realization that her own capacity for love is also limited leads to a feeling of solitude. Because of the connection between the two currents—intensified self-confidence and emotional solitude—the quality of a subjective experience can also be ascribed to the latter. The feeling of solitude arouses exaltation, for example, in the form, "From the watch tower of divine solitude I look down on the common herd."

During adolescence such an orientation can be considered normal. But in many individuals it continues beyond adolescence if their affective life does not outgrow this phase.

Although this feeling of solitude is exalting in a normal development, it also creates a pain that cannot be overcome even with the help of narcissistic self-confidence. An unbearable tension arises from the need not only to be loved but also to love. Because of this tension the youthful person turns to new objects with real avidity and experiences every stirring of emotion with ecstatic exuberance. This is extremely characteristic of the youth of both sexes.

One result of the adolescent's overestimation of his own emotional experiences is his willingness to sacrifice "everything" for the beloved. Actually, this loved object may very easily and very quickly be given up for the sake of another. And the adolescent's explanation is that the previous object was not the true object, but this one is. The erotic readiness to fall in love again and again is stronger in the girl than in the boy, but she is less conscious of the sexual character of these feelings than he. In like manner, the wish to be loved by many and to collect men's "broken hearts" is characteristic of the female adolescent. However, this hunt for masculine hearts rarely expresses a purely narcissistic need. Close investigation usually reveals that these trophies are intended to be shown to definite persons, such as the mother, who in reality or in the imagination of the girl is still trying to deny her daughter adult femininity, or the father, whose respect the girl hopes to win by this indirect method. Often the relation with a girl friend, whose envy or admiration she wishes to excite, spurs her on in this campaign for broken hearts.

The girl's subjective feelings of great love are not always bestowed upon an objectively existing and actually accessible human being; often they are directed toward an object that she barely knows or does not know at all. The deepest ecstasies of love are experienced in fantasy, and these feelings are endowed with the character of object love. In such cases only the experience of loving is important; the beloved person need not necessarily have any objective reality.

We find an excellent example of such a love in the diary of the Russian princess Maria Bashkirtseff.[3] As a rule one cannot put too much faith in diaries. But this one is for the most part sincere and describes Maria's feelings as she actually experienced them, because she had a great gift for introspective analysis and was strongly exhibitionistic. She was precocious, and her adolescence began earlier than that of the average girl. Maria's narcissism was certainly unusually strong; but aside from this, the forms in which she manifested it were typical of adolescence.

For many months Maria was in love with a certain Duke of H——, whom she did not know at all: "I had seen him a dozen times on the street, him, who did not know that I am in existence." Although she might have been loved by many other prominent men, the Duke of H——, who had no interest in her, was at the center of her most ardent love fantasies, and all her feminine ambitious plans for the future were built around this man. She fancied that she would be very famous, that all men would lie at her feet, but that she would choose him alone among all of them. "To see thousands of persons, when you appear upon the stage, await with beating heart the moment when you begin to sing; to know, as you look at them, that a single note of your voice will bring them all to your feet; to look at them with a haughty glance—that is my desire," she wrote. "And then in the midst of this the Duke of H—— will come with the others to throw himself at my feet, but he shall not meet with the same reception as the others. Dear, you will be dazzled by my splendor and you will love me."

This is one of the typical fantasies of an adolescent girl. As we see, all her capacity for experience is purely narcissistic, not

[3] BASHKIRTSEFF, M.: Journal of a young artist. New York: Cassel, 1889.

only as regards the contents of her fantasy, but also as regards the characteristically imaginary object relation. But even here narcissism is not the only factor, for in these fantasies we always find the old object formations and in the platonic, ardently yearned-for lover we often recognize the features of the father. This is probably true also in the case of Maria Bashkirtseff, who was separated from her father at an early age and reconstructed him in her love fantasy.

In other types of adolescent girls the narcissistic-exhibition-istic fantasy is not necessarily connected with an almost unreal love object, as was the case with Maria Bashkirtseff. For many the object is much more real, and the wish, "Love me, I am so wonderful, everyone admires me," is the core of every ambitious aspiration—while often a girl's ambition collapses like a house of cards when the object of this wish disappoints her or is given up. However, in others, ambition and the desire to play an important part on the stage of life dominate the fantasy without centering necessarily on one definite person.

What is true of erotic fantasies, in which the erotic longing in itself and not the beloved person is important, is also true of youthful enthusiasm for an "ideal." One often hears enthusiastic girls exclaim: "Ah, if I only had an aim in life, a great idea for which I could live and die . . . I would be ready to sacrifice everything."

The content of the fantasy is doubtless determined by the girl's cultural milieu. The modern girl, for instance, no longer daydreams of being on the stage and performing solo dances or singing love songs, as her mother did in her adolescence. The daughter may see herself as an orator inflaming the masses to revolutionary deeds or leading an ideologic movement that is of public interest at the moment. The attempt to realize such fantasies is the expression of a maturer stage of development. Even though the motives for this idealistic aspiration are of a selfish-ambitious nature, the activity that expresses it forms a bridge between the youthful ego and the surrounding world.

The realization of such fantasies can be of great social value and simultaneously exert an educational influence in the further development of the young person.

If the fantasies are not ideologic or social but purely egocentric in character, their realization in most cases leads to disappointment. Sometimes the immediate surroundings of the girl influence her fantasies. An ambitious father or a conceited mother often expects a young daughter to fulfil his or her own narcissistic wishes, to become a kind of instrument of these wishes. Such fantasies are doomed to failure when the persons around a young girl make her carry them into practice. The following case history offers an interesting illustration of this point.

Case History of Dorothy

Dorothy is a 15-year-old girl whose mother came to the social agency for advice concerning her daughter's defiant behavior toward her. Dorothy seems fairly intelligent and has some talent as a singer. Although a minor, she has embarked on a more or less professional career, and by giving her age as 18 has been able to get bookings during the summer and small engagements during the winter. She seems to be quite clever at putting a song across and when she appears with a group, she is the featured soloist.

INTERVIEWS WITH THE MOTHER

The mother is a small, thin, tense woman with a rather anxious and unhappy look. She is not particularly attractive and wears glasses, but makes some attempt to dress smartly. She talks readily, enunciating clearly. Her whole manner suggests a deeply deprived and very insecure person, distrustful of other people, somewhat withdrawn, and absorbed in her family.

Recalling her own early life, she described her father as a brutal drunkard who many a time yanked his children out of bed at night in order to beat them. Her mother was not much concerned about them; the daughter feels that she always had to carry the burden and responsibility of the family. At the age of 13 she left home to do housework. She struggled bitterly, never knowing a moment of happiness. She continued to struggle after her marriage, because her husband has never earned much until recently.

There is a son, John, who is two years Dorothy's senior. He is quiet and virtuous and presents no problems. The mother speaks of him with great praise and affection. She says that when they are alone in the house they sing together, because they are so happy with each other.

Dorothy was a very much wanted child. The mother always wanted a girl with curly black hair who would be cute-looking and whom she could dress prettily. The mother's attitude toward the child is at first suggestive of the attitude of the parent of a Hollywood child prodigy: "I suppose I got pleasure from the compliments Dorothy received. Everybody likes her. She is prettier than I ever was."

Neither she nor the father had enough training to enable them to earn a good living and they have known hard times. She says that she began Dorothy's training in singing many years ago and that the child has done very well. She implies by her words that she has a very gifted offspring who has to have special handling and that special rules apply to her.

For a long time it has been understood between them that if the child embarked on a musical career, she must abide strictly by the moral code of her mother; that is the only condition on which the mother will allow her to take her singing engagements, which bring in quite a little money. The mother goes with the girl on her trips as often as she can, but usually Dorothy goes in a group.

The father is apparently a passive partner in this marriage. He sits quietly at one side and says very little unless he is prodded. He has a rather patient face. In appearance Dorothy resembles him quite markedly. He once forgot himself and started to tell me what he was like as an adolescent, and how he enjoyed smoking. He was promptly interrupted by his wife.

The mother tells how terribly worried she is about Dorothy, who is becoming too independent and sophisticated for a girl of her age. Recently she has been very defiant toward her mother. The latter brings out a great deal of resentment against Dorothy, saying that the girl is ungrateful for all that her mother has done for her, although she has slaved to do it. The mother considers herself a martyr; she has sacrificed for Dorothy, and now Dorothy won't obey her at all and that is "unfair." The mother expresses herself in terms like "right," and "wrong," "fair" or "unfair," and throughout stresses her conviction that a child should unquestioningly obey his or her parents.

Dorothy is so cruel to her. The mother supposes that Dorothy must grow away from her and that this is part of it, but it is not right. Sometimes Dorothy says that she hates her mother. The mother tells her right back she hates her. Then the mother begins to cry. "And I mean it! She is so wicked. If I had a choice I would send her to the army instead of John. He is good. Why should the good one have to go and the mean one remain? Of course I love her, too. But why must she act that way to me? It's not right."

She continues to complain that Dorothy is "unfair" to her, that she is "cheap" and "ungrateful." The mother can't endure it. She will tell the whole world and punish her daughter.

"You want me to forgive her, but I can't." She says resentfully and hatefully that she will not be a doormat for Dorothy. "I don't say anything. I keep my feelings inside me and they pile up and then I can't keep them back any longer. I let them out on her. Then she is angry and it happens all over again. . . . It's not right for her to act so and I resent it and I cannot keep from showing it."

The mother displays strong jealousy of her daughter. She obviously resents the fact that everyone thinks that Dorothy is such a fine girl, when actually she is mean. The mother contrasts her own lot with Dorothy's. She was never liked; nobody ever cared for her. This was not "right," because she was a conscientious, hard worker. Things never came easily and effortlessly to her as they have come to Dorothy.

She quotes various people who say that she is to blame for all this trouble because she pushed Dorothy into a singing career, and the theatrical gang the girl now runs with is the cause of her misfortune.

The most recent crisis apparently centers about the fact that Dorothy has begun to smoke. The mother does not approve of this and she has warned the child that it is not good for her breath control. But the girl is quite defiant and answers, "I like to smoke." The mother, however, is very rigid on this subject and declares vehemently that she will never approve of cigarettes and that the girl must not smoke. Smoking becomes a habit like a drug, it is dirty and filthy. Recently there have been a number of spats about this and Dorothy has accused her mother of being old-fashioned and prudish.

The question of Dorothy's interest in boys was brought up; so far the mother does not feel this to be a problem. The mother knows that Dorothy has some interest in boys, but apparently not of a very intense kind. The mother is more troubled about the girl's liking for some rather undesirable girl friends. One of these girls has no father and talks continually about how mean her mother is to her and how she wants to run away from home. It is obvious that the mother fears that Dorothy may do the same thing. In fact, she has talked about getting an apartment of her own, which the mother feels is unwise.

With a gesture of disgust the mother brought up Dorothy's interest in "queer people": "You know, men who like men and women who like women."

She then spoke of the importance of being able to trust one's daughter; she does not know how far she can trust Dorothy.

Again and again she speaks of how concerned she is about her daughter, of how she has no peace of mind, of how she wakes up in the night and thinks about the girl.   Several times she complained that Dorothy does not come directly home after her signing engagements, but goes downtown with the group.   The mother does not know where she is; often it is late at night; she does wonder what Dorothy does with her time.

Throughout the interviews it was evident that the mother is panicky about Dorothy's manner of life, and that she has provoked Dorothy's aggressive protests by her attitude of condemnation and dislike.   Soon it became evident that she hates her daughter, although she tries not to verbalize this. Dorothy has disappointed her by not coming up to her expectations.   She continually connects two themes: her own unhappy youth, and Dorothy's popularity and ingratitude for all that has been done for her.

Plans are made for Dorothy to go to a boarding school.   The mother obviously gives up the idea of Dorothy's singing career with great difficulty. She suggests that Dorothy carry on her singing engagements in the evenings. But at the same time she expresses fears that upon such occasions Dorothy might come into contact with a married man who is interested in her.

DOROTHY'S INTERVIEWS WITH THE WOMAN PSYCHIATRIST

Dorothy says that she is a singer.   She works throughout the school year, entertaining at banquets and night clubs.   She finds it a little difficult, but she makes quite a lot of money.   For example, she gets $7 for singing a few numbers at a banquet and thus she can buy her own clothes and help out quite a bit.   Her story is that she and her mother do not agree on a number of questions.   She feels that her mother doesn't realize that she is more grown up than she appears to be.

The girl is intelligent.   She has made some very keen observations of the people she works with and the people who frequent the night clubs, and feels that her mother is unable completely to understand her point of view.   As an example, she knows that some of the singers and entertainers are homosexual.   She likes one homosexual man very much and feels sorry for him. He is a decent enough fellow and is always very nice to her.

Another bone of contention is her going out in the evening with certain men.   She is always taken to be several years older than she really is and just now she has a young man whom she likes very much   He is 25 years old and a detective.   The mother feels that he is too old and too sophisticated for her, but the girl says that her mother doesn't know that some of the boys she picks out for her daughter are no good at all; they make a good impression but are not nice when they get outside the house.

She is especially resentful because the mother has suddenly taken to accompanying her on her evening engagements.   She would not mind this if her mother had always come with her, but now that she has suddenly become suspicious of her, Dorothy feels that her mother goes with her only to watch her. She finds it especially hard to bear that after the performance the mother criticizes her and says that she should have smiled more or made more gestures. She says with a good deal of feeling: "After all, I know what I'm doing. I must be doing it fairly well or they wouldn't pay me."

Furthermore, the mother doesn't trust her in anything. She lectures her by the hour and goes around and around in circles. Her litany goes something like this: "Girls who smoke sooner or later drink, and when they drink they lose control of themselves, and when they lose control of themselves they become bums. It all starts from smoking."

Dorothy says that that kind of talk is silly, but you cannot change her mother's ideas about such things. She never drinks but she loves to have a cigarette when she is reading. She is now reading a book by John Gunther, in which she is extremely interested.

Dorothy spent a good deal of time telling about the different books she has been reading; a volume of Confucius is one, *Moment in Peking* another. She is not interested in the Christian religion. She has arguments with her mother about that too, and the mother's rigid, unbending attitude only makes matters worse. The girl seems to have a great deal of energy. There is some indication that she feels seriously threatened by the contrast between herself and her brother. Her whole idea seems to be: "Come what may, I am not going to be like him. Mother is not going to squash me."

She has a great many other complaints about her parents. They inhibit her in many ways. Both of them criticize her, especially her mother. They don't like her to go out with older men or to smoke, and her mother, for one, has told everyone that she is a bad girl. She is fed up all around.

It is interesting to hear her because she has a very inquiring mind. She is full of herself at the moment and likes to flaunt what she knows about homosexuals, or let it be known that she has just read a psychologic discussion of some sexual abnormality. She describes an evening at home as being extremely tiresome—first one member of the family grunts, then another one grunts. They don't talk about anything interesting. The mother does nothing but hang around all day gossiping with the women downstairs and leaves the beds for Dorothy to make when she comes home. Therefore she takes a long time walking home from school.

She finds her mother extremely irritating and both her parents boring. She is willing to try to change in some respects, but she is adamant about the cigarettes.

Dorothy and her girl friend have been reading Freud. Recently she had quite a shock because a certain Anna M—— was her ideal woman and she has now learned that this woman is a lesbian. After saying this, Dorothy sat back to watch my reaction and compare it to her mother's. However, I showed great interest and asked her where she got this piece of information.

I also asked her whether she believed everything she heard. Then it came out that she has always been eager to be a boy. She hates being a girl. I had an opportunity to show her that part of her hatred for her mother was due to this feeling of frustration, for which she blames her mother. "That is what it says in Freud's book," she said. "Is it really so?"

Then she wanted to know whether boys have any troubles. I told her that they do, and she seemed relieved and pleased to know that there may be things that bother boys too.

Dorothy continues to bring out a great deal concerning her experiences in the "world of the night club entertainers." She is a sharp observer and is thinking constantly about what goes on around her. She has tried to form her own judgment of what is right and wrong, and says she has talked with all sorts of people. She complains that her mother wants to dominate her, and she is fighting with every ounce of strength in her to break away from this control. She deliberately sets out to do things that she has no real desire to do, simply to show her mother that she cannot rule her. This is quite conscious on Dorothy's part, but often it leaves her with a feeling of remorse.

Dorothy wants to discuss at great length the various anomalies she meets in night club life, for example perversions. She is getting a very good knowledge of the seamy side of life. She has been working about three nights a week and has earned quite a good deal of money lately, singing at private parties and entertaining. She says people treat her very decently, however; nobody "gets fresh."

She dislikes high school intensely. She especially hates American history and simply does not want to go to her particular school any more if she can help it. She has been unhappy about it and that is why she played hooky and went to the movies.

Last year she met a man who fascinated her. She met him in the night club and he is supposed to be quite a man with the ladies. She was very much flattered by his being attracted to her. She saw quite a lot of him last year, much to her mother's alarm, but finally got disgusted with him after she saw him with a young girl who was very much drunk and saw how he treated that girl. She takes quite an adult attitude about everything connected with sex and seems to be extremely irritated with her mother for snooping into her books.

She says that her mother is always checking up on her and looking through her books; she "wishes to goodness" that her mother would stop that. I said we would talk with her mother about that and told her how lucky she was to be back in school.

In an interview with the doctor the mother showed immense improvement. She was able to bring out many of her fears about her daughter and to verbalize the things that worry her most. To quote her words: "To think that I got her into that work, and that it is my fault if she is exposed to all these temptations. And to think that I nearly killed myself to give her the singing lessons."

Since the mother has been gradually giving up her ambition for a Hollywood career for her daughter and since Dorothy has returned to school, there is a better prospect that these two puberties—Dorothy's, and the retarded puberty of her mother—will eventually become relatively harmonious.

Dorothy was a very pretty girl, with shining black eyes and curly black hair. Her figure was slim and supple, and her appearance reminded us of a definite Hollywood type. Her mother had worked hard and sacrificed a great deal to give the girl an opportunity to develop her modest musical talents. Dorothy was at the beginning of a stage career. She specialized in a type of art suitable to little theaters, had had successful summer engagements in resorts, and had also appeared during the winter as a paid singer at private entertainments. What was only a dream for thousands of schoolgirls of her age had become a reality for Dorothy: actually, her experience was Maria Bashkirtseff's dream come true, short of the masses of men at her feet and the Duke of H——. There was no apparent reason why Dorothy, once a part of her fantasy had been realized, should not expect the realization of the rest. What was striking in her interview with the woman doctor was the small part that her artistic career played in her mind. She mentioned her singing only in connection with her job, and her narcissistic gratification assumed the banal form of her argument on her mother's criticisms: "I must be doing fairly well or they would not pay me."

There was no Duke of H—— in her life, in any form. The only audience she mentioned was her mother, who criticized her and said she should have smiled more and made more gestures. Had Dorothy discovered that her talent was slight, or had her mother's criticisms discouraged her and aroused her hatred? Or did this hatred for her mother stem from other sources and was she taking revenge on her by destroying her expectations concerning her daughter's stage career?

We learned that Dorothy's role as a stage star was the realization of her mother's wish dreams and that in reality Dorothy
had only served as her instrument.   The mother had had many
disappointments in her life and described her youth as the gray
existence of an unattractive girl forced into dark corners.
Beaten by her brutal father, this starving and suffering Cinderella probably renounced all her own puberty fantasies and
postponed their realization to some distant future.   Some day
her pretty black-haired daughter would achieve what she herself dared not even dream of.   We knew directly only this part
of the mother's puberty dream; but the other part of it was
revealed in the ambitious plans she made for her daughter's
career.   Dorothy had fulfilled the prerequisite for these plans:
she was a beautiful young girl.   The mother took care of the
rest by her hard, exhausting work, her sacrifices, energy, etc.
Dorothy was a glamor girl; in her mother's fantasy she was
probably a famous movie star.   The former Cinderella felt that
her daughter's fame would bring her too into a bright world.

But Dorothy began to neglect her school work and preferred
to spend her time with the theatrical people who were now her
professional colleagues.   She spoke of her gang with love and
tenderness, saw the defects of its members with extraordinary
keenness, and displayed a remarkable objectivity in her
understanding of the perverted actions that took place in this
group.   She read scientific books that were not only far above
the cultural level of her milieu but also beyond her own intelligence and comprehension.   She learned that her older girl
friend and colleague, who represented a sort of ego ideal for her,
was a homosexual, and she reacted to this upsetting experience
by attempting objectively to understand it.   She read psychologic books, chiefly those of Freud, whose writings, she thought,
dealt with such subjects.   By coming home late at night and
smoking cigarettes she aroused her mother's anger and fear, for
her mother thought that cigarette smoking was the first stage
of moral decline in a young girl.

In several respects Dorothy reminded us of Evelyn and similar young girls. She was happy to belong to a gang and to expose herself to its dangers; she had the feeling of security, and the conviction that nothing could happen to her, that are typical of puberty. The maternal distrust excited her, just as it did Evelyn, to furious protests, and her confidence in herself led her, as did Evelyn's also, into a situation in which she was playing with fire.

The unconscious conflict between Dorothy and her mother seemed clear to us. Dorothy was not going to fulfil her mother's dream: she had completely shifted her dominant interest from her stage ambition to her gang and was taking revenge on her mother because the latter, instead of giving her love and tenderness, made demands upon her. The wish dream typical of her age—of appearing on the stage and being admired and loved—had, because of its realization, become devalued and made banal in her eyes; it was entirely overshadowed by her emotions. Her hatred and revenge feelings were directed against her mother's narcissistic wishes, and she renounced her own gratification in preference to fulfilling her mother's fantasy. She wanted to be grown up, belong to a gang, and feel free—and to her, freedom meant everything that implied a protest against her mother. In other words, Dorothy selected from her puberty wishes only those that she could use in her struggle against her mother. Her behavior was certainly also a reaction to that of her mother, who wavered between a strong feeling of guilt because she had exposed her child to sexual dangers by trying to make her fulfil her own maternal fantasies, and a very aggressive attitude of reproach toward her daughter. She concentrated this reproach on Dorothy's smoking. She seemed to be saying all the time: "You'll never be a famous artist and a princess, you'll be a prostitute."

The woman doctor who treated Dorothy believed that she was jealous of her brother, who was her mother's favorite child. The brother was virtuous and passive, and by her association with the gang Dorothy wanted to show that she was a sort of "tough guy," more masculine and more independent than he. Her smoking was probably connected with this.

The freedom of night life in the present held greater fascination for her than a possible realization of her fantasies about a stage career in the future. When an adolescent has the possibility of gratifying an important part of his desires and emotions through immediate action, he often easily renounces future realization of his most powerful wishes. This was the case with Dorothy. Her emotional life was absorbed in aggressive tendencies in relation to her mother, to which she gave free rein, and her ambitious fantasies about the future gradually became paler and lost their importance.

We were justified in our concern for Dorothy, for it was obvious that she was undertaking certain concrete actions in order to torment her mother. She knew that her mother was afraid of sexual risks and that she felt guilty for having thrust her child into a dangerous milieu. Dorothy deliberately came home late at night, told her mother about the sexual affairs of the members of the gang, and took pleasure in her despair. We were afraid that in a manner typical of puberty Dorothy underestimated the dangers threatening her and had too much confidence in her ability to control the situation. Her wish to identify herself with a new environment could easily lead her into actually assimilating her behavior to that of the gang; her hatred for her mother might induce her to more outspoken and more dangerous actions, and her vengeance might take a form that would intensify her mother's sense of guilt.

So far Dorothy had resorted to a definite defense mechanism in face of the threatening dangers: she had intensified her narcissistic self-assurance by a kind of aloofness and tried to understand intellectually the sexual happenings that probably alarmed her in her new surroundings. For this reason, Dorothy presented an interesting theoretic problem. We knew that this rather intelligent girl, who, however, had previously displayed no intellectual interests, had now suddenly begun to read serious books and shown an interest in sexual problems, perversions, etc. She believed that she did not need to share her mother's fears about the abnormalities of her friends; her own objective attitude was supposed to protect her from the danger of participating emotionally in these abnormalities. Was this what Anna Freud[4] calls a process of "intellectualization," that is to say, did Dorothy's intellectual interests serve directly to check her instincts, did she become learned and scientific because she was afraid of her own sexual impulses? It is possible that a deeper analysis of her psychologic life would lead us to adopt this interpretation, but the impressions gained during our interviews do not support it. We felt that Dorothy's emotional life had become rather empty as a result of her devaluation of her girlish narcissistic fantasies and of her disappointment in her feminine ideal and the object of her first erotic experience. She tried to fill her life with something that would secure her superiority at home (particularly in competition with her brother), win her the respect of her gang, and, last but not least, protect her against the real dangers inherent in the perversions and dark doings of the gang. Through her scientific inquiries she could also gratify her curiosity without running the risk of personal experience. For these reasons, though, we interpret Dorothy's case as one of "objectivization" or "intellectualization," and though the mechanism involved here was a defense mechanism, we believe that it was directed not against instinctual dangers, but against the real situation.

The dramatic character of present day social and political events naturally affects the young girl's fantasy life, and there is no doubt that the war we are living through influences the content of her fantasies and strengthens her urge to realize them in action. However, at this point in our discussion we shall disregard the importance of the war as a psychologic factor and devote our attention to the young girl's personality as it develops under normal conditions. The great majority of

[4] Op. cit.

young girls still pass through a phase, of short or long duration, in which their need to find adequate release for their emotional tensions is expressed in the desire to become an actress (particularly a tragic actress), a newspaperwoman, a detective, or a novelist.

At the age of 16, Andrea, the heroine of the story previously mentioned (p. 32), dreamt that she would be a great poetess. In a manner typical of earlier puberty, she took her future plans very realistically. She thought that in order to become a writer she should, like Balzac, work at night while drinking enormous quantities of black coffee. But as she could not obtain coffee, she tried to substitute water and chocolate. She also planned to wander all night in the woods, because a poet must experience a great deal. "In four years, without anyone having the slightest inkling of it, a thick, thick book written by me will be published: 'Dirges by One Departed.' ... The whole kingdom of Denmark will read it, all the poets, and father and mother too."

This search for experiences, whether because the girl is not yet capable of having them in reality or because her real ones seem too insignificant to her, is particularly typical of puberty. Because of her sense of her own weakness, which is not sufficiently compensated by her narcissistic good opinion of herself, and because of her wish to be strong, mature, important, and a "free human being," the young girl, just like the boy, must constantly struggle for the new position of "being grown up." She must prove herself better and more important than her parents and her brothers and sisters; she must accuse others of repressing her, in order thus to project her own psychologic inhibitions and her perception of her own psychologic limitations in the outside world, and to blame others for what she lacks.

Uncertain of her way, the young girl falls into a conflict between her individualistic feeling that she has duties toward herself and her feeling that she has duties toward her family; to this are added conflicts between various sublimations that express themselves in irresolution: "What shall I be?" This means: "With whom shall I identify myself? Shall it be father, mother, some other ideal figure? Shall I be a *femme fatale* or a career woman, an artist, scientist, or a mother of many children, an ascetic or a believer in free love?"

The individualism and rebelliousness that are strongly accented in adolescence come into conflict with all the old authorities and influences. The girl's fear of her self-exaggerated responsibility and of her own conflicts, her sense of guilt in relation to her family, to which she is still so strongly attached, and above all the difficulties she experiences in trying to harmonize her intensified ideal aspiration with her intensified sexuality, often make such great demands upon her that she easily falls into a state of spiritual and physical exhaustion. Her overweening self-confidence expresses among other things her perception of the psychic expenditure required to solve her numerous conflicts, especially the conflict arising from her renunciation of sexual gratification.

As the old authorities are devaluated, the girl's own conscience, the superego, is strongly heightened. The demands made by conscience in young people of either sex are often greater and harder to fulfil than those made by the people around them. Thus, we often see in the young girl a sense of responsibility and a trustworthiness that seem inconsistent with the strange confusions of adolescence. The girl's youthful ego often collapses under the weight of the demands of her superego, particularly when the onslaught of the sexual needs threatens to triumph over these latter. If these "ideal demands" are accompanied by guilt feelings arising from old or new sources, neurotic disturbances easily arise, manifesting themselves in the most varied symptoms, particularly in characterologic difficulties.

Gradually love fantasies crowd out narcissistic self-satisfaction, and tensions develop that give new features to the psychologic picture of adolescence. An ambitious young girl, for instance, suddenly feels disturbed in her studies or work by her recurrent infatuations and writes a magic word in large

letters over her bed, which serves to remind her every day not
to fall in love any more. The magic word does not suffice for
very long, the girl's self-assured behavior begins to waver, and
her ambitious plans are threatened by her inability to concen-
trate on her work. Her harmonious relation with the milieu
that has accepted her as a grownup (college, office, or factory)
is disturbed.

The young girl's restlessness, her irritability, her conflicts
with herself and her milieu, assume the form: "I am misunderstood, my individuality is threatened, my wings are being
clipped, I must have the right to live my own life. . . ." Even
the most tolerant milieu is unable to meet her demands or
understand them. For the young girl herself does not know
what they are, and her feeling that she is misunderstood really
expresses her own obscure awareness that she does not understand herself. The "misunderstood woman," who so often is
more ridiculous than tragic, is one who has not yet outgrown
this adolescent feeling or who has fallen back into it. The
comical element in her behavior is the fact that it is anachronistic. In reality she deserves to be pitied; she has remained
suspended somewhere in her emotional development and is
only half aware of her lack of emotional freedom of movement.

When the narcissistic attitude begins to develop negative
symptoms, the vacuum between the two object worlds expresses
itself in a different form. The adolescent girl realizes that
she is unequal to her own high demands; her solitude becomes
a desert; depressive moods result. Thus Maria Bashkirtseff
wrote amidst her self-glorification: "Shall I ever find a dog on
the streets, famished and beaten by boys . . . a poor devil of
any kind, sufficiently crushed, sufficiently miserable, sufficiently sorrowful, sufficiently humiliated, sufficiently depressed,
to be compared with me?" And she consoles herself in a manner typical of young girls: "I love to weep, I love to give myself
up to despair, I love to be troubled and sorrowful. I regard
these feelings as so many diversions and while I ask for happiness, I find myself happy in being miserable."

But such narcissistic gratification through suffering usually yields to moods of depression connected with feelings of inferiority, and may crystallize in a real depression that can lead further to a severe adolescence neurosis.

In many girls the depressed mood is overcome by a sudden flare-up of ecstatic feelings and yields to a mood of elation. In such cases we are often inclined to speak of a manic-depressive state or of hysterical emotional fluctuations. Only subsequent developments can show whether pathologic phenomena are involved in such cases or merely intensified difficulties of adolescence.

This emotional solitude may lead to various other more or less typical mental states. Many individuals experience not only depression but feelings of estrangement, depersonalization, unreality, etc.

We have attempted to sketch the state that represents the emotional crisis of the period of life "between two worlds." Besides the characteristic contrast between the poverty of real love objects and the subjective intensity of all experiences, we find still another element that contributes to the morbidity of this period: adolescent "vulnerability," to which we have called attention in discussing our clinical case histories. We have seen how Evelyn ran away from home during puberty and was compelled to return again and again, driven by her longing. Obviously her liberation from the ties of the past was only partial—as is most often the case. We do not know enough about her fully to understand the forces that repeatedly drove her to run away. But we do know that her experiences with her old objects had an unusually traumatic effect, because they took place in the period of puberty with its intensified vulnerability.

The repetition, during adolescence, of a life situation that had a traumatic effect during childhood—an effect later more or less conquered—can provoke a new traumatic reaction leading this time to neurotic illness.

In the case of Nancy we could clearly see her strong reaction when she re-experienced a childhood situation in her relation with her sister.   Nancy reacted to her sister's pregnancy with a grave neurosis; later we learned from her that this reaction had been predetermined by the events of her early childhood. If we knew more about Evelyn we should probably find confirmation of our inference that she found her mother's pregnancy so difficult to endure because it occurred at a time when she was in a state of intensified psychologic tension.   We have reliable indications that she wanted to take the baby under her own tutelage, and we presume that what really took place was the mobilization of a fantasy about having a child herself. Perhaps Evelyn, whose behavior was so completely different from Nancy's, had nevertheless fallen into the same predicament as the latter.   Unfortunately, we know too little of her childhood history to decide whether she, like Nancy, had brought a definite predisposition with her into adolescence, as a result of which she reacted badly to subsequent events, or whether her neurotic reaction must be ascribed only to the vulnerability characteristic of the phase through which she was passing.   We know many young girls who under the pressure of biologic development, and because of the confusions of the maturation process, are prone to react traumatically to real events, even when such predisposing factors are absent.

Thus, for instance, a disappointment in the object on which the girl's own ideal was originally molded can go beyond the normal limits of the devaluation process and lead to disintegration of the ego ideal (we recall the case of Helen, who fell into this dangerous situation).   Or, the sudden loss of a love object from which the girl has not yet been completely detached can lead to the crippling of all her subsequent affective life.   We did not see all this clearly in the case of Evelyn, but we know that she was forced to flee from her home ties, and from her aggressive disappointment reactions and strong feelings of guilt.   When puberty with its increased demands came upon her, she could no longer endure her solitude and abandonment at home and was compelled to seek gratifications in the outside world. In her self-confidence, which was probably fatal for her and which we have just described as typical of puberty, she was sure that she would be able to take responsibility for herself in the outside world better than at home.

Many things in the confused picture of adolescence become clearer if we recognize the clash of two worlds in all the happenings of this period. Of these two worlds one belongs to the future, that is, adulthood, the other to the past, that is, childhood; the present is a time of struggle to bring these two life periods into harmony with each other. This conception gives us a better insight into the workings of the progressive and regressive forces. Where the formation of the ego is involved, the narcissism described above is a progressive trait, for it signifies a stage in the individual's liberation from former objects and the strengthening of his self-confidence; in so far as the libido development is in question, this narcissism is, on the contrary, obstructive and regressive. The stronger demands of the adolescent's own conscience, functioning as inner guardian, are a progressive factor; the inclusion of old feelings of guilt is a regressive factor. Thus every step, every gesture, draws its substance from two opposite factors, and the favorable or unfavorable outcome of adolescence depends on whether the progressive or the regressive forces are victorious.

The task of adolescence is above all to develop from the phase of intensified narcissism to that of object relations and to achieve in these a favorable unification of the affections and instinctual drives. Paradoxically, the impact of childhood experiences, the tenacity of old ideals—in brief, the regressive traits of psychologic development—appear with particular distinctness during this period of enormous progress.

The fact that, shortly before the new objects are found, the rising instinctual drives turn for a time to the old objects, creates a characteristic difficulty of adolescence. Affective struggles take place between an intense desire to "get away" and an equally intense urge to "go back," and this backward movement, which is now endowed with sexual force, actually arises from the re-establishment of an old situation that existed before the beginning of the latency period. For this reason adolescence has been called a new edition of the Oedipus complex, and its task has been defined as the sloughing off of this complex. In my analysis of prepuberty and early puberty, I attempted to show that these two phases, in their forward drive, are clearly repetitions of previous developments. Thus the task of adolescence is not only to master the Oedipus complex, but also to continue the work begun during prepuberty and early puberty, that is, to give adult forms to the old, much deeper, and much more primitive ties with the mother, and to end all bisexual wavering in favor of a definite heterosexual orientation. There is no doubt that the biologic processes make a decisive contribution to the latter achievement.

It is difficult to find one's way in these complicated developments, because the same manifestation may express various and often contradictory tendencies. Thus, for instance, a girl's identification with her mother may signify that she is assuming a woman's role, or it may imply all the difficulties of the Oedipus complex and thus stand in the way of the realization of her feminine wishes. Her perseverance in this identification may also express her inability to develop her own personality. Another result of it may be that the girl clings to her infantile dependence on her mother, that she avoids every conflict with her, and thus leads a shadowy existence at her side. In such a case, instead of reaching a feeling of emancipation and love, the girl has a spiteful and unsuccessful impulse to detach herself from her mother, and this may result in an emotionally crippled personality. If the girl does not succeed in solving the problem of adolescence, she remains, during this period and likewise later as a maturing or mature woman, the child she was during prepuberty, continually aggressive and nervously struggling against this tie with her mother, developing various symptoms in connection with her conflict, and persisting in a completely passive dependence. As mentioned before, a number of conversion symptoms, particularly lack of appetite and similar disturbances, all kinds of phobias and paranoic ideas (fear of poisoning),[5] are connected with such an inability to dissolve the old attachment to the mother.

Adolescent narcissism also assumes a definite form if such a dependence persists, and this may continue in later life. Every gesture, every inner and outer experience, is put before the mother and subjected to her favorable or unfavorable criticism. In some cases this dependence remains fixed on the mother, more often it is transferred to others. The happiness or unhappiness of a person with such an attachment depends absolutely on the judgment of others, and she expends a great deal of energy in finding out the reactions of those around her to everything she does.

We shall begin our survey of the sexual processes with the following question: What requirement must the adolescent fulfil in order to cope adequately with the biologic factors? The answer is clear: the boy must become a man, the girl a woman. The path to be followed by the boy is traced in advance by the functional readiness of his organ; his progressive goal is clearly and unequivocally before him, and the only difficulties he has to solve are the dissolution of old object ties, the discovery of new ones, and the mastering of passive tendencies. The fear that plagues him is: "Am I a man?" and the achievement of a positive answer to this question depends exclusively on the strength of his progressive forces in their struggle against the regressive ones. The clash between the two manifests itself in masturbation, which is the sexual activity of the adolescent boy. Normally his progressive tendencies are expressed in his conscious fantasies, the regressive tendencies in his unconscious fantasies.

We have seen that the female sex organ remains for a long time excluded from direct participation in the girl's sexual life. It is unbelievable how many even very modern girls still

[5] BRUNSWICK, R. M.: The analysis of a case of paranoia. J. Nerv. & Ment. Dis. 70: 1, 151, 1929.

imagine during adolescence that the apertures of their bodies serve only "dirty" purposes and have nothing to do with love. Only psychoanalysts ever learn that progressive girls who sometimes participate in the struggle for woman's political emancipation, and give lectures on the need for the sexual enlightenment of children, still cling in their unconscious to the theories of early childhood, deny anatomic differences, retain the anal idea of childbirth, and base their ideas of sex on the sadistic conception of coitus. The girl has a twofold attitude toward her genitals. This on the one hand expresses the educational influence of her mother, who has advised her to protect a very valuable treasure that must be kept pure and intact until the fateful "sacrifice" to the husband (thus, in dreams, the female genitals often appear symbolically as a hidden treasure, a jewel that must be guarded). On the other hand, the infantile conception that the genitals are a dirty cloaca, of which one must be ashamed, still persists in the unconscious. With regard to this latter valuation, the pubescent girl is in sharp contrast to the normal boy, for whom the genitals have the highest value and whose anxieties center around keeping them intact.

Other differences between the sexual development of the girl and that of the boy attain their full expression during adolescence. It is true that sometimes both are unconscious of sexuality in their yearning for love and their hunger for fulfillment. Even in the period of heterosexual longings, infatuation with persons of the other sex for some time follows a path seemingly independent of the first organic signs of genital excitation. It is difficult to decide whether this split results from a recent repression or whether it constitutes a survival of psychologic states characteristic of the latency period, during which love was to a great extent free from sexual impulses.

In young girls eroticism remains separated from awareness of sexuality for a longer time than in boys. This fact can be explained for the most part on the basis of anatomic differences. The erotic fantasies of boys are soon accompanied by obvious genital processes; they are, so to speak, discredited by these. Because of the temporal coincidence of the yearning for ideal love and the genital urge, it is difficult for the boy to deny the connection between the two.

Girls, however, do not so easily discover that their genitals are the executive agents of their yearning for love, and even if they have had orgastic emotions and have performed masturbatory acts, they still find it easier to keep their psychologic feelings and somatic tensions apart than do boys. Above all, masturbation can assume much more indirect and concealed forms in girls than in boys. The vaginal sensations cannot be compared with the pressure of the male organ, the tension cannot always be exactly localized, excitation and relaxation can take place without conscious control on the part of the girl. The statements of many young girls and women that they have never masturbated rest on a basis of relative truth, because it may very well happen that the entire masturbatory discharge takes place without any direct conscious participation. Thus, it is easy for the girl to undertake unconscious diverting actions based on the fact that the direct excitation in the genital region is easily repressed and manifests itself in sensations in other parts of the body. Such sensations as heart pounding, pressure in the stomach, a feeling of burning in the head, light dizziness, and various other manifestations are often continuations of and substitutes for repressed masturbation.

The turning of the sexual forces toward heterosexual objects, that is to say, the mastering of the new task of puberty, does not proceed without conflicts and disturbances. This progressive aim must be achieved against regressive forces, and because the young girl has no adequate outlet in external reality she can avoid external dangers; but another peril may arise, namely, that of a regressive sexualization of older emotional relations. The theme of prepuberty—liberation from old ties in order to attain adulthood—is now accompanied by another strongly urgent theme, the need to break away from the danger of sexual attachment to the old objects.

The relation to the girl friend, the sexual element of which consisted in common "knowledge," is no longer satisfactory in this form. If the drive of the sexual forces is strong enough before heterosexuality has been stabilized into full feminine readiness, the girl's relation to persons of her own sex may receive an influx of sexual content. Her relation to the friend of the same age now becomes more complicated; in rare cases it has an overtly sexual, genital character, but usually it develops in a platonic but very affective fashion. The differentiation of the active-passive and sadistic-masochistic roles is usually strongly emphasized in these friendships: as we have seen, it had its beginning in early puberty, and during adolescence it often assumes an acute form, in which the passive-masochistic girl is subjected to the other. Sometimes a sudden more or less rationalized break of the friendship takes place, and this can be accompanied by an apparently unmotivated severe depression. Fear of the homosexual component in the friendship has led to flight, followed by isolation and grief.

Very often the homosexual yearning turns toward a more distant object and the love assumes an extraordinarily passionate form. It reaches an even higher degree of intensity than is ever achieved by heterosexual longing. Homosexuality in the adolescent girl very often runs a course as follows. After more or less passionate friendships with mates of the same age, after ardent worshiping of an older girl or a woman teacher, there comes, with the rising sexual instincts, an overwhelming infatuation with a maturer woman who is usually inaccessible and often known only casually. This infatuation has all the characteristics of painful and passionate love. This form of love in adolescence presupposes a strong persistence of the mother tie.

Another form of such dependence upon the mother consists in seemingly heterosexual development. The mother is exchanged for the father, but the infantile form of relation is repeated. This carrying over of the relation to the father[6] rarely leads to adulthood. The path to heterosexual relations is now open; what makes them unsatisfactory is, according to Freud, the fact that the negative feelings formerly directed against the mother are carried over with regard to men. In the relations with the latter, infantile, insatiable, clinging elements are preserved. The hatred for men manifests itself among other things in resentment of the fact that the father could not by his strength and love save the girl from her dependence on her mother. In this infantile type of adolescent girl, the fear of sexual dangers uses a definite defense mechanism—avoidance of dangers, which is the most primitive form of defense. Such girls stay at home with their mothers, renounce all deep experience, and develop more or less perceptible symptoms of agoraphobia.

The following letter of a 15-year old girl to her friend is a clear illustration of such a flight into the infantile relation with the mother under the pressure of fear and sense of guilt.

"Mother wants me to wear a long dress at the big dance party at W.'s— my first long dress. She is surprised that I don't want to. I begged her to let me wear my short pink dress for the last time . . . I am so afraid. The long dress makes me feel as if Mummy were going on a long trip and I did not know when she would return. Isn't that silly? And sometimes she looks at me as though I were still a little girl. Ah, if she knew! She would tie my hands to the bed, and despise me . . ."

It is obvious that the writer of this letter was afraid of growing up, and felt that her mother was deserting her (expressed by the image of the mother's going on a trip). We presume that the girl's desperate "if she knew" relates to her guilt feelings aroused by masturbation. The prohibition ex-

[6] FREUD, S.: New introductory lectures on psychoanalysis. New York: Norton, 1933.

tends to everything sexual, and if staying with the mother
does not give sufficient protection, more complicated protective
measures are resorted to, and neurosis begins.

As we have already pointed out, the heterosexual love of the
young girl is still under strong pressure of regressive forces.
Her relation with her father, which has hitherto been relatively
free from conflict, is now one of inhibition and estrangement.
Often this attitude is intensified to the point of repulsion
about everything that relates to the father's body: his eating
habits are disgusting, his cigar has a penetrating odor, the girl
is reluctant to use the common bathroom—in brief, she avoids
her father's bodily atmosphere, which has become distasteful.
She remains unconscious of the fact that all this represents
a defense against temptation.

The objects in the outside world to which the young girl
does turn her heterosexual love are usually characterized by
the fact that they present no danger of possible realization and
often assume the form described in Maria Bashkirtseff's diary.
One may surmise that Maria's platonic love for the Duke of
H—— was actually the expression of a regressive longing
for her father. Her parents had separated when she was a
little child. But even in persons whose family situations
have been more favorable, such half-real loves contain a mixture
of old feelings and new phantoms.

The girl who rushes hungrily from object to object seems to
display a completely different kind of amorous disposition.
But closer investigation reveals that the two types—the girl
who for many years is constant in her love for an almost unreal
object, and the fickle individual who frequently changes her
objects—are not the psychologic opposites that one might
suppose them to be. Both types seek to gratify a longing for
substitute objects that, although they really exist, have no
actual emotional reality. There are even girls who practice
one of these forms of love for a while and then take up the
other.

Such a thrust for an object, which generally expands into

elaborate daydreaming, may result in behavior that often surprises and even frightens the young girl's intimates. A girl formerly truthful and dependable begins to tell stories of a more or less fantastic character and stubbornly maintains that these stories are true. In boys such stories are gratifications of ambition; in girls, their content is erotic.

We meet girls who, although normal and well adjusted in all other respects, write love letters to themselves, not merely in order to boast about these missives to their friends, but to endow their fantasies with some degree of reality. Lying serves the double purpose of discharging tensions arising from the excessive demands made on one's fantasy life and of protecting oneself from actual realization. What essentially distinguishes such fantasies (pseudology) from daydreams is that they are communicated to others as real happenings. The imaginary gratifications of ambitious or erotic desires—consummated without regard for external reality—that are the principal content of daydreams, also supply material for pseudology. Just as the daydream is sometimes limited to a modest mitigation of some undesirable situation, while at other times it is a fantastic creation in utter contradiction to reality, so the content of pseudology varies from trite love affairs or petty satisfactions of vanity to complicated romantic adventures. Like the daydreamer, the pseudologist fulfils his wishes by inventing lies, and always places himself in the center of his fantasy.

There is, however, one essential difference between the two. While daydreamers are characterized by bashful secrecy broken only rarely to intimate friends, pseudologists importune others with their fantasies, which they relate as real events. In this, their purpose is usually to achieve the satisfaction inherent in the act of communication—one of their motives is obviously the revelation of the fantasy carefully concealed by daydreamers.

Daydreamers, further, are inclined to regard their fantasies as true, and this is part of their pleasure. But the pseudologists'

longing for reality seems to be much more intense—intense
enough for them to represent products of their imagination as
truth even to other people.

The following case is a good illustration of this point.[7] A
girl undergoes a remarkable experience between the ages of
13 and 17. She is an attractive girl, intelligent and of ardent
temperament. She does not lack opportunities for amorous
relations, but always avoids them with the greatest reserve.
A high-school boy of about 17, rather unattractive, whom she
knows only by sight, becomes the hero of her erotic fantasies.
These have an extremely passionate character—consuming
kisses, ardent embraces, sexual ecstasies, the young girl's
imagination creating everything that reality can give to a
sexually mature woman. She becomes so absorbed in this
fantasy that in her seclusion she leads a life full of joys and
sorrows: her eyes are often swollen with tears because her lover
turns out to be tyrannical, covers her with abuse, and even
beats her; then, overflowing with love, he brings her flowers
that actually she buys herself. She manages to get a picture
of him and on it she writes a loving dedication in her own hand,
distorted for the purpose. She has dates with him in forbidden
places, they become secretly engaged, etc. For three years
she keeps a detailed diary about all these imaginary experiences;
when her lover goes away she continues her relations with him
by writing him letters that she never mails, and to which she
replies herself.

What interests us in this case is the fact that she tells everyone about these mysterious relations, representing them as real,
so that she exposes herself to unpleasantness and punishment;
when reprimanded, she always admits contritely not that she
is lying, but that she is still involved in the forbidden relationship. Her descriptions are so convincing that no one doubts
the truth of them, even though the innocent boy has denied
having any relations with her.

As we have said, this girl had every opportunity to experience

[7] DEUTSCH, H.: Über die pathologische Lüge (pseudologia phantastica). Internat.
Ztschr. f. Psychoanal., vol. 8, 1922.

in reality what she invented pseudologically. But she had several motives for preferring the latter course. The fact that her erotic life consisted in fantasies woven around a chosen object is, as we noted earlier, normal for a girl in the pubescent stage (we saw a similar example in Maria Bashkirtseff's diary). In her choice she was determined by her unconscious attitude toward her brother; this too is a regressive although normal determinant of erotic choice. The regressive nature of adolescent fantasies is manifested in the fact that as a rule the real objects that are chosen strongly resemble earlier objects—that is to say, father or brother. Under the impact of puberty our pseudologic girl tries to center her longing on a real object, but succeeds only partially. She chooses one object after the model of her brother, but she is incapable of a real love relation. The kind of relation she wants must be imaginary, not real. The girl strictly avoided every opportunity to become acquainted with the hero of her fantasies. She preferred the fantasy; in it her brother, to whom she was unconsciously faithful, and her real object could merge. In her childhood she had had various real experiences with her brother that were preserved in her unconscious and that at a given moment were revived with all the force of a fresh experience. The old experience was attributed to the new object, and former reality endowed the present love fantasy with a real character.

This resurrection of snatches of remembered real events distinguishes pseudology from more normal puberty fantasies. Fenichel[7a] rightly notes that pseudology is a special method of negating reality. During puberty every reality that might gratify sexual wishes may appear dangerous, and a regression to fantasy or pseudology takes place. Pseudology is used as a defense; the adolescent girl takes her fantasy for reality in order to renounce a reality that she regards as perhaps more dangerous.

Another form of escape from a present that is unsatisfactory or conceals dangers is the postponement of realization. Young

[7a] FENICHEL, O.: Zur Oekonomie der Pseudologia phantastica. Internat. Ztschr. f. Psychoanal., vol. 24, 1938.

girls indulge in detailed plans for the future that they think up alone or with appropriate collaborators. These plans vary from the most trite and prosaic pictures to the most fantastic and impossible. Many a young girl debates in her own mind the most insignificant fixture in the kitchen of her future home, before the slightest chance of marriage has presented itself. Others see themselves eloping under the most romantic circumstances and build splendid castles in the air for their future residences. The erotic plans vary between being desired with burning passion and suffering poignantly for the sake of the imaginary lover.

However, absorption in daydreams is also not without dangers, and the young girl tries to tear herself away from these experiences. Often she takes the same path she took during prepuberty to liberate herself from childhood dependency. She turns actively toward reality and under normal conditions succeeds in achieving a compromise. In this case, reality must contain a sufficient amount of pleasure elements, must offer sufficient gratification, and be interesting enough to compete with her fantasies. But this step into reality does not always succeed. In the first place, the outside world opposes the desire for sexual pleasure in adolescence and thrusts the girl back into her dreams. In the second place, the imaginary world is often so full and rich that reality is in comparison pale and unsatisfactory. In such cases colorful fantasy is preferred to gray reality. We have also seen that the fear of real fulfillment, which makes fantasy appear a less dangerous refuge, also drives the girl away from reality.

In many girls the orientation toward reality takes a form that easily creates new problems. For instance, I have met young girls who, because of a fear of passive sexual experiences, plunged into intense sexual activity. They tried to overcome fear by the tested method of "active intervention," but the experiences they themselves provoked usually weighed upon them just as heavily, and their fear only changed its content. The fear of fulfilling sexual wishes is replaced by guilty self-reproach for having too rashly overruled sexual inhibitions.

Many modern young girls have sexual experiences before they are psychologically ready for them, endeavoring to skip the stages necessary for real psychologic preparation. They are ashamed of their sexual inhibitions, disown them, and become a prey to anxiety and depression. Sometimes this sexual pseudofreedom assumes a directly obsessive character. The young girl engages in numerous sexual relations, is deserted by her lovers or deserts them again and again, regards her behavior as "emancipated," and fails to realize that her actions are those of a creature enslaved by largely unconscious urges and fantasies rather than those of a "free human being." But the opposite course of action also involves dangers for the young girl. Avoidance of real experiences because of an exaggerated fear of them leads to an overburdening of the fantasy life, to neurotic symptoms and rather pathologic behavior. The various forms of runaway behavior, not always as primitive and direct as Evelyn's, result from such an avoidance. With somewhat more mature girls running away assumes the form of taking up professions for which they have no real inclination or interest, or of joining political groups, cults, or religious communities. The real purpose of such actions is not to emancipate themselves from their milieu but to escape from their own strongly sexualized fantasies. Such girls often have a tendency to eliminate love from their lives entirely. Even though they frequently aspire to high humanitarian, social, or scientific goals, they lack the spiritual richness that comes from emotional experience. This type of girl, having given up all emotional life, usually indulges in narcissistic and emotionless "objectivity" for long periods: the danger here is that the success of this total sublimation may permanently mutilate her affective life. Such girls are threatened with neurotic derangement in later life.

The essentially sound activity and the social and intellectual energy developed by the young girl who renounces her fantasies, often blight her emotional life and prevent her from achieving complete femininity and, later, motherhood. That women frequently remain entangled in infantile forms of emotional life while their minds and activities are extremely well developed, is an interesting fact that still requires explanation. It appears that the development from fantasy life into fully mature femininity is a psychologic achievement that can be inhibited by intellectualization.

Later we shall discuss at greater length the relation between the type of the ambitious and energetic young girl who achieves her aims by great exertions, thanks to her ability to repress her sexual drives, but whose emotional life is stunted in the process, and the so-called masculinity complex. In direct contrast to this type is the woman who achieves complete femininity in eroticism and sexuality at the price of completely subordinating every ambition and talent to this purpose. Normal growth is consistent with the harmonious coexistence of the two developments.

Some adolescent girls who have been subjected from earliest childhood to the harmful influence of an excessively severe morality, or who have felt the impact of strong unconscious guilt feelings, react in a definite manner to the psychologic processes of their maturation. All the free stirrings of the future are in this case prematurely petrified, and the adolescent urge for freedom and the hunger for love are replaced by rigid moral principles. Every time a danger of violating these principles arises, the voice of the inner law makes itself heard as a "signal of fear." New renunciations are added to the old, and although freedom from guilt feelings can be achieved, it is only at the price of renunciation. This is the ascetic girl, who usually has a predisposition to obsessional neurosis; this predisposition was no doubt present before, but it is intensified through the struggles and fears of puberty. After the storms of adolescence the tension may relax and subsequently the girl may develop more freely. If she fails to develop in a less inhibited way, such a girl will become an obsessional neurotic or a conscientious old maid.

The opposite type manifests a childish lack of restraint even during adolescence; because of her lack of developed inhibitions, such a girl has a hard time adjusting herself to the restrictions of her milieu and becomes an "adolescence problem" more frequently than the other type. But as a rule, given favorable environmental influences, she has much greater inner possibilities for further development.

Adolescent girls, though they may be reared in the same cultural conditions and though they are subject to the same biologic processes, present great differences in their still immature but already sharply outlined personalities. One dynamically challenges her milieu; another passively and limply submits to guidance and "fate"; still another is overactive, unable to wait passively for the future and to invent fantasies about it. Some put no limit on their longings and must have boundless elbow room for their effervescent fantasies. Such exuberant fantasy life certainly increases the danger of morbid reactions, but it also offers more opportunities for development of femininity and makes for greater richness in the whole personality. Another type has rigidly defined objectives, determined wishes and apprehensions. This girl is mature and formed at an early age; her fate follows a predetermined direction that she cannot change. She will at first outstrip the youthfully effervescent, unbalanced, undependable girl of the same age, but will have fewer possibilities of further development.

No matter how much they differ in characteristics, all these young girls consider their lives in the present provisional and are beset by inner conflicts until a path of fulfillment opens before them. Young people of both sexes are tormented by a feeling of insecurity, uncertainty, and inner restlessness throughout adolescence. The straight line of development and the effort of the ego to adjust itself and master reality are over and over again interrupted by the rising tides of sexuality. During this phase of life, the anatomic difference between the sexes assumes greater importance than it had before. The organic contrast between the extroverted activity of the boy's sexual apparatus and the veiled, less consciously perceived, and less urgent activity of the girl's is reproduced in the life of the psyche.

During this entire period young people show a tendency to turn away from reality and indulge in fantasies. But it seems that the boy's more active sexuality leads to a stronger turn toward reality and toward conquering the outside world than is the case with the young girl. Hence an important psychologic difference between the sexes: man's attention is principally directed outward, and woman's inward. That typical trait of adolescence that we discussed before—keen observation of one's own psychologic processes—is as a rule more intense in the girl than in the boy. Preoccupation with her own mind continues in the woman's later life and determines two important and distinctive feminine characteristics, namely, woman's greater intuition and greater subjectivity in assimilating and appreciating the life processes. The cornerstones of these fundamental feminine characteristics are laid during adolescence.

Another important difference between the sexes with regard to the relative completion of adolescence lies in their tendencies to identification. The tendency itself is not peculiar only to girls during adolescence. Naturally there are differences between boys and girls as regards the objects of their identifications, their purpose, etc., but the process itself stems from the same needs of the weak ego and serves the same general end in both sexes.

The young man emerges less scathed than the girl from the phase of intensified identifications; in the formation of his personality he has assimilated them more successfully. True, only a few boys develop personalities so powerful and independent that they can completely renounce identifications with others. But the feminine ego seems to remain longer—to some degree it remains throughout life—in that phase of adolescence in which the tendency toward identification is strengthened. The question whether this is explained by definite dispositional elements in woman or by the boy's more active turning toward reality, is not difficult to answer. The same dispositional factors strengthen woman's tendency to identification and obstruct those of her activities that are directed toward the outside world. These forces are also responsible for other characteristic feminine traits, such as those we have mentioned above, i.e., woman's greater intuition and subjectivity. The common denominator of all these qualities is woman's greater deep-rooted passivity with regard to all life processes outside of the reproductive function.

With regard to woman's tendency to identification, it is to be emphasized that this feminine quality shows great individual variations. Identification must not overstep certain limits, otherwise it constitutes a danger for the ego. The more stable the woman's self-confidence and feeling of strength, the less dangerous is this tendency. Once certain limits are crossed, the ego is endangered and the process of identification deprives the individual of the full possession of his own personality. Freud[8] speaks of the "multiple personality" as resulting from a process in which numerous identifications lead to a disruption of the ego. He refers to a purely inner process of ego formation in contrast to a type I have described, in which the ego constantly identifies itself with objects in the outer world instead of forming emotional relationships with them.[9] The psychologic process of identification will in one case have a pathologic outcome that may be more or less severe and in another a more normal resolution. Women give us a better opportunity than men to observe a large gamut of various kinds of identifications that take place within normal limits.

The tendency displayed by many women to renounce their

---

[8] FREUD, S.: The ego and the id. London: Hogarth, 1927.
[9] DEUTSCH, H.: Some forms of emotional disturbance and their relationship to schizophrenia. Psychoanalyt. Quart., vol. 11, 1942.

own judgment and adopt by identification the opinions of their love objects is very typical. Women are also frequently enthusiastic partisans of ideas that apparently have been given them by others. But closer observation reveals that such ideas were previously conceived and developed in their own fantasy. The adoption or carrying out of these ideas is possible only through identification with other people. Even talented women are often uncertain of the value of their own ideas until they receive them from someone else whom they respect. This remarkable combination of projection and identification is doubtless connected with woman's generally passive attitude. The feeling of insecurity in creative activity corresponds to the deep-rooted need of woman to be fecundated from outside in order to be creative.

The tendency to identification sometimes assumes very valuable forms. Thus, many women put their qualities, which may be excellent, at the disposal of the object of their identification and content themselves with thinking: "What a magnificent man I am in love with." They prefer to love and enjoy their own qualities in others. Vice versa, ambitious women who, because they are not active or not talented enough, have not found any direct gratification for their ambition, try to compensate themselves through identification with their men. They strive with the greatest energy to win recognition for their husbands, are full of aggressive hostility to those who do not share their admiration, and behave as though their overestimation were an expression of their love. At bottom they often do not believe in the value of the men they admire with such enthusiasm not out of love, but in order to gratify their own ambitions projected in them.

There are women endowed with rich natural gifts that cannot, however, develop beyond certain limits. Such women are exposed to outside influences and changing identifications to such an extent that they never succeed in consolidating their achievements. Instead of making a reasonable choice among numerous opportunities at their disposal, they constantly get involved in confusion that exerts a destructive influence on their own lives and the lives of those around them.

It might be supposed that this facility in identification with others favorably influences the capacity for adjustment. However, in women, these two processes do not always coincide; on the contrary, there have been most interesting observations suggesting that the opposite is true. The woman who comes close to the type of multiple personality described by Freud is capable of completely renouncing her own personality as she absorbs the man's interests and assimilates herself entirely to him. The intellectual interests, hobbies, and talents, even the handwriting and posture of the man, are acquired. Such women make use of the absorbed traits as though they were their own and often turn them as weapons against the men from whom they have taken them. Something that begins as amiable imitation can gradually assume a hostile character in the form of "I don't need you, I am like you!" A woman largely identified with a man may at the same time destructively oppose him and try to retain her rights and ways in all matters of life.

In contrast with this, we often observe that the more completely a woman preserves her own personality, the more easily does she adjust herself to a man. In such cases it is as though the façade were made of a pliable material that adapts itself perfectly to reality, while the material behind it is as hard and inflexible as marble. This type of adjustment, which we sometimes encounter in women of character, also distinguishes certain races and nations. These adjust themselves with striking facility to a new environment, yet they seem to possess solid, deep-rooted qualities that are almost inaccessible to outside influences, and they thus stubbornly resist complete assimilation. There is perhaps a close connection between these two qualities—the capacity for adjustment and the preservation of a firm, immalleable kernel.

The facility with which woman identifies often exposes her to accusations (sometimes justified) of falseness (deceitfulness

of women).   A certain type of clever woman has a knack of
sensing which side of herself she should show to a man in order
to make him feel big.   Many women owe their success in
important fields to this kind of capacity for adjustment.
What they tell one man they withhold from another; with
one they make themselves small and insignificant, with another
they stand on their toes to show him that they can reach up
to his level.   They do all this because of their more or less
conscious tendency to give the other person narcissistic gratification in such a way that he feels himself to be wonderful
and at the same time admires his flattering admirer.   These
women usually do not strive for love but use the sympathy
they arouse in others for their own ambitious purposes.   They
are particularly dangerous when they compete with other
women often more gifted than themselves, who, because they
openly pursue their ambitious aims, are feared and rejected by
men.   We shall return to this latter type of woman.   At this
point we wish to emphasize the fact that woman's peculiar facility for identification reveals a whole gamut of possibilities.   It is
an innate feminine quality that, born of weakness and passivity, can serve varied and often opposite purposes.   It makes a
great difference whether identification serves the purpose of
love or hate, whether it stems from the cold source of a
masculinity (desire to *be* "like him") or from the warm source
of femininity (desire to "understand him" by *feeling* "like
him").

We spoke above of a phase of adolescence during which boys
and girls display a particularly keen understanding of their
own psychologic states.   We explained this by the narcis-
sistically intensified self-observation and heightened interest
in the processes of their own psychic life that are characteristic
of this period.   In my psychoanalytic practice I have encountered a type of patient who by his pathologic intensification of this behavior was able to throw much light upon it.
Distinguished by extraordinary intuition about their own psy-

chologic processes and by the ability to observe and understand them, persons of this type turn all their activity upon
their own psychologic life, while they are strikingly passive
in their attitude toward the world around them. They are
as well adjusted to reality as can be, but they quite passively
let themselves be dominated by people and things. Analysis
shows that their inner perception amounts to a more intensive
self-observation for the purpose of defense against inner dangers.
We are thus confronted with a defensive process in which the
individual behaves like someone anxiously listening in the
dark and perceiving every noise with special acuteness. One
patient of this type declared that he observed himself so at-
tentively in order not to go insane, thus clearly defining his
inner perception as a defense mechanism. It was also ascertainable that in these patients the repressed anxiety increased
in intensity as soon the defensive self-observation failed. In
one case the anxiety grew constantly stronger during the
treatment, until finally the patient began to develop paranoic
ideas. It was thus possible to observe *statu nascendi* the
transformation of the inner perception into a projection in
which the inner observer became the persecutor in the outside
world.

Our experience with these patients brought us closer to an
understanding of that "inner perception" that women possess
in a greater degree than men. To understand it is all the more
important because the most striking feminine characteristic,
intuition, can be derived from it.

Let us once again recall the final phase of adolescence, during
which the young boy strongly and actively turns toward reality,
while the girl perseveres for a longer time and to a greater degree
in her fantasy life. An excessive preoccupation with one's
fantasy life involves dangers for the ego and requires a heightened inner alertness, a more acute "listening in the dark." The
faculty of self-observation developed during adolescence is at
the woman's disposal for fighting this psychologic danger. At
first this faculty functions as a defense mechanism, and if the

adolescent's development toward womanhood follows a favorable course, it crystallizes into a positive characterologic quality.   If this self-observation does not play the part of a rigid governess during adolescence and drive the young girl into flight from fear of her own fantasy life, the combination of rich fantasy and emotional life, of subjectivity and inner perception, gives rise to *intuition*, an important component of what Goethe called the "eternal feminine."   A part of adolescent narcissism is included in this formation, and when it does not evolve into egoistic self-love it endows the woman with that winning quality, that charm that seems to say: "Love me, for I too have something to give."

Woman's understanding of other people's minds, her intuition, is the result of an unconscious process through which the subjective experience of another person is made one's own by association and thus is immediately understood.   The other person's subjective experience manifests itself in an external happening that is sometimes barely perceptible, but that in an intuitive person evokes by quick association a definite inner state; the conscious perception rapidly tames the inner reaction, incorporates the impression received into a harmonious series of ideas, masters the "inspirational" element, and translates it into the sober form of conscious knowledge.   Since the whole process is very rapid, its second phase, that is, the intellectual elaboration, is barely perceived—everything seem to take place in the unconscious and affective element, because the conscious ingredient does not come to the fore.

What we see in intuition is not a logical concatenation of impressions; on the contrary, in each intuitive experience, the other person's mental state is emotionally and unconsciously "re-experienced," that is, felt as one's own.   The ability to do this will naturally depend on one's sympathy and love for and spiritual affinity with the other person; and the extent of this spiritual affinity, for which the German language has the term *Einfühlung* (sometimes translated by "empathy"), depends on the richness of one's own emotional experiences, which underlie the "inner perception" or the ability to understand one's own feelings and psychologic relations and, by analogy, those of others. This brief definition of intuition describes an ability that is to a high degree characteristic of women. For the sake of caution let us replace the term "ability" with "potentiality," to indicate that women are not always, perhaps not even frequently, in position to make use of their intuition. For other factors too determine its functioning. All human beings develop prejudices—psychoanalysis calls them resistances—against their own inclinations and potentialities.[10] These prejudices may naturally obstruct intuition and the ability to understand other persons. Also, the practical application of women's intuition often fails. They make serious errors in their judgment and treatment of other people even when they are endowed with strong intuition. After every error and every disappointment they discover that as a matter of fact they expected and knew in advance what would happen, but "something" prevented them from making the right use of their intuitive ability. It is not our aim here to discuss the possible deeper motives of such behavior. No doubt, self-injurious masochistic tendencies are often involved in these cases, and they create unfavorable conditions for the practical use of the intuition. Nor is intuition always a sufficient means for mastering the outside world; more objective methods of rational critique are often needed in order to use this faculty effectively

However, the type of woman under discussion here is usually restricted in the use of her intuition by other motives. These women have mistakingly and unfortunately transferred their self-valuation to another field. They refuse to admit their feminine qualities, which are of the subjective and emotional order, and instead of drawing an advantage from these positive feminine qualities, strive for more "objectivity" and "unemotionalness," that is, for qualities less inherent in their natures. A young woman with whom I had the opportunity of discussing

[10] DEUTSCH, H.: A discussion of certain forms of resistance. Internat. J. Psycho-Analysis, vol. 20, 1939.

such difficulties in the practical application of her intuition told me that she always recalled with horror her mother's irrational, purely emotional behavior. "Are not all women like that?" she asked.

We can answer this question objectively: Yes, many women are like that, for every human potentiality can be abused or used badly, just as it can be used effectively. Furthermore, this apparently "irrational" tendency can become a blessing, and flight from it leads to inner impoverishment that only pretends to be rational objectivity. The value of woman lies in the good management of the irrational component of her psyche.

While ascribing a greater degree of intuition to women, we do not deny its existence in men. In men too the experiences of adolescence can have a fruitful and lasting effect. But a sensitive, intuitive man probably has a strong feminine component in his entire personality. This seems particularly true of artistically gifted men and of those whose professions require psychologic understanding of other people. It has rightly been stressed that literary works written by men often reveal deep psychologic understanding of the feminine soul. These men obviously used the sublimated forces of their own femininity for a successful identification with women. On the other hand, world literature, including modern literature, contains a large number of works by women that are distinguished by psychologic genius. Our personal impression, for which we naturally do not claim any general validity, is that women whose literary achievements are brilliant as long as they confine themselves to a field in which they can make use of their psychologic gifts, often prove inadequate when for political or other reasons they switch to intellectual fields in which the objective approach is paramount. When their literary talent draws from the horn of plenty of feminine intuition, their achievement is worth while; but their intellect is not on a level with their innate feminine intuition.

In our effort to find the sources of specific feminine qualities we seem always to return to our starting point. The sequence constituted by (1) greater proneness to identification, (2) stronger fantasy, (3) subjectivity, (4) inner perception, and (5) intuition, leads us back to the common origin of all these traits, feminine passivity. For the sake of clarity it will be useful to keep this passivity in mind while analyzing its individual components.

One of these components is the young girl's inclination to fantasying. We have pointed out that the boy because of his anatomic and physiologic characteristics is better prepared for the task of mastering reality—has built up a greater "reality potential," so to speak—than the girl. Attempts are often made to explain the young girl's perseverance in fantasy life by the double sexual standard, which gives the young man better opportunities for sexual gratification, thus protecting him from being overburdened by fantasies. Observation of modern youth has permitted us to correct this view. Today the double sexual standard is being eliminated by pressure from two opposite directions: the young girl behaves with greater freedom, and the young man is willing to postpone his sexual gratification until he achieves greater capacity for love. These new developments, however, do not seem to have much effect upon the sexual differences with which we are dealing here, and we are compelled to assume that much more elemental motives, rooted in biology, are responsible for them.

The approach of the reproductive task while the possibility or capacity for fulfilling it is lacking, is another factor that intensifies the girl's tendency to fantasying. Again we are confronted with a developmental situation in which a progressive tendency releases regressive forces. The hypothesis that the motherhood fantasies of young girls, because they are physically mature, have a greater reality value than the childhood experiences relating to them, is based on a kind of optic illusion. The woman approaching maturity is in exactly the same situation that she was in as a little girl, when she laid the first cornerstones for her future womanhood in her fantasy life. At that time she played with dolls in active identification with

her mother. As a maturing girl she normally gives up thi
identification and now identifies herself with herself, in the rol
that she will play in the future. Her possibilities of realizatio:
are still distant, she is still separated from them by her anxieties
her wishes, and her preparations for the sexual act. Now tha
fulfillment is nearer, it is felt as a greater danger, and th
awakening psychologic processes connected with the reproduc
tive function are driven into the more inward sphere of fantas}
life, just as they were in the girl's childhood. This inclinatio:
to fantasying, born from the inner more than from the oute
impossibility of realization, that is to say, from passivity, i:
turn increases the passivity of woman, in a kind of vicious circle
The fantasies can become a prelude to action, but their gratifi
cation takes place on a psychologic plane, and while they inten
sify and enrich psychologic life, they weaken the impulse t(
realization.

Thus woman acquires a tendency to passivity that intensifie:
the passive nature inherent in her biology and anatomy. Sh(
passively awaits fecundation: her life is fully active and rootec
in reality only when she becomes a mother. Until then every
thing that is feminine in the woman, physiology and psychology
is passive, receptive. This speculation, which is based on m}
experience, can perhaps be confirmed by a more objectiv(
observation: no human being has as great a sense of reality a:
a mother. It is often striking how with the achievement o
motherhood, implying, as it does, the strongest possible turning
to reality, the young girl who previously had developed a pro
found intuition, loses this valuable gift and replaces it witl
other, more realistic qualities.

The girl's strong bent toward fantasy and subjective experi
ence, while giving birth to the positive qualities of intuition anc
empathy, involves certain dangers. Excessive withdrawal from
reality strengthens neurotic tendencies. The girl's intellectua
development, her social adjustment, and her professional activ
ity can naturally be disturbed by excessive fantasying.

Fantasies, subjective experiences, and strengthening of th(

intuitive faculty appear in the course of the girl's development. They are also products of a sublimation that remains subjective and emotional and that is typical of women; for this reason premature realization of vital goals does not seem to be advantageous even under favorable circumstances. All the fruits of psychic experience that begin to mature during adolescence must complete the process of maturation. Only a mother who has partly sublimated her motherliness during the waiting period will become a real mother. Observation shows that a too early maternity involves the danger of retarding this process of maturation. It is true also, however, that there is a kind of "late maturation" in motherhood. Thus, we often see emotionally infantile women who prematurely, without being psychologically prepared for motherhood, become mothers and who catch up with the maturation process during pregnancy or with the birth of the child. War mothers provide us with ample opportunities to observe this. Another danger is that early motherhood makes such demands on the girl's incomplete personality that all her activity is put to the service of the reproductive function and her personality is crippled as a result.

These passive tendencies in the girl are not contradictory to the frequently intense active strivings that she develops during adolescence. Many girls are forced by the pressure of social conditions to work at some occupation, but they regard such occupations as provisional. Even today it is striking how many women engaged in active professional work await the moment when they will be supported by their husbands, and bitterly reproach a husband who is unable to satisfy this demand. Many girls take up professions because it is the fashion to do so or because of their social convictions; most of them are moved by the desire to share in active life. One might think that this activity, particularly intensified in our generation, is in contradiction to what we have described as specifically feminine. But actually, absurd and paradoxic as it may sound, the psychic structure of woman does not consist exclusively in the "eternal feminine." It is true that femininity is her essential core, but around this core there are layers and wrappings that are equally genuine elements of the feminine soul and frequently very valuable ones, indispensable for the preservation and development of the core. If we follow the subsequent development of these elements, we find that they stem from the active, sometimes masculine components that, even though always more or less present in woman, originate in the masculine part of the bisexual disposition. They are continuations of elements present in the undifferentiated phase of childhood, identifications with masculine prototypes, survivals of the prepuberty thrust of activity—in brief, they are sublimations of active currents in woman.

Even superficial observation shows that a girl who has previously been intelligent, brilliant, and promising, often lets all these personality values burst like a soap bubble during puberty, when she is overtaxed by her awakening femininity, the intensification of her inner world. The inverse is also true. We often see an intellectual girl who is ambitious, pedantically conscientious, and neurotically dutiful, strengthening these qualities in adolescence and making of them an armor to protect herself from the development of feminine qualities. Such a girl seems to me the most miserable feminine type in existence, for, exactly like her rustic twin sister Dulcinea, she is often an excellent but usually an incomplete man. She too is disturbed by motherhood, not by emotional but by real maternity. In her effort to make life perfect she achieves motherhood, and her particularly dutiful devotion to her children often comes into real conflict with her other aspirations. Such women are all intellect or all strength, and their subjective experience, emotional development, and intuition are completely lost. They will always do their work thoroughly but will never produce anything original stemming from the treasure of intuition, the source of woman's genius.

Dulcinea types, intellectuals or sportswomen, are extraordinarily frequent in colleges. Their teachers are pleased with them, because they are cooperative and reliable. But their affective lives are dry, sterile, and impoverished. Only exceptionally talented girls can carry a surplus of intellect without injuring their affective lives, for woman's intellect, her capacity for objectively understanding life, thrives at the expense of her subjective, emotional qualities. Modern education unfortunately neglects this truth, and girls are very often intellectually overburdened. Sports are not an adequate substitute for deep affective experiences, nor do amusements and artistic enjoyment answer the need for real relaxation and communion with oneself.

At the other extreme there is the completely passive girl. She does not reach the point of sublimating her fantasies. She fails to develop her active femininity with its passive goal, because her fear of what may come or of what she has already found lurking within her cripples her psychologically; she abandons herself to her fate and becomes a completely passive object for outside influences to work upon. This passive orientation can assume various forms. When it has a sexual character it leads to passive abandon without any other motive than that of weak-minded passivity; or it may extend to all the situations in the girl's life and make her a passive foil for every outside stimulus. Sometimes she perseveres in some sort of activity, but only when its goal is prescribed by others. This type of girl is not identical with the type mentioned above (p. 131). While the latter passively follows others as a result of her emotional emptiness, the former has many emotional potentialities but fails to develop them actively out of fear and inhibition. She is neurotic without knowing it. She is feminine, but an alien disturbing element has distorted her feminine passivity. She has not sublimated this essential tendency of her nature into profound subjective experience, because she has abandoned herself to it too completely. Every strong emotional excitation causes such girls to have fainting fits; they are subject to narcoleptic states, and excessive sleeping, as a reaction to feelings of fatigue, takes up much of their lives. They use sleep to escape from life, not to restore their strength.

Another difference between masculine and feminine development stems from the fact that during the years of greatest psychologic growth, that is, in adolescence, women show a definitely stronger tendency than men to spiritualization of the sexual instinct. In the history of mankind the spiritualization of this instinct has taken various forms. Primitive religion raised sexuality to the status of a divine function and thus decreased the need for individual spiritualization. Later, sexuality was considered an instrument of the devil, and asceticism was preached in behalf of spiritualization that could not be undertaken directly. In individual life this spiritualization proceeds along several paths. Through fantasy activity that begins early in childhood, the sexual instinct is from the start connected with unconscious psychologic contents. The same process is repeated with greater intensity during puberty. The interval of time between the reawakening of the sexual urge and its direct gratification is filled with fantasy activity, and thus the endowment of the sexual instinct with psychologic content is further advanced. In the animal kingdom, sexual stimulation is connected with the sensory organs, above all with the sense of smell. (This connection is even more marked in the maternal instinct of animals and is responsible for the radical difference between "motherliness," an emotional complex in women, and "maternal instinct" in animals.) To be sure, in human beings the sensory organs are likewise an important intermediary between the sexual sphere and the psychic elements, but the development of fantasy life establishes a relation between sexuality and the various spiritual functions, especially the emotional life. We shall see that the character of this relation between the instinct and the emotional life constitutes one of the essential sex differences between men and women.

What we have observed directly in the processes of adolescence again reminds us that many psychologic phenomena may paradoxically exert both inhibiting and furthering influences. The intensification of the sexual instinct mobilizes counterforces that serve to resist it.[11] The same forces of resistance make important contributions to the development of the ego by simultaneously serving sublimation. They exert a lasting instinct-inhibiting influence that is utilized to the advantage of the personality as a whole, so long as it remains, quantitatively and qualitatively, within normal limits. If these defense mechanisms become rigid, steadily opposing instinctual gratifications and other developments, they acquire the character of an inner resistance that manifests itself in the form of neurotic symptoms and pathologic personality formation.

The girl's mechanisms of defense against the onslaught of sexuality are to some extent identical in character with the boy's. The girl with intellectual interests and a disposition to obsessional neurosis will strengthen her intellectuality and tendency to objectification and thus repel the threat of the rising sexuality. She will even use these qualities as weapons against the outside world when her increasing feminine charms fire men's lust and place her in real and immediate danger. We have seen that even the nonintellectual Dorothy suddenly began to develop an observant objective curiosity when she found herself in a dangerous milieu.

Connected with woman's greater passivity and more intense inner life and fantasy is the specifically feminine tendency to disregard the coarse sexual claims and express them in the form of idealized love yearning and sublimated eroticism. During the first stages of adolescence the tendency to idealize the sexual instinct is common to boys and girls. It manifests itself above all in the choice of the love object, the nature and significance of which for the young preclude any coarse sexual aspect in it. In men this attitude is reduced to a minimum in later life and

[11] FREUD, A.: Op. cit.

persists only in abnormal cases. Men who cannot sexually desire the object they love, and vice versa, are numerous, but they are neurotic. The same split in erotic feelings is encountered in girls, but, as we have seen above, rarely with regard to the love object. In them, this split affects themselves, that is to say, they either lower themselves to the status of a purely sexual object or raise themselves to that of an "unattainable."

At any rate, the girl represses the conscious realization of the direct instinctual claim for a much longer time and in a much more successful manner than the boy. This claim manifests itself indirectly in her intensified love yearnings and the erotic orientation of her fantasies—in brief, in the endowment of her inner life with those emotional qualities that we recognize as specifically feminine. In the psychologic household of women these qualities represent a process of sublimation and at the same time serve as a defense against direct sexual instinctual demands. A great Polish poet called passion the "poetry of the body," and sensuality its "prose." This striving to throw off the prosaic instinct and attain poetic richness of emotion distinguishes the adolescence of girls from that of boys, in whom fantasy gradually gives way to masculine activity that is turned toward reality. In the boy, as opposed to the girl, at the end of the conflict between the instinct and the defense mechanism, the sexual instinct emerges largely independent of its sublimations.

It must be mentioned here that these differences between the sexes, although basic, have a quantitative as well as a qualitative character. We have spoken of certain "masculine" qualities as normal components of feminine psychology. It is not to be concluded from these observations on the differences between the sexes that the normal man is an instinctual being —well adjusted to reality and often endowed with great spiritual qualities—whose sexuality, uninfluenced by the emotions, strives actively and without inhibitions to achieve its direct goal. Such men exist, but they cannot be considered representative of the masculine sex. What we consider the essential feature of women—the fact that their sexuality and other life interests are heavily laden with emotion—is also a factor in the development of man, and as a "feminine" component perhaps plays the same part in his psychology as the masculine component plays in woman's. But the social valuation of these components furthers masculinity in women and discourages femininity in men. Just as during puberty the epithet "sissy" is an insult, while "tomboy" is often an expression of praise (p. 85), so in later life masculine qualities in women frequently have a high social value, while femininity in a man makes him ridiculous and even despised if it manifests itself too clearly. The fact that many men owe their artistic gifts and some of their professional excellence to this component is often overlooked.

However, we wish here to stress the quantitative element without making any value judgments. We assume that all the forms of development of sexuality and personality are shared by both sexes, that the same defense mechanisms and types of sublimation are at their disposal, but that one sex makes greater use of some of them, and the other of others. These quantitative differences contribute a great deal to the differentiation of the sexes.

When discussing the goal-inhibited manifestations of the girl's sexual development, we maintained that they moved in the emotional sphere. Feminine sexuality is sublimated into definite emotional values to a much greater extent than masculine sexuality. Later we shall have an opportunity to return to the direct manifestations of feminine sexuality in adolescence.

Let us now examine the relations between the young girl's sexual and reproductive functions. We reject the suggestion of a "negotiated peace" between these two functions if its purpose is to deprive the feminine sexual instinct of an independent tendency that serves only the aim of pleasure. Such peace proposals originate in the demands of the church, and in certain racial ideals and social aims, rather than in real understanding, based on experience, of the feminine functions. We disagree, however, with the other view, often expressed by psychoanalysts, that reproduction is only a consequence of the sexual

act and not its ultimate aim.   It is precisely in adolescence that
the two currents can be seen juxtaposed, separate yet influencing each other.   The maternal instinct manifests itself in fantasies, fears, and symptoms that appear most markedly during
the first menstruation.   At this time its character is so infantile,
so full of regressive elements, so close to the old ideas of the
little girl, that we are hardly able to treat it as a fully awakened
urge to maternity.   We shall call this group of ideas and emotions the "motherhood complex" and assign to it in this life
period the role of a psychologic "outpost" that heralds and prepares the subsequent development of the reproductive instinct.
Whether it owes its existence only to psychologic factors or
whether we have here the inner perception of a hormonal process is difficult to decide.

The really characteristic feature of the young girl's erotic
longing and its unconscious content is the expectation of the
sexual experience as distinct from motherhood.   The origin of
this longing in primitive, unsublimated instinctual drives manifests itself in various ways.   Ardent wishes to be desired, strong
aspirations to exclusive egoistic possession, a normally completely passive attitude with regard to the first attack, and the
desire to be raped that asserts itself in dreams and fears, are
characteristic attributes of feminine sexuality.   They are so
fundamentally different from the emotional manifestations of
motherhood that we are compelled to accept the opposition of
sexuality and eroticism on one hand and reproductive instinct
and motherhood on the other.   Thus the double sexual role of
woman expresses itself in the beginning, when we can see the
psychologic manifestations of both aspects at the same time.
Only later and gradually, perhaps not until the actual sexual
experience has taken place, do the two tasks become closely
interwoven; they either support and strengthen each other or
come into conflict.   Later we shall see how sexuality and
motherhood are often in absolute emotional contradiction, and
how they nevertheless merge in the deeper and unconscious life
of the soul.

CHAPTER FOUR

Menstruation

THE most important event of puberty is menstruation. A biologic sign of sexual maturity, the first genital bleeding mobilizes psychic reactions so numerous and varied that we are justified in speaking of the "psychology of menstruation" as a specific problem. The intermingling of biologic hormonal events and psychologic reactions, the cyclic course of the somatic process, and the periodic return of menstruation, make it one of the most interesting of psychosomatic problems. The extent to which the two spheres of life—the organic and the psychic—influence each other, is a matter for experimental investigations.[1]

What interests us here is menstruation as a psychologic experience. Even before it begins, young girls have definite expectations about it and typical emotional relations to it, with individual variations. Although we can speak of a "period of expectation," it is not easy to give an exact definition of this period, which may be conceived in two different ways—either as the period of maturation immediately preceding the first menstruation, or as the whole long period of the girl's unconscious preparation for femininity. During the longer period, menstruation, even when the girl does not know about it intellectually, acquires a psychologic existence that is of the greatest importance in determining her reaction to the later real and personal experience.

One of the essential elements of this period of expectation is that the girl's childhood impressions of her mother's "secrets" connected with menstruation come into play. An obscure awareness of her mother's monthly indisposition manifests

[1] BENEDEK, T., and RUBENSTEIN, B. B.: The sexual cycle in women. Psychosom. Med. Monog., vol. 3. Washington, D. C.: National Research Council, 1942.

itself at an early date in the girl's fantasy life, and it is not always possible to ascertain whether, when, and to what extent she became familiar with the real nature of this process. Her mother's menstrual discomforts, blood-stained garments, and casual remarks can all make a very strong impression on the girl's mind. The younger she is and the more incapable of assimilating these impressions, the more painful, bloody, cruel, and threatening are these manifestations of femininity in relation to her fantasy life.

Psychoanalytic observations were the first to reveal the relation between the psychologic reactions to the first menstruation and the female castration complex.[2] But the connection between menstruation and the reproductive function is also manifested in the contents of fantasy life as revealed by psychoanalysis, to such an extent that we might almost speak of an unconscious knowledge of the biologic significance of menstruation.[3] The discoveries of M. Klein[4] and other authors of the English school demonstrated that the psychic reaction to the idea of a bleeding part of the body is not confined to the genital organ, and that the young girl's interest in her anatomy is transferred from the genital to the internal organs. In the anxieties provoked by the sight or imagined presence of blood, the idea of being torn and dismembered internally plays an extremely important part.

All such ideas are deeply buried in the girl's unconscious Childhood events, educational factors during the latency period, and prepuberty experiences strongly influence them. They form the psychic content of the period of expectation, in the larger sense of that term. In a narrower sense we can give this name to the time when the girl awaits the approaching event in

---

[2] We replace the term "female castration complex" by "genital trauma," which more exactly expresses our own view of the process referred to. In chapter vi the exact significance of this term will be discussed in detail.

[3] DEUTSCH, H.: Psychoanalyse der weiblichen Sexualfunktionen. Vienna: Internat. Psychoanal. Verlag, 1925.

[4] KLEIN, M.: Introduction to child analysis. London: 1932.

full awareness of its nature, or, if the milieu is unfavorable, in half-awareness. But in my opinion complete "surprise," to which many authors refer, can be the result only of repressions on the part of the girl or unusual neglect on the part of the persons around her. In the latter case the girl's elders must not only have omitted to inform her but must also have made it impossible for her to get information from others. Such a situation can arise only under exceptionally unfavorable circumstances. The daughter of an inhibited mother who because of her own difficulties does her utmost to prevent her child from gaining any insight into sexual processes, usually has abundant opportunities of getting information elsewhere. Only if the girl is excessively shy and reserved in her contacts with friends of the same age can she remain unenlightened for long.

But even under the most unfavorable circumstances it is extremely rare that a girl's lack of knowledge is due to any other factor than her own unwillingness to know. Such "ignorance" usually results from an earlier strong curiosity that has been repressed. Psychologic investigation in most instances reveals that it is precisely the "surprised" girl who once had the wildest and most exotic ideas about the expected physiologic phenomenon. Out of fear and a sense of guilt, these irrational ideas are repressed and forgotten, and any rational ideas on the same subject seem to meet the same fate.

Unfortunately the irrational ideas, cut off from intellectual influences, later produce much stronger effects than the rational ones. The sources of these irrational notions lie mostly in early childhood. Either they remain entirely unconscious or they assert themselves in the form of distorted ideas about menstruation. But they may also be the product of later fantasy life, misunderstanding, false interpretation of real impressions, misinformation, etc.

Let us assume that the young girl in the premenstrual period has a normal, uninhibited attitude, that is to say, she is ready to receive rational information. Educators are inclined to believe that the most appropriate source of information is the

girl's own mother.   Yet we must take the mother's psychology
into account.   Menstruation is very often the one thing that
the mother conceals from her children with particular discretion; it is a secret, and the idea of revealing it meets with
great psychologic resistance on her part.   Many mothers find
it much easier to talk with their daughters about conception,
pregnancy, and birth than about menstruation.   One often
encounters profound obstacles in the mother even before finding
them in the daughter.   The writings of Daly[5] and Chadwick[6]
throw light on the motives for this concealment of menstruation
by the mother.   The anthropologic studies from which these
two authors have drawn their data show that in many countries
and cultures, both in the modern and in the ancient world,
among the most primitive as well the most civilized peoples,
menstruation was and still is connected with ideas of horror,
danger, shame, and sin.   Between the strict taboos of primitives and the many prejudices and fears of civilized peoples
there is a bond of strong and deep-rooted identity.   The superstitions of the semi-educated, the fears of the immature and the
neurotic, and the fantasies and dreams of most of us, all have a
fatal similarity to the rules and prohibitions of primitives
regarding menstruation.   This will surprise us less if we realize
that primitive taboos, like the fantasies of civilized people, are
reflections of processes in that part of the mind that seems im-
pervious to the influence of civilization.

The anthropologists have been chiefly concerned with the
reactions of the environment to the menstruating woman.
Chadwick says: "The taboos and superstitions which surrounded the menstruating woman were often increased in
severity respecting the girl after the first menstrual period.
She was, *equally* with the older woman, considered a grave
public danger."[7]

[5] DALY, C. D.: Der Menstruationskomplex.   Imago, vol. 14, 1928.
[6] CHADWICK, M.: The psychological problems in menstruation.   New York: Nerv.
      & Ment. Dis. Pub. Co., 1932.
[7] Ibid., p. 4.

According to anthropologic data, all events, beliefs, and restrictions connected with menstruating women express the general idea that women at this time are dangerous and dirty. Chadwick observes that the evil powers ascribed to menstruating women are identical with those ascribed to witches in folklore. She quotes a passage in Pliny's *Natural History:* "The menstruating women blighted crops, blasted gardens, killed seedlings, brought down fruit from trees, killed bees, caused mares to miscarry. If they touched wine, it turned to vinegar; milk became sour, etc."[8]

The widespread taboos against cohabitation with menstruating women, the Jewish custom of purificatory baths, the horror associated with the sight of a naked woman during her menstruation, the similarities between witch cults and ceremonials and the anxieties connected with menstruation, are all very significant.

If it is true that prejudices against menstruating women are found everywhere in people's unconscious minds and that menstruating women and witches are endowed with the same attributes—hatred, threat of death, magic powers, cannibalism, and poisoning potencies—then the mother's motive in concealing her menstruation becomes clearer. Undoubtedly she fears her daughter's probable reaction to it.

Many authors stress the importance of enlightening girls about menstruation. Havelock Ellis[9] vigorously advocates this step and points to the bad effects of ignorance as observed by numerous physicians:

A large number of girls are not prepared by their mothers or teachers for the first onset of the menstrual flow, sometimes with disastrous results, both to their bodily and mental health.

In a study of one hundred and twenty-five American high-school girls, Dr. Helen Kennedy ("Effects of Highschool Work upon Girls during Adolescence," Pedagogical Seminary, June, 1896) refers to the "modesty" which

---

[8] Ibid.

[9] ELLIS, H.: Studies in the psychology of sex. New York: Random House, 1928, vol. 2, pt. 3, p. 64.

makes it impossible even for mothers and daughters to speak to each other concerning menstrual functions. "Thirty-six girls in this high school passed into womanhood with no knowledge whatever, from a proper source, of all that makes them women. Thirty-nine were probably not much wiser, for they stated that they had received some instruction, but had not talked freely on the matter. From the fact that the curious girl did not talk freely of what naturally interested her, it is possible that she was put off with a few words as to personal care, and a reprimand for her curiosity. Less than half of the girls felt free to talk with their mothers of this important matter."

Edmond de Goncourt, in *Chérie*,[10] describes the terror of his young heroine at the appearance of the first menstrual period, for which she had never been prepared. He adds: "It is very seldom, indeed, that women speak of this eventuality. Mothers fear to warn their daughters, elder sisters dislike confidences with their younger sisters, governesses are generally mute with girls who have no mother or sister."

This demand for enlightenment is to a great extent justified. Those responsible for the upbringing of young girls commit a serious sin of omission if they fail to explain the facts to them. Psychoanalytic experience, however, shows that violent reactions to the appearance of the first menstruation have very little to do with intellectual ignorance. The latter, as has been said, is the result of a repression in the overwhelming majority of cases: the girl had more or less conscious strong motives for cutting herself off from knowledge or for repressing it after she had gained it. The emotional motives responsible for the rejection of conscious knowledge manifest themselves in other forms also.

Observation shows that horror at being surprised, accusations against the mother, nervousness, and symptom formation are independent of intellectual knowledge. The girl's accusation that her mother failed to enlighten her about menstruation— already instanced as encountered in prepuberty as well as in later stages—may stem from different sources. It is often a reproach referring to all sorts of other situations in which her

[10] Op. cit., p. 65.

mother had secrets, a reproach transferred from something else to menstruation.   Even more frequently, the girl has reacted with a strong sense of guilt to her own curiosity and knowledge of hidden things, until she has succeeded in negating them, and her reproachful "Why didn't you tell me about this?" makes the mother indirectly responsible for this guilty knowledge, now repressed.

Naturally not all girls react in the same way to this new manifestation of their femininity.   A young girl who awaits her menstruation in an environment of sisters or friends already mature seldom feels "surprised."   For her, the onset of this process is a welcome sign of long-desired progress and she takes it for granted.   Another girl, given the same conditions of enlightenment and conscious expectation, may react with excitement, anxieties, and depressions that can be very intense and result in more complicated neurotic manifestations.   Havelock Ellis describes one attempt at suicide as follows:

> A few years ago the case was reported in the French newspapers of a young girl of 15, who threw herself into the Seine at Saint-Ouen.   She was rescued, and on being brought before the police commissioner said that she had been attacked by an "unknown disease" which had driven her to despair.   Discreet inquiry revealed that the mysterious malady was one common to all women and the girl was restored to her insufficiently punished parents.[11]

Reports exist of a number of cases of girls who attempted suicide during menstruation because they were tormented by terrible fear of a painful disease, in spite of the fact that they were enlightened.   The motives for such a reaction will be discussed later.

In spite of the diversity of these manifestations, investigation reveals elements common to all of them—anxiety, defense against the physiologic event, definite forms of accepting or negating it, self-accusations or charges against others, and various fantasy formations that, however, stem from common roots.   The chief expression is anxiety, in which the approach-

[11] Ibid.

ing adulthood and sexuality are experienced as a threatening danger. The forms in which this anxiety manifests itself exert a great influence on the processes of puberty.

During prepuberty menstruation is for many girls one of the important subjects of "secrets." The little friends observe the older girls with curiosity and envy, they respect, admire, and pity them, and wonder in a strong spirit of competition whose turn will come next. This conscious and whipped-up expectation typically ends in great disappointment. The young girl hopes that with the onset of menstruation her role with regard to her environment will change, that she herself will experience something new and momentous. Above all, she hopes to be recognized as a grownup and to acquire new rights. "Grown-up-ness" for her means freedom from her own inability to achieve anything and, above all, from the restrictions and renunciations that she has to suffer as a child and that are imposed upon her by the grownups, especially her mother. These restrictions are chiefly directed against the aggressions and sexual activities of childhood. We know that the former are intensified during prepuberty and that during puberty sexuality also manifests itself in increased tension, although it has not as yet a definite aim. However, menstruation, that important sign of maturity, does not bring about any advantageous change. On the contrary, the girl's aggressiveness comes into even stronger conflict with her sense of guilt, and the increased wave of sexuality only leads to a more intensive struggle against masturbation. Young girls who have reacted to the first menstruation with depressions often openly admit that they were previously informed about the facts and yet experienced a painful feeling of being surprised. The surprising element was the sense of disappointment that may be expressed thus: "Here is the longed-for, tremendous event, yet nothing has changed around me or inside me."

Very often mothers accused of not having enlightened their daughters tell us that what prevented them from speaking was not their own shyness but the girl's unwillingness to be enlightened by them. We recall that Evelyn's mother (p. 38) was a shy and inhibited woman who was incapable of discussing sexual matters with her daughters; for reasons rooted in her own psychology she left the job of enlightening Evelyn to the latter's older sister. But many more emancipated and modern mothers have observed that their young daughters prefer by far to be instructed by their friends and sisters. The cause of this attitude seems clear to us. During the girl's early childhood her mother's menstruation was associated with cruelty, uncleanness, bad odors, and reactions of disgust. All these emotions are mobilized again when the mother broaches the subject of menstruation and they create in the daughter a feeling of repulsion toward the mother.

All observations suggest that, whether or not the girl is given intellectual knowledge, even when she has the best possible information about the biologic aspects of the process, and despite its wish-fulfilling character, the first menstruation is usually experienced as a trauma. Naturally much depends upon the age of the girl, her level of psychologic development, her milieu, etc. According to some educators, early onset of menstruation, that is, at an age when the young girl is still very much dependent on her family for the care of her body, is felt as a new burden, another irksome duty imposed by the grown-ups, like taking her baths, changing her underwear, seeing to it that her bowel movements are regular, etc. The child protests strongly against these new requirements, sticks her dirty underclothes into bureau drawers or hides them in various corners of the house, and refuses to bother with the necessary protective measures. She also feels restricted in her normal activities, such as sports—gymnastics, swimming, etc. The fact that menstruation is a mark of approaching adulthood has no effect upon her and the knowledge that she is ahead of other girls is small compensation for her discomforts.

It is my impression that every phase of puberty has its own typical reaction to menstruation. If its first occurrence comes at a time when the girl has not yet psychologically advanced beyond the stage of prepuberty, genital bleeding is treated as though it were a new eliminatory function. The young girl is extraordinarily ashamed of this phenomenon, tries to conceal it, and each time she is detected feels as though she had been caught doing something unclean. This view of menstruation as unclean is a direct descendant of the cloaca theory, according to which everything coming from the lower apertures of the body is dirty and distasteful. The idea of dirtiness can in fantasy be extended to the entire body and the girl feels "unclean" and depreciated as a whole. Her relation to herself now corresponds to her old relation to her menstruating mother, mentioned above, and to those taboos and superstitions in which a girl who is menstruating for the first time is treated as unclean in the highest degree.

This attitude relating the first menstruation with excretory functions is particularly strong in girls who have suffered from enuresis or enteritis. If they are surprised at night by the wetness of the blood, they are sure their old troubles have returned; if they notice stains on their underwear during the day, they try to combat the evil by dietary measures, etc.

It is a well known fact that many young girls, during several years of childhood and sometimes even beyond puberty, suffer from involuntary discharge of small quantities of urine when going up or down stairs, climbing hills, making sudden motions, and particularly during laughing fits. This widespread and well known symptom of "weak bladder" can to some degree be explained by purely physiologic factors: many authorities believe that the organic sphincter control of the bladder is weaker in females than in males. Psychologically, this incontinence can have very unpleasant effects upon girls. They feel restricted in their freedom of movement and often renounce social pleasures lest they stain their dresses or chairs during a fit of gaiety. Sometimes one hears young girls complain that they have lost the habit of "real laughter" out of fear of wetting themselves.

Whether this bladder difficulty is psychologically determined is difficult to decide; at any rate, it has far reaching psychologic repercussions. The girl denies herself every joy of life, every pleasurable emotion, justifying her renunciation by her fear of being embarrassed as a result of incontinence. In other words, she thinks that any gratification will be paid for with a disgraceful penalty. The old infantile theory that the boy has a kind of spigot that can be shut off, while the girl has only an opening that is difficult to control, can be reactivated and bring about a new devaluation of the entire female organism. Under these circumstances, the first menstruation may likewise easily be experienced as an uncontrollable discharge of body fluid. In later life, when such a girl is a grown-up woman, she will have a tendency to avoid social contacts during her periods and will justify this attitude by experiencing pain and a feeling of weakness. She often feels that she has an enormously copious flow, tries to protect herself by using several pads, does not have the courage to leave home, and uses menstruation as a restrictive factor of great importance in her whole life. Thus at every menstrual period she repeats the difficulties that she once experienced because of her sphincter weakness.

Many women have the habit of spending a few days in bed during their periods, although they have no complaints that could serve as a pretext for doing so. It is true that usually such women belong to social classes in which feminine idleness is taken for granted. But in most cases this is not a simple manifestation of fastidousness, nor an effort to "forestall aging," although in many women the latter is the conscious motive for their voluntary isolation. The real motive is the desire of these women to flee from the reactions of their environment (taboos) and from their own intensified aggressions and sexual dangers, their intensified readiness to enter into conflicts with others, etc. This general motive is usually accompanied by more specific and personal ones. During their first menstruations, these women were treated with particular tenderness and forbearance by their families, usually their mothers. The "poor child" was surrounded with the greatest solicitude, and the attitude of her family made her feel that she was entitled to have the ruthlessness of nature compensated by particular consideration. There are women who admit that the days of their menses are the most peaceful and happiest for them. They achieve complete serenity and relaxation, allow themselves to be lovingly cared for, and free themselves from their usual obligations, including those toward their own children; often in the subdued light of her warm room this mature woman feels like a baby in its mother's lap or in the cradle. For such women, in contrast to most others, these days are days of particularly good understanding with their mothers. The childhood experience of having received more tender care from their mothers during illness, or having had the right to make greater demands upon them during those days, is repeated by these adult women, and now during the "monthly illness" their relation to their mothers is affectionate.

Other women, while they demand considerate treatment from those around them, display an angry aggressive mood particularly toward their mothers and substitute persons. These women, like those discussed above, were as a rule psychologically immature when they began to menstruate; they were either attached to their mothers in an infantile fashion or began to menstruate prematurely. In later life, by a kind of inner compulsion, they repeat this behavior during each subsequent menstrual period.

Girls who have a disposition to obsessional neurosis usually regard menstruation as something "filthy," but in this case not because they are immature. In the obsessional neurotics we have something deeper that manifests itself throughout life. They are extremely clean in other respects, too, but during menstruation they pay particular attention to their bodies, especially their genitals, and are obsessionally preoccupied with cleanness of these organs and thoroughly and pedantically wash out every vestige of blood.

The idea that menstruation is something filthy often leads to excessive modesty. It has been observed during criminal trials that a woman will more easily acknowledge that she has committed an aggressive crime involving bloodshed than that a given blood stain is from her own menstruation. It has often happened that women whose blood-stained underwear is adduced as an evidence of their guilt have hesitated to use menstruation as an alibi.

Faithful River, a novel by the great Polish writer Zeromski, depicts the episode of a Russian attack on a country house during a Polish insurrection. A wounded Polish rebel is hidden by the young daughter of the family. The Russian soldiers find blood stains on the bed used by the wounded man. Questioned by the Russians, the girl, who is in love with the rebel, calmly replies: "That is my blood."

The novelist, who has a deep knowledge of the feminine soul, adds: "After she had said these heroic words and made this unprecedented sacrifice for her lover, she was consumed by shame. She had the feeling that she was drowning in blood and that she would choke with mortification."

It is also known that even professional prostitutes find nothing so humiliating and mortifying as the baring of menstruation before men.

Often the young girl develops an attitude of absolute negation toward her first menstruation. She simply refuses to concern herself with it, does not change her manner of living, and denies the existence of her monthly indisposition. Many preserve this attitude later too, and even say defiantly that they will not be bothered by menstruation. Often this negation goes so far that these girls are particularly enterprising and active in sports, dancing, swimming, etc., during their menses. This kind of reaction is characteristic of the boyish or tomboyish girl, who thus tries to express her defiant feeling— "It is true that I am not a boy, but I don't see what difference it makes." If this tendency grows stronger, the girl turns away from her femininity more and more, constantly behaves in a boyish fashion, and if at the time of her first menstruation she is still in the phase of bisexual irresolution, the first flow nca paradoxically exert a negative influence on her final decision to be a woman.

Girls who have achieved a certain degree of psychologic maturity display a completely different attitude toward their first menses.

In order fully to understand this complicated reaction to a normal biologic process, one must constantly keep before one's eyes the total picture of puberty. In the preceding chapter we spoke of the emotional life of the young, as well as of the intensified vulnerability that is characteristic of it. We tried to explain adolescent narcissism on the basis of the entire course of development of the individual, and we learned that the more intensified demands of the sexual drives, the conflict between the desire for gratification and the resistance to it, are important elements in the picture as a whole.

We are justified in expecting that during this period of life every experience—particularly experiences that seem important—should easily excite the whole personality, and that the reactions to it should stem from various parts of the psychologic whole. The young girl's narcissistic ego may welcome menstruation as a satisfying step along the road to adulthood. But deep-lying regressive forces influence, disturb, and often even paralyze this progressive attitude. During the first menses the sexual forces to a greater or lesser extent take possession of the psychic scene and find powerful allies in unconscious elements that now re-emerge from repression. Thus we are confronted here too, as in all other functions of puberty, with a conflict between progressive and regressive forces. In this conflict, the biologic significance of menstruation is on the progressive side, the emotional reactions on the regressive.

Let us once again recall how intently the young, with their heightened self-love, listen to outside voices that confirm their own valuations of themselves, how intently they observe their own subjective experiences, and how they try to utilize these to develop self-confidence. They admire their own intellectual capacities, try to strengthen them, emphasize their superiority by an "objective attitude," and forge weapons for defending themselves against their own anxieties.

But is it not only the psychic life that in this phase of development receives intensified self-observation and self-love. The young girl takes her own body as the object of her self-love much more often than the boy. Sometimes the pubescent girl changes the forms of her self-love: first she delights in admiration given by those around her to her femininity, and in this the competitive drive to be prettier than other girls (usually certain other girls) is of the greatest importance for her. Often, after a phase marked by vanity, interest in clothes, parties, and flirtations, the girl turns away completely from this kind of pleasure, becomes interested in "higher things," and develops her ambition in new directions. The "flight from femininity" is not always the motive force here; it is often a certain blasé feeling, a surfeit of this type of success, that leads her to seek new gratifications. The hunger for new possibilities of narcissistic gratification induces the girl to rise above the emptiness of her previous existence and turn to better things. It is often striking that in the course of this metamorphosis she suddenly begins to neglect herself physically, loses her previous charm, and shows her disregard of externals in her clothing, behavior, etc.

This abrupt change in the girl's relation to herself, the displacement of her interest from physical to spiritual matters, can also take place in an inverse sequence: suddenly, after a period of intense spiritualization, the girl devotes more attention to the bodily processes, but only from the point of view of "beauty" and outward appearance. The secondary sex characteristics (breasts, hair) attract her attention first and she either accepts or rejects them. Efforts to flatten out the chest and cutting or plucking out of pelvic hair are common manifestations of a negative attitude. In this narcissistic puberty phase, when love for her own body increases in the girl, we can observe a particularly anxious concern for its welfare.

Narcissistic vulnerability in relation to the body as a whole is expressed principally in the rejection of anything that might destroy its integrity. This attitude, acquired in early childhood, becomes a permanent part of the unconscious and is preserved for many years. Throughout their lives individuals of both sexes react to wounds on their own bodies in a manner that betrays the influence of the infantile "castration complex."

Because of the sexual stimuli and especially because of the menstrual bleeding, the genitals become the center of uneasy attention and feelings of injury. They are conceived as a part of the entire body that regains a special importance during menstruation because it is the site of increased tension. The reactions to these feelings are varied; injuries and other morbid processes in the body may later mobilize the same reactions in the unconscious as menstruation. Peculiarities in the behavior of many women when they suffer minor wounds, nosebleeds, etc., illustrate this point.

The most primitive of these reactions expresses the desire to "heal" the part of the body that is now felt to have experienced a "wound"—in this case the genitals—by reconstituting the well integrated intact whole, which is felt to be damaged during menstruation. This elementary fantasy centered around the reconstruction of the body also has a more complicated motive. In our opinion, this is the repetition of a definite phase of childhood during which the girl wanted to have an active organ like the boy's. However, it would be false to assume that we have here merely a repetition compulsion and a revival of traces of old memories. This wish of the girl arises in puberty for the same reasons that it arose in childhood—under the pressure of active sexual drives and masturbatory impulses. That is why the reactions to the first menstruation are so largely dependent upon what has taken place with regard to masturbation. Most observers agree that with the onset of the first menstruation there is an intensification of sexual excitability. It is of the greatest importance whether the girl, at the onset of menstruation, masturbates or has already given up masturbation under the pressure of guilt feelings or is still struggling to wean herself away from masturbation. Menstruation either leads the girl to abandon masturbation, or conversely, the biologically determined tension accompanying this process incites her to masturbate. Anxiety and guilt feelings in the latter case endow the bleedings with associations of cruelty, suffering, and punishment, and mobilize the old childhood reactions connected with the genital problem, anatomic differences, etc.

Later, the monthly bleedings often cause a repetition of this behavior for many years: masturbatory practices, often of a compulsive character, are given up with the onset of the flow (sometimes shortly before), only to be taken up again as soon as it ceases; or the reverse may be the case, these practices being carried on only during the menses, even where there is a completely satisfactory sex life.

Abnormal reactions to the first menses are extremely varied. Intensified excitability, feelings of discomfort, greater susceptibility to fatigue, and depressions are frequent manifestations of puberty as a whole; usually they increase during menstruation.

The tendency to develop anxiety states, which is intensified during the entire period preceding adulthood, is particularly strong at the time of the first menses. Girls previously relatively free from anxiety now suddenly display this state and to a varying extent display it again every month. This anxiety manifests itself in general tension or irritability.

If the young girl has a neurotic disposition that has not yet broken through, and if the whole course of her prepuberty has been under the sign of unresolved inner conflicts, her first menstruation may cause the outbreak of a neurosis or morbid activities, as in the case of Evelyn (p. 37). Often the anxiety assumes a phobic character; the girl's interest in her own body may develop into hypochondriasis, and the guilty feelings may lead to paranoid reactions.

However, the entire process of maturation is marked by

heightened inner tension and the whole personality of the young individual is engrossed in the struggle for liberation and adjustment to reality on the one hand, and the effort to master the sexual drives on the other. It is clear that menstruation is also involved in this struggle. It intensifies the already existing problems and creates others, and its accompanying psychologic manifestations correspond to the existing stimuli from within and without.

There are also more direct reactions to the physiologic experience; these are connected with its acceptance or rejection. They may manifest themselves even during the "period of expectation" and in this case are mostly defensive, simple functional inhibitions. They lead to a kind of retention of menstruation, which, despite all the symptoms of physical and psychologic maturity, begins extraordinarily late. Or, just as frequently, menstruation begins and then is interrupted for years. As a rule, it is very difficult to influence this functional disturbance by organic treatment, but psychologic treatment sometimes removes it with surprising rapidity. Such therapeutic success does not result in every instance, nor is the treatment always successful in the same degree; yet our experience in this field gives strong proof of the psychogenic nature of these disturbances. The stoppage of menstruation after a single appearance is usually found upon examination to be a "shock reaction" provoked by the horror with which the first bleeding was received. The organic process by which this violent physical reaction is brought about is still to be discovered. Analytic experience suggests that psychogenic amenorrhea appearing in later life often has a very complicated psychologic structure stemming from many sources. The same is probably true of the events of puberty. The inhibiting shock reaction is also the expression of a process that has many roots.

Menstrual pains constitute another complication of the normal course of development. This manifestation, too, has many causes, of which some are general and some individual.

Most authors who have studied the psychologic processes accompanying such pains connect them with birth fantasies. It is true that this determinant is present most of the time, but even with the application of psychoanalytic technic it is hard to ascertain whether the pains originate in the fantasies, or vice versa. A certain naïve motivation of the pains seems to me very typical of the first menstruation. The still very young girl is embarrassed by this physiologic process and finds it most convenient to regard it as a mere "illness." Thus she escapes from the sexual significance of the process and at the same time negates its disturbing content relating to the future. For the child, pain is always the symptom of illness, for which she is not responsible, which entitles her to loving care, and which surely passes away. Now too her mother assures her that "everything will soon be fine again." Pain is a sort of diversion maneuver in the conflict, and the bodily processes give sufficient opportunities for using this way out.

Yet the experience of the first menstruation as a "disease" can take a much more pathologic course. Thus in the case described by Havelock Ellis (p. 155), the young girl wanted to commit suicide because she had an "unknown disease." Can one really believe that a disease, just because it is unknown, would induce someone to commit suicide if it did not have a deeper psychologic significance? The impulsive attempt at suicide could only have been the product of an old and tormenting psychologic conflict, the solution of which was made more difficult by the onset of menstruation. In this girl's eyes, menstruation was perhaps the obvious fulfillment of a subconscious threat and thus increased her anxiety to such an extent that she could no longer overcome it. Some measure of depressive mood during menstruation is extraordinarily frequent, and an attempt at suicide could easily have resulted from a deeper depression.

This girl perhaps belonged to that group of women who harbor strong sadistic impulses and can control them only so long as no *agent provocateur* makes continued control impossible.

That aggressive drives intensify during menstruation is a generally known fact; the laws of many countries treat it as an extenuating circumstance in crime. And it has often been shown that intensified aggression can turn against one's own self and lead to suicide. It was perhaps the blood itself that had an irritating and provoking character; or perhaps, even during her period of expectation, the girl had imagined intensely that something "terrible" would happen to her body when she grew up. For all girls the future contains many mysterious and terrifying elements with regard to their bodies, and their expectation ideas often arouse anxiety.

We have pointed out that menstruation is experienced as an illness even in simpler cases. Thus, the girl's attitude toward menstruation is a kind of rationalization that strips the process of its mystery and profound meaning.

Another extremely interesting attempt to solve the menstruation conflict is of an anatomic character. The bleeding in this case is not eliminated as in amenorrhea, but the psychologic influence on the physiologic process is such that the bleeding takes place in another part of the body. I have seen several cases of so-called vicarious menstruation in which bleeding took place every month or at irregular intervals, but never affected the genitals. Often it is transferred to a part of the body removed as far as possible from the genitals (nose, chin, etc.), and the choice of the substitute organ is usually psychologically determined. One of the strangest examples I know is that of a patient whose psychoanalytic treatment started when she was 22 years old and who had suffered from amenorrhea for seven years. At the age of 15 she had one normal menstruation; later she suffered from irregular bleedings under the skin of one ear lobe, to which she always reacted with the most violent hypochondriac anxieties. Each time she imagined that she had cancer and would inevitably die as a result of the bleeding ulcer under her ear lobe. Her case was diagnosed as one of vicarious menstruation; all attempts of gynecologists to restore the normal menstrual cycle failed. Later, the bleedings under the ear lobe ceased, but she failed to menstruate for many years.

In the course of her psychoanalytic treatment, the patient developed fantasies in which the vagina was avoided as an organ and everything connected with femininity was centered in her back. She complained of pains in her back at almost periodic intervals, and their psychologic origin was evident from the analysis. One day the patient was informed by a telegram that her sister had given birth to a child. The following day she complained of terrible pains in her back and told me that she could feel a lump there. I sent her to a gynecologist, who found that an operation was indicated. Later he told me that he had discovered something he had never seen before in all his practice: biopsy revealed a large number of blood-filled cysts in the tissues around the vertebrae, and the consistency of the blood showed them to be of both old and new formation. There was no doubt that they were vicarious menstruations that, in conformity with the patient's fantasies, had avoided the genitals and were localized in her back. It is quite possible, however, that certain physiologic factors had intensified and influenced her fantasy life, as is always the case in the formation of a psychosomatic symptom.

In our patient, the psychologic components of the bleeding ear lobe symptom were easily ascertainable, but the organic process remains obscure and hypothetic. Even in her early childhood the patient had been a "diversionist via the ear," and in her struggle against masturbation she used the device of "plucking" her ear. It is true that the ear lobes are used for this purpose mostly by boys; girls favor the hair, fingernails, etc., but it is impossible to formulate any general rule on this point. It is noteworthy that during her puberty our patient resorted to the same organ as a substitute for her genitals that she had chosen during her childhood—the ear.

Little Andrea in the story quoted above (p. 32) also said that she would prefer "to bleed every day from her nose or the pulse artery in her wrist, so that it could be seen." In other words, she directly and consciously proposed to menstruate vicariously, in order to avoid the genitals.

Other forms of menstrual disorders will be discussed below.

As the young girl's personality develops, as her adjustment to reality progresses and her attitude to her entire body becomes transformed, her valuation of her genitals undergoes a change. Just as her whole personality is torn during puberty between narcissistic vanity and feelings of inferiority, just as she sometimes ardently admires and sometimes sharply criticizes her oft-contemplated image in the mirror, so her attitude toward her genitals during this period is full of contradictions. Let us recall the girl's double valuation of the genital organ—a "cloaca" and a "jewel." Now the girl begins to be concerned with preserving this "treasure" intact. This positive narcissistic attitude is her soundest and most reliable chastity belt. But exaggeration of this attitude and intensification of anxious worries about the genitals can be a symptom of neurotic disturbance. The more narcissistic the girl's relation to her body, the stronger will be the anxious reaction, which sometimes is transferred from the genitals to other parts of the body and expresses itself in typical puberty hypochondriasis.

One manifestation of such a narcissistic attitude is the girl's overestimation of herself as a sexual object, which leads her to believe that the man who will one day possess her sexually will receive an unusual and particularly desirable gift. Later she can barely grasp the fact that what she possessed and was able to give is not unique at all. Even a harmless approach on the part of a man may result in grave depressive reactions in such girls; they feel that they have been dragged down from their pedestal of inaccessiblity. Sometimes depersonalization states appear and the young girl maintains that she is no longer "herself"; she is alienated from herself, and her previous lofty opinion of herself is shaken. Adolescence, with its typical intensification of narcissism, creates particular proneness to such reactions.

In girls of morbid disposition, the onset of menstruation, or the first erotic experience connected with a strong genital excitation, may release psychotic symptoms. The physiologic changes are interpreted as "enchantment," as induced by "some strange machinery," etc. To save her own person from guilt and destruction, the patient transforms her whole body into someone else's. In one case I found that this transformation consisted in identification with a girl who had been sexually seduced and later deserted by the patient's own fiancé. The patient's own sexual excitation and the sexual approach of the fiancé shattered her narcissistic seclusion as well as her overestimation of her own person and her hitherto "unapproachable jewel," thus mobilizing the psychotic reaction.

This estimation of the genitals as a "jewel" is partly the result of education, partly of the young girl's narcissistic appraisal of her own femininity during adolescence, and above all, of the overcompensation of all the emotions connected with the old genital trauma.

I have always supported the theory that, while the anatomic difference has important consequences, the importance of these derives from physiologic processes, particularly from the subjectively felt sexual excitation. Thus we see that the little girl's interest in her genitals appears especially when masturbatory activity and somatic sensations steer her attention in this direction. Without this prerequisite, her interest in the anatomic difference does not involve very far reaching psychologic consequences.[12] During puberty, as a result of bodily growth and the rise of sexual excitation that is physiologically conditioned, this interest is reawakened and psychologic expressions of the genital trauma are again mobilized. Anger, shame, depression, feelings of inferiority and guilt, everything rooted in the girl's old genital conflict, now comes to the fore. Unless the genital trauma has been greatly intensi-

[12] Deutsch, H.: Op. cit.

fied by individual experiences, it is mastered by the feminine tendencies mobilized by the first menstruation. Emotional contents of a decidedly feminine character take the place of the penis wish and penis envy. Fears of defloration and rape, mobilized and strengthened by the onset of menstruation, accompany the young girl's sexual fantasies at this time. Menstruation becomes a decisive experience in this process of feminization.

The intensification of sexual excitation and the formation of numerous psychologic phenomena relating to it are still under the sign of an individual personal experience. Inner preparation for sexual pleasure that is the prize of maturity, obscure premonitions of a painful experience, fears of defloration and rape, attempts to escape, defensive processes, etc.—all these are preliminaries to the gratification of the sexual instinct. This goal is biologically determined and identical for both sexes; the intensity and strength of the urge is different in each. Only in the methods of achieving it do we find the full differentiation between man and woman.

When we investigate the psychologic phenomena accompanying the first menstruation, we discover that there is hardly a young girl who is not at this time confronted with the problem of the reproductive function in some form. For the first time in the girl's development, we are faced with the double function of the female as a sexual creature and as a servant of the species. In this double function woman tends much more strongly than man in the nonindividualistic direction, that is to say, her inclination is in favor of the species, in favor of the reproductive functions. From now on the problems of the girl who has become a woman are clearly defined: they are a conflict or a harmony of many contradictory elements. In addition to the questions of masculine versus feminine and active versus passive, there is now perhaps the most complicated question of them all—the alternative between individual being and servant of the species. No matter how great the girl's psychologic preparation for taking over the last-named role has been, there is no doubt that with her first menstruation her fantasy life turns strongly toward the reproductive function. During her menstruation, whether her reaction is that of wish fulfillment or anxiety, whether the biologic phenomenon appears as a promise or a disappointment, again and again the girl's unconscious shows psychologic contents resulting from biologic processes connected with propagation. It remains an open question whether the connection between the two is causal. Closer examination almost always reveals that these fantasies that emerge during menstruation date from an earlier period in which the causal connection did not yet exist.

The fantasies mobilized by the first menstruation express wishes and fears relating to pregnancy and childbirth; in part these are obscure unconscious forebodings, in part they derive from vague bits of information picked up from the secrets of the grownups; in other cases they relate to clear intellectual knowledge about the physiologic meaning of menstruation. Knowledge plays a greater role under conditions of modern education than under those of the old-fashioned training of young girls.

The connection between the physiologic fact and the psychologic reactions is surprisingly far reaching. In addition to the anxieties and hopes mobilized by the first menstruation, the girls' unconscious fantasies suggest that psychologically too the process is vested with what is actually its biologic meaning and what will later be realized consciously—disappointment in the expectation of a child.

The depressive moods that, as we have seen, so frequently accompany menstruation, usually contain this element of disappointment. We do not observe them before the onset of the first menstruation; sometimes they appear before the second, but as a rule premenstrual depressions set in only after several years. This can be explained by the fact that in the course of the menstrual cycle the premenstrual bodily sensations are repeated over and over again. This experience teaches women to be sensitive to the preliminary stages of the

organic processes.   Here the parallelism between the biologic
process and the psychologic reactions may express an inner
perception originating in experience.

Why many women suffer menstrual depressions before the
menstrual period, and others during it, is not clear.   Many
women who suffer from premenstrual depressions report that
with the onset of the flow they experience a joyful feeling of
liberation.   They forget from month to month that their
periodic depression is caused by the approach of the menses
and breathe relief when onset of menstruation supplies a
rational explanation of this depression.   Most of these women
have preserved the prepuberty expectation that something
terrible is about to happen to them and are pleasantly surprised every month when the event they have awaited with
such anxiety turns out to be only the ordinary physiologic
occurrence.

The consequences of the psychologic influences of early
childhood will come to the fore later too in all the reproductive
functions.   Developments in early years, identification with
feminine objects, especially the mother, environmental influences, etc., create in the young girl an inner disposition that
will manifest itself when a suitable provocation occurs.   The
first menstruation gives this inner disposition an occasion
to emerge into the light of day.   Thus, the psychic reactions
connected with the problem of the reproductive functions
always have an individual character.   But there is one thing
that is common in all women: with or without intellectual
preparation, knowing or only sensing, the young girl connects
menstruation with childbirth. The naïve and ignorant Andrea
(p. 32), when she notices the bleeding, says wistfully: "It is
ridiculous, but I cannot help thinking about what happens
when one has children."

Many young girls believe that during menstruation they
must avoid contact with men; with some this attitude originates
in their own perception of their intensified sexual excitability;
in others it is an old traditional prejudice that has been passed

on by the mother (or another woman); in many others it expresses the unconscious fear of pregnancy that is psychologically closely connected with menstruation. The observer comes to realize that the young girl suffering from grave anxiety states and pregnancy symptoms is only expressing her alarm at her own sexual excitation that she cannot understand. The fear of having been made pregnant by use of the bathroom, by sitting on a warm chair, by a kiss or an ardent embrace, etc., is much more frequent than the uninitiated would suspect and, paradoxically, is not always influenced by sexual enlightenment or experience. The degree of consciousness or unconsciousness of these fears depends upon the girl's intellectual knowledge. A girl who is sexually enlightened has pregnancy symptoms without explaining them on the basis of a kiss, but in her unconscious the excitation felt during a kiss can become the theme of a pregnancy fantasy, while an unenlightened girl naïvely believes that the kiss has caused her to be pregnant. An interesting example of the fear of pregnancy and of typical reactions to the first menstruation was given me by a 14-year-old girl whom I had an opportunity to observe during her stay in the hospital. Most of the material quoted below is taken from her hospital records.

CASE HISTORY OF MOLLY

The 14-year old patient was brought to the clinic by her mother. She complains of various fears, especially the fear of fainting and the fear of dying. She avoids going into the street, as she is afraid she will faint there and does not wish to be seen lying down. Her fear also becomes more intense in a closed room and she has to reassure herself constantly that she will be able to leave such a room; she cannot sit or stand still in the house, has to open the windows, go to the ice box, or wander around eating an apple or drinking a glass of milk. Her fear of dying is especially great at night; she keeps herself awake for fear of dying in her sleep. She is afraid of contracting a heart disease, like one of her girl friends who has a rheumatic heart. At times everything is unreal and she feels far away from everybody. At other times, everything seems strangely close to her—she can see herself somewhere in the Pacific, fighting with the troops, etc. In large groups she feels isolated and unreal. She had to stop going to school, to the movies, or on buses.

The girl is the fourth of five siblings. Her father is described as extremely strict and narrow-minded. He criticizes the appearance and behavior of his children at every meal. The mother is a worried, unhappy person who resents the fact that she had to have four babies in four years. Ever so often the parents are not on speaking terms for weeks, especially after attempts of the mother to defend the patient. Several times the mother has left the house for three or four days, threatening never to come back.

The patient's older sister married an actor against the mother's will; two brothers, also older than the patient, had difficulties of adjustment in adolescence and one of them ran away from home.

The patient was a gifted youngster. At the age of 13 she was a good tap dancer but gave up performing on account of stage fright. Although she made friends, she was fundamentally shy. She has written a good deal of poetry. In adolescence she became very close to a girl friend two years older than herself who had to stay at home most of the time on account of heart disease. She took the troubles of the family very seriously and often felt that she ought to take the mother's burdens on her shoulders. She has always believed that her father has not liked her as much as her younger sister, except at a time when she broke her arm; he shows some feeling for her now since she has "the nerves." The quarrels between her parents weigh heavily upon her, but she has a feeling that through her illness they have been reunited. Whereas all her siblings have decided that in case of a parental divorce they will stay with either the father or the mother, the patient is the only one who wants to stay only with both of them. She likes to think about boys, but shrinks from going out with them, for she cannot defend herself except by blushing, and one girl in her school became pregnant. She took the greatest interest in her older sister's pregnancy and delivery and recalls that her present fear of death actually began when she heard after the birth that women often die in childbirth.

Her present illness first manifested itself after two of her classmates fainted in school when the teacher told the class that during the first world war corpses were found in garbage cans. Although she herself did not faint, the patient felt the faints, and her fantasies centered around the experience of losing consciousness, which was described by one of the girls affected as most dreadful, and by the other as "wonderful." Closer study revealed that the patient had had fears of fainting and dying for quite a while. One episode that excited such symptoms occurred when her sister left home with the baby, when the baby was about 2 months old. During the preceding weeks the patient had taken entire care of the child and had expected to keep it. The morning of the departure, the patient's father drove the sister to the station. The mother, who was extremely upset by her older daughter's leaving and by a previous quarrel with her husband, threatened to run away and kill herself.

The patient and her brother prevented her from leaving the house. At first the mother resisted, then she fainted, and the children carried her to her bed. The patient's thoughts were very much concerned with separation, fainting, and death.

The mother reported that the patient had begun to menstruate several months previously. She acted rather embarrassed about it and told her mother, "That thing is here."

The mother did not know what she was referring to because, although she had prepared the patient for this event, the child had not developed physically in any way and the mother did not expect it so soon. The patient went with her sister to buy some menstrual pads. On meeting a man on the street, she hung her head. In general she acted "disgusted with herself." She has never had any pain during her periods, but the mother comments that it seems funny to her that the patient always attempts to hide the fact of her menses from her. Once she noticed a stain on the sheet and asked the patient if she was menstruating. When the child denied it, the mother wondered a little whether the 12-year old sister might have started to menstruate, but she soon realized that the patient had "fibbed" to her. At the onset of her menses Molly said: "Anything might happen to me now. I might have a baby."

The mother thinks that the older sister was too frank about her pregnancy. When Molly made the remark quoted above, the sister said to her: "Well, you have to live with a man for that."

The girl replied: "Well, I am living with two men—my father and your husband."

The patient knew all about the birth of her sister's baby. The sister was confined at a hospital; she was given twilight sleep, and forceps had to be used.

The mother occasionally makes references to the father's strictness. He will not allow the girls to go out after dark, because of the large number of soldiers in the town. There have been two instances of rape, or something of the sort, that have got the community all aroused.

The mother describes the girl's symptoms as a terrible anxiety about leaving home. Sometimes it is impossible to get her out of her bed, which seems to be her favored protection. Sometimes she goes out in the afternoon to play with her friends on the street, but she cannot bring herself to leave her own block; if faced with the prospect of leaving the immediate neighborhood, she has an attack of "shaking." She is fearful of cars and trains. One night when the family went to a crowded restaurant, the patient got up and hid in the ladies' room. She cannot sleep and lies awake listening to noises and imagining that somebody is trying to enter the house. She has fits of weeping that come upon her at any time; she daydreams and writes poetry and short stories. These are mostly spy and murder mysteries in which she herself, thinly disguised, is the heroine. She has eating spells, feeling that eating will keep her from fainting, and it is the fear of fainting that constantly haunts her. She nibbles her way through the day. The mother has the impression that the girl is very jealous of her younger sister. The mother herself is "ill"; she is afraid to go out alone and to ride in cars and she once jokingly said to the patient: "Well, let's go and die together."

The mother gives no information about the fights between her husband and herself nor about any plans for a separation or divorce.

We do not intend here to explain in detail the morbid symptoms of this girl. Her attitude toward menstruation was so typical that it can be considered normal, although subsequently she was stricken by a severe neurosis. Her revulsion and embarrassment when she said, "That thing is here," her "disgust with herself," her tendency to conceal her menstruation from her mother every month and even to deny having it, as though it were something bad and forbidden, her preference for her sister's rather than her mother's help—all these manifestations are quite familiar to us. Nancy (p. 63), for instance, acted in exactly the same way before she was influenced by her psychotherapeutic treatment. Molly's remark at the beginning of her first menstruation—"Anything might happen to me now, I might have a baby"—represents an idea that fills the minds of many girls with expectation and fear. We have noted that her reply to her sister's statement, "You have to live with a man for that," was, "Well, I am living with two men, my father and your husband." This reply expresses a fantasy that remains deeply buried in the unconscious in most young girls and usually comes to the surface only as a result of psychoanalytic treatment. We know little about Molly's relations with her parents. The little that we have learned from her directly reminds us of Andrea, who wanted to unite her parents through her sickness and death. Molly brings Nancy to mind also; this girl's older sister also was pregnant and later gave birth to a child. We are aware that in puberty the tendency to identification is intensified. We see this tendency in Molly too: in her fainting spells she identifies herself with her schoolmates, in the nature of her symptoms with her mother, and in her pregnancy fantasies presumably with her older sister. Young girls whose fantasy life is full of pregnancy and birth ideas are particularly inclined to identify themselves with pregnant women, especially their mothers or sisters. If these fantasies are to a considerable extent accompanied by feelings of hatred and by aggressive impulses, they result in morbid symptoms and fears of death. The girl's life in such a case is, like Molly's, marked by actions of avoidance; every shadow of a sexual attempt is felt as a threat to which she reacts with anxieties or fainting fits. We are particularly interested in Molly's attitude toward death, because in young girls' fears we constantly discover a close connection between the idea of death and the ideas of pregnancy and childbirth.

Molly's father watched strictly over the chastity of his growing daughters, talked a great deal about the danger of rape, and warned them against going out alone. The problems of pregnancy and childbirth assumed real urgency for Molly, because of her sister. She had also heard that women may die in labor. All these impressions from the outside can mobilize the fantasies and anxieties that fill all young girl's minds. With the onset of menstruation, the associative connection between death and birth is particularly strengthened. It is true that outside events contribute to revive this connection; but actually it is more elemental, more primitive. It is innate in the feminine psyche to bring blood, conception, birth, and death into close connection with one another. Some authors, basing themselves on folklore and myths, believe that it is blood that constitutes the connecting link between death and birth.

For our understanding of subsequent psychologic phenomena in the life of woman as the servant of the species, it is important to note that the foundations for later experiences are laid in puberty and during the first menstruation. If the psychologic disposition existing in puberty is accompanied by external experiences, these latter can be of paramount importance for the future. For instance, knowing of the death of a woman, or even only of her having been in danger of death during childbirth, can produce an irreparable traumatic impression leading to grave disturbances in the girl's development toward motherhood. If the young girl has a strong tendency to identify herself with such a woman, all her ideas connected with the reproductive function, beginning with the sexual act, will be filled with the fear of death. Molly has given us an insight into such a fear of death in relation to pregnancy and childbirth. She used her neurosis to escape the threat of death by avoiding life.

Fainting fits during puberty express the girl's flight from dangers or her passive abandonment of herself to them. Epileptiform fits express her aggressive motor defense against the same dangers, as occurred in the case of Nancy.

Another 14-year-old girl was stricken with an acute psychosis on the second day of her first menses. This girl was brought to a psychiatric clinic in Vienna dancing and laughing. Her face was covered with rouge, her hair was dishevelled, she raised her skirt and used obscene language, constantly repeating the word *Politik*. When she became accessible to treatment it was found that this German word was for her a composite of two other German words—*Polizei* ("police") and *dick* ("fat"). These two words symbolized her puberty anxieties. *Polizei* was related to the prohibited and feared idea of prostitution, which in her native country is under police supervision; the second word connoted the danger of pregnancy—"getting fat." It is difficult to imagine a more graphic representation of the typical anxieties besetting a girl in puberty than this composite word. According to her mother, the patient had always shown a tendency to solitude and withdrawal. However, until the onset of menstruation she was for all practical purposes healthy and attended school regularly, so that it was possible to speak of an acute onset of a psychosis that later became chronic. Once again the first menstruation played the part of *agent provocateur*; it obviously overburdened the girl's whole psychologic structure and her limit of tolerance was overstepped.

Every modern physician knows to what extent the function of menstruation is subject to psychologic influences, not only in puberty but also in later life. The realization that psychologic factors can express themselves in various menstrual disturbances is becoming more and more widespread.

Many years ago, as a young medical student, I followed with great interest a court case concerning a marriage problem. A husband had asked for a divorce and as his only reason told the court the following story. By profession he was a traveling salesman who returned home only at irregular intervals. In the preceding two years, he said, every time he returned he had found his wife menstruating. In his eyes this was sufficient proof that she no longer wished to have marital relations with him, even though she assured him in all sincerity that it was only a coincidence, a kind of bad luck for which she was not responsible. The psychiatrists rejected the husband's theory, even though it was already well known that menstruation can exert a tremendous influence upon psychologic life. They were ready to admit that mood changes could accelerate or retard menstruation for a short period, but the enormous and recurrent influence described to them by the husband seemed to these experts impossible. The only person ready to accept the husband's interpretation was the old judge, who had a keen intuition and a broad knowledge of human nature. He granted the divorce, and subsequent events proved the husband's theory to be correct.

Since that time we have learned a great deal about the influence of the emotions on the bodily functions in general, and about the psychology of menstruation in particular. Menstruation is important not only because of its connection with puberty and the difficulties of that period, not only because it is the expression of sexual maturity and has a special relation to reproduction, not only because it is the center of the

demolition of the climacteric and the psychology of that phase
of development, but also because it is a bleeding, which mobilizes many aggressions, ideas of self-destruction, and anxieties.

Menstrual disorders represent the most important group
of genital disturbances in women, and the most common. The
typical, almost "normal" disturbances are amenorrhea, dys-
menorrhea, menstrual irregularities like the one instanced in
the court case described above, continuous bleeding, intermit-
tent and vicarious menstruation, etc.

We have briefly described a few of these disturbances, chiefly
in cases in which they arose in connection with the first menstruation. Our experience with them is very rich. There is
scarcely any neurosis, any emotional difficulty, that does not
provoke a more or less marked reaction of the genital apparatus,
and this is most strikingly and objectively apparent in the
monthly bleedings. However, it must not be forgotten that
menstruation is a biologic process, that possible organic or
hormonal disturbances must always be taken into account,
and that treatment of menstrual disturbances must always
be undertaken in collaboration with a gynecologist. Clinical
observations of various menstrual disturbances connected
with psychologic influences have been recorded in numerous
publications. They come not only from psychoanalysts and
psychiatrists, but also from investigators who usually attach
more importance to the organic aspects of the problem.

In our discussion of the psychology of female puberty we
have devoted particular attention to the first menstruation.
We deviated from chronology in our exposition of feminine
development in order to trace a complete picture of the psychology of the menstrual processes.

In the course of a woman's lifetime the subjective events
connected with the first menstruation have a tendency to
recur at every other menstruation, but normally in a very
weakened form. Gradually the woman accepts the physiologic process as such, and its psychologic significance recedes

into the background. As a result of this transformation, the memory of the first menstruation often grows dim and sometimes is subjected to so much repression that there may be an amnesia concerning the event. In such cases we are told by the subject that her menstruation has always been completely normal and that from the very beginning she interpreted it as what it really is, a biologic process. Analysis usually reveals that such declarations are false and refer not to the first menstruation, but to later ones. The manifestations accompanying the first experience may be the object of similar falsification, for instance with regard to the fact of knowledge or surprise, the manner in which the event was communicated to the mother or friends, etc. This point is illustrated by the behavior of a 26-year-old patient regarding a letter she received from a girl friend when she was 16 years old. The patient failed to mention a postscript in this letter until the analyst brought up the subject of what really happened during the first menstruation. This is what the friend wrote:

> You still haven't got it? ... You lucky girl! I am beginning to think that you are the only one of us who will not be subjected to it. A. says that if with all your strength you want it not to happen, it will not happen, but unfortunately this is rare.

In connection with this postscript, our patient gradually recalled that she was the last of her circle of friends to menstruate, and that she had been convinced, to her great satisfaction, that she never would. When her wish seemed to be fulfilled, she grew fearful, because she began to think that she would never be loved by a man and would never be able to have children. Later, at the age of 17, she at last began to menstruate; she was glad of it, but had the feeling that her flow was "too sparse and too pale," and that, as a matter of fact, she still was different from other women, just as she had been before. She preserved this feeling until her pregnancy. It is hard to decide whether she originally retarded menstruation by her unconscious "will"; but it is certain that during her analysis she tried to conceal important data about it by unconscious falsifications of her recollections.

The motive for forgetting and falsifying events relating to the first menstruation is the reluctance of women to admit that they once gave a deep psychologic meaning to events that they have since understood better. "It is a biologic process," they maintain, and do not want to be reminded of the fact that it was something else when they were young girls. It is natural for people to resist the idea that somatic processes have psychologic significance.

CHAPTER FIVE

Eroticism: the Feminine Woman

U NDER normal conditions we may expect adolescence successfully to complete its specific tasks. One of the most important of these is to master the instinctual tendencies and to bring them into a harmonious relation with the demands of the outside world and the ego. But even under the most favorable conditions, this function of adolescence is performed only to a limited extent. The "end of adolescence" is thus a relative concept, and the phase it represents varies greatly among individuals. Many adolescent features are carried over to the years of maturity, and this is especially true of women.

Above all, the young girl's puberty does not seem to fulfil one of its biologic tasks: woman's sexual life remains more inhibited than man's. We shall discuss the causes of this difference in chapter VI; for the time being we shall content ourselves with noting that we are confronted here with specific biologic and anatomic factors. The effect of these is doubtless strengthened by the young girl's education, that is to say, by social influences, but their role, however important, remains subsidiary. Our understanding of feminine frigidity, which has so often been a problem of psychoanalytic investigation, can be complete only if we take into consideration the fact that there is a constitutional inhibition that has no parallel in men.

Woman owes many of the most valuable and interesting features of her psychic life to the processes connected with this inhibition. These are fashioned during adolescence, and we have become acquainted with them as normal manifestations of that phase of life.

One of the consequences of woman's intensification of her inner life is, in our opinion, her specific eroticism.

We have seen that eroticism, which is a direct continuation of the young girl's ardent reveries, draws its strength from the instinctual force acting in the unconscious. As a result of a process of sublimation, woman's sexuality is more spiritualized than man's. The need for sublimated eroticism is so inherent in the feminine psyche that young girls who deny the necessity of a platonic love ideal, and prematurely engage in sexual activity, usually react to it with feelings of emptiness and disappointment. Because of this experience, they are even more prone later to create an unsatisfactory split between sexuality and the erotic longing for a love ideal. There are many such women who all their lives long for erotic love and the experience of the *grande passion*, even if they are happily married and sexually satisfied.

Normally, women strictly subordinate sensuality to the condition of love or longing for love. Sensual fantasy and the yearning for fulfillment can for a long time be more satisfactory than realization, and more conducive to happiness, and thus the adolescent split between eroticism and sexuality is continued. The ability gradually to shape the erotic longing in such a way that it does not negate the direct experience of sexuality, or does not impose too severe erotic conditions, is one of the goals of woman's adulthood and sexual maturity.

This process of sublimation enriches woman's entire erotic affective life and makes it more individually varied than man's, but it endangers her capacity for direct sexual gratification. The constitutional inhibition of woman's sexuality is all the more difficult to overcome because, as a result of sublimation, it is more complicated (and the conditions for its gratification more exacting) than the primitive desire to get rid of sexual tension that more commonly characterizes masculine sexuality.

We have shown that intensification of narcissism is one of the most interesting phenomena of adolescence. We pointed out that it protects the young person's ego from feelings of weakness during his efforts to master reality, as well as from being diffused in identifications, and that it supplies both sexes with the capacity for self-observation that is characteristic of this period of life.

In our view the continuation of this function of narcissism beyond adolescence is a specific and differentiating trait of *femininity*. "The narcissistic woman" or "feminine narcissism" has become a kind of byword, often even an insult. Thus it seems necessary to discuss this concept.

Freud's definition of narcissism relates it to the early childhood phase of the ego during which the libido, the emotional energy, takes the ego for its object. During the individual's entire life, the ego remains the great reservoir of this energy, from which emotions are sent out toward outside objects. The positive values of narcissism have been noted. Strength of character is often connected with it; the greater the narcissistic self-exactions, self-confidence, and self-respect, the stronger the character. Freud[1] ascribes to each person's narcissism a great force of attraction for other persons, and thinks that feminine charm derives from this self-loving, wanting-to-be-loved narcissistic quality. Many people are inclined to explain the fact that woman's narcissism is stronger than man's on the basis of her mortification over her organic genital inferiority, which she expresses by constantly demanding compensations for her offended self-love. This hypothesis also explains why narcissism is lessened in motherhood: through the possession of her child woman feels compensated for her previous disadvantage, and she can spend her capacity for love on others, especially on her child.

While granting that this explanation contributes to some extent to our understanding of feminine narcissism, we do not think that it is complete nor even that it takes the most essential factor into account. In our opinion, the intensification or preservation of the narcissism that was strengthened during adolescence results from a conflict between definite sexual tendencies and that part of the ego which expresses the instinct

[1] FREUD, S.: On narcissism: An introduction. Collected Papers, vol. 4.

of self-preservation. Since the sexual tendencies of woman are directed toward goals that are dangerous for her ego, the latter defends itself and strengthens its inner security by intensifying its self-love, which then manifests itself as "narcissism." Woman's sexual goals are dangerous for her ego because they are masochistic in character, and the riddle of feminine narcissism can be solved only if we understand feminine masochism, the aggressor in the inner conflict. In all situations marked by intensified masochistic tendencies, the narcissistic protective reaction seems to come into play. For this purpose it is taken over from adolescence into womanhood and continues to play a positive role in the psyche. As we shall see, *most erotic feminine types can be derived from the interplay between narcissism and masochism.*

The effects of narcissism vary in women. It may enrich or impoverish their psychologic life. In some cases it performs a useful function and contributes to psychologic health; in others it is a grave pathologic symptom. We shall illustrate these variations by a few simple examples taken from Tolstoy's *War and Peace*, in which several "narcissistic" women belonging to a small social group are depicted.

For instance, there is Princess Hélène, who is in love with herself and her beauty. Tolstoy gives a vivid picture of her.

The princess smiled. She rose with the same unchanging smile with which she had first entered the room—the smile of a perfectly beautiful woman. With a slight rustle of her white dress trimmed with moss and ivy, with a gleam of white shoulders, glossy hair, and sparkling diamonds, she passed between the men who made way for her, not looking at any of them, but smiling on all, as if graciously allowing each the privilege of admiring her beautiful figure and shapely shoulders, back, and bosom—which in the fashion of those days were very much exposed—and she seemed to bring the glamor of a ballroom with her as she moved toward A. P. Hélène was so lovely that she not only did not show any trace of coquetry, but on the contrary even appeared shy of her unquestionable and all too victorious beauty. She seemed to wish, but to be unable, to diminish its effect.

The company is listening to a fascinating story.

> All the time the story was being told she sat upright, glancing now at her beautiful round arm, altered in its shape by the pressure on the table, now at her still more beautiful bosom, on which she readjusted a diamond necklace. From time to time she smoothed the folds of her dress, and whenever the story produced an effect, she glanced at A. P., at once adopted just the expression she saw on the maid of honor's face, and again relapsed into her radiant smile.

Hélène's narcissism is so great that in her infatuation with her own beauty she feels the admiration of others as natural and even as burdensome. A beautiful woman less narcissistic than Hélène is more dependent on the reactions of other people, and their admiration always arouses the same joy in her, just as being loved always arouses joy in a loving woman. Narcissism is often accompanied by the question mark of insecurity, and tensely awaits an affirmative answer from the environment. Hélène's narcissism has to a large extent freed itself from this dependence. Nor does she try to win social approval; her adjustment is so complete that she simply adopts the expression of another authoritative person and then relapses into her impersonal smile. In love with herself, she cannot love anyone else; the joys of motherhood do not tempt her, and marriage means to her only social position and money.

Vera, a minor character in the novel, is still more withdrawn from the world in her narcissism. She cannot even produce the winning smile that Hélène always has in readiness, and the success of which seems natural to her. Even when Vera smiled, Tolstoy writes,

> The smile did not enhance her beauty as smiles generally do; on the contrary it gave her an unnatural and therefore unpleasant expression. Vera was good-looking, not at all stupid, quick at learning, was well brought up, and had a pleasant voice; what she said was true and appropriate; yet... the handsome Vera, who produced such an irritating and unpleasant effect on everyone, smiled and, evidently unmoved by what had been said to her, went to the looking glass and arranged her hair and scarf. Looking at her handsome face she seemed to become still colder and calmer.

While Hélène's smile expresses the need for human contact and arouses admiration, Vera's smile is a stereotyped mask that arouses only irritation. Her own reflection in the mirror is the only thing that interests her.

When Natasha, the character who represents the lovely feminine girl, makes her first appearance in society, she is consumed with the desire to make an impression and to be admired and loved by everyone. Her narcissistic need to be loved, and her inability to resist ardent wooing even from the "wrong man," lead her to commit the tragic error through which she attains full maturity. Natasha's narcissism emanates warmth and willingness to return love for love: "Natasha fell in love the very moment she entered the ballroom. She was not in love with anyone in particular, but with everyone."

Like all Tolstoy's characters, Natasha is taken from real life. Women like her are a living refutation of Freud's assertion[2] that a feminine woman does not love but lets herself be loved. Feminine love, the core of the "feminine woman," is naturally passive-narcissistic. If this love is not pathologically distorted, it can be likened to a fire that radiates warmth. One must come near to such a fire, sometimes one must even stir it up; but it sends out rays of various kinds in many directions, and the value of its "passive" achievement is not inferior to that of the most "active" love.

As further traits of femininity we have cited a strong tendency toward passivity and an intensification of masochism. If we replace the expression "turn toward passivity" by "activity directed inward," the term "feminine passivity" acquires a more vital content, and the ideas of inactivity, emptiness, and immobility are eliminated from its connotation. The term "activity directed inward" indicates a function, expresses something positive, and can satisfy the feminists among us who often feel that the term "feminine passivity" has derogatory implications.

[2] Op. cit.

"Feminine masochism" follows the same path as "activity directed inward." By analogy we can say that woman's activity directed inward is parallel to man's intensified activity directed outward, and her masochism is parallel to the masculine aggression that accompanies his activity, particularly at the end of adolescence. To reassure the reader, we shall anticipate our discussion of feminine masochism by pointing out that it lacks the cruelty, destructive drive, suffering, and pain by which masochism manifests itself in perversions and neuroses.

Before describing our feminine-erotic types, we shall briefly outline the fundamental elements of their psychologic structure. These are: (1) the instinctual life, which in the feminine woman has a passive-masochistic character (later we shall show the genesis and development of this instinct formation); (2) the narcissistic components of the ego (the nature and development of feminine narcissism were dealt with above); (3) the emotional harbingers of woman's reproductive functions, which exist in her before real motherhood occurs.

The relative weight of each of these elements is influenced by each woman's childhood history, especially by the outcome of her effort to liberate herself from old objects during adolescence. The woman's choice of love objects is to a great extent determined by her past emotional ties and her psychologic readiness for motherhood.

A harmonious interplay of the elements defined above characterizes the feminine woman, whose predominant trait is eroticism. The form of this eroticism and the ways and means by which it achieves its aims give the total personality of each of the three feminine types described below their special color. What is common to all of these types is facility in identifying with man in a manner that is most conducive to the happiness of both partners. The narcissistic prerequisite of this identification is psychologic affinity, the similarity of the egos. To the woman falls the larger share of the work of adjustment: she leaves the initiative to the man and out of her own need renounces originality, experiencing her own self through identification. Some of these women need to overestimate their objects, and their narcissistic method of making the man happy can be expressed in the formula, "He is wonderful and I am a part of him."

These women are not only ideal life companions for men; if they possess the feminine quality of intuition to a great degree, they are ideal collaborators who often inspire their men and are themselves happiest in this role. They seem to be easily influenceable, and adapt themselves to their companions and understand them. They are the loveliest and most unaggressive of helpmates and they want to remain in that role; they do not insist on their own rights—quite the contrary. They are easy to handle in every way—if one only loves them. Sexually, they are easily excited and rarely frigid; but precisely in the sexual field they impose narcissistic conditions that must be fulfilled absolutely. They demand love and ardent desire, finding in these a satisfying compensation for the renunciation of their own active tendencies.

If gifted in any direction, they preserve the capacity for being original and productive, but without entering into competitive struggles. They are always willing to renounce their own achievements without feeling that they are sacrificing anything and they rejoice in the achievements of their companions, which they have often inspired. They have an extraordinary need of support when engaged in any *activity directed outward*, but are absolutely independent in such thinking and feeling as relate to their inner life, that is to say, in their *activity directed inward*. Their capacity for identification is not an expression of inner poverty, but of inner wealth.

Naturally such an attitude involves the danger of masochistic subjection and of the loss of one's own personality. If these dangers are successfully avoided, we have here the most gratifying type of the "feminine woman." What is fascinating and enigmatic in such women is not the part of their personality we have just described. The tendency to identification, passive reception, masochistic renunciation in favor of others, the effects of intuition—all these are qualities that we have recognized as typical of the "feminine woman." Her fascination lies rather in the protective mechanisms she develops to offset the dangers mentioned above. These mechanisms are entrusted to the narcissistic forces of the psyche, and, paradoxic as this may sound, only the effects of these forces endow such women with their full personality value. We recall that narcissism performs not only a negative function, hostile to the external object. In women it serves as an important counterweight to masochism and performs a positive function. It plays the part of a guardian protecting them from passive-masochistic decline. The post chosen by this guardian in the psychologic structure determines the difference between our first and our second feminine type.

The *first* type of feminine personality is the woman, who, when erotically desired and urged, finds it very difficult to refuse and is easily conquered. Here the guardian obviously has not established his post at the entrance door. The gratified man feels himself loved, enjoys the woman who psychologically and physically gives herself to him, but soon discovers that he has received only an insignificant part of her feelings, that he is outside a closed door behind which are deeply hidden psychologic treasures that can be won only with great effort.

As we see, the harmony of this type is constituted by a definite characteristic relationship between the passive-masochistic tendencies and feminine narcissism. Behind a protective narcissistic wall, severely guarded, there is a strong personality and a rich world of inner activity. The gates of the front yard often remain open, because this type of woman feels so secure behind her protective wall.

The *second* type of feminine woman is the woman whose narcissistic guardian is posted at the very entrance door to her erotic and emotional life. She is difficult to conquer and defends her personality both physically and psychologically, because she is well aware of the danger of masochistic yielding. During the period of preliminary struggles in the attempt to win her, she fortifies and secures her position and steers the man's love and valuation into the correct channels. Through her own identification she solidly ties the man's life to her own. After the guardian has been overcome and the outer gates opened, all the inner gates too are opened without reservation. The narcissistic guardian has seen to it that this woman's personality is preserved. From now on her behavior is similar to that of the first type of feminine woman.

The integration of these erotic personalities is evident from the fact that they behave in the manner described above not only in their erotic life, but also in all other fields. In their friendships with women and men—and they have many friends, thanks to their intuition and their lack of envy, competitive feelings, and other forms of aggression—they display the same harmonious attitude, that is, narcissistic protection of their own personalities and passive subordination to others through identification. They are distinguished by very great tolerance. In their relationship to other people they go beyond the principle that to understand everything is to forgive everything; for them, to understand everything is to have nothing to forgive. What distinguishes them from many men and women of other types is that envy is alien to them and that they experience jealousy only to the normal extent of their eroticism. Perhaps a particularly favorable mastering of penis envy contributes to the formation of the personalities of these women. At any rate, through love and heightened self-confidence they brilliantly succeed in overcoming the "narcissistic mortification" that in the opinion of many psychoanalysts is the result of woman's penis envy. Their masochism does not need to seek protection in that escape into masculinity to which other types of women resort, because it has created for itself a well defended position within femininity. I permit myself this conjecture with regard to penis envy although I do not consider penis envy the main source of feminine narcissism. Nor do I regard envy as a specifically feminine quality.

The woman described here is easily influenced, yet knows

how to express a quiet but firm veto.   If her male companion or any other person in her entourage oversteps proper limits in his demands by increasing her masochistic burden or running counter to her ethical or esthetic needs, she breaks her ties despite her devotion and tolerance.

It seems that these types of women, particularly the first, have such a tremendous readiness to give and receive love that no disappointment they experience can keep them from eventually entering into a new relationship—under the same conditions—of identifying devotion.

Sometimes they create the impression of being too easily accessible.   But with experience the psychologic observer learns that identical behavior in different people does not always have an identical meaning.   A popular Latin proverb says: *Si duae faciunt idem, non est idem.*   For the psychologist the deeper motives are decisive.   From this point of view we must carefully distinguish the women who "can be easily had" from our feminine type.   The former, in contrast to the latter, can also be easily deserted.

It is an old truth that has not changed very much, in spite of the transformation of our standards, that man's sexual desire is intensified if he has to overcome obstacles before achieving sexual communion with woman.   Just as in prehistoric times, women are more gratified when they grant sexual intimacy only after a long wooing.   In this old and ever new form of relationship, the two conditions of feminine eroticism are fulfilled—the masochistic condition, because woman wants to be fought for and conquered and awaits her "defeat" in joyful excitation, and the narcissistic condition, because this struggle increases man's desire, which is so gratifying to woman.   Social questions have no relation to all this.   The psychologic factor rules here, independently of the social order; it only changes its form.   In the Middle Ages, when women were most subjected socially, chivalrous love and the knight's humble service of his lady were most widespread.   And even in the Moslem countries, there are, side by side with the easy acquisition of the woman as a sexual object, methods of making this conquest difficult in order to heighten her value as an object of pleasure.

In our culture, many women renounce this prize of being conquered for reasons that are often contradictory. The inability to say no may express nothing more than an infantile inability to give up an immediate pleasure for the sake of a greater but delayed one. These women display in all their behavior a childishly uncontrolled nature. Another motive may lie in the woman's narcissistic hunger, which seeks gratification in a continuous series of situations of being desired; still another may be the masochistic wish to be humiliated and deserted. The urge to break her chains, to be as sexually free as man, to appropriate "a certain amount" of man's active drive, to satisfy aggressive impulses in continuous unfaithfulness—all these motives, emanating from woman's masculine component, lead her to uninhibited, "free" erotic activity. Wittels[3] cites as examples of such androgynous women the wicked Messalina and lovely Helen of Troy.

The "primitive woman" who yields happily and without conflicts to her sexual desires is as unknown to me as is the "primitive man." In fiction we sometimes encounter characters who approach this type. And yet, upon closer examination, how complex is the promiscuous Jaga, for instance, in Ladislas Reymont's *The Peasants*, and the sexually disreputable, yet so motherly Verinea in the novel by Seifulina.

Experience teaches us that manifestations of a too great sexual freedom are not found where there is harmonious femininity. They express inner confusion just as much as—and sometimes even more than—excessive abstinence and sexual inhibition. Our concept of the normal feminine woman is built not upon such manifestations, but on the harmonious interplay of various psychologic forces; thus, our type is clearly different from types that are similar to it in appearance only.

The difference between our two types of feminine women can

[3] WITTELS, F.: Die libidinöse Struktur des kriminellen Psychopathen. Internat. Ztschr. f. Psychoanal., vol. 23, 1937.

be great, despite their profound identity. The first type is more easily moved, not only erotically, but in all her emotions; gentle and tolerant, she makes great demands, but at all times is ready to let the object affect her as it is, even sometimes to accept it without overestimating it, and to identify herself with it. The danger for this woman lies in her masochism; for it may happen that her narcissistic guardian is bribed. A definite type of man can succeed in this bribing of the guardian; he, too, is highly erotic and narcissistic, very aggressive in his ardent wooing and his desire. He is so seductive in his will to possess completely, and seems to have so much to give, that the woman cannot resist him. As such a man is often endowed with great gifts and is also able to stimulate and hold the woman's intellectual interests, he succeeds in weakening her narcissistic self-defense, and she becomes the victim of her own masochism. In that case, her inner harmony is destroyed; unless she succeeds in saving herself and rebuilding her narcissistic wall, she will repeatedly experience her masochistic fate, either by remaining tied to a man of whom she cannot rid herself, or by changing from one aggressive object to another. She becomes neurotic and ceases to be a harmonious "feminine woman."

The second type of woman is less masochistic but more intolerant; her demands are greater, and she assumes the passive feminine role only under definite conditions of far reaching narcissistic gratification. The danger for this woman, in contrast to the first type, lies in narcissism. Her excessive demands result in impoverishing her object relations and can easily lead to frustrations and disappointments.

Of course the separation between the two types is not always sharp. There are many transitional types, and even the pure types are for the most part "mixed formations." The modes of reaction too diverge from the "typical." How often does the sweetest woman, who has behaved in a completely passive-feminine way, suddenly assume an aggressive, vindictive attitude when she suffers a narcissistic injury. When the narcissistic guardian of her erotic masochism fails, masochism is transformed into sadism and turns more aggressively against her own ego.   Suicides of women who have suffered disappointments in love usually result not from the loss of the object, but from a narcissistic injury.   I knew a woman who, because of such an injury, wept for many weeks, day and night, mourning the loss of a man whom she had devaluated long before and whom she had ceased to love, as she well realized.   I also had the opportunity of studying a gentle and lovely woman who, without the slightest conscious trace of love grief, murdered a man because he inflicted a narcissistic injury upon her.   In the course of her trial, which caused a sensation, the prosecution looked for political motives, because no one could understand the importance of a narcissistic injury to this woman.

We know numerous feminine types that are psychically sound and mature and yet show very adolescent features in their behavior.   Erotic, strongly emotional, and impulsive women regard each relation they leave behind them as a mistake and during their full maturity behave like the adolescent girl who with each infatuation thinks, "The other man was not the right one, this one is."   Others display a marked faith in the permanence and exclusiveness of their feelings and a desire for "eternal love."   The narcissistic demand, "Love me exclusively and forever," is usually connected with a fear of loss, and in this fear lies the source of the masochistic gratification that often degenerates into self-tormenting jealousy.   Paradoxically, it is the same masochistic need that induces an erotically experienced woman to write to her lover: "Give me insecurity, for it alone can give value to my love for you."   With many women, the feeling of exclusiveness causes anxiety, and they can engage in a relationship only if it is understood that both parties are free to brush it off when the feeling is no longer mutual.

The most erotic lovers are often incapable of maintaining a harmonious relationship under prosaic, humdrum conditions, because for them love is possible only as an ecstasy of admiration and of being constantly desired.   It is hard to satisfy this narcissistic need in the grind of everyday life.   Strongly erotic women refuse to engage in marriages involving a prosaic life, if their social position enables them to do so, or they have different partners in rapid succession (artists, etc.). Women with strong social conscience and great erotic longings break up an erotically unsatisfactory relation in a different manner: they invent a special ideology for the purpose and declare that a sexual companionship that lacks the intensity of erotic experience that they demand is immoral and must therefore be given up. The same type of women, when they fall into a conflict between their maternal duties and their erotic longings, usually take the rationalizing attitude that it is better for the children to have their parents separated than to live in a "cold, loveless" atmosphere.

In some corner of her heart, every woman has a masochistic need to experience the torments of longing and the sufferings that deep love can bring. In the same recess there is a narcissistic wish for great proofs of the partner's love and readiness for self-sacrifice. When Edward of England broadcast to the world that he had given up his throne for "the woman I love," his words aroused a curious and unforgettable echo in the hearts of many women between 16 and 60 years of age. This profession of love awakened in them the longing "to be loved." What really moved them was the king's announcement of the sacrifice he was willing to make for the sake of his beloved. The erotic woman wants to have a throne and a crown at her feet, even if her lover does not possess them. "But if he had them . . ."

We have said that the woman's choice of a love object and her attitude toward it are also determined by the manner in which she coped with her old emotional ties and by the motherly component in her psyche. Our two types choose one of two models: the overestimated man, very active and masculine, after the pattern of the idealized father, and the promising young man who needs to have the woman identify herself with him in order to develop his self-confidence. The latter choice is usually conditioned by the motherly component of feminine eroticism. One thing, however, must be stressed here: the more masochistic (in the feminine sense of the term) the woman's instinctual tendencies, the farther removed is her erotic ideal from the man who needs help or is sick.   If the woman's unconscious instinctually conditioned masochistic attitude coincides with the conscious sacrifice of her ego, that is to say, if pity or any form of altruism enters into her relationship with the man, she is strongly inhibited from being stirred erotically.   It can often be observed that even the kindest woman of this type must make a great effort to suppress her repugnance when her lover is ill and needs her care.   The motherly-erotic woman can give much active help without being diverted from her erotic enthusiasm, but only under certain conditions.   She can, for instance, encourage the continued development of the man in the sense of common ideal formation or other interests, provided she believes in his strength.   In this she completely differs from the ambitious woman who demands in an aggressive-active manner that her man achieve something and who in doing this transfers her own ambition to him.

These two forms of love choice—a daughter relation to a father ideal, and a mother relation to a man—also have their dangers.   The former is so tied up with infantile conditions that it can easily lead to neurotic complications.   Women who all their lives remain erotically bound to a man they have had to renounce and women who frequently change their love objects are often only using two different ways of expressing their deep father tie.   In contrast to the latter, the female Don Juan is more narcissistic; she cannot bear renunciation and negates it by changing her love objects—"I am loved in spite of everything."

The woman who is harmoniously erotic, who is most "feminine" and represents the best achievement of her Creator, often declares in the evening of her rich and happy love life: "I have not always been faithful, but actually I have been in love only once."   Some crumpled picture in her album or an image in her memory represents for her a figure to which in her early youth she attached her great yearning and readiness to love, and through which she unconsciously preserves her faith to her first love object, her father.

There are two very trivial and fully conscious fantasies of the normal young girl that relate to the father. In one he is a great man who deserves a better fate, a victim of the prosaic mother who has tied him to the gray business of earning a living. She, the little daughter, would be a more suitable object for him, though he must painfully renounce it. In a large number of instances, a psychologically sound woman may have as her first love object—an object to which she often remains attached for life—an unfree man, often a married man, who fans her love and responds to it, but cannot break his old tie. Such a man reproduces the situation described above. The fantasy of his painful love yearning and the woman's own suffering, shared with him, often prove stronger motives for faithfulness than the fulfillment of love.

The other girlish fantasy that often exerts a great influence on woman's erotic life is based on the idea that the father loves the mother as a sexual object, but gives his better self, his ideal ego, to his daughter. She is the one, she thinks, who understands him and possesses his soul. The erotic woman who after each sexual gratification anxiously asks her beloved, "Do you still love me?" is not necessarily moved to do this by her education and the existing double standards of morality, according to which woman is devalued when she gives herself sexually. She is really expressing the little girl's wish to share the "better things" with her man, and her own devaluation of sexuality. In neurotic women the idea that men make a cleavage between ideal and sexual love leads to sexual anxiety and inhibition.

There is another type of adolescent love that continues throughout life in some women and that may occur in women who are excellently adjusted to reality. For instance, a happily married woman who has children and a career, and who is in every respect an adult and mature person, is constantly entangled in a painfully blissful and platonic love for some man

who is usually a father figure for her, such as her working superior, or an important man in a field in which she is interested,
etc. One woman called this love her "Sunday happiness"; for
only on Sundays did she have time to indulge in fantasies
relating to it.

In *Much Ado about Nothing* (Act 2, scene 1) we find an interesting illustration of this division of emotional life into everyday
gratification and Sunday high seriousness.

> DON PEDRO: Will you have me, lady?
> BEATRICE: No, my lord, unless I might have another for working days;
>   your grace is too costly to wear every day."

The erotic woman's *motherliness* probably comes to the fore
to a greater extent when the chosen love object is a young man
than when he is modeled after her father. But this is not always
absolutely the case. The growing daughter, especially if there
is no mother, frequently plays the latter's protective role with
regard to the father. How she scolds him when he forgets his
raincoat or deviates from the diet the doctor has prescribed for
him! And how fond she is of listening to his account of the
great deeds he has accomplished during the day! Whether he
is a subordinate employe or a prominent public personage, in
her eyes he is always an important figure. In the same way, the
erotic-motherly adult woman listens to her man and tries to
preserve for herself the illusion of his importance and for him
the knowledge of her faith in him. She repeats this behavior
with regard to her son. Both mother and son need to have
faith in the boy's great future, and the motherly woman knows
how to give her son this faith. She calms his fear of the tasks
he has to perform, because she does not demand that he perform
them. Nor does she devaluate him if he achieves his aims only
to a modest extent. The erotic-motherly woman has this
gratifying attitude toward her husband too.

Elsewhere we shall try to throw more light on the concept of
motherliness; for the time being we shall confine ourselves to a
brief definition. The motherly woman in her behavior toward

her environment reveals the ability to subordinate her individual interests to those of the species. The species is represented by the child; but the motherly attitude can be directed toward other persons or things. This feeling is very different from every other kind of love, even the most "selfless"; in erotic women it often contributes substantially toward weakening their narcissistic needs in their relations with men.

We might expect that the erotic-motherly woman would, as a result of her constitution, find the best outlet for her feelings in motherhood; but this is not always the case. This most womanly of all women is the very one who most often encounters difficulties in her motherhood. A conflict arises between eroticism and motherliness, a conflict all the more acute because eroticism can use many motherly feelings for its own purposes and thus compete with real motherhood. Vice versa, the woman may direct toward her child such a large part of her self-denying, identifying, and masochistic feelings that her eroticism is endangered.

The narcissistic guardian that functions so well with regard to the man often fails with regard to the child, and the mother's masochistic self-sacrifice becomes a danger for her, and later for the child as well. The fact that the most womanly woman, with all her wealth of motherly feelings, is often unable to bring into the world as many children as she yearns for, probably saves her feminine ego. Nor can such a woman, in her relations with her children, always create that harmony which she develops in all other life situations. Her motherhood lacks one active ingredient of a definite character—a solid, broad, obvious motherliness, in which love for her children is more important than eroticism and which, in the conflict between motherhood and love, decides in favor of the former. For that reason— and this is regrettable—erotic-motherly women are often childless or limit themselves to one child. They put too much, often their whole rich emotional world, at the disposal of this one child. One such woman succeeded, after many years, in solving the riddle of why she had had only one child, although motherhood was in her eyes the highest value.   She had identified herself with her child to such an extent that the idea of giving birth to another, who would compete with him for her motherly love, seemed unbearable to her.   This woman was experienced and shrewd, and *consciously* she wanted to protect her child from the unfavorable situation of being an only child; but unconsciously she yielded to the power of her identification with him and remained monogamous as a mother just as she was in all her other relations.

Here a question arises that is asked with monotonous frequency: Is the feminine woman polygamous or monogamous? Let us begin by paying our respects to the social factors involved in this question.   Human society created monogamy to meet the needs of a definite social order and economic organization. Monogamy was imposed for the sake of preserving the species, because the human child, in contrast to other living creatures, needs help and protection for a long time after birth, and some form of monogamy upheld by the law seems to offer the best guaranty of this protection.   Thus monogamy became a law in most civilized nations and acquired a compulsory character. Whether this institution also has a basis in human nature is a psychologic problem.   We know women who have grown up in social conditions that freed them from monogamy, women who freed themselves from its requirements individually, and women who, as a result of their passivity, have discarded it under the influence of others.   Thus we have rich material at our disposal. Our impression is that the feminine woman in an overwhelming majority of cases is fundamentally monogamous.   This monogamy does not necessarily require the exclusiveness of marriage or confine sexuality to one object for life.   A woman may even change her love objects quite frequently; but during each relation she is absolutely monogamous and has a conservative need to continue the given relation as long as possible.   This normal behavior presupposes that no disturbing countertendencies are at work.

The psychologic explanation of this phenomenon seems clear

We have only to go back a little in the development of the woman.   Let us recall that we left the pubescent girl in a triangular situation and expressed the hope that later she would dissolve the sexually mixed triangle, a reflection of her bisexuality, in favor of heterosexuality.   This formulation was made for the sake of simplification.   Actually, whether a constitutional bisexual factor contributes to the creation of such a triangle or not, this triangle can never be given up completely. The deepest and most ineradicable emotional relations with both parents share in its formation.   It succeeds another relation, even older and more enduring—the relation between mother and child, which every man or woman preserves from his birth to his death.   It is erroneous to say that the little girl gives up her first mother relation in favor of the father.   She only gradually draws him into the alliance, develops from the mother-child exclusiveness toward the triangular parent-child relation and continues the latter, just as she does the former, although in a weaker and less elemental form, all her life.   Only the principal part changes: now the mother, now the father plays it.   The ineradicability of affective constellations manifests itself in later repetitions.

In her relation to her own child, woman repeats her own mother-child history, and seeks to continue the regular psychologic process in a new triangle.

While waiting for motherhood, even before its beginning, woman psychologically prepares for the triangle.   Sometimes this is expressed directly and consciously in the wish, "I want to have a child by him, *with him*."   The role of the man in the triangle is here clearly defined from the beginning.   At other times the wish may be, "I want *a child*," and then the man is partly moved into the background.   The normal feminine woman always more or less includes the man, and this not only in the physical sense, because the formation of a triangle is a deep need for her.   This need often asserts itself under the most unexpected conditions, and the failure to satisfy it can considerably disturb her relation to her child.   This can be illustrated trom many cases, but we shall choose only a few very striking examples.

One is that of a young revolutionary who came from a country in which the formula *pater incertus est* has become a fundamental social convention. This liberal-minded young woman suffered from depression. She was psychologically unable to be happy as the mother of her beloved child because she could not bear his fatherlessness, that is, the absence of the third member of the triangle. She herself had been reared in a traditional family and it was clear that she had consciously and intellectually liberated herself from her old dependence. But in her emotional and unconscious life she was a victim of her reactionary repetition tendencies. Only experience can show how many generations must work to effect a change in such deep-rooted patterns.

Another example is that of a young woman who tenderly loved her husband. As a result of tuberculosis of the testicles, the husband became incapable of begetting children, and the woman felt extremely disappointed in her longing for motherhood. The couple lived in a country where adoption is out of the question. With the full consent of her husband, the woman made up her mind to be impregnated by another man, but in order to obscure the traces of fatherhood, she had sexual relations with two men at the same period, once with each. She gave birth to a beautiful, healthy child, but, like our first example, collapsed under the feeling that the child's father was for her an empty concept. Because of her feelings of guilt and her resentment against her husband, she was unable to consider him her child's father and accused him of not being interested in it. She railed that it was fatherless and that she wanted to renounce it. Neither her longed-for pregnancy nor the suckling of the child nor all the numerous threads that connect mother and child could make this motherly woman a mother as long as the part of the father in the triangle remained unfilled. Only after her own emotional difficulties had been overcome, and after she agreed to accept her husband as the child's father, could she become a happy mother.

An even more striking example is offered by the following case, that of a woman who was more neurotic. At the age of 23 she married a man of 43 with whom she had fallen in love. The marriage turned out to be a very happy one, although during the first six months the couple did not achieve complete sexual relations. Immediately after these began, the young woman's menses stopped, to the great joy of both herself and her husband. In the fourth month of her supposed pregnancy, during the summer, she went to the country to stay with a relative. There she engaged in a love relation with a young man who was a few years younger than she. It was only a passing affair, without particular passion on her part or subsequent conscious guilt feelings. She thought that this affair had no importance at all, as she was pregnant anyhow. Her pregnancy created in her the feeling that actually "nothing counted now." She returned home from her vacation, and her sexual relations with her husband were even more gratifying than before. In what she thought was the sixth month of her pregnancy she consulted an obstetrician for the first time and to her surprise learned that she had really been pregnant for only two months. This discovery caused her no concern, nor did it disturb her husband; the woman at that time still had no doubt that her pregnancy was the result of her intercourse with her husband, especially as he had come to see her during her period of sexual unfaithfulness. Only after the birth of the child, during the suckling period, did it occur to her that the paternity of the child was uncertain. At first this was only a fleeting idea that came to her while she was looking at the child, whom she worshiped and to whom she devoted herself with the greatest solicitude. Gradually her doubt took a greater and greater hold on her, and her joy in her child was overshadowed by the tormenting question, "Whose child is it?" By the end of one year the child had ceased to be a child for her, and she herself had ceased to be a mother. It was now only an object for which she mechanically fulfilled the duties of a mother, but to which she had no emotional relation, because this relation was dis-

turbed by her tormenting doubt.   Every gesture of the child,
every smile or cry, was met not by motherly joy or concern, but
by the question, "From whom did he get that?"   To all the
attempts of her friends to help her overcome this feeling she
replied: "How can I take any joy in my child when it is fatherless? A child must have a father."

After a long psychologic effort the woman resolved emotionally to accept her husband as her child's father, whether he had
begotten it or not.   With the reconstitution of the triangle she
was able to accept motherhood.

Unmarried mothers seem to us particularly suitable as subjects for the study of the psychologic problem raised here.   The
interesting observations made by Beata Rank[4] and F. Clothier[5]
provide us with fascinating examples that confirm our own
views.   Many of these unmarried mothers, from morbid
motives, eliminate paternity from the outset and destroy the
triangle.   But those in whom normal motherliness, even though
under difficult external (and usually also internal) conditions,
succeeds in asserting itself, clearly reveal the existence of a
triangle.   The fatherless child, often conceived in conditions
that really make the father *incertus*, has nevertheless a paternal
"representative" in the mother's fantasy.   The power of this
father proxy can be so great that a real father seems completely unimportant.

The feminine woman manifests this deeply conditioned and
never mastered triangular situation of childhood in her demand
that the father be "certain" and this demand makes her
monogamous.   And as every love relation of the feminine
woman psychically contains the germ of a child, she must secure
and protect monogamy even when she changes her love objects.
The fact that the role of the father may be assigned to a man
who has not begotten the child, does not change anything in the
psychologic situation, as we have seen in two of our examples.

[4] RANK, B.: Understanding of the unmarried mother.   Unpublished manuscript.
[5] CLOTHIER, F.: Psychological implications of unmarried parenthood.   Am. J. Ortho-
    psychiat., vol. 13, no. 2, 1943.

Mary, the mother of Jesus, in accordance with the deep human need for chastity in motherhood, is represented as having given birth to a child by immaculate conception. But the same human need added Joseph to the legend as a father figure.

We have studied two types of the feminine woman together because, despite certain differences, they are closely related to each other. There is still a *third* type that we class with this group, although certain additional elements give it the character of a borderline type; more concretely, it contains an admixture of active drives that we generally ascribe to masculinity. Women of this type possess to a high degree the basic valuable feminine qualities—a passive-erotic attitude toward men, intensified inner life, intuition, deepened emotional life, and a tendency to fantasying. But they also manifest other features that are absent from typical femininity. Their masochism, for instance, has not the relatively pure form of a pleasure function; it is accompanied by considerable elements of "moral masochism." This kind of masochism is much more severe, imperious, and aggressive against the woman's own ego than feminine masochism and manifests itself in a stronger tendency to conscious and unconscious guilt feelings. As a result, the moral qualities of this third type of woman are more imposing than those of the other two types and she seems more reliable, ethically and socially. This difference is sometimes only apparent.

The gamut of individual characterologic differences in our purely feminine type is very large. Her warmth and sensitiveness, her nonaggressiveness, and the fact that she seldom provokes aggressions in others, create around her a calmer and more harmonious atmosphere, decrease her guilt feelings, and leave her moral faculties unoccupied, so to speak. But when conflicts arise that do mobilize these moral faculties, these women often turn out to be relentless toward themselves and others. On the other hand, it may occur that feminine women, excessively gentle and passive, trust the judgment of others, disa-

vow their own better intuitive knowledge, or subordinate their
own value judgments to their erotic needs.

In our third type the individual differences are less pronounced, the outline of the total personality is more general and
uniform.   The narcissistic guardian here can afford to be less
careful, for moral masochism takes over the greatest part of the
work of psychologic management.   In this type too, the basic
feminine combination of masochism-narcissism is preserved,
but the two factors have lost their original proportions.   Masochistic passivity is less marked, for the moral ingredient of this
woman's masochism is more insistent and more active.   It
tolerates the narcissistic element only to a limited extent, and
chiefly in so far as it heightens self-respect and self-exactions.
The erotic wish to be loved, which is another aspect of this
narcissism, is minimized.

Women of this type love with feminine abandon, but withdraw
their readiness for erotic abandon in narcissistic pride when their
demands for reciprocal love are not sufficiently met.   In purely
feminine fashion, they tend toward erotic fantasies and are full
of longing and romantic expectations, just as the women of the
other two types.   But they are prouder and more intolerant
toward the objects of their immediate emotional relationships
and above all toward themselves.   Their erotic fantasies easily
arouse guilt feelings in them, and they often defend themselves
against such fantasies.   This tendency to guilt considerably
limits their erotic freedom of movement.

The social anxiety of these women is strong and their sense
of duty demands that they put their feminine qualities at the
service of real and social values, rather than of eroticism.   They
are less artistic and esthetic, and their orientation is more
ethical than is the case in our first two types, although the cultural level is the same.   They are strictly monogamous, not
only out of an emotional need, but because they follow the
characterologic commandment of faithfulness.   At the same
time they are extremely sensitive to every suspicion of emotional unfaithfulness on the part of their lovers or husbands,

and are as intolerant toward them as they are toward themselves. But this arises less from moral than from feminine-
narcissistic motives. Their ideal demands with regard to their
love objects are very great, and they are not inclined to moder-
ate or adapt these demands through overestimation of the
object. They are ready to assume a completely feminine behavior, but only on condition that the man's activity and the
goals of this activity conform to their wishes and expectations.
In this respect they should not be confused, however, with the
masculine-ambitious women who demand that their men be
successful in order to gratify their own ambitions.

What the type we are describing here expects of her partner
is not external success, but proof of his strength of character.
In conflicts between eroticism and values like religion, social
obligations, and ethical commands they usually—in contrast
to our other types—choose the latter. If they choose in favor
of eroticism, they spoil their love happiness by subsequent guilt
feelings. Their erotic enthusiasm can be kindled only by
moral values, and it is destroyed by actions they morally con-
demn. Their choice of object is usually motivated by the desire
to complement their own personality, that is, they are ready to
give up much of their activity drive in favor of the man if his
own activity in love and work is strong enough to satisfy them.
They completely reject the passive man who is willing to play
a subordinate role. These women rarely run the risk of masochistically submitting to the man's aggression, although their
sexual interest tends strongly in that direction. Obviously the
necessary warning signals function in them and protect them
from this danger. It seems that moral masochism has sufficient
power to weaken its erotic partner, feminine masochism.

The love object of such a woman usually has the features of
the person in whose image she formed her ego ideal. Usually
this is the father; in families where the mother represented the
ideal, the ideal is formed after her image and the object is later
chosen accordingly. Despite a certain danger of homosexuality
inherent in their type, these women completely avoid it in their

sexual life. However, they have a marked tendency to strong sublimated relationships with other women.

Women of this type are very motherly, but their motherliness is entirely different from that of the other two types. It is of the active form that under normal conditions leads to a large family. These mothers are usually the center of the home, leaving all activity outside the home to the man, on condition that they themselves direct the education of the children and set the tone of the home. Their feminine intuition usually saves them from the matriarchal attitude, which might lead the children to devaluate their father in favor of their mother. They want to uphold the paternal authority, but in this connection they often fall into conflict: they demand that their husbands display great authority before the children, but at the same time they by their own activity unconsciously deprive the fathers of authority. In one respect the relation of these women to their children is different from that of the other types. In the event of a conflict between motherhood and eroticism, they usually decide more easily than the others in favor of their children. But they also demand more of their children, are more intolerant toward them, and from their earliest years show an anxious concern about the formation of their characters. A striking although trivial example of the difference between this type and the other two lies in their reactions to masturbation in their children. Simple motherly women of the feminine-passive type feel, without any need for the slightest enlightenment, that in masturbation they are confronted with a normal process, and intuitively treat this matter as a modern educator does. The women of our third type, unless intellectually informed, fall into despair, and their intuition suffices only to keep them from inflicting harsh punishments. By kindly reprimands they develop their children's sense of guilt, as a kind of family inheritance. They often spoil their own joy in their children by constantly worrying about whether they are doing everything they should to give them an education consonant with their ideals.

In identification processes they differ from the other types in that they have a tendency to expect others to identify with themselves rather than vice versa. This does not stem from an egotistic desire that others adjust themselves to their wishes, but only from the moral desire that others should conform to their ideal demands.

Outside their immediate surroundings, to which they are attached with strong emotional ties and for which they feel responsible, they develop not only all their intuitive qualities but also great tolerance. They defend the underdog in society and all those who need help, and in their case this is not a reaction stemming from a repressed aggression. They are really and fundamentally ready to help others, because their active motherliness extends beyond the circle of their own children. Wherever these women are not subject to the tensions of anxiety and guilt feelings, they have a real inner capacity for developing all feminine and motherly qualities.

Their erotic freedom is exposed to entirely different dangers than that of the previously discussed types: the ascetic ideal of these women can effectively inhibit their sexual experience and rob them of the erotic joys of which they are perfectly capable. We have seen that, in contrast to this type, the previous types showed excessive psychologic dependence on eroticism.

We are inclined to think that the differences between the first two and the third type of femininity are to a large extent determined by the milieu. The feminine-erotic type is more frequent in Latin and Slavic countries, while the feminine-active-moral type is more characteristic of the Calvinistic countries with their tradition of severity. In cases of neurotic distortions of the personality or of neuroses, the erotic types are more likely to be victims of hysteria, and the moral type of obsessional neurosis. Thus we also take constitutional factors into account in the construction of these types. Particularly as regards our third type, the familial disposition to obsessional neurosis plays an important part. But in contradiction to their disposition to obsessional neurosis, these women have an

emotional life that in warmth and capacity for positive unam-
bivalent relations reminds us rather of normal and hysterical
women. The obsessional-neurotic elements in their personalities suggest either a constitutionally fixed substratum or effects
of environmental influences; however, they are able to develop
an emotional personality that, to a great extent, is freed from
this substratum.

Upon closer examination of all these feminine types, we are
particularly struck by the usually positive relation of the
woman to her mother. But this relation seems to have a
different character in the feminine-passive types than in the
more active ones. In the latter, it is more like a reaction; it
follows a phase of aggressive animosity that is very successfully
overcome. Their excessive tendency to guilt feelings reveals
their still existing aggressive impulses. The real personality of
the mother seems here to have had a strong effect. It is usually
the very active, domineering mother who provokes the hatred
of the daughter and nourishes strong self-exactions in her.

The feminine-passive type displays considerably fewer
reactive features. In this case the original tender, loving,
and more passive dependence on the mother seems to weather
all the stormy periods of hatred that must be expected in the
development of every girl. Many women of this type appear
to have taken the mother's part against the father's from
earliest youth. The common grief of being neglected by the
father, or the premature loss of the father, combined with the
mother's loving kindness, create an emotional relationship
with her that involves great dangers. The continuation
of this early infantile tie to the mother may lead to very
childish and passive dependence upon her. The tendency
to definite forms of hysteria, particularly those with organic
symptoms, is conected with this kind of mother relationship.[6]
Certain forms of homosexuality likewise belong here.

If the dangers are successfully avoided in the course of

[6] COBB, S.: Borderlines of psychiatry. Harvard University Press, 1943.

further development, a thoroughly positive relation to the mother seems to lead to an ideal outcome; it supplies a contribution toward and perhaps even a basic condition for the development of the feminine woman.

Observation seems to show that normal feminine-passive women, even in complete adulthood, also reveal certain tendencies to infantilism that often manifest themselves in body structure, voice, gestures, etc., even where the physiologic functions are normal. In contrast to them, feminine-active women are more robust, with larger bones than the other types of feminine women, or with a width through the pelvis that reminds us of their reproductive function.

During their depressive moods (to which they have a normally human disposition), psychologic contents associated with guilt feelings predominate in the feminine-active type; the feminine-passive type is more prone to feelings of solitude and nostalgia; she prefers to brood and become absorbed in herself. A somewhat more obvious remainder of her mother tie manifests itself in the form of an intensified urge to eat. The compulsive nature of this urge is revealed in frequent trips to the ice box or in the consumption of huge quantities of sweets, which cannot be replaced by cigarettes, even in the case of passionate smokers. These little eating obsessions usually remain within normal proportions and can be overcome by will power. It is interesting to note that in such cases depression seems to coincide with signs of childish longing for the mother, the first food giver.

Although all of them are capable of love, and in most of them heterosexual love is a condition of their existence, feminine-passive-erotic women do not content themselves with *love* alone; they need the ecstasy, sufferings, and bliss of *being in love*.

The types described above should not be confused with others that outwardly resemble them but are essentially different.

There are, for example, women who know only *being in love*

but not *love;* in other words, they can experience love only as an uncritically overestimating ecstasy of feeling that has nothing to do with the real value of the object. Happiness here consists in the complete gratification of the unconscious determinants of the love relation, rather than in harmonious object love with its real overcoming of ambivalence. As soon as the ecstasy has passed, the love disappears. What remains is indifference or hatred with regard to the man so ardently loved before. Partly to escape the guilt feelings connected with hatred, partly to make up for the loss, the woman begins to devaluate the formerly overestimated object. But for the most part this is an automatic process in which all the negative feelings and anxieties overcompensated and suppressed by the ecstasy now come to the fore. All the former love happiness is distorted in memory, and only the seamy side of the relationship is recalled. The intensive process of overestimating infatuation swings in the opposite direction, all the good qualities of the object are denied, and his defects are tremendously exaggerated. The woman who only a short time ago was ardently in love feels cheated and disappointed, no matter whether her lover deserted her or she deserted him. Closer examination shows that this woman loved only a phantom, a fictitious ideal to which she temporarily gave a real name. After a shorter or longer period she experiences the same love enthusiasm for another phantom, and this will suffer the same fate. These women are in their behavior like the type who, driven by their narcissistic hunger, always want to be ardently desired and to experience their object's love ecstasy. Both types are incapable of love, but in the latter type of woman it is her own need to be in love that gives her the illusion of loving. This woman also seems to be much more disturbed in her emotional life than the other.

In striking contrast to this type, our feminine woman, despite her longing for the ecstasies of being in love, has a very great capacity for real love. In her, unless severe disappointments exert a disturbing effect, the acute state of infatuation usually passes over into love. She is also capable of repeatedly experiencing love ecstasy in relation to her chosen object because she loves him—provided of course that her erotic conditions are fulfilled.

The feminine-active type, even though capable of love ecstasy, is willing to choose a life companion according to the demands of her ego and the objective value of her choice, his social position, etc., and she can be happy and satisfied in such a partnership. The instinctual wishes that in her case are often frustrated are successfully repressed.

More or less erotic, more or less dependent on love for their happiness, the women described here are the prototype of femininity as a psychologic concept. They bring this sharply defined personality into all their life situations, from sexual love to the highest sublimations. We meet these types among charwomen, cooks, and nurses, in offices and in the church. They are also capable of the most spiritual sublimations. The more passive ones completely develop their deepest natures when they engage in occupations that give full play to their intuition—that is to say, artistic and psychologic work. They also fulfill their destinies when, silent and in the background, they inspire their husbands, always stimulating, encouraging, and understanding them.

The more active ones are, by their psychologic constitution, creators and organizers in all the departments of peaceful life. Destruction and preparation for destruction is not their domain. All these women are valuable if they develop their feminine peculiarity in the sense described above.

They differ among themselves according to their education, nationality, religion, race, and the period in which they live. But their essential kernel always remains the same. We find this type of woman even in prehistoric times as Autonoë, the Intuitive One, in whom dwells the feeling of what is right and what is wrong, who is wise and understanding even though lacking that strength of intellect which is man's instrument for acquiring knowledge.

All these women, in so far as they remain within the normal limits of their psychologic structure, show complete sexual readiness toward their partners, provided, however, that certain definite conditions are fulfilled. Because of their passivity, in them more than in any other type the awakening of the orgastic response depends largely on the man's ability to arouse the existing readiness and overcome the normal inhibition. What is in question here is not at all the so frequently overstressed and even ridiculous demand made upon men by several sexologists, that they heighten the woman's erotic excitability (in the physical sense) by their dexterity. The road to the feminine woman as a sexual object leads through the psyche, and all the four fundamental factors noted above must be taken into account if her conditions are to be met. Her inhibition can be strengthened as a result of her narcissism, masochism, tie to former objects, and motherliness; and each of these four factors, if present to an excessive degree, can become a source of frigidity. Especially in favor of the last-named component does the feminine woman often renounce orgastic gratification, without in the least suffering in her psychic health. But even if motherliness is not involved, she often tolerates her own sexual inhibition without losing her all-embracing warmth and harmony.

CHAPTER SIX

Feminine Passivity

IN OUR preceding discussions we have repeatedly referred to woman's passivity and have held it largely responsible for the specifically feminine sublimations and the nature of feminine personality. Freud[1] came to question his own initial assumption that the "masculine" is identical with the "active" and the "feminine" with the "passive." He points out that while in the animal world the aggressions that initiate the sexual act do usually emanate from the male, in some species the male's activity is restricted to copulation, and in all the other functions the females are the stronger and more active partners. He illustrates his point by citing the much discussed behavior of various female spiders that are passive in the sexual act, but extremely active in all the other processes of life.

It is interesting to note that man's unconscious considers the spider a "masculine female," and in dreams and folklore it serves as the symbol of the "phallic" or "masculine" woman. This suggests that the connection between "activity" and "masculinity" is deeply rooted in our mental life.

It cannot be denied that the animal world contains examples of females that also play an active role in the process of copulation. To mention only a few: the female of a certain species of cricket (*Nemobius sylvestris*) is the sole active partner and mounts the male, who is stretched out motionless, from the rear. (The males of all other *Locustidae* are, however, extremely active.) In several species of butterflies, the male approaches the female very actively and takes possession of her in an aggressive manner, but after penetration has been effected, a complicated position is assumed by the pair, in which the

[1] FREUD, S.: New introductory lectures on psychoanalysis, p. 156.

male clings passively to the female, who drags him along in her flight.

Among the mammals likewise the activity of the female is strongly marked in certain cases. Meisenheimer's book *Geschlecht und Geschlechter* ("Sex and Species")[2] contains observations, made in detailed investigations, that frequently take note of this activity of the female. Yet the same book contains the following passage: "In the processes of copulation it is the male animal and its organism that display activity; the passive role belongs to the female. Only rarely is this relation reversed." Thus, even though the cases of female activity are fairly numerous, they are only exceptions to the general rule.

If the sexual "passivity" of the female is generally regarded as typical, it still remains to be seen to what extent other, nonsexual manifestations of woman's life are patterned after this behavior.

The theory that I have long supported[3]—according to which feminity is largely associated with passivity and masochism—has been confirmed in the course of years by clinical observations. All my views on this subject are based on clinical experience, and daily observations of animals have strengthened my conviction that my theory is correct.

Viewed in retrospect, the evolution of the sexual act seems to show that the female's passivity in this act came to the fore at the very moment when external fecundation was replaced by internal fecundation. But for a long time after that her passivity was not identical with her subordination. The sexual stimulation came from her, and for a considerable period in the evolution of the species the time of copulation was determined by the female. Among the higher mammals, the male seeks out the female, becomes excited by her proximity through his sensory organs, and tries to conquer her. The

---

[2] MEISENHEIMER, J.: Geschlecht und Geschlechter. Jena: Fischer, 1921.

[3] DEUTSCH, H.: The significance of masochism in the mental life of women. Internat. J. Psycho-Analysis, vol. 11, 1930.

female, although bound by evolutionary transformations of the sexual stimulation to community with the male, has from the earliest times preserved an initial indifference and independence with regard to him. At first she flees his wooing, and she must gradually be won or overpowered by him.

In the animal world the rhythm of sexual activity is determined by the female. This is most clearly seen in those species in which the male reproductive cells detach themselves after the ova are deposited. This feature of sexual life is preserved up to the highly developed organism of the mammal. The ovum fecundated internally before it leaves the mother's body enjoys much more favorable conditions of development than the ovum fertilized outside, where it is exposed to a number of hazards that can easily prove fatal. As the female organism does not produce mature eggs continuously, but only at definite periods, the sexual activity of the male obviously has to depend on these periods. Among the higher animals, the female has genital secretions at the time of maturation of the ovum. These secretions enhance the sexual impulse of the male and his activity designed to conquer the female; and it is during these periods—and only during these periods— that she shows herself accessible to the male's desire for sexual intercourse. The female's willingness has a passive-receptive character, although in this phase she displays all the symptoms of heightened excitation and motor agitation.

In the human species this law still seems to assert itself to some extent. Here too the last vestiges of rhythmically heightened sexual willingness in woman can be recognized. But because of further evolutionary transformations, this old rhythm has now almost entirely disappeared in the sexual intercourse of men and women. The woman's sexual activity no longer follows the stirrings of her own rhythm or the summons of the reproductive function. She has obviously subordinated herself to the sexual will and domination of the male. At the same time, the male's sexuality has followed an opposite course of development and made itself almost completely

independent of the female rhythm. How was such a paradoxic situation brought about? What factors caused this
development that is contrary to the old law that the rhythm
of sexual activity in both sexes is dependent upon maturation
of the ovum?

Our hypothesis is that with the final differentiation of the
human species, with the displacement of the body's center of
gravity, the development of the upright posture, and the
formation of powerful prehensile appendages, the male could
free himself from his dependence upon the feminine rhythm
and take sexual possession of the female even without her consent. It is no exaggeration to say that among all living
creatures, only man, because of his prehensile appendages, is
capable of rape in the full meaning of this term—that is, sexual
possession of the female against her will. Every time I see
one of the numerous pictures in popular movies or magazines
showing an anthropomorphous ape or a powerful, bearlike
masculine creature with a completely helpless female in his
arms, I am reminded of my old favorite speculation: thus it was
that primitive man took possession of woman and subjected
her to sexual desire. Interestingly enough, in many myths
and fantasy formations, brutal possession is interpreted as a
kindly act of rescue. Thus the ape with his powerful arms, or
the bear, saves the girl from a threatening disaster that is
mostly of a sexual nature—and the threat comes from someone
else, not from the rescuer. In young girls' dreams the mighty
hairy human-animal figure often appears not as a seducer, but
as a savior from sexual dangers. This metamorphosis of the
seducer into a savior reveals the wish-fulfilling character of the
girl's dreams and her masochistic longings, which reproduce
the situation of the primitive conquered woman.

We conjecture that the sexual act, which originally was an
act of violence, and which the woman, weaker and more taxed
by the reproductive function than the man, could not resist,
was gradually transformed for her into an act of pleasure. The
violent penetration and mighty embrace, perhaps accompanied

by wooing and caresses, thus became the woman's sexual enjoyment. Her dependence upon the sexual rhythm was broken, and the act of pleasure was separated from the reproductive function. If further speculation is permissible, I should like to advance the hypothesis that the powerful embrace of the prehensile arms, combined with the defensive counterpressure, induced strong pleasure sensations in the woman's entire body. The particular disposition in the feminine skin surface to be pleasurably excited perhaps originates in these primitive situations. The psychoanalytic hypothesis that this quality of woman's skin can be explained by the anatomic sex difference, and corresponds to a transfer from the unsatisfactory genitals to the entire body, does not necessarily contradict my hypothesis. The latter is beautifully illustrated in the Greek myth of the seduction of Leda by Zeus. The story of the god who assumes the shape of a swan and envelops the woman with his plumage seems to express the feminine wish to feel the seducer's might with the whole surface of her body.

If my phylogenetic hypothesis is correct, the wooing and possession of the human female involved the surface of her body before her genital zone came into play, while the male was already in a state of definite genital excitation that drove him to active or aggressive behavior. This very ancient development seems to me to be the prototype of a definite sexual sensitivity that has persisted to this day. The stronger need for tenderness characteristic of the woman, her need for the embrace as a prelude or even a prerequisite to sexual excitement, would according to this view be a primitive feminine quality, perhaps a continuation of the primitive situation. Her more developed desire for contact has a thoroughly passive character that also plays a part in the differentiation of the sexes.

This behavior is repeated in the functions of the sexual cells: the ovum is relatively motionless, passively expectant, while the spermatozoid is active and mobile. The behavior of the sexual partners during intercourse continues this differentiation between the masculine-active and the feminine-passive. The anatomy of the sex organs leaves no doubt as to the character of their aims: the masculine organ is made for active penetration, the feminine for passive reception. The objection that many and even most normal women develop a high degree of activity during sexual intercourse does not refute the view presented here. There are facts that seemingly contradict the natural law but are nevertheless of great significance. They are secondary forms of behavior, for the most part psychologically determined. Woman's protest against her passive role and her tendency to identification may play a part in this active behavior.

So far, physiology and anatomy support our view. Our further task will be to ascertain to what extent this organic disposition expresses itself in the total psychologic picture of the feminine personality. Up until this point, our attempt to defend the view that femininity is characterized by passivity related only to the sexual functions. It might be sufficient to point out here that psychoanalysis has demonstrated the great influence that sexuality exerts on all other manifestations of life; but actually this theory has never denied the fact that all psychic phenomena are influenced by education, the social order, cultural conditions, and similar factors. Nor must it be forgotten that, in addition to the sexual drives, psychoanalysis takes into account other important psychic forces whose power often proves greater and more decisive than that of sexuality. For instance, the analytic interpretation of neurotic conflicts is based on the assumption of factors that directly oppose the drives of sexuality and so create conflicts. In its investigations of human psychology, psychoanalysis has never ignored the interaction of the psychic, inner forces, nor has it failed to note the constant interplay between the outer and the inner world.

Nevertheless, while fully recognizing that woman's position is subjected to external influences, I venture to say that the fundamental identities "feminine-passive" and "masculine-active" assert themselves in all known cultures and races, in various forms and various quantitative proportions. Margaret Mead's interesting anthropologic study[4] of a primitive tribe in which women play an active and aggressive role, while men perform social functions regarded elsewhere as feminine, seems to prove no more than does the sexual behavior of several animal species in which the roles of the partners are reversed. Such exceptions cannot change the general principle; and we can assume that this principle will continue to assert itself until we succeed in influencing the internal, hormonal constitution of the human body. But even then the anatomy of the sexes, which is surely less subject to modification, will exercise its veto. The reproductive function too will have to undergo radical transformations before entirely new paths are opened to feminine activity.

Experimental data collected by psychoanalysts show that very often woman resists this characteristic given her by nature and, in spite of certain advantages she derives from it, displays many modes of behavior that suggest that she is not entirely content with her own constitution. Our task will be to find out how woman's personality develops against this constitutional background and what ways and means she has at her disposal to preserve her feminine nature and, at the same time, to ward off and master the dangers for the ego that are inherent in passivity and masochism.

We have seen that the feminine woman finds these means in her own ego. We have also found that passivity, while it is the central attribute of femininity, is a relative concept. Many active tendencies can accompany this passivity—and this does not contradict our conception of the feminine woman. Only if the methods of coping with passivity that we see used by our feminine women proves unsuccessful, does woman's

[4] MEAD, M.: Sex and temperament in three primitive societies. New York: Morrow, 1935.

dissatisfaction with her own constitution come to the fore. The expression of this dissatisfaction, combined with attempts to remedy it, result in woman's "masculinity complex."

For a long time psychoanalytic research made this masculinity complex responsible for many typical manifestations of femininity, and as a result the independent significance of many of woman's psychologic processes was denied. Her positive achievements were usually interpreted as a successful sublimation of tendencies contained in this complex, while a number of her neurotic conflicts and specific traits of feminine character were believed to result from her lack of a penis.

There is no doubt that penis envy exists in woman's psyche and has a great influence on the development of her personality. But the theory that makes penis envy the basis of her most essential conflicts is untenable. Penis envy is generally ascribed to the reaction experienced by the little girl when she first sees the masculine organ; even a priori it seems unlikely that a trauma of external and accidental origin should play a fundamental part in the formation of feminine personality. As we shall see later, penis envy is not a primary factor, but a secondary one; it is essentially due not to external but to internal developments; and if we did not realize this before, it is because we mistook the rationalization of the genital trauma for the trauma itself.[5]

While the importance of penis envy cannot be denied, a full understanding of woman's passivity can be obtained only from an investigation of the development of her sexual instincts and her ego. We shall now take up the first part of this task and study passivity as a result of the girl's instinctual development in so far as it is determined by her anatomy. In doing this, we must first of all keep in mind that at all periods of the child's development, when one kind of gratification is given up it is always compensated by another. For instance, when the child gives up the oral gratification of the

[5] According to E. Jones, "the sight of the boy's penis is not the sole traumatic event that changes her life; it is only the last link in a long chain": Papers on Psychoanalysis. London: Bailliere, 1938, p. 615.

nursing period, the mother (or whoever takes her place) associates the new method of feeding with the tenderness formerly connected with breast feeding, and the pleasure of being suckled is replaced by that of sucking. In addition, the child now derives pleasure from its excretory functions. During this period, the child's ego grows and his interests are not limited to the gratification of his sexual instincts. New sources of pleasure are available—the active conquest of the outside world in all its forms, new relations to objects, etc. Thus we see that the possibilities of gratification have two sources—direct instinctual satisfaction and the child's relationship to the environment, a relationship that grows gradually more independent of the sexual instincts.

The last or phallic phase of the little boy's sexual development is concentrated around an organ whose full activity he can enjoy until fears and prohibitions compel him to renounce his pleasure in it. The immense importance of the fear of castration in man results from his high valuation of his own genital organ. It must not be supposed that this valuation has a purely narcissistic origin. It is the dynamic energy, the physiologically conditioned urge that manifests itself in masturbation, that endows this organ with its importance and makes it the focus of the little boy's interests and fears. This urge has not only an active character; it also contains more elementary infantile aggressive tendencies. These express themselves in the boy's entire personality during this period. His pugnacity, which in the eyes of the grown-up observer is a troublesome, perfectly useless activity, is an expression of this aggressive need, in the gratification of which the healthy normal boy feels happiest. By and by he can transfer his activity and aggression to other forces within him. The drive for adjustment to reality, active sublimation, and the growth of his ego will now engross him for several years. He needs no compensation for his loss of gratification, because he has new possibilities of gratification in other fields.

But how about the girl? She too as a result of her heightened genital urge needs an organ in which this urge can be focused. The clitoris is the only part of her genital apparatus available for this purpose. Hence in girls the phallic phase is also called the "clitoris phase." We can disregard here the common embryonic origin of this organ and the penis; its anatomic structure, tumescent character, innervation, and erectility make the clitoris an organ comparable to the penis. The comparison must naturally prove unfavorable to the clitoris, because this organ lacks the forward thrusting, penetrating qualities of the penis.

It might be assumed that either the little girl's sexual excitability is from the outset less active and intensive than the boy's, or that she has an inferior organ with which to attain the same instinctual goals. Actually it seems that both these assumptions are correct and that two factors are at play in the girl's sexual development: on the one hand, her instincts are constitutionally less active and aggressive than the boy's; on the other hand, psychoanalysis has discovered a sufficient amount of active-aggressive components in the little girl's fantasy life to support the view that her genital organ is an inadequate outlet for them. Although in some cases this organ can be touched and seen, its development is often so rudimentary that it can barely be considered an organ. As a result, the little girl is frequently "organless" in the phallic (clitoris) phase of her development. But even girls in whom the clitoris is more developed go through a period of rising and actively directed instinctual energy for which this organ can only prove inadequate. This inadequacy is probably one of the motives that induce little girls to give up masturbation during the clitoris period of their childhood. The assertion they so frequently make at this period, that they once had a penis, stems now from sources other than the later lying boasts: although it is based on a false inference, the feeling behind it is real. According to many mothers who are good observers of their children, the transfer of the alleged posession to the past appears as a rule after the little girl has given up masturbation. Her obscure memories of the clitoris activity during the masturbation period seem to lead her subsequently to endow the clitoris with the reality value of an adequate organ that existed in the past.[6]

We feel compelled to assume that this real inability of the organ to gratify the active and aggressive instinctual impulses must entail important consequences. In the first place—and this is in contrast with the boy's behavior—those impulses that need an active organ are given up. Thus the inadequacy of the organ can be considered a biologic and physiologic cause of the psychologic sex differences. If this is so, we are dealing here with a normal occurrence, and we should expect that its consequences follow a biologically predetermined path that leads to the further development of femininity. However, the clinical material at our disposal shows that this path is in reality extremely circuitous. While in the preceding phases, when one method of instinctual gratification fails, it is automatically replaced by another, this time the process is attended by many complications, and to understand it one must follow it from the beginning. The consequences of the inhibition that now takes place in the operation of the actively directed instincts may be twofold. One consequence is the attempt to overcome the inhibition, an attempt attended by all the reactions that lie within the framework of the female castration complex (p. 317). The other is to be found in the line of normal feminine development that is in accordance with the girl's constitutional predisposition, that is to say, the inhibited activity undergoes a turn toward passivity. The place of the active organ is taken by a passive-receptive one, the vagina. This process does take place, but later; and the aggravating and portentous element in the process is that between the turn to passivity and the full availibility of the corresponding organ a long period of time elapses, during which the little girl does not have this organ at her disposal— at this moment of development it is simply not there! Thus the little girl is for the second time confronted with organless-

---

[6] Rado's "illusory penis" seems to stem from this fantasy. Psychoanalyt. Quart., vol. 2, 1933.

ness: the first time she lacked an active organ, now she lacks
a passive organ.   It is only these two events together that
produce her genital trauma.   As we have seen, the consequences of the first may be the manifestations of the castration
complex.   We regard as the consequences of the second the
mobilization of regressive tendencies.   The little girl's feminine
fantasies are centered on other passive organs: the anal and
oral components of the sexual instincts reappear.[7]   The
anxieties and fantasies relating to childbirth and all other
sexual contents are tied up with alimentary and excretory
functions; they accompany woman into her adult years and
often give rise to hysterical somatic symptoms connected with
these functions.   The vagina—a completely passive, receptive
organ—awaits an active agent to become a functioning excitable organ.

   In the psychologic material gathered from the analyses of
adult women, particularly neurotic ones, we find repeated
expressions of the lack of an organ, feelings of inferiority, etc.
According to my present view, the assumption that these complaints result from the lack of a penis is one-sided.   Their real
origin is the fact that during a period of biologic development
in which the inadequacy of an organ leads to a constitutionally
predetermined transformation of the active tendencies into
passive ones, no ready organ exists for the latter—in other
words, the little girl continues to be organless in a functional
sense.   Her genital trauma, with its numerous consequent
manifestations, lies between the Scylla of having no penis
and the Charybdis of lacking the responsiveness of the vagina.

   One might keep faith in the purposefulness of nature and
find a deeper meaning in the fact that among the developmental
processes in the girl something takes place that looks like a
short circuit.   Logically these processes should result in the
functional readiness of the vagina to intercept the sexual
stimulations and thus prepare the feminine organ for its

[7] DEUTSCH, H.: Psychoanalyse der weiblichen Sexualfunktionen.

future functions.   But, as we have seen, this is not the case. True, several authors support the view that the vagina shows itself even in childhood.   Josine Mueller,[8] for instance, reports from her practice some cases of obvious vaginal activity in children.

According to K. Horney,[9] our failure to perceive the existence of the vagina in childhood more clearly is due to a negation and repression of it.   She assumes that vaginal sensations and psychologic contents relating to them exist in childhood. It is undeniable that fantasies of masochistic-passive character appear at an early age, and, as Melanie Klein has pointed out,[10] they are characterized by particular cruelty.   Dismemberment of the "insides" through the penetration of a gigantic body and through the expulsion of a child are often found in the little girl's fantasy life.   But I believe that such ideas have nothing to do with vaginal sensations.   They refer to the internal organs of the body, that is to say, the stomach and intestines, and the paths of penetration and expulsion are represented by the mouth and the anus.   The cruelty of these fantasies corresponds to the strength of the aggressions directed inward.   Thus, what seems to be in preparation for later femininity during the childhood phase is passivity and masochism; what is added subsequently, if the development is favorable, is their *correct elaboration* and the discovery of the vagina as a functioning organ.

I should like to clarify my theory that the vagina is not a functioning sexual organ in childhood by an example that shows that when the tension of a need is felt in an organ, even in an organ whose goals are passive and receptive, arrangements are made for gratifying this need.   I refer to the child's oral needs, and I have in mind not only suckling.   It can be observed that children whose oral needs are not suf-

---

[8] MUELLER, J.: A contribution to the problem of libidinal development of the genital phase in girls.   Internat. J. Psycho-Analysis, vol. 13, 1932.
[9] HORNEY, K.: The denial of the vagina.   Internat. J. Psycho-Analysis, vol. 14, 1933.
[10] KLEIN, M.: The psychoanalysis of children.   London: Hogarth, 1932.

ficiently gratified stick everything into their mouths—often in a frantic fashion—whether they are hungry or not. Such a child, if satiated, will vigorously protest against taking any more food and yet will put in its mouth a pacifier, nipple, or any other object. It is generally known that children who are deprived of this sucking gratification are disturbed in their sleep. The association of this urge with the pleasure of eating is not the chief cause of its persistence. The newborn child sticks its fingers in its mouth before being fed, and the restlessness of babies upon awakening can for some time be eliminated only by sucking. Personal observation has made me suspect that our patients' reproaches against their mothers, and their feelings of having been injured that go back to the period of weaning, do not always and not solely relate to the withdrawal of their mothers' milk-giving breasts. Children who because of educational prejudices were consistently kept from sucking are particularly prone to develop a reaction to this deprivation that lasts a long time. The analogy of the mouth is all the more valid because the subsequent sucking-receptive function of the vagina strongly resembles that of the mouth.

Although we see in the child reactions to the deprivation of sucking, we find no sign of an analogous vaginal urge sufficient to drive the little girl to actions such as sticking objects into her vagina, etc. From time to time we observe manifestations that seem to imply vaginal sensations—manipulations with the hand, even impulsive sticking of objects into the genitals, etc. But a careful study of these observations shows that all such actions have nothing in common with *spontaneous* vaginal sensations and that their causes are usually external: worms, catarrh of the bladder, washing procedures, or direct seduction. Acute irritations of the posterior vaginal wall through the anus, as a result of constipation and enemas, are often mistaken for vaginal irritations.[11]

---

[11] DEUTSCH, H.: Op. cit. I am greatly indebted to Dr. F. Clothier, of the New England Home for Little Wanderers, for her kindness in putting her own observations of a large number of children at my disposal. These show that excessive vaginal masturbation in little girls is almost always the result of a previous seduction.

A further proof that the vagina has no independent function during childhood is the fact that even when the little girl's passive-masochistic tendencies assert themselves in masturbatory activities, these remain tied to the clitoris. I am able absolutely to confirm Fenichel's observations[12] on this score. It is as though the clitoris offered its services to the feminine tendencies after having failed to serve the active tendencies. In many women the clitoris retains this function throughout life, and very frequently the childish masturbation of the clitoris turns out to be particularly important. If the little girl renounced every sexual function as a result of her double organlessness during the period of excitation, she would be exposed to the danger of losing her capacity for obtaining any sexual gratification—the danger of aphanisis, as E. Jones has called it.[13]

The awakening of the vagina to full sexual functioning is entirely dependent upon the man's activity; and this absence of spontaneous vaginal activity constitutes the physiologic background of feminine passivity. The competition of the clitoris, which intercepts the excitations unable to reach the vagina, and the genital trauma then create the dispositional basis of a permanent sexual inhibition, i.e., frigidity.[14] It is this disposition acquired in childhood that is responsible for the very large number of frigid women. It goes without saying that overcoming of the inhibition depends upon subsequent psychic events and especially upon the events of puberty. For instance, a neurotic illness is often responsible for a given woman's inability to overcome her predisposition to frigidity. On the other hand, one can see even extremely severe neuroses that do not diminish potential sexual sensitiveness; inversely, they are psychically healthy women who have not been able to overcome their sexual inhibition but tolerate it well.[15]

[12] FENICHEL, O.: Weiteres zur preoedipalen Phase der Mädchen. Internat. Ztschr. f. Psychoanal., vol. 22, 1934.

[13] JONES, E.: Early development of female sexuality. Papers on psychoanalysis, p. 558.

[14] DEUTSCH, H.: The significance of masochism in the mental life of women.

[15] IDEM: Psychoanalyse der weiblichen Sexualfunktionen.

Very often in such cases the sexual energy is diverted to the reproductive functions, and motherliness fully takes the place of sexuality. That the social restrictions upon feminine sexuality can intensify the dispositional inhibition is indisputable.

We can now leave the problem involved in the origin of feminine passivity and turn to another connected with it, namely, penis envy and its consequences. But as we do not intend to place upon it all the responsibility for the girl's feelings of envy, we must go back a little farther.

I believe that every child, boy or girl, whatever its situation in the family, whether loved and pampered or neglected and unappreciated, an only child or one among many, reacts with great envy to the birth of a brother or sister. It envies everything: what the new child has and what it has not. The little boy does not notice that he has an advantage over his little sister. If he is sufficiently advanced in his development, this discovery arouses his fear, because he is already involved in genital anxiety. If he is still little and interested in the urinary function, he notices that the new child lacks something; he reacts with interest to this discovery, but his principal feeling is that of envy over the love, care, food, etc., enjoyed by the newcomer. The birth of a rival makes him experience a new feeling or strengthens an old one. According to his development, his envy has an oral character and bears upon the alimentary processes or refers chiefly to the excretory functions and cleansing procedures.

The little girl's envy likewise is excited by rivalry, and, just as in the case of the boy, this envy bears upon everything the new child receives, whether she herself has the same or not. There are also adults who envy others regardless of their own possessions. When the little girl is still very young, she is not very much impressed by her little brother's penis. She is more interested in his excretory processes and often herself begins to behave like a baby in this respect, in order to be like the little intruder. She is jealous over the physical care given him, or else she feels terribly offended because her mother fails to appreciate her merit in being clean and loves the dirty little one just as much as herself. Out of revenge she soils herself and may for the rest of her life retain something of this reaction— "it is not worth while being good and trying to earn praise, for one is not appreciated anyhow."

Out of this general tendency to envy, the little girl may develop a penis envy even if she regards the possession of the penis as an inferiority of the newborn baby; and this happens quite frequently. I once had a case of perversion—a woman who could be sexually aroused only by humpbacked men—that involved just such an evaluation of the penis as an abnormality. Little girls, especially if they had no brothers before, often say: "Oh, I had this thing, too," or "I have one, too." In this they are conscious pseudologists who out of pride refuse to admit that they do not possess something. Many girls imagine that all babies have something like a penis when they are little and do not need it any more when they grow older. This view is very popular and is sometimes used as self-consolation when envy is aroused. On the other hand we can observe that little girls from whom we do not yet expect any real genital interest display symptoms of violent penis envy. They reach out for the organ of a brother or playmate and with great feeling express the wish to take it away from him. Such a wish is an expression of envy, but it has not yet the significance that it will acquire later in the girl's development; it only expresses an envious desire for possession common to all children and extending to everything they see in others and do not have themselves. It is true, however, that even at this stage early characterologic differences can be noted in children. These early envy reactions partly determine how the girl will react to the genital trauma later, in the clitoris phase. As for the characterologic reaction, it will depend to a great extent upon the influences of the environment, above all upon the kind of preparations made for the expected new child, the home atmosphere, the mother's behavior toward the child, etc. In short, the influence of the environment on character formation has achieved its effect before the new impressions begin to operate. And it must not be forgotten that every child is born with a specific characterologic disposition.

The child's tendency to envy also expresses itself independently of the birth of a new sister or brother. An only child manifests envy every time the interest of the persons around it, especially the mother, seems diverted from the child to something else. We do not intend here to analyze in detail the psychologic differences between an only child and a child that has brothers or sisters. We desire only to stress that envy as a characterologic property of children of both sexes manifests itself at a very early stage, regardless of the presence or absence of brothers or sisters, and independently of the genital interest.

The anatomic difference becomes significant only in that phase of the girl's development in which her genitals (that is to say, her clitoris) assume functional importance. I recall an observation of many years ago that was later confirmed by Jones,[16] Rado,[17] and Lampl–de Groot.[18] An 18-month-old girl displayed complete indifference at sight of the penis; only later, in the period of heightened interest in her own genitals, did she develop a strong emotional reaction to the phenomenon. I reiterate my view that in this phase processes with a traumatic effect take place in the girl regardless of whether outside impressions have produced a real basis for the development of penis envy or not.

These internal processes create in the girl a heightened interest in her own and other people's genitals. She encounters two types of reactions in the outside world—first the prohibition of her mother, who is particularly alert during this period, then the actions of her brother, cousin, or little neighbor who wants to see and above all to show. In this way the girl discovers the difference and, as a result, develops reactions whose intensity and effect will depend on previously existing factors. These

[16] JONES, E.: Papers on psychoanalysis, p. 562.
[17] RADO, S.: Fear of castration in women. Psychoanalyt. Quart. 2: 425, 1933.
[18] LAMPL–DE GROOT, J.: The evolution of the Oedipus complex in women. Internat. J. Psycho-Analysis 9: 332, 1928.

are on the one hand her characterologic development, especially her disposition to envy, and, on the other, the strength of the genital trauma, which in turn depends upon the strength of the sexual urge, masturbatory processes, etc. Penis envy and its consequences develop in the soil thus prepared.

But the process may also have an opposite sequence. The perception of the anatomic difference between the sexes may heighten the girl's interest in her own genitals and induce her to exciting investigations of it. The excitement in this case has been prepared by internal instinctual processes but is provoked from the outside, and thus from the outset appears connected with penis envy.

Later the sequence of events is blurred, and in the analysis of adults it is impossible to separate the primary genital trauma from penis envy. I believe that this chronologic confusion is responsible for the mistaken theory that the difficulties of woman's development are caused by her penis envy. This theory displaces the emphasis from a constitutional difficulty of development to a secondary affective and characterologic reaction to it.

Let us briefly recapitulate our analyses. In her instinctual development the little girl encounters a difficulty. This difficulty may either have general, normal consequences, or lead to more individual or abnormal reactions. We have discussed the former: they contribute to normal feminine passivity and, as we shall see later, to masochism. The latter can have a disturbing character and are an indication that the difficulty was not mastered and had a really traumatic effect. These traumatic reactions are extremely varied, and we designate them collectively as the female castration complex. Penis envy plays an important part in it as one of the forms in which the trauma manifests itself; sometimes this envy provokes the trauma, but it is never the primary cause of it. The girl's discovery of her anatomic difference from the boy is for her the confirmation of a lack that she has previously felt herself—its rationalization, so to speak. She gives an internal process real content by projecting it in the outside world. "Such an organ does exist," she seems to think," so I am right in feeling the lack of it!" Penis envy will depend, as we have said, upon the girl's characterologic disposition and upon the other conditions outlined above. We have also admitted the possibility of a reverse sequence.

Thus the inner conflict is projected into reality and, as a result, all the later reactions seem to be caused exclusively by the real discovery of the penis. We are familiar with such rationalizations from many other psychologic situations. Probably the discovery of the penis has intensifying and consolidating effects; at any rate it is a real experience and provokes manifestations of envy. The little girl now wants consciously to possess the organ and she gives her wish a very real content: here is a positive possession that can serve various purposes (playing, urinating).[19] But the really dynamic cause of penis envy lies deeper and is the prerequisite to the real experience.

Even though penis envy has secondary and traumatic significance, it is a component of the feminine soul that so regularly appears in analytic treatment that we must regard it as "normal." Only when it is excessive and has disturbing effects does it acquire an abnormal character. Nor does it remain isolated in the psychic structure; rather, it associates itself with various other psychologic contents, is intensified and often brought to the fore only by them, and in such combinations becomes a part or the center of the feminine masculinity complex that we shall discuss later.

[19] HORNEY, K.; On the genesis of the castration complex. Internat. J. Psycho-Analysis, vol. 5, 1924.

CHAPTER SEVEN

Feminine Masochism

W E HAVE dealt with the genesis of feminine passivity in so far as it is connected with the genital trauma and the fate of the sexual instincts. This part of our analysis thus took cognizance only of woman's sexual tendencies. But even though we ascribe great power to the influence of sexuality on the personality as a whole, "we must remember," as Freud[1] put it, "that an individual woman may be a human being apart from this." Hence we must look for other sources of feminine passivity. Methodologically it seems simpler to discuss these sources together with the problem of feminine masochism. These two problems are not identical, but the origins of masochism and passivity are intimately connected. They are both the outcome of the feminine constitution and of a mechanism of instinctual reversion related to it that turns energies directed toward the outer world inward; and in so far as activity is concerned, we have considered passivity simply as a state of inhibition.

We know that the child's activity and entire instinctual life are strongly impregnated with aggressive tendencies, and we assume that whenever the activity is inhibited, the aggressive tendencies suffer the same fate. Their dynamic force does not allow them to remain in a state of mere inhibition, they continue to be active, and only their direction changes. This aggression turned against one's own ego would lead to dangerous self-destruction if the process were not subjected to further transformation. Freud[2] assumes that the "development of strong masochistic impulses has the effect of binding erotically

[1] FREUD, S.: The psychology of women. New introductory lectures on psychoanalysis, p. 185.
[2] Ibid., p. 158.

the destructive tendencies that have been turned inward."
This hypothetic assumption rests upon another hypothesis,
namely, that such masochistic impulses were present earlier,
before the aggressive turn, and now are further strengthened.
We do not intend here to attempt a solution of this problem.
Perhaps the interplay between narcissism and masochism that
we invoked for explaining feminine psychology has a prehistory,
a period during which narcissistic self-love mastered the destructive impulse directed against the ego, creating a disposition to masochism.   In this process self-love achieves a complete triumph, for normal women display no signs of a tendency
to inflict physical pain and moral suffering *upon themselves* in
order to derive pleasure from such actions.   Only later, in relation to the world of objects and in various acts connected with
the feminine reproductive functions, is their tendency to associate pleasure and pain revealed.

To avoid misunderstandings, we must differentiate feminine
masochism from "moral" masochism, which is a consequence of
the unconscious feeling of guilt and serves the self-punishing
tendencies, not erotic pleasure.[3]   Naturally, the boundaries
between the two are sometimes uncertain, and in appraising
feminine masochistic manifestations we can take the quantitative element into account for purposes of differentiation: an
excess of masochistic attitudes, an obvious tendency to suffer
without compensation through love, etc., make us suspect the

---

[3] Freud refers to "erotogenic" or "feminine" masochism, as distinguished from "moral"
masochism: The economic problem in masochism, Collected Papers, vol. 2.

presence of the moral ingredient. Nor must we confuse feminine masochism with conscious masochistic perversion.

All human life is built on the striving to decrease discomfort and pain, and the idea that women, who constitute the majority of the human race, are masochistic and seek pain and suffering, quite naturally meets with wide skepticism and opposition.

A normal woman, when told that masochism and passivity are essential elements of her psychology, will no doubt dispute this. She will use against the charge of passivity the fact that she is active all day long, that she cannot bear to remain idle. She will resist the charge of masochism even more strongly, declaring that she is strong-willed and would not tolerate subjection to the will of any man; the idea that she is fond of suffering and pain and seeks them seems to her absurd. If told that masochism is part of her sexuality, she may reply that the pain of defloration spoiled her honeymoon and that only her love and tenderness for her husband made this pain bearable. A modern woman, asked to endure labor pains without recourse to the modern devices for easing childbirth, and thus to abide by the Bible's commandment, "In sorrow shalt thou bring forth children," would certainly reject the proposal with indignation. Obstetricians tell us that pregnant women often make them promise at the very first consultation that everything possible will be done to alleviate their labor pains. In fact the doctor's soothing words on this score play an important part in easing the woman's anxiety over childbirth. From this conscious rejection of pain, we can infer that the desire for it—if it does exist—is unconscious, and that the woman herself resists it. If we assume a constitutional and anatomic factor as the basis of feminine masochism, we are confronted with the problem: How does woman succeed in favorably managing her masochistic tendencies? Here we shall try to trace the paths of the further development of masochism and passivity and find out how woman accepts masochism and assimilates it in the formation of her personality.

Let us recall the girl's prepuberty phase. In this phase, as we saw, the young girl is very active, she is relatively free from sexual instincts, and in her activity we discovered no symptoms of repugnance to femininity, no reaction formations, no evidence of flights into masculinity, etc. A normal and healthy girl actively tries to conquer her environment. In this she repeats or continues an effort initiated in early childhood—the drive toward adjustment, toward mastery of reality, a drive particularly potent in prepuberty.

We have already pointed out that we do not regard the processes of maturation as mere products of instinctual developments or as solutions of conflicts with these developments; rather, in agreement with many writers within the psychoanalytic school and outside it, we assume the existence of "primary functions of the ego, defined as that organization of integrated functions by which we perceive, appraise, and manipulate the environment."[4] Hartmann urges us to include "the totality of these functions in so far as they factually, individually, or generally operate beyond the field of psychic conflicts," under the provisional name of "a conflict-free sphere of the ego."[5]

For the clarification of our conception of feminine passivity and masochism, the hypothesis of an independently operating active tendency in the ego will be extremely useful. In the light of this hypothesis, adjustment signifies not passive acceptance but active collaboration, with the purpose of influencing and transforming the environment.

It is difficult for psychoanalytic theory to conceive ego functions operating outside the sphere of instinctual conflicts. The freedom of ego functions with regard to the environment seems to be extremely relative. Every new developmental phase in the "conflict-free sphere of the ego" is conditioned by memories of former phases and by environmental factors. The individual thus has two problems to solve: he must repeatedly

[4] HENDRICK, I.: Work and the pleasure principle. Psychoanalyt. Quart. 12: 313, 1943.

[5] HARTMANN, H.: Ich-Psychologie und Anpassungsproblem. Internat. Ztschr. f. Psychoanal. 24: 66, 1939.

liberate himself from past dependencies, and he must master
difficulties in the outside world. These problems are difficult,
and the individual may fail in either of them; usually they are
connected, and when one is not solved, the other likewise remains unliquidated.

Observing this struggle for liberation of the ego, we realize
that the object world of early childhood that must be given up
piecemeal with each new drive toward activity, is represented
by the mother. Here sex differences do not seem to play any
part. Boys and girls have passively received gratification of
their instinctual needs from the mother and have for a long
period of life depended on her help and support precisely in
their most active ego functions. Getting up from the ground,
walking upright, taking food, becoming aware of dangers and
how to avoid them—all these took place with the mother's
active collaboration. The child's dependence upon her thus
not only has a libidinous character, but is also a necessary result
of the long period of helplessness. From the beginning the
passive drives of the ego were centripetally directed toward the
mother, the active ones centrifugally away from her. If we
investigate the libidinous and aggressive influences to which
these ego drives are subjected, we shall discover that very complicated relationships arise here, in which the two factors sometimes further and sometimes hinder each other.

As the child with gradually increasing intensity turns away
from the mother and childhood dependencies in favor of active
adjustment to reality, this reality is represented more and more
by the *father*—and this is true of both boys and girls. The
relation of parents to children parallels that of children to
parents: the mother is most strongly tied to the child in the
period of its greatest helplessness; the father begins to show real
interest in the child when it becomes susceptible to his influence
and shows a stronger interest in the outside world.

No emotional tie is given up without the accompaniment of
negative feelings; and in the child's primitive emotional life,
dependence is always identical with love, and the struggle for

independence is accompanied by hostility. This struggle must use negative feelings to overcome the mother tie and the fear of losing her. Thus the infantile anxieties of the period of struggle for liberation stem from two sources—from the aggression that is used to achieve this liberation, and from the fear of losing the mother.

In this struggle both boys and girls turn from the mother to the father. Both use negative feelings, i.e., hostility to the mother, as a motive force for liberation.

It is impossible for us to ascertain whether the active ego drives would prove sufficient in the individual's turn from the mother toward reality if they were not accompanied by deeper and more instinctual forces. We are acquainted with a number of motives that induce children of both sexes to turn away from the mother—frustrations, slights, jealousy, restriction of sexual freedom, and the infantile tendency to aggression and emotional ambivalence. In girls, an additional motive arises from emotional reactions connected with the genital trauma, since they turn their resentment of their own inferiority against their mothers and make them responsible for it. While we are not quite clear about the temporal sequence of these developments, we can assume that all these motives support the drive toward independence and are perhaps even prerequisites for this drive.

What is the purpose of the turn toward the father? What does the boy or the girl expect of him? Principally, an alliance against the mother in favor of reality. The father is the representative of reality and the outside world in which the children want to live as grownups. In contrast to him, the mother is too much tied up with old infantile gratifications, with helplessness and dependence. To be grown up means to move away from the mother.

The father (or his substitute) has an affirmative attitude toward his son's desire. We know from experience that the lack of such a relation with a father is extremely unfavorable to the boy. A masculine alliance, unencumbered by emotional complications resulting from rivalry for the mother's love, is welcomed by both parties. Thus the father supports his son's early masculinity and from now on both are engaged in a struggle not for the mother's love, but against her. A kind of condescending, patronizing, slightly devaluating attitude toward her characterizes the boy in various active life phases, and, interestingly enough, the father usually shows himself willing to enter into an alliance based on this attitude. But if the father is brutal to the mother or mistreats her, the son refuses to become his ally, and under the pressure of guilt feelings his alliance with the mother is strengthened. In such a case the boy's adjustment to reality is thwarted by a strengthening of the Oedipus complex. This constitutes the most dangerous disturbance in his development, because it is the most lasting.

A feminine and sensitive mother helps her son in the turn toward reality just described, and facilitates his activity and the development of his ego even when it involves her renunciation of his tender attachment to herself.

We must consider the fate of the boy further in order to gain an insight into that of the girl. The man to man relation does not always remain harmonious. Father and son undertake common actions in the outside world, the type of action depending on the cultural milieu—the father for educational reasons, in order to make his son strong and manly, the son in order to be as manly as the father. "Rough-housing" and playful competition with the father is a natural outlet for boys' aggressiveness. In time, however, the boy must suffer a defeat in the still playful struggles with his father. In normal cases he transfers the idea of competitive struggle to persons of equal or lesser strength, and his later task will consist in conquering the "tyrant" with the help of his brothers (friends). In prepuberty and puberty we find the normal boy engaged in the continuation of these struggles, which are now directed against the father and his substitutes.

The son-father relation may also assume a more passive character. The boy accepts his defeat and wants to be loved

by his father, or makes a compromise.   Sons who preserve their
manliness but throughout life aspire never to primary but only
to secondary positions, in which they want to be loved and
valued by their superiors as the "best," illustrate such a compromise.

It is certain that these active tendencies emanating from the
ego are disturbed or furthered by instinctual conflicts.   For
instance, the alliance with the father entered into for the purpose of strengthening the ego can, if disturbed by instinctual
processes, easily lead to a passive-homosexual development, etc.

Let us now investigate the case of the girl.   How does the
environment affect her turn toward the father?   Here the
influence of the mother is much more inhibiting than it is with
regard to the boy.   The mother feels—and her feeling is supported by objective facts—that the girl is weaker and needs
more help than does the boy, and that the girl cannot pursue
her drive toward activity without exposing herself to dangers.
In brief, the inhibiting influence of the environment asserts
itself in terms of the girl's *biologic* structure.   The girl, like
the boy, appeals to the father and tries to enlist his aid.
The process is more complicated and the solution more varied
than in the case of the boy.   The father often accepts his little
daughter's demand, especially when he has no son.   One might
suppose that in this intensification of activity supported by the
father the little girl's femininity would be endangered.   But
this does not seem always to be the case.   The reasonable gratification of the need for activity and liberation from the mother's
inhibiting tutelage offers better prospects for later sublimations
and for the development of a positive tender relation to the
mother that is of the greatest importance for the girl's femininity.   In every development, the inhibition of normal tendencies
at any point contains the germ of later disturbances.   We
regard the achievements of each developmental phase as dispositional acquisitions for the future.   Puberty will bring these
acquisitions to the fore.   An active relation of the girl to the
father—if it has not suffered any distortion in the interval—will

manifest itself also during puberty in active sublimation tendencies that often have the character of identification with the
father, without bringing in their train any danger to the development of femininity.

But this normal development toward activity may undergo
various disturbances; of these we shall consider only the most
frequent and typical. The girl's relation to the father may, for
instance, exhaust all the emotional sources that would otherwise be directed toward heterosexual objects when the girl
reaches sexual maturity. The overestimation of the father
developed in this active relationship can only with difficulty be
transferred to another man, upon whom extremely high demands will be made. This complicates the task of finding a
love object and the constantly renewed demands made upon
the man may prove a great obstacle to happiness in love and
marriage.

In other cases, there occurs, at a very early age, a split of
which we have spoken before: the girl's active sublimating
tendencies are attached to the father, while her sexual fantasies
assume an extraordinarily passive and masochistic character.
It is remarkable how many women who preserve the activity of
their egos, and use it for sublimation purposes, are extremely
passive and masochistic in their sexual behavior; either they
remain erotically isolated, avoiding all dangers, or fall victims
to brutal men. This split is very often the result of an identification with the father, later continuing in a favorable sublimation, in which the feminine erotic component remains on the
level of infantile masochism. The whole attitude of these
women toward life may be very active and masculine, and they
may display particular resistance and aggressiveness in the
struggle for life. Sometimes this masculine attitude is an
abortive reaction formation, an attempt to flee from excessively masochistic femininity. But the reaction has not affected
the whole instinctual tendency, and the masochistic impulse
recurs in each feminine feeling. The flight could succeed here
only if femininity were given up completely.

This split already begins with the active father relationship discussed above; the sensual current, which remains unconscious, joins it only later and gradually. The object of the two tendencies (active and passive-masochistic) is the father. The psychologic effect is as though the young girl had two fathers—the "day father" with whom her relation is conscious, with an active emphasis, and the "night father," who brings all the dangers of cruelty and seduction in his train and mobilizes anxious nightmares. In the fantasy formation that is called the family romance, this split comes to the fore with especial clarity. The girl has a feeling, which is perceived with full reality, that she has two fathers. One is the real father; the masochistic current that was directed also toward him, may assert itself consciously if it has been displaced to another father through fantasy activity. Sometimes the split in the father relationship appears only in puberty, when emotional life is seized by such a powerful sensual current that the tender relationship to the father and the active identification with him can no longer resist the sensual impulses. The latter are split off, the normal connection between the active and passive currents does not take place, and as a final result we obtain active masculinity and intensified masochism.

But these difficulties can also be avoided. Often such a relation to the father continues from earliest childhood; sometimes it begins only with the young girl's intellectual maturity. It can be conducive to happiness and gratifying even if the girl's erotic capacity remains excessively fixed in the sublimated father relationship. The girl's renunciation of erotic fulfillment must not be judged by stereotyped standards. Observation teaches us that a strongly sublimated daughter-father tie does not necessarily involve neurosis or feelings of frustration and privation, even if it impairs the girl's erotic life. Fulfillment of the positive goal of life is not necessarily connected with normal sexuality.

Such a relation to the father is often provoked by him, and the psychologic motive for maintaining it often lies in him.

Sometimes he wants the daughter to replace the son he never had or who was a failure, and to inherit his spiritual values; often the man's love for his mother is transferred to the daughter and brought into a gratifying form on condition that the sublimation has been completely successful. Interestingly enough, such a relation very often obtains with the third daughter, especially if she is also the youngest. It is as though the father's relation to the daughter has got rid of its dangers and freed itself from the fear of incest with the two older daughters. The third one—Cinderella—seems to be particularly suitable for the father's love choice because of her helplessness and apparent innocuousness. The need to save the little daughter from the aggressions of the mother and the older sisters certainly plays a great part here. We shall not go here into the deeper motives for such a relation.[6]

Very often the danger of such a relation to the father arises from the fact that sometimes he grants his daughter's request for an alliance and later abruptly breaks this bond. The father suddenly realizes, often under the prompting of the mother, that his daughter is approaching sexual maturity and should have more feminine interests; he refuses to have "active" communion with her. Very often his own subsequent anxiety drives him to repudiate this relation.

Another form of the girl's activity consists in banding together with boys; this is most likely to occur if she has brothers. It is fascinating to observe how easily the urge to boyish activity is transformed into a masochistic trend. The boys admit the girl to their games as an equal if she allows herself to be beaten from time to time and is willing to perform exhibitionistic and humiliating acts. There are desperate cries and tearful complaints; soon afterward the boyish masochist is consoled and again engages in the same games. This is a simple example of double gratification. It might be thought that the little girl accepts suffering for the sake of gratifying her natural need for

[6] Freud subjects the role of the third sister to a profound psychoanalytic investigation in: Motiv der Kästchenwahl. Gesammelte Schriften, vol. 10, p. 243.

activity.   But this is not the case: actually, she is already a
little woman, in whom the active and masochistic ingredients
are operating parallel to each other.   Later her ego will not
easily accept this double game, and conflicts will arise the solution of which will become one of her most difficult tasks.

We have tried so far to follow the ways of feminine activity
in those cases in which it was seemingly afforded special possibilities for development.   These are obviously favorable to the
purposes of activity, but not always to the harmony of the
personality as a whole.   We do not wish to maintain that under
less favorable conditions the girl's activity is doomed to extinc-
tion; its forms are different from the boy's and her urge lacks the
fighting, driving element.   In contrast to the development of
the boy, the activity of the female child, on the path toward
adjustment to reality by way of the breaking of the mother tie,
encounters an inhibition of her ego development imposed by
the outside world.

It seems that all forms of childhood activity, whatever its
origin, are accompanied by aggressive tendencies, and that the
fate of the latter constitutes a decisive factor in the psychologic
differences between man and woman.   The boy who frees himself from his dependence upon his mother is more than active:
he fights for his active position and thus finds an outlet for his
aggressions.   As he matures physically and psychologically,
his active and aggressive forces are distributed in a manner that
strengthens the ego and that is accepted by society.

With regard to the girl, however, the environment exerts an
inhibiting influence as regards both her aggressions and her
activity.   The effect of this inhibition depends on the intensity
of the environmental influences and on the strength of the girl's
active urge.   Here the forces of the outer and the inner world
act in the same direction—that is, the urge toward activity in
woman is weaker and the external inhibition stronger.   It is
above all the aggressive components that are inhibited; the
social environment not only rejects them but also offers the
woman's ego a kind of prize or bribe for renouncing them.   For

the sake of simplifying our exposition, we have divided the
child's environment into two parts—on the one hand the world
of the mother, who loves and inhibits her child, and who, beginning with a definite point in its development, condemns it to
passivity, and, on the other, the fighting, activity-encouraging
world of the father. The developmental processes take place
within the triangular situation that we meet again and again.
We have seen that children of both sexes ask the father as the
representative of reality to help them liberate themselves from
the mother. This request is sometimes granted the girl with
regard to activity, but never with regard to aggression. Has
anyone ever seen a father romping with his little daughter in
any manner except lovingly? Does he ever encourage her to
competitive struggles? The bribe offered to the little girl by
the father, as a representative of the environment, is love and
tenderness. For its sake she renounces any further intensification of her activity, most particularly of her aggressions.

In brief, the girl gives up her aggressions partly as a result of
her own weakness, partly because of the taboos of the environment, and chiefly because of the love prize given her as compensation. Here we come to a development that again and again
takes place in the woman: activity becomes passivity, and
aggression is renounced for the sake of being loved. In this
renunciation the aggressive forces that are not actively spent
must find an outlet, and they do this by endowing the passive
state of being loved with a masochistic character. Earlier we
have tried to explain feminine passivity on the basis of the
anatomic difference between the sexes. The same explanation
applies to feminine masochism. The absence of an active organ
brought the turn toward passivity and masochism in its train.
It is noteworthy that the processes in the ego and the instincts,
the constitutional, anatomic, and environmental factors, all
seem to work together to produce femininity.

We have observed that apparently even the most successful
active sublimations of woman do not insure freedom from
masochistic drives. We have mentioned the active-masculine

type, in whom the strong masochistic tendencies are repressed or split off. To make this more clear, it seems that the feminine kind of sublimation of masochistic drives is more successful than the active forms. The type of feminine woman we encountered in the previous chapter justifies us in this conclusion. The feminine woman is evidently much better equipped to control her feminine masochism than is the active type.

Our observations seem to call for a few corrections of the psychoanalytic hypotheses concerning the development of girls.[7] The former psychoanalytic observations of the little girl's development dealt chiefly with her sexual instincts. It was found that with her detachment from her mother, the little girl—already a miniature woman—has an erotic-passive attitude toward her father, an attitude that constitutes the kernel of the feminine Oedipus complex. But we have overlooked the fact that, contrary to our previous views, the girl's first turn toward the father has an active, not a passive character, and her passive attitude is only a secondary development. The active turn results from a process of growth and adjustment to reality. In prepuberty this process is repeated and continues for a time in the almost regular identification with the father in puberty.

This activity thrust of the girl is usually met by an attitude on the part of the father that exerts an inhibiting influence on her active drive. In this function the father is a representative of the environment, which later will again and again exert this inhibiting influence on the woman's activity and drive her back into her constitutionally predetermined passive role This attitude of the father contains another element of decisive importance in feminine development. He appears, without being conscious of it, as a seducer, with whose help the girl's aggressive instinctual components are transformed into masochistic ones. The masochistic ingredient in the relation to the father appears in the active games with him, which later assume an increasingly erotic character. It is enough to observe the little girl's

[7] FREUD, S.: Op. cit., p. 174.

fearful jubilation when the father performs acrobatic tricks with her that are often painful, when he throws her up in the air, or lets her ride "piggy back" on his shoulders. When this seduction on the part of the father is lacking, the girl will encounter difficulties in her feminine development.

Our theory of the girl's relation to the mother also requires modification. The especially hate-filled attitude that we observe in our female patients represents usually a neurotic intensification of hostility. In a more normal development, the detachment from the mother proceeds gradually, step by step. The process is a conflict between attachment and detachment; the latter acquires new hate components from the now intensified rivalry for the father's love, but in favorable cases the process ends with a positive, tender, and forgiving relation to the mother—and such a relation is one of the most important prerequisites for psychologic harmony in later femininity. Before this is achieved, the girl's mother relation passes through various phases, each of which contains its own dangers. To understand these we must considerably modify the accepted notions of pre-oedipal, oedipal, and postoedipal mother relations. There is only one mother relation from birth until death, though it undergoes various changes in accordance with the childhood development.

Paradoxically, the girl's mother relation is more persistent, and often more intense and dangerous, than the boy's. The inhibition she encounters when she turns toward reality brings her back to her mother for a period marked by heightened and more infantile love demands. This regression is very often responsible for feminine neuroses and severe disturbances in character formation. The renewed aspiration to go forward aggressively is laden with masochistic elements; it dangerously inclines the girl to assume a passive-masochistic attitude toward her mother and probably predisposes her to homosexuality more than her own masculinity does (see chap. ix).

It is a remarkable fact that the types of neurosis we encounter nowadays with increasing frequency reveal just such a passive-masochistic, infantile relation to the mother more clearly than did the older types, whose main content was found to be dependence on the father tie and the masculinity complex. In the cases we have in mind the relation to the father often takes the form of a twofold accusation. There is first the reproach that he did not help the girl sufficiently in her *active effort* to liberate herself from her mother; second—and this reproach has a more erotic character—he is accused of having failed to prevent by his love the girl's return to her mother.

This regressive relation to the mother involves dangers that obviously surpass even those involved in a masochistic attitude toward the father. We can now understand why female homosexuality is often repelled with panic. For the fulfillment of this erotic desire signifies not only return to an infantile form of existence, but also a profound union with the mother, a union that is of a deeply regressive character and that contains the threat of psychosis and even of death.

The regression toward the mother that we regard as a normal process, although it is not without its dangers, provides the girl with an opportunity for reconciliation with her mother and simultaneously for freeing herself from her aggressions as well as from her masochistic dependence. Early puberty, during which this conflict between aggression and dependence is repeated, gives us the best opportunity to observe its unfolding.

The passive-masochistic attitude toward the father—that is to say, toward men and toward life as a whole—can be seen with particular clarity in puberty. But analysts of children tell us also of the cruelty of childish aggressions and of children's sadistic-masochistic interpretation of coitus. Reconstructions of childhood fantasies in the analyses of adults confirm these observations; we do not know to what extent real occurrences, such as actually overhearing parents during cohabitation or observing the sexual acts of animals, contribute to these fantasies, and to what extent we have to deal here with deeper-rooted, perhaps phylogenetically conditioned fantasies. Psychoanalysis can, for the moment, clearly determine only their existence,

not their genesis. From reliable observation of the development of little girls, one gains the impression that dreams and
fears relating to penetration of the body—usually not through
the genitals—appear independently of real observation of
coitus.

The fantasy life of girls in puberty reveals an unmistakably
masochistic content. Girlish fantasies relating to rape often
remain unconscious but evince their content in dreams, sometimes in symptoms, and often accompany masturbating actions.
In dreams the rape is symbolic: the terrifying male persecutor
with knife in hand, the burglar who breaks in at the window,
the thief who steals a particularly valuable object, are the most
typical and frequently recurring figures in the dreams of young
girls. They are connected with fear, not with pleasure, and
thus differ from the boy's puberty dreams, the clearly sexual
character of which is revealed by their effect, the nocturnal
seminal emission.

The conscious masochistic rape fantasies, however, are in-
dubitably erotic, since they are connected with masturbation
They are less genital in character than the symbolic dreams,
and involve blows and humiliations; in fact, in rare cases the
genitals themselves are the target of the act of violence. In
other cases, they are less cruel, and the attack as well as the
overpowering of the girl's will constitute the erotic element.
Often the fantasy is divided into two acts: the first, the masochistic act, produces the sexual tension, and the second, the
amorous act, supplies all the delights of being loved and desired.
These fantasies vanish with the giving up of masturbation and
yield to erotic infatuations detached from direct sexuality.
The masochistic tendency now betrays itself only in the painful
longing and wish to suffer for the lover (often unknown). The
predominance of the narcissistic element in the erotic fantasies
is in itself a triumph over the masochistic element. Many
women retain these masochistic fantasies until an advanced
age. Such women are far removed from any manifest perversion; on the contrary, they are often extraordinarily sensitive

and resentful of any psychic or physical pain.   In these women
especially, the narcissistic wish to be loved and desired predominates as far as their consciously sought experiences are concerned.

We learn—often even without deeper analytic investigation
—that rape fantasies are variants of the seduction fantasies so
familiar to us in the lying accounts of hysterical women patients.   Both rape and seduction fantasies are deliberately
passed on to other persons as true, and they have the typical
pseudologic character we found in the more romantic and fantastic lies of puberty (p. 123).   That is, they draw their
appearance of truth from the fact that underlying them is a real
but repressed experience.   It is precisely rape fantasies that
often have such irresistible verisimilitude that even the most
experienced judges are misled in trials of innocent men accused
of rape by hysterical women.   My own experience of accounts
by white women of rape by Negroes (who are often subjected
to terrible penalties as a result of these accusations) has convinced me that many fantastic stories are produced by the
masochistic yearnings of these women.[8]   Freud[9] calls attention
to the fact that hysterical patients often speak of having been
seduced by their fathers, and that the same seduction fantasy
sometimes involves the mother.   He thinks that seduction by
the mother—as contrasted with that by the father—"has a real
basis, for the mother, who took care of her child's body, must
actually have aroused pleasure sensations in the genitals."

My own observations suggest that the fantasies relating to
the father are also based on a real seduction.   The crueler
character of these fantasies results from the fact that this seduction took place at the height of the masochistic turn, when the
girl's activity was inhibited by her father's tenderness.   We
have already mentioned the games with the father, which are

[8] DOLLARD, J.: Caste and class in a southern town.   Published for the Institute of
    Human Relations by Yale University Press, 1937.
[9] FREUD, S.: The psychology of women.   New introductory lectures on psycho-
    analysis, p. 164.

full of a directly experienced fearful pleasure very close to masochism.

Another very frequent rape fantasy is a sort of masochistic orgy within a triangular situation. In this characteristic fantasy a female figure forces the girl to submit to sexual acts performed by men whom the female urges on. The female figure ties the girl, gags her, and prepares red-hot objects; these are applied by the men to the girl's genitals. Sometimes the female figure introduces a number of men who one after the other abuse the girl sexually. Compulsion by a woman plays the principal part in these practices. The superficial elements of these fantasies are easy to grasp: the pain decreases the guilt feeling produced by the pleasure, the rape frees the girl from responsibility, the compulsion exerted by the woman, who represents the mother, is a counterweight to the latter's prohibitions. To be sure, every masochistic function contains a component of moral masochism that serves to gratify guilt feelings. But the principal motive force of all these methods of achieving masochistic pleasure stems from the erotic needs of instinctual components that have been repressed and that assert themselves in this open form in fantasy life. It is no doubt only by sanction of pain and by negation of the object's identity that these fantasies can come before consciousness.

Everything that takes place in puberty is so important to us because during this phase the second cornerstone of the future personality is laid (the first was laid in childhood). Moreover, the same instinctual motives that operated in childhood again come into play. This life period cannot escape the returning ghosts and for that reason it gives us important insights into earlier developments. Among these ghosts are the rekindled masochistic tendencies that now, as we see, are no longer dark, unconscious premonitions, but clearly defined fantasies in close contact with reality. The task of puberty is to bring these into normal channels.

The rape and seduction fantasy, with its primitive sexual content directly relating to the body, is less dangerous than other masochistic fantasies, mostly unconscious, that do not work directly toward the gross sexual goal. If the rape fantasies were directly gratified they would lead to perversion, but this is extremely rare; it is known that the masochistic perversion is less frequently found in women than in men. Where it exists, its content is completely different from that of the rape fantasy: its essence is the wish to be beaten. Women with such perversions whom I have had an opportunity to examine maintained that they felt no pleasure sensations while being beaten, and that they agreed to be beaten partly for professional-financial reasons (if they were prostitutes) and partly in order to offer themselves as "love sacrifices" to sadistic lovers. It is interesting to note that the masochistic wish is gratified here by a detour, that is to say, by the choice of a sadistic love object and the toleration of his perversions, while direct gratification is rejected. A somewhat more dangerous group of sexual fantasies are the prostitution fantasies that, especially in big cities, are based on occasional exciting observations of street life at night, stories, and popular "thrillers." The dangers of their realization are particularly great for growing girls from social strata in which economic motives, for instance poverty, can serve as a rationalization and can incite to action. We have touched on this point in our discussion of the case of Evelyn. We discuss these fantasies in connection with feminine masochism because such masochism usually serves as the principal theme of the prostitution fantasy.

Two factors are particularly responsible for this fantasy formation in puberty. The first lies in the dark stirrings of sexual excitation, and has a rather undefined, not genitally localized character; the second lies in the simultaneous intensification of the idealistic-narcissistic demands upon the ego that we have described as characteristic of puberty.

As a result of the tension between these two forces acting in opposite directions, anxiety states and symptoms and prostitution fantasies arise. We learn of their existence in various ways. Sometimes they make their way into consciousness and are confidentially communicated to other persons; in other cases they are acted out, and their bizarreness and monotony reveal the inner contents. But the best method of reaching them is psychoanalysis. Once they have been recognized analytically as typical, they can easily be unmasked in less direct manifestations. There are various types of prostitution fantasies, especially in puberty. In one of these types, we find an extremely ascetic and narcissistic ego ideal, while sexuality is conceived of as extremely low and sinful. The sexual act is connected with the idea of the subjection of woman to man—an idea whose roots are so deep that it is inaccessible to any intellectual correction.

Here the ego ideal repudiates all sexual freedom, even the freedom to imagine. The inner perception of the sexual drive is condemned with a harsh "You are a whore!" and every stirring assumes the form of the masochistic, humiliating admission, "I am a whore." Fantasies of such a type have a particularly humiliating character. The very approach of a man is regarded as a sexually humiliating attack; this is accompanied by the self-accusation, "I myself have provoked it"—a confession of the unconscious or conscious fantasy life. When this attitude is fixed, either the ego ideal has won (this leads to an ascetic mode of life) or the prostitution fantasy; this can then assume various forms. It can be realized in a respectable marriage, in which the sexual approach of the husband is experienced as a degradation and humiliation, or it may result in the obsessional acting out of prostitution accompanied by the severest conflicts and feelings of guilt. One woman whom I observed managed to express the split directly by leading a strictly respectable life interspersed with lapses during which she went out into the streets and offered herself to passers-by for insignificant sums of money.

Another type of fantasy more or less consciously involves the mother. According to the fantasy, the mother led a sexual life not for her own pleasure—for she was a respectable woman— but only for the sake of the father. The girl includes in her fantasy memories of events that suggest to her, rightly or wrongly, the idea that her father's erotic advances were painful and humiliating to her mother. It may be that the mother, as a reaction to a new and undesired pregnancy, either sincerely, or in order to excuse herself before her children, said something that aroused this impression and left its mark on the young girl's mind. The girl decides, at least in her fantasies, not to suffer her mother's fate. She wants to enjoy her sexuality, that is, not to be respectable like her mother, but to love freely, to be a "whore." Although this solution is intended as opposition to the mother's way of life, identity with the mother asserts itself in the fact that the prostitution fantasy likewise contains the masochistic element of subjection to the man's will.

Still another type of fantasy appears to be the opposite of the foregoing. Here the respectable mother, from the very fact that she has had children, that is, a sexual life, is reduced to the status of a whore, and the girl's consciousness energetically rejects identity with her. The devaluation of the mother may reach a height of intense hatred and rage; the prostitution fantasy is mobilized against her and frequently acted out. Especially when the depreciated mother begins to restrict the girl's freedom of movement and to display fears for her morality, does she provoke actions that at first are directed only against herself, but that under certain circumstances can become very dangerous for the young girl. The masochistic element here is the fact that the girl's adventures are usually very unsatisfactory and bring her into unpleasant conflicts with the outside world. Many young runaways begin their careers after a violent struggle with their mothers. The identification with the mother here too asserts itself unconsciously.

Similar to this is the behavior of the girl who rightly or wrongly imagines that her mother was or is a prostitute. She builds her own life, in a compulsive manner, on the model of this mother. This happens frequently with girls who have been adopted or reared in foster homes. The absence of the real mother, or the lack of knowledge about her, furthers this fantasy and leads to identification with the imagined unknown mother.

It is noteworthy that a truly disreputable mother is less likely to induce the formation of prostitution fantasies and their realization than an imaginary and completely unreal version of a disreputable mother. In the former case the daughter can consciously control her course of life and refuse to resemble her mother, in the latter she is a tool of unconscious motives that cannot be influenced by the will.

Various other types of prostitution fantasies are directly connected with the father. For instance, a daughter who has a particularly well sublimated relation to her father and sees this relation broken off with the approach of sexual maturity—the father often being responsible for such a break—avenges herself in a masochistic way and is repeatedly faithless to him with other men. The masochistic element is often concealed behind aggressive actions. The girl feels devaluated because she has been rejected by her father and she continues the devaluation by reducing herself to the role of a sexual object for anybody. The previous sharing of her father's love with her mother, in which she took the "better," spiritual part and left the sexual part to her mother, now breaks down, and the girl's repressed sexual drives come to the fore and are transferred to other men. In many such cases the relation to the father is very tender, particularly when the girl is the youngest or one of the youngest among several sisters. As she grows up she loses her privileged position with her father and is treated like his other daughters. She retaliates for this faithlessness with faithlessness—"all men instead of one man." She lowers herself to the sexual role that she formerly assigned to her mother. This rejection of the father in puberty is a very frequent motive not only for fantasies but also for revenge reactions whose masochistic content reveals the formerly repressed relation to the father.

The real personality of the father plays a particularly important part in puberty. Paradoxically, promiscuity may express the quest for a highly estimable father after the real father has been devaluated. It is almost unbelievable how often a young and intelligent girl who has previously been quite strong-minded, gives herself to the first man she meets

in order to re-experience rejection, and over and over again
naïvely trusts a lover whom she barely knows, saying to
herself, "He is a wonderful man."   One young girl who became
pregnant as a result of a casual affair expected with complete
confidence that her friend of one day would come to her as
soon as he learned that she was in difficulties.   For after all
her father was always there when she needed his help.

Fathers who are brutal toward their wives, or who drink
heavily and induce in their children a state of constant anxiety,
are doubtless more likely to further the triumph of ascetic
tendencies in their daughters than fathers who are passive
and weak toward their wives.   Only if the brutal father, as is
so frequently the case, wavers between brutality and tenderness toward his daughter, does he strengthen her masochistic
ties, which she later continues, often promiscuously.   The
passive father who fails to protect his daughter in her frequent
conflicts with her mother during puberty, often provokes more
revenge tendencies than the brutal father.   It is striking how
many young runaways are found to have such passive fathers.

Of the many determinants of the prostitution fantasy, we
have singled out only the most typical.   Whatever the cultural
milieu, the psychologic background remains constant, although the forms and methods of realization of these fantasies
vary greatly.   The strictly reared daughter acts differently
from the proletarian girl.   One meets the latter in social
agencies, the former in private practice and sanatoriums;
the latter rationalizes her action by explaining that she was
never properly cared for, or by adducing her economic difficulties as the cause of her troubles; the former has a "neurosis."

The prostitution fantasies briefly outlined here may be very
richly elaborated, and then every detail corresponds to an
unconscious content.   Kidnaping, forced stay in a brothel,
without the possibility of contact with the outside world,
sexual abuse by various men of all descriptions, sale as merchan-
dise in the white slave market, exotic trips to foreign lands,

the figure of a wicked woman who usually plays an important part and directs the white slave trade, and at the end a "rescuer" whose love saves the fallen woman—all these are condensations of things heard or read, combined with the girl's own psychologic life and her fantastic ideas about sex.

Those who have investigated the life of professional prostitutes are often surprised to find that their existence is greatly reminiscent of these fantasies. The lies that prostitutes are so fond of telling to naïve men coincide literally with the contents of puberty fantasies. At the beginning there is usually the wonderful man who seduced and deserted the girl or, in a more tragic version, lost his life. He is responsible for all her misery. There is the wicked woman who has made her a slave, and there is the envy of the older prostitutes who make her life miserable, etc. More naïve "customers" are also told stories of kidnaping, white slave traffic, cruel fetters, etc. These "whore lies" are in fact ordinary daydreams forged by the customer and the prostitute together. Intuitive or experienced prostitutes know how to adapt the content of their lies to the psychology of the customer. The masochistic boy easily identifies himself with the "persecuted" girl and is full of anger against the guilty "brute." He even attempts to save her and is extremely disappointed when the victim does not accept his offer. The sadist vicariously experiences the atrocities in the stories and in his fantasy takes over the active role of the seducer; thus he can remain free of guilt feelings and of the onus of perversion.

We are interested here in the problem of prostitution from the psychologic point of view. To be sure, among professional prostitutes there are girls who are spiritually and morally weak, who have embraced this profession as the only solution of their social problem; it provides them with an opportunity to earn a living and they attach no emotional significance to their "trade." The fact that society condemns them does not bother them; moreover—this is often overlooked— the world of prostitution is a community with its own code and its members must more or less strictly observe that code. The moral demands of society do not inhibit them; the only way to touch them is by punishment. For many prostitutes this way of life is merely a continuation of the moral development that led or forced them in this direction from the beginning of their lives.

Even the simplest moral laws have absolutely no influence on these women, because these sanctions express values that are completely alien to them. In their eyes, moral laws conceal unbearable wrongs and are full of the most contradictory requirements. To moral indignation, to every attempt to influence them to change their ways, they react with cynicism. And why should they accept moralistic proposals, if the tangible social norms are represented for them only by the police and the authorities whom they hate and struggle against? The promise of happiness in an orderly family does not tempt them because, according to their ideas, family life is only a source of unhappiness and disappointment or of deadly boredom.

Their psychic infantilism makes of the entire world a nursery in which social institutions are personified by their representatives, and their emotions are turned against these representatives. Many investigators of the problem believe that prostitutes are "born" as such, and to prove it they argue that whenever a prostitute is removed from her milieu and placed in a new, more favorable one, she returns to her previous way of life out of her own desire and impulse. We grant that in these cases a powerful urge is present that proves stronger than everything else. The motives operating here are of course psychologic, but they are acquired, not innate.

The following history of a prostitute will provide a good example of social rationalization of a behavior determined psychologically. This prostitute—let us call her Anna—was one of the unwelcome patients at a psychiatric clinic to which she was sent from time to time to be treated for attacks of rage. She was registered (as is the custom in Europe), and at almost every regular police inspection forcibly resisted examination. Once, suspected of having a venereal disease, she was taken to the medical examiner; she staged the usual "prostitute riot" and as a result was sent for psychiatric observation. In her later hospitalization the doctors were afraid of her, because she hated them all, aggressively demanded release, fought with everyone, and was so shameless in her behavior that she had to be isolated, out of regard for the other patients; she was, however, much more accessible to the women nurses and women doctors. After some time I succeeded in winning her confidence and throughout a period of three years I had regular contacts with her.

It was remarkable how her profession had left no trace on Anna's appearance. A blonde girl with innocent blue eyes, she had a transparent white skin through which in some places her blue veins could be seen, giving her face a peculiar charm. Her life history was very typical. She came of a proletarian family; her father had taken to drink, her mother was sickly, tormented, prematurely aged by work and worries; left to herself, Anna was encouraged by the young people of her neighborhood to take this way of making easy money. Although later in the hospital she behaved like a real psychopath, she showed no genuine psychopathic symptoms. She seemed no more pathologic than the average girl. She took up prostitution from economic motives, and quickly adapted herself to her profession, which became her whole world. She had no moral opinion on the subject of prostitution, and her contempt for the outside world was genuine. The social order was for her represented by men occupying high and important positions, among whom she also numbered the doctors at the hospital. Asked why she so hated and despised these men, she would answer: "Why not? Don't we know better than anyone that these men easily drop their masks of gentility, self-control, and importance, and behave like beasts? . . . These men come to us expecting to have their way with us for money. If they meet the slightest resistance, they snivel and beg or fly into a rage."

Thus this was a world of men who simulated tenderness and

love only in order to behave like beasts. And whenever this world wanted to impose its authority on her, Anna replied by discharging all her fury and disappointment; for she always associated these men with a situation in which they were lowered to the status of animals. Anna became a prostitute out of economic motives, but she practiced her profession according to her own psychologically compulsive plan. Once she had loved her father and respected his paternal authority. After she had witnessed brutal scenes in which he made sexual demands on her mother, she began to despise and hate this respectable man; later she discharged her fury against her father—a fury that was impotent while she was still a child—on other "respectable" men. She no longer believed in their respectability, even when they behaved in the most correct fashion. Anna had many opportunities to get married, but she rejected all proposals, discouraged by the family life she had known in her childhood. That she was actually continuing the masochistic role of her mother in her profession, she did not suspect.

Anna led a double life—and she maintained that many prostitutes lead such lives in certain respects. She liked books and music and had a fervent desire for a clear-cut morality that she was willing to accept; only such a morality no longer existed for her. She was aggressive only with regard to "important" men; to young, poor, inexperienced men she was very helpful and sweet. She clung faithfully to the head nurse of our department and to me also, for years, but we were never able to exert the slightest influence on her behavior. She never told lying stories, except once to the head nurse and once to me. To the former she spoke of a child she claimed to have had and asked the nurse to adopt it if she died. She gave the exact address where it could be found and other data concerning it. To me she spoke of a little box of jewels that she claimed to have deposited in a safe; she commissioned me to remove this after her death and to use the proceeds for charities. Neither of us, the head nurse nor I, knew the particular secret she had entrusted to the other—for Anna had asked us not to mention it.   After Anna died of tuberculosis, both these stories turned out to be pseudologic.   Characteristically, in her stories the child and the jewels had come from the man with whom she had first had intercourse as a professional prostitute.   According to her story, this man loved her and wanted to marry her, but already had a wife and children.

Although the problem of prostitution is a complex and special field and should be left to the specialist, we shall discuss additional features of the phenomenon, because they present great psychologic interest.

One is the prostitute's relation to her pimp. If the connection between prostitution (as fantasy or profession) and masochistic tendencies is a psychologic construction, this relation proves that masochism plays a great part in the life of the prostitute   There is no girl practicing this profession who does not have a "protector."   Attempts are made to interpret this institution too as a by-product of the social conditions of the prostitute.   She is defenselessly exploited by the "madam."   The "protector" (pimp) defends her against attacks coming from the outside world, like a father or older brother.   But he himself exploits her in the most brutal manner, makes her work hard to increase his earnings, takes her money, whips and maltreats her while offering her the pleasures of love.   The prostitute, frigid by profession, experiences the loftiest ecstasies of love after a masochistic orgy with her consistently brutal lover.   She clings to him with the greatest tenderness, cares for him like a mother when he is sick, in need, or in danger; in short, she experiences with him all the happiness of womanly love.   The only aberration here is that this happiness comes about under masochistic conditions.

This relationship has features that are quite familiar to us. The man protecting the girl from the wicked woman—is he not the same who in the pubescent girl's fantasy rescues her from the claws of the wicked witch, the knight of the fairy tale who frees her from the witch's enchantment? Let us recall the young girl's unconscious reproach against her father for not having saved her from her mother's power. We all know how often this role is ascribed also to the older brother, and how often he really does defend his little sister when her mother wants to punish her. And does not the girl boast of her "big brother's" strength to her friends, just as the little prostitute praises her muscular and frivolous "handsome Louis?" And, on the other hand, what older brother has not subjected his little sister to his own extremely humiliating aggression? And has not every woman passed through a phase during which she has again and again unconsciously provoked this mistreatment?

Another figure present in the affective life of the prostitute is the "wicked woman," to whom the girl is often attached by the most intense hatred and yet by indissoluble ties of love. Observers dealing with the problem of prostitution often find it hard to understand why these girls are incapable of freeing themselves from the clutches of such women, even when they are given an opportunity to do so. What makes it impossible is the deeply masochistic love tie that exists between the prostitute and her "madam." Who would recognize, in these female dregs of human society, a variation of that ideal feminine figure for which the ecstatic pubescent girl felt such a wild love, a love usually mixed with pain and pleasure, and for which she wanted to suffer and yearn?

The Spirit of Youth and the City Streets, by Jane Addams,[10] whose pioneering work in the field of social welfare is known to everyone, contains life histories of women that are tragic examples of masochistic love bondage. Their heroism is fed by masochistic self-destructiveness, their love sacrifice stems from compulsive urges, and can naturally be understood only from psychologic experience. One story tells us of Molly,

[10] ADDAMS, J.: The spirit of youth and the city streets. New York: Macmillan, 1930, pp. 37–43.

a young girl who married a professional criminal named Joe. He was imprisoned for two years. Molly was faithful to him for one year and then decided to get a divorce, which she obtained without difficulty. She married a wealthy and respectable man, moved to a well-to-do neighborhood, gave birth to a child, and was a good mother to it. All her dreams seemed to have been realized. One day while out airing her baby she learned that Joe had returned to their old apartment and was "mighty sore" at her for having deserted him. Without a moment's hesitation she went back to him. She entered upon a life of misery and humiliation. She lived in the most sordid surroundings, moved from one furnished room to another, and was socially ostracized; Joe refused to remarry her, but she had a number of illegitimate children by him and asserted blissfully: "I am all right as long as Joe keeps out of the jug." She never expressed the slightest regret.

Another charming young girl came quivering to Hull House, her tear-stained face swollen and bloody from the blows her lover had dealt her. "He is apt to abuse me when he is drunk," was the only explanation—and that given by way of apology—that could be extracted from her.

She was not married, had no children, and her man beat her so violently that twice she almost died. The social workers wanted to help her and kept her at Hull House for a time. As soon as she had recovered a little, she insisted on being released, saying that she had to clean up her place for Pierre, who was always very weak when he returned from his drinking bouts. Nobody could dissuade her from returning to him. She was enslaved by her masochism, the strongest of all forms of love.

A great many of the psychologic problems that social agencies have to deal with in their women clients are based on such masochistic ties. The greatest difficulty in these problems is that they are usually much more unconscious and better rationalized than in the tragic cases quoted by Jane Addams. These women get in touch with welfare agencies

only as a result of financial complications. Their psychic
dependence is concealed behind the economic one; all attempts
to help them fail because, even when freed of their external
dependence, they again and again find skilfully rationalized
ways of falling under the subjection of brutal, weak, or un-
reliable men. It is especially when the man's unfaithfulness
and the known existence of a mistress are involved, that all
the efforts of the social worker are futile. Somehow or other,
even after the situation has been financially rearranged, even
after the apparently sincere wishes of the tormented woman to
find peace and quiet have been satisfied, the old difficulties
start all over again. Badly managed feminine masochism
is a serious psychologic and often sociologic problem.

Inasmuch as we consider the processes described here to be
intensifications of "normal" feminine psychologic states, we
assume that woman is exposed to very great dangers in her
development. At this point, however, we must anticipate a
little. We have seen these processes as through a magnifying
glass, and determined their typical properties, which are
inherent in woman's disposition; but as yet we have not discussed the methods by which the ego can master the dangers
threatening it.

The reader must further have been struck by the fact that the
masochistic disposition is in the cases quoted here accompanied
by a number of psychologic processes, the existence of which
endows this disposition with its vitality and effectiveness.
Memories are activated, reminiscences are assimilated, various
unconscious justifications are invoked, numerous individual
impressions are used, and, above all, identifications are produced as an important motive for fantasy formations and
real actions. All these elements are joined by aggressive forces
that are completely outside the "masochistic turn," while their
participation often becomes the factor that touches off the
difficulties.

These additional elements are responsible for an "overflow"
of the masochistic tendencies. This overflow can take place

under various conditions. Direct environmental influences can contribute to it, or experiences that intensify the aggressive tendencies; these can then turn against the individual's own ego. We have also seen the great part played by identification and we know that this process is particularly important in puberty. But what most contributes to the overflow of feminine masochism and gives it its self-destructive character is moral masochism, that is, the sense of guilt and its effects. Here a fundamental difference between man and woman manifests itself. When we encounter a passive-masochistic, feminine orientation in a man, we fairly always find that it came about under the pressure of guilt feelings and that his "moral masochism" acquired feminine erotic character only secondarily. This is reversed in women: in them feminine masochism is primary and moral masochism is secondary. The latter then sails under the false flag of eroticism and appears as such, but its destructive character gives it away. A classic example is the case of Molly cited by Jane Addams, in which we were allowed to see only the power of love and could only guess the effects of a cruel sense of guilt.

In milder cases it is even more difficult to draw a sharp line. Experienced social workers try to discover the secondary psychologic motives that wrecked the lives of these women; but it is not always possible to master these motives. Woman's masochistic-erotic subjection shows extreme variations in intensity, and as long as it produces more gratification than grief it is difficult to influence her. We shall not deal here with the problem of mastering feminine masochism complicated by other elements (especially moral masochism). This belongs to the theory of the neuroses.

Let us now clearly formulate the questions that we still have to answer. We have assumed the presence of an inhibiting process in woman's development, and we want to discover how she can employ the passive-masochistic psychic energies that dwell in her ego while at the same time avoiding dangers for her personality.

In discussing puberty, we have purposely dealt first with those processes that take place outside the sphere of instinct development. The human ego is endowed with a vast self-love that, under relatively normal conditions, suffices to prevent a self-destructive action. We have seen that puberty is the period in which narcissistic self-love is at its height; we also assign the intensification and mobilization of feminine masochism to the same period. It seems that in normal development, that is to say, if the processes are not excessively intense, we can rely on the ability of the self-loving ego to escape all existing dangers.

By what methods does the ego achieve this? The simplest and most direct way is the method we have seen used by the normal young girl. She sublimates the erotic urge, thus indirectly bringing the masochistic component under narcissistic control and gratifying it without danger. She opposes the masturbatory rape fantasy with all the weapons against masturbation that she has at her disposal. I believe that normally masturbation is automatically given up in childhood and puberty, if the ego, absorbed in other outside interests, renounces the gratification of the urge. The ego behaves like the educator who diverts the child from masturbatory procedures by other activities rather than by threatening or inflicting punishments. This diversion does not always succeed—and then there arise all the struggles around masturbation that we see as mainly responsible for the difficulties of puberty and that result in neurotic conflicts. We shall not discuss these conflicts here; we shall only recall the anxiety dreams, anxiety states, and various other temporary symptoms that remind us of these struggles even in normal conditions.

Sublimation of sexuality into eroticism is a process that outlasts adolescence and is a permanent component of feminine psychologic life. We have described one of the typical results of this process—as a definite form of a sublimation in which the distribution of forces between the narcissistic ego and feminine masochism leads to complete harmony. We have called this process "intensification of inner life," and "activity directed inward." The prerequisite of such a harmonious development is that no psychologic component contributing to it should overflow, and particularly that guilt feelings, moral masochism, should not exert any disturbing influence. It seems that this harmony depends to a great extent upon the overcoming of a surplus of aggressions; above all, the girl's hatred and fear of her mother must yield to a feeling of love and tenderness.

What the woman belonging to our erotic type achieves through love, other women achieve by more circuitous, more social paths. The willingness to serve a cause or a human being with love and abnegation may be a reflection of feminine masochism. Here too, just as when it takes a direct sexual turn, it can overstep the normal limits: then the woman gladly exposes herself to privations, sufferings, and even the danger of death. In her contempt for the dangers that threaten her, she experiences—just like the erotic type of woman in her more normal manner—two gratifications: masochism assumes the false name of heroism, and the ego draws great advantages from this situation, particularly in satisfying its self-love. Thus, in both cases, there is created a possibility of compromise between self-injury and self-love, that is, between masochism and narcissism.

Often the masochistic readiness for sacrifice is a mask for sadistic impulses that must be avoided for fear of loss of love in the outside world and the inner sense of guilt. Here we no longer have feminine masochism, although it is not always easy to see the difference. How often we encounter women who have failed to achieve a harmonious overcoming of their masochism and who strike us as neurotic characters of a definite type. They cannot live without narcissistic gratification, but every form of it, whether in love or in ambition, is so shot through with masochistic motives that they must shy away from any fulfillment. They confess their helplessness, complain of their futile efforts to find something to satisfy them either in love or in activity. Outwardly their lives do not seem neurotic, nor do they directly seek suffering, which would reveal their behavior to be really masochistic. On the contrary, because of their very avoidance of direct masochistic dangers, their lives are empty, without content; their masochism asserts itself in the form of a renunciation of the positive values of life.

Another type we encounter frequently is that of the woman who, in order to avoid and to gratify her masochistic wishes, uses methods acquired in adolescence and preserved in maturity. She lets herself be seduced by the delusions and sublimations of eroticism. She is inclined to have a forbidden or secret dream that permits her to forget and repress her daily privations. She is induced to take part in ideologic movements, often of a very abstract nature, and indulges in fantasies about the importance and grandeur of her activities, only to suffer disappointments again and again. As such women are often endowed with excellent critical minds, it is clear that some sort of unconscious motive must be at work in their behavior. Most often the motive is unconscious masochism that has not been normally assimilated because of its excessive intensity. In men we find similar situations only in adolescence or in states of serious neurosis. In women this is possible with a simultaneously existing good adjustment to reality; above all, it is much more general and frequent. *The attraction of suffering is incomparably stronger for women than for men.*

Women are often prone to expressions of the most active indignation. They often participate in violent anonymous protests and join revolutionary movements. Most of the time they are unconsciously protesting against their own fate. By identifying themselves with the socially oppressed or the nonpossessing class, they take up a position against their own unsatisfying role. In many women this expresses a kind of "masculine protest" and their sublimated and socialized dissatisfaction with their feminine destiny. If one has an opportunity to observe these women and is not misled by the part played by the masculinity complex, great as it may be, one learns that they have strongly masochistic pasts and have often experienced real masochistic tyranny. In the childhood history of these women we find tyrannical fathers, and their sublimated activity is unconsciously directed against those who oppressed their mothers and limited their own freedom. It is interesting to note that the revolutionary woman leaders of the anti-tsarist movement, for example, were often daughters of authoritarian generals or—and this only an apparent contradiction—oppressed minor officials. They were all distinguished by an extraordinary readiness for sacrifice and a need to suffer for their ideas. In their love life they were either absolutely ascetic and had no erotic interests, because they had devoted all their femininity to the cause, or else they here too suffered the torments of longing and privation because their work as a rule actually separated them from their lovers; sometimes they devotedly and masochistically loved their own leaders and often had real affairs with them. In the behavior of daughters of passively tolerant fathers, identification with these fathers plays a part, for these women have actively taken up suppressed protests of the latter. Precisely such women usually seek and find a "tyrant" for a lover, and he gives them what their fathers failed to give them.

In some women repressed masochism emerges far from its sources; others catch up directly with a masochism that they formerly failed to gratify. This most powerful factor of femininity asserts itself directly in some, by detours in others; in erotic love in some, under a mask of masculinity in others. At this point psychologic insight inevitably comes close to value judgments. It is not a matter of indifference whether woman employs her surplus masochism for prostitution or for impressive heroism, just as it is not a matter of indifference whether a man as a result of his exuberant active-aggressive forces becomes a gangster or a hero in the service of a great idea. Nor is it one and the same thing whether the narcissistic guardian, by repelling masochism, contributes to the inner harmony of the erotic woman, or renounces direct gratification by permitting the masochistic sacrifice for an impersonal aim. In women whose achievements for society are great, one can often observe the harmonious operation of the two com-

ponents in areas remote from eroticism. What strikes one for
example in the diary of Vera Figner,[11] the Russian revolutionary, is the fact that the word "I" is seldom used in an
egotistic sense. It always represents a part of a whole; the
personal achievement is modestly concealed behind the heroism
of the movement. The psychologist should not be misled by
his knowledge of the sources and mechanisms of psychologic
phenomena and should appraise them according to their
social value.

The little stenographer who worships her boss, whoever he
may be, and who bears with him in his worst moods, allegedly
in order to keep her job, the sensitive woman who cannot
leave her brutal husband because she loves him "despite"
(actually because of) his brutality, and the active and talented
woman collaborator who devotes all her intuitive gifts to her
master's productions, are all happy in these roles and repress
their erotic longings. The Slavic peasant woman who lets
her drunken husband beat her and declares sadly, "He does
not love me, he has stopped beating me," the heroine and
the prostitute—all of them are happy or wretched according
to the extent of their feminine masochism and the degree to
which they can utilize and assimilate it. The success or failure
of this assimilation determines whether the woman develops
a harmonious femininity, becomes neurotic, or forms a pathologic masochistic personality.

In all the examples we have given, the borderline between
"normal" and "pathologic" is fluid. What is common to
both is the fact that whatever the form that the masochistic
component may assume, it remains completely *unconscious* as
a source or condition of pleasure. Even those whose masochism is quantitatively far beyond the "normal" limit are not
aware of the fact that they provoke the masochistic situation
or bear up with it because of—not in spite of—the suffering it
brings them.

In one of her functions woman must have a certain amount
of masochism if she is to be adjusted to reality. This is the

[11] FIGNER, V.: Nacht über Russland. Berlin: Malik, 1928.

reproductive function: from beginning to the end, even where it most serves the purpose of pleasure, it requires toleration of considerable pain. The real dangers inherent in woman's service to the species impel her to assimilate her feminine masochism and her human anxiety. This achievement seems to run counter to the individual striving for pleasure. In the functions of the genital apparatus, two contradictory interests, that of the individual who strives for pleasure and that of the species, involving pain, must be unified. They can become connected only if pain is endowed with the character of pleasure. Woman's entire psychologic preparation for the sexual and reproductive functions is connected with masochistic ideas.[12] In these ideas, coitus is closely associated with the act of defloration, and defloration with rape and a painful penetration of the body. The sexual readiness, the psychologic pleasure-affirming preparation for the sexual act, draws its masochistic components from two sources—one infantile, regressive, and dispositional, and the other *real*. For defloration is really painful and involves the destruction of a part of the body. The rape fantasy reveals itself as only an exaggeration of reality. Acceptance of pain associated with pleasure, or of pleasure associated with pain, may result in such a close connection between the two that the sexual pleasure becomes dependent on pain. Thus feminine sexuality acquires a masochistic character. Actually a certain amount of masochism as psychologic preparation for adjustment to the sexual functions is necessary in woman, but it is clear that the danger of "too much," and of pathologic distortion, arises from this situation.

The second motive for the association between pain and pleasure derives directly from the reproductive function. All the conscious and unconscious fantasies relating to childbirth, in all its phases, have throughout a painful and dangerous character. As a result, the wish for a child acquires a masochistic character through being closely associated with the fantasies. Here again it is the *reality* of labor pains and of

[12] DEUTSCH, H.: The significance of masochism in the mental life of women.

the whole bloody process of birth that endows masochism with the function of adjustment to reality. And here there is the same danger of pathologic distortion. The pleasure in the child may be replaced by the pain of childbirth and the sufferings of motherhood, and thus the whole reproductive function is given an abnormally masochistic character.

Woman's relation to her genitals, the scar of the genital trauma, the emotional components of the female castration complex, of which we shall speak later, as well as menstruation, naturally contribute to the masochistic character of her sexual functions.

Thus, we see that masochism plays a dual role in the feminine sexual and reproductive functions: on the one hand, it helps in the adjustment to reality through the necessary consent to pain; on the other hand, an excess of masochism naturally provokes a defense, and, fleeing from the dangers of an excessive masochism, woman turns away from her tasks, from her femininity. Masochism will then have the same effect as an abnormally intensified sensitivity to pain produced by excessive self-love. This sensitivity mobilizes a defense that can result in all sorts of disturbances of the feminine functions. Thus, fear of pain may stem either from excessive masochism or the excessive narcissistic intolerance of the ego, which refuses to accept any discomfort. Each of these two important factors of the psyche, masochism and narcissism, may work against the requirements of the reproductive function. Thus the destiny of woman as the servant of reproduction likewise depends on the harmonious cooperation of masochism and narcissism.[13]

[13] At this point I should like to defend my previous work against a misinterpretation. K. Horney contends that I regard feminine masochism as an "elemental power in feminine mental life" and that, according to my view, "what woman ultimately wants in intercourse is to be raped and violated; what she wants in mental life is to be humiliated." It is true that I consider masochism "an elemental power in feminine life," but in my previous studies and also in this one I have tried to show that one of woman's tasks is to govern this masochism, to steer it into the right paths, and thus to protect herself against those dangers that Horney thinks I consider woman's "normal" lot. Cf. K. Horney: New ways in psychoanalysis. New York: Norton, 1938, p. 110.

CHAPTER EIGHT

The "Active" Woman:
The Masculinity Complex

W E HAVE tried to define our concept of femininity and have done so in terms that seem to contradict several accepted facts and can therefore be of value only after these latter have been clarified.

One of our psychoanalytic concepts that seems still to need further clarification is that of the masculinity complex in women, and the popular and yet provoking and objectionable—this not without reason—concept of penis envy.

To femininity, as we have defined it, we ascribe the role of a nucleus that combines biologic, physiologic, anatomic, and psychologic elements. The organic factors are relatively constant; the psychologic factors vary with the individual, according to her inner processes and the influence of the environment.

Although the interaction of all these elements results in great individual variations, the nucleus crystallizes from their combined effects. It forms the quintessence of femininity. Various and multiform additional elements come to join it, some of which may figure in the constant psychic inventory of the feminine personality. Other psychic phenomena arising from conflicts, compromises, defense mechanisms, etc., can be called "marginal phenomena," because they move away from the central core, yet are typical and frequent. If the mental ingredients outside femininity are not in a harmonious relation with the feminine core, insoluble conflicts arise, these being manifested in neurotic phenomena. Sometimes a subsidiary element may succeed in occupying the central position and endow the woman with a less feminine character that is not, however, necessarily abnormal or pathologic.

We have identified certain tendencies with femininity. If a trait we ascribe to femininity is occasionally found in a man, it is recognized as feminine. A relatively large degree of passivity, for example, lends a man a feminine character as a subsidiary result of abnormal psychic processes.

In so far as the direct manifestations of sexuality are concerned, the principle of what might be called division of labor is clearly prescribed organically; that is to say, activity is the share of man, passivity that of woman. Here too, it must be emphasized, passivity does not mean apathy or lack of sexual energy. This energy may even be quantitatively very large; in that case it manifests itself in the intensity of passive-receptive readiness. Likewise with masochism: if we find a large amount of it in a man, we rightly derive it from his sense of guilt, and understand it as moral masochism. In contrast to this, female masochism is integrated with the woman's personality, is assimilable and capable of being definitively sublimated, so that it hardly emerges as an independent factor. Only when it reaches an excessive intensity can it come into conflict with the rest of the woman's personality and be regarded as a pathologic phenomenon.

We have conceived the realization of femininity as a result of the "turn" of active-aggressive forces. For the sake of greater clarity and to avoid possible misunderstanding, we shall briefly summarize our idea of the processes involved.

Our view of the girl's early childhood rejects the psychoanalytic hypothesis that the young girl in this period is masculine. Direct observation shows that the girl from the very beginning has pronounced feminine traits. Nevertheless, there is considerable similarity between children of both sexes; this results not, however, from their being both masculine, but from the fact that definitive differentiation takes place later. This identity is both passive and active; the first kind predominates. Children of both sexes are suckled at the mother's breast, have to be taught to be clean, restrict their object relations to one person (the mother), have aggressive impulses, and adjust themselves to reality by similar devices.

The definite differentiation of the sexes occurs in the phase in which the increasing activity of the instincts and of the ego meets with different outcomes in the girl and the boy. The boy's task is to get rid of the aggressive ingredient and for the time being to put all his active tendencies at the disposal of the ego and its adjustment to reality. Through experiencing the disorders and anxieties of his development, the boy finally achieves normal boyish activity in the outside world. His aggressive and actively genital instinctual tendencies show him the way; he is aided by educational measures and his own urge to master reality. Gradually he grows less dependent upon his instinctual impulses. Parallel with his instinctual development, his ego is formed, and if the result of his progress is favorable, he can turn his active forces toward the outside world.

The same striving for activity also characterizes the little girl's ego. But in contrast to the boy's situation, the active and aggressive forces of the girl are subjected to external and internal inhibition. All the factors involved—biologic-constitutional, anatomic, and environmental—combine to produce this inhibition. At this point we must correct and supplement our previous exposition: this inhibition is only partial. Many of the active and aggressive forces are preserved as positive ingredients of feminine mental life. As a rule they are harmoniously integrated into the total structure, even if we assign to them the character of masculinity. In this interpretation, the "feminine core" is a product of inhibition that is accompanied by a number of uninhibited active and aggressive tendencies. To achieve equilibrium, a system must be built in which these tendencies lead not to abnormal phenomena, but to normal and positive results. By this we mean that woman's activity acquires an abnormal and disturbing character if it comes into conflict with the rest of her personality, that is to say, with the feminine core. Only then can we speak of the masculinity complex. But before discussing this, let us examine woman's normal activity. What are its sources and aims? We are particularly interested in the activity of the ego, which reveals itself as an inherent force in psychic development.

We have seen before that the increasing urge to master reality plays an extraordinarily important part in causing children of both sexes to turn away from their mothers toward their fathers. We have also learned that in the ego's drive toward adulthood, identification with the active mother proves a useful instrument in the girl's development toward active aims. The active mother is for the little girl the prototype of the active tendencies associated with motherhood. The identification with this active mother is for the most part expressed in the little girl's games, and is shown in her relationship with her younger siblings, with little animals, dolls, etc. We cannot be sure whether this is a psychologic or biologic factor in which, even in childhood, something like the maternal instinct is involved. At any rate the activity we see in the little girl as a product of her identification with the active mother acquires a permanent psychologic representation, which lends woman a definite character. Actually it is always there, and is particularly intensified in puberty, when it is a new manifestation that we have called the harbinger of motherhood. The nature of this activity is very characteristic, and its content goes beyond having children and nursing and rearing them; it is closely akin to those attitudes by which the little girl distinguishes herself from the little boy at an early date. The preliminary signs of the difference between the sexes are clearly discernible in children's games. The little male's activity is directed outward; forward aspiring movement, repeated additions from the outside to things built, and eventual destruction of them, characterize the boy. The little female builds houses in order always to put something inside them, to close gates and carefully preserve what has been built. Her games have the character of nest-building activity, of putting things in order and keeping them together.

When this form of activity takes the central role in the framework of the personality, a feminine type develops that under suitable cultural conditions is identical with that of the active "domineering" mother.   The nature of this woman's activity is not necessarily intellectual, her personal aspirations are not particularly ambitious or competitive with regard to men. She creates an atmosphere of will power and certainty of purpose that predisposes her to matriarchy.

This feminine type is closest to that which we have called the erotic-active.   It differs from this latter chiefly in the fact that the erotic and passive components are weaker, but, in common with our feminine type, this woman, in addition to her greater outward activity, develops an activity directed inward, which, however, serves aims other than erotic ones.   Because her activity is of a motherly character, she is predisposed, under suitable social conditions, to have many children or to create substitute products in activities intended to take the place of direct motherhood.   She founds childrens' homes and nurseries, on a small or large scale, real or symbolic.   Along with this, as an expression of her activity directed inward, she has a deep religiousness, not always of an institutional character.   She has cultural and ideologic interests and her values are conservative.   She usually lacks revolutionary impetus, but is capable of decisive actions in support of her values such as they are.   In families with this type of mother there prevails a kind of matriarchate, for the mother not only rules in the home but also directs the fate of her kin.   In brief, she is the same woman that Bachofen, the discoverer of the institution of matriarchy, found in early human history.[1]

While today this figure acts under different cultural condi-

---

[1] BACHOFEN, J. J.: Mutterrecht und Urreligion. Leipzig: Koerner.   We need not take sides here in the polemics over the historical correctness of Bachofen's theories.   It may be disputed whether there ever existed a "telluric gynecocracy," with the mother at the head of the social order, and Bachofen's presentation of the evidence may be subjective and open to question.   But there is no doubt that such a powerful mother figure exists in myths and various very ancient fantasy formations.   We are indebted for an interesting study of these problems to Beata Rank: Zur Rolle der Frau in der Entwicklung der menschlichen Gesellschaft.   Imago, vol. 10, 1924.

tions, she represents the same mother principle, which has a deep
psychologic foundation. She bears witness to the fact that
although in the course of human history various forms of life
and social organization have been discarded and replaced by
new ones, and religions, ideals, and ethical commandments and
valuations have changed, certain psychic features in the development of the individual have remained for centuries uninfluenced by all these outer transformations.

These features combine into units, sometimes in myths,
sometimes in highly differentiated cultural organizations; some
of them emerge, others disappear, to reappear again later.

The following lines are from Bachofen's *Mutterrecht und Urreligion* ("Matriarchy and Primitive Religion"):

> More ancient than the male prophet is feminine prophecy; more constant
> in loyalty, firmer in faith is the feminine soul; woman, weaker than man, is
> nevertheless occasionally capable of rising far above him; she is more conserv-
> ative, particularly in cults and when it comes to the preservation of the
> ceremonial element. . . . Traced back to the prototype of Demeter, the
> earthly mother becomes, as it were, the mortal representative of the telluric
> primeval mother, her priestess, and as hierophantic priestess, is entrusted
> with the administration of her mysteries. The religious primacy of birth-
> giving motherhood leads to that of the mortal woman. . . . The mysterious
> constitutes the true nature of every religion, and wherever woman plays a
> leading part in the cult and in life, she shows a bias for the mysterious. This
> is warranted by her natural disposition, which indissolubly connects the sen-
> sual and the suprasensual, by her close kinship with the life of nature and
> with matter, whose eternal death first arouses in her the need of a comforting
> thought.

Thus, the Demeter mother rule is, according to Bachofen,
associated with the cultivation and development of the mysterious, the supernatural, the religious, and is distinguished by
the appearance of sublime priestly feminine figures. The
gynecocratic civilization consecrates motherhood and is characterized by an intensification of the mystic, the religious, and
similar elements; woman in it is the severe guardian of the
mysteries, of law and peace.

This is the prototype of that active-motherly woman who

has a primitive feminine quality in her spirituality. This quality constitutes a bridge between her and the inwardly erotic-
feminine woman, even though the two are essentially different.

We emphasize again that our classifications are intended only
for purposes of exposition; when we speak of types it is always
with the reservation that pure types are almost nonexistent,
and that in each real type one can always find traits of another,
sometimes directly opposite type. Thus, among our active-
feminine types we often encounter women who, for all their
eligibility to be chiefs of a matriarchy, display tendencies that
do not quite tally with the pure type: indeed, such "impure"
traits sometimes manifest themselves even in women of Bachofen's matriarchy. Even in the period of her domination,
woman, weaker than man, displays an inclination, arising from
her feeling of weakness, to subject the stronger sex through
religious influences and moral values. "Equipped with such
forces the weaker sex was enabled to undertake the struggle
against the stronger one and to triumph."   In exactly the same
way, without being conscious of their aims, the modern representative of this type of woman often supports tendencies that
serve to weaken and enslave man. It is no accident that the
husbands of such women, although living in a patriarchal civilization and having all paternal rights and duties, are very often
pushed out of the role of the forceful father. Nor is it an accident that the sons of these women, full of reverence and admiration for their active mothers and accepting their lofty ideology,
remain passive, feminine, and strongly dependent upon them.
It seems that when woman's activity goes beyond a definite
degree of intensity, it is accompanied by forces that inhibit the
activity of the persons in her entourage and thus becomes dangerous especially for the male members of the family.

Similarity to the primitive matriarchy in many families goes
so far that the daughters inherit not the material goods of the
family as in primitive society, but the spiritual goods. The
men carry on their business outside the home, pursue money,
exhaust themselves in competitive struggles, while the women—

mothers and daughters—cultivate spiritual values in religious, intellectual, or artistic fields.

So long as their environment accepts the motherly-active women in this role, they are not subject to the manifestations of the masculinity complex. Only when their motherly activity is inhibited from outside do reactions appear that point to a large number of aggressions. These are often concealed behind depressive moods or lead to alterations of character that are contrary to thoughtful, self-sacrificing motherliness.

It seems that as a rule, despite its motherly-feminine form, woman's activity, if it oversteps definite limits, leads to the renunciation of feminine-erotic experiences or to the restriction of her capacity for them.

It is difficult to decide whether we should infer from this that increased activity always develops at the expense of the other elements of femininity; there is no doubt that frequently the sensual attraction of the motherly woman is unfavorably influenced by her active behavior. But here as elsewhere one must not indulge in generalizations.

The disposition to this type is founded, as we have said, in the successful identification with an active mother. Thus the turn toward passivity assumed a milder form, the aggressive tendencies were poured into a specific kind of activity.

We have seen that the prepuberal activity thrust constituted an offensive that, independently of the sexual instinctual tendencies, aimed at the conquest of reality. This intensified activity may outlast the girl's turn toward passivity, a process that takes place in puberty. The woman "colleague" or "comrade," the ambitious or "pushing" type, can preserve her femininity provided that even in her unconscious she does not make her activity depend on the condition of masculinity. Sometimes she behaves like the little girl we have mentioned before, who insisted on playing with boys as their equal only in order to be whipped from time to time. Later the situation takes place in the conscious erotic experience, and the whipping loses its literal meaning.

Another form of woman's activity stems from her active identification with her father, in which she renounces her feminine-erotic role and achieves a satisfactory sublimation; the fact that she is not a man does not give her any inferiority feelings in this situation. Here too femininity is in danger: sometimes it splits off from the sublimated elements and, as we have mentioned above, assumes an overpassive and overmasochistic character. In other cases, it is gratified by detours (for instance, through professional activity of a motherly-feminine character, like pedagogy, etc.). This identification, which comes to the fore especially in puberty, as a link in the normal development, can also become the starting point of complications.

Active-erotic behavior, coquetry, for instance, is part of feminine equipment, but paradoxically enough, it is precisely here that the borderline between active and aggressive is very fluid. The feminine-erotic woman practices her art of seduction in an unconscious, more passive manner. Active provocative coquetry is generally felt to be an aggression. Circe and Lorelei only wear the mask of femininity—just like their modern counterpart, the "vamp." It is interesting to note that conversely also a woman's aggression can constitute a flight and a mask for deeply feminine instinctual desires that are dangerous for her and are therefore repressed. And what is repressed often re-emerges in a tragic fashion. A wonderful illustration of this is the figure of Carmen, the Spanish cigarette worker, immortalized in Bizet's opera. Probably based on a real character, she is the heroine of numerous popular tales and short stories (the best known of these is by Prosper Mérimée). An infinite feminine narcissistic charm is always ascribed to her, by means of which she catches masculine hearts only to play a cruel sadistic game with them.

How is it possible that so much cruelty and heartlessness does not scandalize us and lead us to reject her fascination? The reason is that while following her destiny we constantly feel that Carmen directs the weapon of her aggressions not only against other people, but also and principally against herself, to gratify her own cruel masochism.   Sadistically enjoying the torment of others, she at the same time masochistically enjoys her own panic fear of the ultimate outcome that she herself prepares with iron fatality.   In this clandestine anticipated enjoyment lies the whole subtle power of the masochistic impulse.   How easily and quickly Carmen could have died at the hand of the *torero;* but she chooses a passive, powerless man for the slow seduction to murder.   The flight and reconciliation with the weak soldier and the certainty of the desired end attract Carmen as a child is attracted by the cruel play with a fly whose wings are to be torn off.   In this case, the fly is her own feminine heart burning in masochistic desire.

Many women—feminine women—are deeply stirred by Carmen's fate and—sometimes sobbingly—confess their identity with her.   It would be a mistake to think that they consider themselves like her in the charm with which she seduces men or in her cold-blooded sadism.   What stirs up the unconscious in these women is Carmen's archfeminine, tragically whipped-up masochism.

In "modern-minded" circles the view seems to prevail that woman's passivity in sexual matters is outmoded and that now it is the woman who chooses the object and takes the sexual initiative.   Such behavior goes against biologic and psychologic laws.   Those who regard it as an expression of a social-evolutionary development are the victims of an illusion.   What takes place here is not, as is believed, the "liberation" of woman from a social evil that condemns her to passivity.   In the light of psychology, this reversal of roles can be seen in many cases as arising from the interplay of two anxieties: women use activity as a mechanism of defense against the fear of their passivity, just as Carmen uses her excessive aggression against masochism. Men escape the responsibility and effort connected with active wooing.   Apparent progress conceals the neurotic disturbance of both sexes.

When we speak of woman's activity we often add the adjective "masculine." Yet we assume the existence of a feminine activity; thus we seem to fall into a contradiction. Nevertheless the two notions are connected—because of their genesis, the history of their development, and their affinity with aggressive instinctual components. These components lead the boy in a straight line to masculinity; in the girl they are subjected to an inhibition. The remaining active forces in woman, under definite conditions, also reveal their masculine origin, especially when they are accompanied by stronger aggressive tendencies. As we have seen, the final differentiation of the two sexes into masculine and feminine is preceded by a bisexual phase that leaves more or less strong traces in both. Our psychoanalytic investigations show that usually we are confronted here by a psychologic process, whether or not it is founded on a biologic factor.

This brings us to woman's masculinity complex.

In our view, the masculinity complex is characterized by the predominance of active and aggressive tendencies that lead to conflicts with the woman's environment and above all with the remaining feminine inner world. The various forms of these conflicts determine various types. In its most primitive manifestation, masculinity appears as the direct enemy of feminine tendencies, disturbing their function. Such disturbances manifest themselves especially in the affective life as well as in all specifically feminine phases of life (menstruation, pregnancy, childbirth, etc.) Here again we may encounter a vicious circle: fear of femininity mobilizes the masculine tendencies, which in their turn increase the disturbance. As this fear chiefly relates to the reproductive functions, it is not surprising that in the pathology of these we often find manifestations of the masculinity complex. From a therapeutic point of view it is important to realize that the masculinity complex often conceals not a protest against but a fear of the feminine functions.

Another form of the conflict between femininity and masculinity results from the fact that the woman's psychologic interest is here turned toward aims in the pursuit of which femininity is felt as troublesome and is rejected. Here a feeling of inferiority may develop, stemming from the perception that the feminine components of the personality hinder achievement of the desired aims. In this case, the manifestations of the masculinity complex may assume a more depressive character: the woman feels that she is inefficient, that she will never achieve her ends.

In other cases, the masculine-active forces are to a great extent successfully sublimated, but this is accomplished either at the expense of feminine values or in constant conflict with them. The simplest example of such a conflict is provided by the mother who, after each success she achieves in her professional activity, or after each ambition-gratifying situation, instead of feeling satisfaction, is tormented by guilt feelings with regard to her children. This category also includes those women who constantly waver between two kinds of duties—those of wife and mother on the one hand, and those of a professional career on the other—and who find satisfaction in neither. The clash between these two kinds of real duties is usually caused by a displacement of a deeper emotional conflict to a reality situation. The active woman actually does transfer to other goals psychic energies that she otherwise would spend directly on the objects of her environment, particularly on her children. And, conversely, not all her psychic energies are available for these goals, because, as a woman, she has spent them emotionally on more direct object relations.

More complicated and veiled is the masculinity complex in those women who have brilliantly succeeded in sublimating their masculine activity but are not aware of the fact that they have paid a high price for it in their feminine values. Woman's intellectuality is to a large extent paid for by the loss of valuable feminine qualities: it feeds on the sap of the affective life and results in impoverishment of this life either as a whole or in specific emotional qualities. The intellectual woman is not Autonoë, the Wise One, who draws her wisdom from the deep sources of intuition, for intuition is God's gift to the feminine woman; everything relating to exploration and cognition, all the forms and kinds of human cultural aspiration that require a strictly objective approach, are with few exceptions the domain of the masculine intellect, of man's spiritual power, against which woman can rarely compete. All observations point to the fact that the intellectual woman is masculinized; in her, warm intuitive knowledge has yielded to cold unproductive thinking. To her particularly Goethe's saying applies:

> Believe me, a fellow who speculates
> Is like a beast on an arid heath,
> Led 'round in circles by an evil spirit
> While close by a green meadow lies.

The "green meadow" stands here for feminine affectivity, and the "arid heath" for the speculating intellectuality to which woman is led by her masculinity complex.

Innumerable types of intellectual-masculine women could be cited; we shall mention one of them particularly, for we encounter this woman rather frequently, and she is quite interesting. A comparison of this type with other, feminine types of women brings her psychic structure into clear relief. She replaces the charming warmth of the feminine-erotic woman by flattery. Usually she does not compete with men, for she is intelligent enough to realize the limitations of her talents. She tries to achieve superiority over other, often more talented women through being respected and appreciated by men as their equal. She likes to show her identification with men, but unlike the feminine woman, she proposes to do so not by intuitive sympathy, but by a kind of shrewd grasp of masculine ideas and a flattering appreciation of them. Her intellectuality moves within limited forms; she often succeeds in reproducing respectably the achievements of others, thanks to a formal talent (as reviewer, orator, teacher, etc.). She explains her lack of productivity, of which she is not unconscious, by inhibitions from which she hopes to free herself.

The masculinity complex of this intellectual type usually has a specific origin: it comes into being indirectly as a result of thwarted femininity. A comparison with the active-motherly woman will further clarify our point: the latter is the Demeter type of woman, whose strong mother-daughter relationship, identification with the active mother, has endowed all her personality with its specific character. The intellectual woman of the nonfeminine type discussed here has no mother in the psychologic sense of the term. She is, continuing our mythologic parallel, like Pallas Athene, the woman born out of her father's head. She also differs from the active woman mentioned above in whom identification with the father may play a part, by the fact that her own ego has been extremely impoverished through the elimination of the mother. Interestingly enough, the childhood history of this type shows no competitive or jealous attitude toward her brothers, as we might expect. On the contrary, she is allied with her brothers, after the manner of Pallas Athene. This alliance is usually motivated by jealousy of a prettier or more loved older or younger sister. By joining her brothers, this type of woman achieves superiority over her sister and dismisses her mother, her sisters, and her own femininity from her emotional life.

Other active-masculine types show the surplus of active-aggressive forces in a more direct manner. The sadistic witch riding on a broom, the herb gatherer and healer, with a big stick in her hand and a bagful of mysterious things on her back, and many other figures out of mythology and folklore, clearly reveal the connection between aggression and masculinity in woman. This connection seems to us of decisive importance; for our repeatedly advanced conception of woman's development implies that woman's masculinity originates in a surplus of aggressive forces that were not subjected to inhibition and that lack the possibility of an outlet such as is open to man. For this reason, the masculine woman is also the aggressive woman.

Classic examples of active-aggressive personalities that constantly strive to give their excessive activity a rational purpose, and can never achieve peace, are provided by women whose behavior has a decided hypomanic character.   On closer examination these very women reveal the intimate connection of activity with aggression and masculinity.   Their perpetual actions and accomplishments serve a twofold purpose: they are a direct expression of the excess of aggressive forces for which they always seek outlets, and a manifestation of denial of the passive-feminine element and of the absence of a masculine organ.

I had an opportunity to observe over a long period a woman whose personality must have seemed odd indeed until she was unmasked by analysis.[2]   The many mishaps that had marked her life had left no trace upon her; she reacted to every misfortune with philosophic superiority, each time stressing all the good things that still remained to her.   There was no question of apathy in her case, because she had an exuberant temperament, constantly engaged in new friendships and love affairs, in successful studies of new subjects, etc.   Her unconcern with her outward fate could be observed in the course of her treatment.   During that period she was deserted by her husband and lover, lost a large part of her fortune, and personally experienced the tragic fate of the mother who is given up by her grown-up son (this woman was strongly attached to her son) in favor of another woman.   Nothing of all that could disturb her euphoria; she always and immediately found a way out by depreciating what she had just lost or by immediately creating substitute values that nipped in the bud the reaction to the loss and negated it.   The result was always: "Actually, I have not lost anything."

In this patient I saw quite clearly how the entire mechanism of denial had begun in connection with the birth of her brother. When this event took place, her behavior was so striking that all her family remembered it as a kind of family saga.   For a

---

[2] DEUTSCH, H.: Zur Psychologie der manisch-depressiven Zustände, insbesondere der chronischen Hypomanie.   Internat. Ztschr. f. Psychoanal., vol. 19, 1933.

short period—the patient was then a little girl—she developed furious aggressions against the newborn child; this was followed by a phase in which she declared that she possessed all the things that she knew would be denied her.   For some time her behavior was pseudologic; she told all sorts of fantastic stories intended to show that she actually possessed all the things she claimed to possess.   For instance, she once said during her religion lesson that her father had given her Mount Ararat and that she had built a house for her doll on it.

In later years she accepted a certain compromise with reality: while trying to transform it in line with her wishes, she did this in such way as to be able constantly to negate her privations as well as her own aggressions; but she stopped telling fantastic lies.   She became conscious of the morbid character of her efforts to negate frustrations only during treatment.

We have cited this neurotic woman as an example because her behavior differs only in degree from that of many sound and worth while women.   Many such women, pioneers in important fields, prominent because of their initiative and indefatigable efforts, who have made valuable contributions to the welfare of mankind because of their will and energy, resemble my hypomanic patient to a great degree.   I do not cite their names, out of respect for their achievements.

In their love life these women usually suffer great disappointments.   The overactivity and frequent change of aims characteristic of them are manifested usually in their masculine fields.   Erotically they are very often more stable, that is, they do not change their love objects, and love does not play an important part in their lives.   Their choice of men is made difficult as a result of their preference for passive men, whom they later furiously urge to become active and whom they persecute with the eternal reproach of not being sufficiently energetic.   Like Brunhilde, these women vainly seek a Siegfried who could make them feminine, for they avoid active men, and the passive ones can hardly develop into Siegfrieds, especially in the atmosphere created by these women.   Their relationships with active men always end in conflicts, in which both partners are filled with hate and aggression.

Another type of overactive woman operates in the sexual field also. Just as the former changes her nonerotic interests, the latter changes her love objects. We also meet with this type in prostitution, the nature of which is partly explained by the masculinity complex. The type of prostitute described in the previous chapter is, in contrast to this latter type, determined by masochism.

In all the groups described so far, the women are just as unconscious of their turn toward masculinity as of their turn away from femininity. In some cases they are feminine in appearance, and even try to emphasize the fact that they belong to the feminine sex. Their efforts to be feminine are incessant and futile, just as are their efforts to be masculine.

Psychologic observation shows that such a turning away from femininity or turning toward masculinity involves a complicated process that often has many determinants.[3] The basis of the mental conflicts and difficulties that arise here is a dispositional readiness for them, created by the developmental processes we have described.

The psychologic motives of these conflicts are extraordinarily numerous. We shall take up only a few of them here with regard to the masculinity complex. A disturbance in the identification with the mother certainly plays a great part in the development toward femininity. What is most ominous is not pure and simple rejection of the mother, but a conflict between rejecting and clinging to her. For instance, a girl in puberty forming her ego ideal can completely reject identification with her mother through her consciously or unconsciously determined depreciation, and follow a different model. If the mother is excluded from the ego formation in this period of the girl's life, the model is only the father. The girl's emotional

[3] HORNEY, K.: The flight from womanhood. Internat. J. Psycho-Analysis, 1926. The author points especially to the Oedipus complex as motive for such a flight.

personality may still be formed after her mother, partly as a result of a continuation of her early infantile identification with her, partly as a result of rivalry for the father's love.   This leads to a conflict between two identifications that is solved favorably, or creates an inner tension the resolution of which is possible only through repression of one component and excessive growth of the other.   If the motherly part of the personality is the one that is repressed, the fatherly part will, by reaction, manifest great intensity, in order to negate the other; then we shall be confronted with a reactive form of masculinity. Women with this kind of masculinity repress every feminine gesture or emotional expression and do everything they can to appear masculine.   Such repression may completely impoverish and devastate the woman's emotional life, for she depreciates and rejects everything emotional.   Some women boast of this coldness as a proof of strength, others complain of it without realizing that their emotional poverty is a prerequisite for the masculine component of the psyche, which they have accepted.

A phenomenon frequently found, especially among talented young persons successful intellectually or professionally, is the sudden overwhelming fear that the feminine role must be given up and the gratification of feminine desires completely renounced in favor of activity.   This fear is sometimes neurotically related to the body and may be expressed as: "Something is wrong with my body, I have hair like a man, my genitals are not normal."   The feeling that the genitals have a masculine appearance expresses the unsatisfied wish to be loved and to love as a woman; through her inner perception of her masculine tendencies, the girl feels disturbed in her femininity and displaces the psychologic difficulty to the body.   One might object that in this case, as in many others, dissatisfaction with one's own body indirectly expresses the absence of a masculine organ. But this is not the case; it must not be overlooked that we are confronted here with a conflict situation that is fed from two sides, and that no choice has been made between two wishes:

the girl would gladly be a man but refuses to renounce the fulfillment of her feminine wishes, and vice versa.

In other cases this lack of harmony between two identifications leads to a rift, and one part of the personality, for instance the emotional part, remains feminine; the intellect, turned toward real life and work, acts in a masculine manner. The emotional, feminine part can be exclusively related to sexuality and eroticism or it may include part of the sublimations. Such a solution might lead to great harmony and excellent achievements; but usually the harmony is lost when stronger demands are made either upon the affective-feminine life or on the masculine efficiency.

An extraordinarily clear example of a conflict between femininity and masculinity is represented by George Sand, the French novelist. Her conflicts are so typical and so clear that she is a perfect illustration of our theoretic views.[4]

George Sand has always fascinated biographers of various nationalities, and there is a large body of literature concerning her. I select from her life only a few facts so typical that they can well serve to illustrate our problem.

There are two photographs of George Sand that present a striking contrast.

In one we see a rather stout, motherly type of woman, holding her children in her lap; in the other, a masculine person, in man's clothes, with short hair and a cigar in her mouth—and it should be borne in mind that George Sand lived in a period in which the general masculinization of women we see today had not yet taken place, so that her appearance in the photograph is more extreme and individualistic than would be the same degree of masculinity in a woman's appearance today. These two pictures indicate at once a kind of double personality, a split, a conflict between masculine and feminine tendencies. This double personality expresses itself even in the artist's name. As a female her name was Aurore Dupin, and when she

[4] The discussion that follows is an excerpt from an earlier published extensive essay by the writer: Ein Frauenschicksal: George Sand. Imago, vol. 14, 1928.

married she became Madame Dudevant.   But the name that
as a writer she made famous was her masculine name, George
Sand.

She is the classic type of man-woman, the strange being who
seems to carry a masculine soul in a feminine body.   Close
examination of her life shows that the masculinity complex,
even in its pure form, results from an unsuccessful striving for
a feminine realization of happiness; it is a stake in the happiness
lying outside the boundary of the feminine.   We shall see that
this frustration of the feminine lay deeply hidden in her childhood experiences.   It was because of these that her femininity
could never attain happy fulfillment.

It is known that George Sand, as a woman, led a very promiscuous life and ruined many men.   As lovers she chose so-called
feminine men.   People spoke jestingly of "Monsieur Sand" and
"Madame de Musset."   It was also a matter of common
knowledge that Chopin, one of her love victims, was of a feminine nature.   It was thought natural for her to choose this type
of lover, for thus the masculine and feminine could balance each
other.   Hence it was said that the masculine George Sand loved
feminine men.

Each of George Sand's numerous love affairs terminated in
literally the selfsame catastrophe: the man was destroyed—
George Sand's masculinity prospered.   But there was also
something within her that was broken and destroyed.   We
shall devote particular attention to this part of her personality,
because in it lies the secret of her masculinity that we are
trying to penetrate.

To open the closed doors that lead to the hidden secret of her
fate, we have two keys: her voluminous autobiographic writings[5] and her novels.   We shall not concern ourselves, for the
present, with her scientific, philosophic, and social ideas, which
incidentally were on a high plane of masculine intellectuality.
Sainte-Beuve, Delatouche, Pierre Leroux, Lamennais, Flaubert,

[5] Journal intime (posthumous).   Paris: Calmann-Lévy, 1926.
Histoire de ma vie (3 vols.).   Paris: Calmann-Lévy, 1926.

the brothers Goncourt, Balzac, Delacroix, and many others treated her as an equal.

Now, despite her tremendous intuitiveness, which approached the level of genius, despite her effort to understand herself, George Sand's creative personality was split. One part supplied her autobiographic works with material from her conscious life, the other appears in her novels under various names and in numerous characters, betraying what was deeply rooted in her unconscious.

In her hours of artistic creation George Sand would fall into a kind of twilight state during which she made a decisive break with reality and set down in novels what she inwardly experienced. Her contemporaries said that she used to sit brooding for hours and days with a dazed expression, lost in the experiences of the heroines of her novels. She dreamed and rambled on in her dreams exactly as she had done as a child: even as a little girl she was a terror and an enigma to all who beheld her. George Sand herself said that she never experienced what she described in her novels—so far was her writing removed from her conscious existence. The heroines of her novels could at once, and in every case, by anyone who knew her life, be recognized as George Sand; but she was by no means willing to acknowledge this identity. When I studied her writings I was always able to find the parallelism between the experience behind her autobiographic works and that behind her novels—between conscious experience in the former, and unconscious experience in the latter.

With the aid of the analytic method we shall try to find out how the unresolved psychic experiences of George Sand's childhood, repressed into her unconscious, were compulsively repeated in her adult experience, and how the later enigmatic events in her life were faithful reproductions of a pattern previously stamped upon her emotions.

Even before her birth, a definite family constellation had already to some degree determined her fate. Her father was Maurice Dupin, son of Aurore de Saxe, and grandson of Prince

Maurice de Saxe, after whom he had been named. Prince Maurice was the son of the Polish king Frederick Augustus II and of the princess Aurore Königsmark, after whom George Sand was named Aurore. I mention this genealogy in order to explain the family pride evidenced by George Sand's grandmother, the elder Madame Dupin. George Sand's mother, on the other hand, was of humble origin, the daughter of a bird seller from the banks of the Seine. Now Grandmother Dupin completely transferred the intense attachment she felt for her famous father to her son. Maurice junior was to become the reincarnation of Maurice senior. The love demands that the father had not satisfied were to be satisfied by the son. It is not infrequent for mothers to make such dangerous demands on their sons. The mother's expectations are to be gratified in two ways: her pride in her son is to be satisfied, as well as her claim to being the sole recipient of his love. Grandmother Dupin, possessing unusual intellectual gifts, drove her only son Maurice to laborious study, just as she herself had already trained and formed her own intellect on the paternal model.

The ardent, intense bonds of love between Madame Dupin and Maurice were of an intellectual nature, based on a community of interests that had been created by study. This relation was terminated characteristically by the son: he made an attempt to free himself and chose a wife who was his mother's precise opposite. This woman, Sophie, George Sand's mother —in contrast to the highly aristocratic grandmother—was a plebeian. She could scarcely write grammatically. A prostitute type, she was clearly the antithesis of Madame Dupin, who was the essence of sexual chastity. While the grandmother was reserved and self-controlled, Sophie was undisciplined and unmannerly. Whereas for Madame Dupin motherhood was inconceivable without the sacrament of marriage, Sophie had illegitimate children.

Between these two women there developed a life and death struggle, such as could arise only between two rivals for the love of one man. Maurice stood between the two women, bound to each. He could renounce neither, for they corresponded to two separate strivings of his psyche: his need for tenderness tied him to his mother, and his sensuality to Sophie. His whole life was a sacrifice to this typical split, and the competitive struggle of the two women to possess the man was later transferred to the child. Both women, who became veritable furies, fought to win the child's heart, as once they had fought for Maurice. Little Aurore herself was a very feminine creature; she was quite like any normal girl. Like her grandmother and mother, she wanted to be the sole love object of her father, and engaged in the competitive struggle along with the two older women. In her diaries these things are not mentioned, for of course George Sand was not conscious of them; but her artistic inspiration, her novels, the fantasies produced in states of reverie by her unconscious double, relate indirectly to these events.

It is quite common for girls to hate their mothers for being the love objects of their fathers, but at the same time they try to identify themselves with their mothers and to resemble them, precisely in order to win the affection of their fathers. This is the normal way of attaining womanhood. Gradually hatred is abandoned, and the mothers are retained as models of femininity.

The stability of a girl's character formation depends on whether her ego ideal has developed in harmony with the father-mother model. At this point poor Aurore failed completely. Her personality did not develop harmoniously, and her ego ideal collapsed. Her childhood contained two mothers: both loved the father and were loved by the father in turn. Upon which of the two models was she to create her mother-woman ideal? Which would she take as a model to guide her in her relations with men? The grandmother loved little Aurore like a son, called her "my son," and insisted that she be equipped with the virtues of a boy. She put little Aurore into a position disastrous to her femininity by declaring: "I am like your father."

But to be loved by the father—so the grandmother reasoned

—meant that Aurore should become like her, the older woman whom he treasured, honored, and idolized. That other woman, thought the grandmother, that stranger and enemy, could appeal only to his sensuality.

As a result Aurore's approach to men was modeled on her grandmother's love for Maurice; she acted toward men as a mother to a boy who needs her guidance.

Unfortunately the psychic machinery is such that it keeps on working even beyond the desired end; Aurore, enacting the mother-son relationship in her subsequent love affairs again and again, must like her grandmother be betrayed in favor of a prostitute. This is the one constant feature of her love affairs. The pattern was foreshadowed in the events of her early childhood; and, unmodified in any respect, it cropped up again and again in her subsequent experiences.

Aurore's mother hated the grandmother and contrived by constant criticism to fill her daughter with the same hatred. The mother displayed the utmost contempt for the aristocratic feudal values of the grandmother, her self-control, distinction, and pride of ancestry; she ascribed the grandmother's reserve to emotional coldness. And here the temperamental, tender Sophie was the victor. All the hatred that Aurore felt for her mother was channeled toward *bonne-maman*, as she called her grandmother. And the problem of her ambivalent feeling was resolved in this way: hatred was the grandmother's portion and love the mother's. Later a reversal took place: the grandmother was loved and the mother was hated, because she disappointed her daughter. This disappointment was the really disastrous factor in George Sand's life.

The struggle between the two women ended with Sophie's leaving the family to live her own life in Paris. She left Aurore behind with the promise that she would take her to Paris soon. Aurore impatiently waited for the promise to be fulfilled, and her *bonne-maman* discovered that the girl's heart was more alienated from her than ever. In a fit of jealousy the grandmother revealed to the 12-year-old girl the past of the mother whom the child still loved, making it clear that the mother had resumed her previous shameful course. The revelation that her mother was a prostitute was a fatal blow to the girl's femininity.

From then on Aurore was without a mother ideal, and her masculinity, already foreshadowed by her education, was further encouraged. In her later life, she made passionate spasmodic but unsuccessful efforts to restore her mother ideal, and thus to save her own femininity. The question has been asked again and again: How is it that George Sand's heroines are so womanly, maternal, and sweet, while she herself was their antithesis? The fact is that Aurore tried to achieve in fiction the feminine ideal and the model mother she had been deprived of in real life.

Another device she employed to save her femininity was to assert, in the name of social justice, the right of all women to behave as her mother had. After all, men were not despised for promiscuity. She was the first feminist. Equal rights for women in every field became her program. This program sprang of course not only from logical conviction; it also answered the need of her injured daughter heart. Her insistence on legal rights for natural children is certainly connected with the fact that she had heard her jealous grandmother tell of her brother Hippolyte's uncertain parentage.

Bonne-maman could not have done better if her deliberate aim had been to destroy the girl's mother ideal. But she failed to take Sophie's place in Aurore's heart; on the contrary, the girl's unconscious hatred for her mother was now entirely directed against her grandmother. All that her grandmother had offered her in the way of intellectual values was now cast away. From then on Aurore refused to study and became like a mischievous, wild, and undisciplined boy. She set herself against all things feminine, dressed in mannish garb, and in every way tried to ruin her good reputation as a woman. She did indeed bring down on herself the condemnation of society. People spoke of her as a wicked witch and accused her of blasphemy and sorcery.

This escape to the masculine recurred whenever Aurore expe-

rienced a disappointment in love.   This was the second source
of her masculinity.   The first was identification with her father,
the aim of her grandmother's educational policy.   This identification was placed at the service of her unusual intellectual
gifts, to which she owes the part she played in cultural history,
and perhaps even a bit of immortality.   The second form of her
masculinity contained an evil sadistic element that reacted to
disappointment with hatred and revenge.   While her intellectuality in later life served her as a kind of refuge from disappointments in love, her sadistic tendencies led her to disaster.
Both forms of masculinity—here so largely determined by the
personal experiences of childhood—are quite common.   In
other cases similarly the augmentation of masculine tendencies
in a woman is a reaction to disappointed femininity.

Generally speaking, wherever woman's masculinity is not
raised to the plane of creative activity, it is associated with
intensified sadistic reactions.   George Sand herself, in a letter
to Flaubert, said that the importance of the anatomic difference
between the sexes was overestimated and had no psychologic
significance.   Poor George Sand!   Had she been able to understand the causes of her own sufferings, she would have spoken
differently.   She would have recognized that the evil she did to
men was merely one of the results of the anatomic difference.
Woman's masculinity often resorts to aggressiveness because it
lacks the anatomic means to express the active masculine act.
So it came about that George Sand's motherly love ended in the
sadistic destruction of her lovers (Chopin, De Musset).   But
her cruel acts were followed by catastrophic fits of remorse, an
annihilating sense of guilt that created terrible depressions and
led her to contemplate suicide.

My thesis is that George Sand's sadistic-masculine reactions
to disappointment followed the pattern of her first reactions to
her grandmother's destruction of her mother ideal.   We shall
try to find evidence for this in her own writings.

In her novel, *La petite Fadette* ("The Cricket"), she describes
a girl who is exactly like the little Aurore of her diaries after the

disclosures made by her grandmother. Little Fadette acts like a naughty, sadistic boy: "Mother Fadette's granddaughter was known in the surrounding country as 'little Fadette'—partly because she was familiar with the black arts. Everyone knows that Fadette Farfadette is a malicious witch."

At the age of 10 Fadette is abandoned by her mother, who leaves her to become a prostitute following the camps. At the age of 10 Aurore's mother abandoned her to go to Paris and lead a loose life. Later her grandmother told her that Sophie had met her father during the war, when she followed the army as a prostitute. Fadette's grandmother knows medicinal herbs and is skilled in other arts, which she teaches Fadette. Fadette's grandmother, instead of taking the place of parents, treats her in a harsh and loveless manner. The hostility of Fadette's environment is due to the fact that the neighbors transfer the mother's guilt to the child. This, declares Fadette-Aurore, is the cause of her own mischievous hooliganism.

But Fadette grows up to be a sweet and kindly woman; sadistic aggression in her is transformed into a woman's loving, passive attitude. The transformation takes place when a man's love awakens her to femininity. Thus George Sand in her artistic fancies gratified the wishes that life had not granted her. Her deepest wish was to be a woman; when put to the test by a man's love, this wish was never realized, since in each of her numerous love affairs the psychologic compulsion to repeat her disappointing experience proved more powerful. Only in artistic dreaming did George Sand realize her aborted femininity.

The question arises: Were George Sand's relations with men determined exclusively by her relations with her "two mothers"? Must we not, according to psychoanalytic method, take her relation to her father into account?

When Aurore was a child, the contemporary scene was dominated by a heroic figure that had captured everyone's imagination—Napoleon. Aurore's admiration for Napoleon was mixed with her longing for her absent father, who, at Murat's side, headed the southward march of the French armies. We can see today that any child whose father is in the armed forces, even in the most insignificant capacity, imagines that the whole fate of the war depends on him. And Maurice de Saxe was no mean figure in the army of Napoleon.

When red flashes appeared in the sky, little Aurore's mother would say: "Look, there's a battle going on, and no doubt your father is in it."

Little Aurore built a fortress with four chairs and an old stove. She made violent gestures, struck out at the invisible foe, hid in imaginary forests, gathered cruelly mutilated corpses on imaginary battlefields, fought victoriously—herself in the role of the hero, another Maurice de Saxe. George Sand, in her memoirs, is quite aware of this identification with her always absent father. When the object of our love is withdrawn, we imitate the traits of the absent one in order to find consolation for our loss. So little Aurore became warlike and satisfied her sadistic impulses in imaginary battles.

These battles in which Aurore played the part of Maurice de Saxe laid the final base of her subsequent masculinity. Her later tragic experience with her two mothers did the rest.

Absorption in an imaginary life and an inclination to cruelty characterized George Sand's childhood. She would spend the day in her fortress, plucking at the straw of the chairs. At night she would lie awake in bed for hours, plucking the fringes of the curtains. The noise thus produced was a sort of musical accompaniment to her fantasies. In the adjoining room her mother would say: "Aurore is playing with the fringe now."

Yet in the very midst of her gratifying fancies, fears and oppressions would trouble her, and one incident became the focus of these childish anxieties.

A punchinello—a clown dressed in red and gold—found his way into her solitude. Aurore received the gift with mixed feelings. The clown could not be kept in the same box with her much loved doll, her little daughter. She had a foreboding that something terrible, something sinister would befall the little

feminine creature from such intimate relation with the clown
She hung him from the stove, opposite her bed.   His masculine
glance pursued her till she fell asleep, and she awoke screaming
with fright and drenched with sweat.   She had dreamt that the
clown had caught fire, and, all aflame, had pursued her and her
doll.   After this dream the child suffered from pyrophobia, i.e.,
a dread of everything associated with fire.   George Sand later
came to see in this dread an experience that afflicts all children
in one way or another.   She termed it the great *souffrance
morale*, the "psychic anguish" of childhood.   She also asserted
—anticipating the experiences of psychoanalysis—that these
anxieties were in some way connected with typically female
nervous disorders and that what was needed was to "find a
psychic means to counteract a psychic cause."   When she
rested her head against the breast of the servant Pierre, her
fear vanished.   This Pierre, whom she loved tenderly and
whose figure frequently appears in her novels, served her as a
kind of father substitute.

Little Aurore slew her military enemies from her fortress of
four chairs, and she mutilated her dolls, respecting only those
that were so well constructed that they were unbreakable.   This
attitude continued throughout her life.   While her novels were
taking shape, even at 60, she still kept reaching for some adequate object.   The men whom she loved were dolls that could
be smashed.   She mutilated them and yearned for some
sturdier comrade with whom to play life's game.   The gold and
crimson punchinello, terror-inspiring and brilliant with flame,
seems to have been the only male before whom George Sand
felt wholly feminine.

Her father returned from the wars from time to time and was
jealously monopolized by the sensual Sophie.   He was an
affectionate father and seems to have been inclined to spoil the
little girl.   The mother would intervene and insist on greater
severity.   The passionate child in her great need for love seems
to have felt bitterly every form of love refusal.

Self-contradiction was constant in George Sand; the very

things that she understood and elaborated artistically with incredible intuition were the ones she overlooked and denied entirely with her conscious mind.

Thus, for example, she described her childhood as sunny, radiant, and happy. Her actual reminiscences, however, always contain a note of disappointment. A fall from her nurse's arms, which drew blood, a song of cut laurel branches—these are her earliest childhood recollections. This little song filled her heart with boundless sadness and years later tears would come to her eyes when she remembered:

> Nous n'irons plus au bois,
> Les lauriers sont coupés.
>
> (No more to the woods we'll go,
> The laurels have been cut.)

"Explain childhood's eccentricities to me," says George Sand. "I could never wipe out the mysterious impression made upon me when I recalled this song."

Such childhood memories as bloody injuries or a cut branch are lasting and create depressive reactions throughout a woman's life because they symbolically express the unmastered genital trauma. Little Aurore admired a certain white dress and thought it the loveliest thing in the world. Her mother made a harmless remark: "The dress seems yellowish"—and at once the little girl became terribly sad, as though at some serious disappointment.

Such a reaction is common to both adults and children who have experienced so many disappointments that they confront every situation with a complete readiness for new disappointment. In such a case it is pleasanter to stick to fantasy, for fantasies gratify all one's wishes. Thus from earliest childhood George Sand unwittingly widened the gap between her dream life and reality.

When she was not quite 4 years old, she looked forward to a journey to Spain that had been planned. There she would see her heroic father again, and receive his love. What a disappointment was in store for her! The adventure did not come up to her expectation. The little girl felt more lonely and abandoned than ever. As a boy, uniformed like her father, she was introduced by her mother to Murat as "my son." As once the figures of Napoleon and her father had merged in her imagination, so now Napoleon's representative Murat merged with her father to form one heroic figure. In later life—once—her longing for love led her into the arms of a masculine, paternal man. Yet here too the disastrous power of the unconscious repetition compulsion intruded; Michel, philosopher and art historian, called her "my son." Michel was a masculine man and wanted a woman for a sexual partner. The love episode could only end in disappointment.

In Spain, filled with unsatisfied longings for affection and left to her own resources, the little girl stood in front of a large mirror and played: now she was her father, now her mother; now she was dressed as a boy, now like the elegant Sophie. Later George Sand saw herself in these two forms when she learned to look into the mirror of her own divided soul. She called out as though trying to reach someone who might understand her. The only reply was a hollow sound that rang through the great halls of Murat's palace. Her mother explained to her that this was Echo. And full of joy, little Aurore called to her new friend, "*Bonjour, Echo!*" Such was her loneliness even then— and all her life she remained lonely.

The Spanish journey that was to be a triumph for her girlish heart had a tragic epilogue. Her father fell from his horse and was brought home dead. Four-year-old Aurore remained in her seemingly unemotional abstracted state. She did not accept her father's death as real and impatiently asked from time to time: "When will father come back from death?"

Her longing for her father expressed itself in a very striking way. A curious imaginary figure accompanied George Sand throughout life. This figure was named Corambé in her fantasy and was in reality a self-created godhead, occupying the center of her great religious feeling. George Sand was extraordinarily religious, yet she rejected any existing religious institution. She believed in the divine power of love, of erotic passion. She was full of longing for a superhuman being and in addition erected altars to Eros, the god of sexual love. She considered love the profoundest act of piety. She held to these two beliefs, which met only on the common ground of never fulfilled longing.

Corambé, George Sand's god, emerged when the 12-year-old Aurore, lonely, abandoned by her mother, was seeking an object for her love. In this period of potential and unsatisfied longing for love, every girl is reawakened to her original desire for her father. The unconscious longing is then diverted to enthusiastic adoration of some heroic figure of romance or reality. But George Sand was seeking an ideal with which life could not supply her. Her father—as she saw him in her first childish imaginings—could only be represented by a god. One night the ideal assumed the name of Corambé in her dreams. She declared that the letters shaped themselves into this word before the eyes of her mind. The name became "the title of her romance and the god of her worship." Corambé was the secret of her dreams and for a long time her religious ideal. She built him an altar and offered sacrifices to him; her life was filled by his constant presence. He was ever beside her, observing her behavior, rejoicing and suffering with her. She laid her love gifts on his altar, but Corambé never wanted bloody sacrifices. Evidently he had forbidden her to indulge her sadistic impulses. She told him endless stories— her dreams and fantasies—but he did not wish to hear tales of erotic love. In the stories she told, man and woman always appeared united only by friendship, thus symbolizing her repressed sexuality.

Throughout her whole life the god Corambé played the same role. In her artistic creation he was in her pen, in her ink; he was the object of her inspiration. This platonic relationship to her god became warmer and more passionate during one ecstasy she experienced. Aurore's rebellion against her grandmother, after the disastrous depreciation of her mother, had ended up with her being sent to a convent. Here she continued to be a "bad boy," and was known as a *diable* ("devil"). One day while playing near Titian's painting of the dying Christ, she was seized with compassion for the sufferer and overcome by deep sorrow. She had a dizzy spell and heard a voice crying: "*Tolle, lege*"—a hallucination, recognized by her as such. She experienced the perfect rapture of ectasy. She felt God within her, beating in her heart, flowing in her veins. She was overcome by a shattering joy, she became one with God—he was in her, she was in him. She herself compared this miracle to the experience of St. Theresa—except that, as with Corambé, God, while father, brother, eternity, was never a spouse. She is most emphatic about this.

The story of Corambé's origin is clear: the longed-for father, exalted to an ideal figure, is once more personified and endowed with all the virtues for which the imagination yearns. He is disavowed as a sexual object and the relation to him is raised to the plane of religious belief. The ecstasy, as experienced and described by George Sand, is one with which psychoanalysis is well acquainted. It is a most intimate, intense union with God the Father, a sublimated form of—and one might almost say the opposite pole to—sexual union. George Sand's religious adoration of Corambé is a continuation of her relation to her father. Instead of giving her love to some man of flesh and blood, her love remains chained to her childish dreams. The great, wish-fulfilling virtue of the divine Corambé seems to be that he *never* leaves her and is always at hand. The Latin word *coram* stands for "in presence of." Was not George Sand at the time assiduously studying Latin? But the *-bé* is not clear. I should like to try to construe this suffix analytically.

When Aurore was small and her father was away, her mother tried to teach her the alphabet. The little one showed application and talent. But she had one curious difficulty: the letter *b* did not exist for her. For a long time she obstinately omitted it from her list and neither punishment nor prayers could correct this error. "Whoso says *a* must say *b*," says the proverb. Yet when asked why she refused to write and read the letter *b* she answered with a curious obstinacy: "Because I do not know *b*."

It seems to me that the *b* repressed in her childhood is identical with the *-bé* that later turned up as the suffix to *coram*. The whole word could then mean, "in the presence of *b*." If the *b* repressed in childhood referred to the absent father, whom she hardly knew at the time, then its turning up in Corambé would be quite understandable.

This attachment to Corambé seems to have been a great obstacle to her feminine love life. All her love affairs, except the unsuccessful one with Michel, have clearly the character of a mother-child relation. Her disastrous affair with De Musset is typical. It began as a friendship, the tender union of a boy genius and an inspired mother. She always called him "my good" or "my bad" child. She felt that she was not in sexual danger with him, until with motherly kindness she yielded to his tears and complied with his sexual desire. De Musset was always a "mother's pet" and his choice in love was determined by a neurotic mother attachment.

Before the journey to Italy and its famous terrible epilogue in Venice, she received him in motherly fashion from his mother's hands with the promise to watch over him as a mother would.

The first stage of their relation followed the stereotyped pattern. George Sand was the *bonne-maman*, affectionate, solicitous, stimulating. In her role as a mother she abandoned herself completely. She identified herself with the beloved child. But just as the grandmother was separated from Maurice by a prostitute, so in Venice De Musset began to betray mother-George with prostitutes. He claimed that it was she, with her coldness and interest in things outside him, that drove him to do so. She denied this. Both were right. She did what he accused her of doing, automatically, as a result of a repetition compulsion. He behaved like an irritated, capricious child trying to torment his mother. When George fell sick, De Musset reacted as children sometimes do: he felt insulted and revenged himself. Then came the famous night in Venice, when at the delirious Alfred's sickbed George kissed and embraced the physician Pagello. She denied this, but her denial is as unacceptable as Alfred's delirious accusations—for George Sand sometimes followed her unconscious impulses so blindly that falsifications of memory would not be surprising.

Whatever the true facts of this episode, she could not be simply a kindly mother in the mother-child relation. Her own mother had cruelly deserted her, and she was compelled to desert and disappoint in turn. The mother-child relation is clearly revealed in a letter by De Musset that admits of but one interpretation: "You thought that you were my sweetheart? But you were only a mother. Heaven made us for each other, yet our embrace was incest."

In her eternally unsatisfied longing for love, George Sand went from one man to another. No relation could be successful, for she always found a weak, infantile boy in need of assistance. What she sought was the love of a great, strong, powerful divine father. This desire had to be repressed and sublimated into religion.

Her relation with Chopin was a replica of her relation with De Musset. She saved the tubercular boy only to be tormented in her mother role by his passionate jealousy. George Sand in this case too devoted herself to her lover heart and soul, but, obedient to the sinister demands of her unconscious, broke her fragile toy. Ardently seeking the strong father, she found only the weakling son; herself disappointed, she disappointed in turn; causing sorrow, she herself suffered most bitterly.

Every woman's love for a man is nourished by two springs: her love for her father and her love for her son, even before the latter is born. These two forms of love must unite and flow toward the same object. In George Sand's case both tendencies suffered severe disturbances in their development. Plunged from earliest youth into a life of fantasy, she mingled the realities of the external world with the content of her fantasies. Her experiences in love could never be completely freed from this bondage. Each tendency was determined by childhood memories and could only lead to tragedy. Even her attempt to save her femininity by marriage was unsuccessful. She loved her son Maurice as a mother, yet she troubled and complicated even this relation by her relations with sons not of her flesh.

Ardently longing for femininity, each new disappointment as a woman pushed her into masculinity again and again. She was George Sand intellectually, and "Piffoel" in her emotions. Piffoel was the name she always gave herself in her inconsolable sorrow, after each new loss of femininity. *Bête mélancolique et abominable* ("melancholy and abominable beast") was what she called her masculine double, whom she held responsible for her wretchedness.

George Sand's psychic split can be seen both in her love life and in her sublimations. Although her intellectual personality was masculine, her creative work tapped sources other than her intellect. As a novelist she was feminine-intuitive par excellence; she reached the extreme of the quality that we have found characteristic of our feminine type. George Sand's turn toward herself, her activity directed inward, sometimes even verged on twilight states, and in her novels she projected her own psychic experiences in figures created after the image of her own unconscious self. When we uncover the instinctual components behind the sublimations, we find confirmation of our view that her intellect concealed aggressive-masculine components, and her poetic intuition passive-feminine ones.

In conclusion let us look once more at the two photographs of Aurore–George Sand mentioned above. They certainly suggest the problem of the bisexual disposition, but we are nevertheless inclined to hold psychologic motives responsible for the split between the masculine and feminine components. Whatever may be the endocrinologic findings of the future, we have seen in the case of George Sand that her masculinity complex was only a consequence of her thwarted thrust toward femininity.

In George Sand we have seen conflicts between different identifications that could not be resolved because of the gravity of the affective experiences. True, George Sand reacted to her love disappointments by escaping into masculinity, but the disappointments themselves were provoked by her incapacity for feminine experiences.

Once again we are confronted with a vicious circle. One psychic situation provokes the other, and the sequence is gradually lost, so that the question whether she was masculine because her femininity was disturbed, or whether her femininity was inadequate because it was disturbed by a masculine disposition, is practically unanswerable. Psychoanalysts tend to regard the masculinity complex or penis envy as the primary cause of feminine psychic difficulties. But examination of the life of George Sand and of many other, perhaps less fascinating and less rich but essentially similar lives, shows the inadequacy of this hypothesis.

But if we assume that human beings have organically bisexual dispositions, that woman and man originate in a common primeval source, we are compelled to conclude that in the psychic economy of the individual, the two components, masculine and feminine, must be united to form a harmonious whole. The feminine component should predominate in women and the masculine in men. When the harmony of the masculine and feminine tendencies is disturbed in an individual, an inner conflict arises. The sources of this disturbance, as I have tried to show, are psychologic.

The life of a woman under the impact of the masculinity complex is not always rich in love disappointments and poetic and intellectual achievements. In women who lack George

Sand's gifts, the confusion of masculine and feminine assumes more primitive forms. Sublimation is replaced by aggression, and in their relations with men, such women use "love" or instinctual sexuality as a pretext for gratifying their aggressions and revenge impulses.

In many masculine-aggressive women it is the fear of men, or the desire to take an anticipated revenge for the rape they expect, that leads them to an aggressive reversal of the normal situation; these women do the seducing, abusing, and deserting. Thus they escape anxious expectation and renounce tenderness and feminine gratification in favor of the aggressive masculinity they imitate. This state of mind frequently leads to prostitution—not only in the literal sense but also in that of psychologic behavior—just as does a really experienced and repressed love disappointment. Such women can seduce and disappoint one man after another, in order to take revenge for their own disappointment. Wherever we find the aggressive form of prostitution, we also find other signs of masculine tendencies. But we must not forget the Carmen type, who conceals her masochistic opposite behind her aggressions.

In some of these prostitutional types, masculinity manifests itself in the negation of motherhood. To them, as women, sexuality has the same meaning as to men—a pleasurable discharge without the consequence of motherhood. This does not imply that woman's sexual experience does not always serve immediately pleasurable ends. But the emphasis on the exclusiveness of sexual pleasure, the active negation of the other goal, is, in woman, masculine.

This evaluation is also expressed in the attitude of men, to whom the prostitute signifies the opposite of the mother. The sexual-emotional experience of the prostitute—who is usually frigid—is changed into money values, and here again it would be a mistake to explain the cupidity of the aggressive prostitute by purely economic motives. The economic motive is often the primary one, but sometimes, just as in the case of the masochist, it is a rationalization of emotional motives

Returning to George Sand, we shall have occasion to study in her still other forms of masculinity. Her preference for young men was wholly personal and arose from her childhood experiences. Many women choose this kind of object relation not from motherliness, as was the case with George Sand, but from their own longing in puberty to be boys. In such women the fantasy we have mentioned earlier asserts itself in this realization. Probably this was true of George Sand also, and augmented her other motivations. George Sand's vivid disguises before a mirror, sometimes impersonating a boy and sometimes a girl, provide us with an impressive illustration of this deep-rooted double nature, stemming from bisexuality, that seeks playful gratification.

Women who later love younger men give their longing to be a boy a less playful character through this projection. Very feminine and passive women are most given to preserving their wish for masculinity in this form. At the same time they usually try through such an erotic choice to escape the masculine man, who is particularly dangerous for their masochism.

Mental life is confusing because it has innumerable contents and disposes over only a limited number of expressive possibilities. For that reason, every event, action, and gesture can express something definite and its opposite. And because side by side with the most aggressive masculinity, the most tender feminine emotions appear in the same woman, the purpose of an individual action is not always clear.

In our exposition of the masculinity complex we have thus far disregarded the idea of penis envy or the female castration complex. We shall now take this up in detail.

In psychoanalytic terminology "female castration complex" has a specific meaning. It refers to the disturbances that derive from penis envy and that prove that fundamentally woman does not renounce the masculine organ and that her attempt to repress the envy and desire for possession of it is abortive. The repressed elements manifest themselves in various psychic reactions that together constitute the female castration complex. The basic material for this view was provided by Abraham,[6] who followed Freud[7] and van Ophuijsen.[8]

Abraham distinguishes two reactive types in women who have not mastered penis envy: the wish fulfillment and the revengeful type. The woman of the first type is dominated by the unconscious fantasy that she possesses a penis and tries to assume a masculine role. In the course of our description of types we have called the reader's attention to such women. Especially the intellectual woman, with her typical overestimation of intellectual values, falls into this category. According to Abraham, such a woman tries to achieve something great or masculine in the intellectual field in order to compensate for her lack of a penis. The vindictive type is filled with the desire to take revenge on man for his advantage. Numerous difficulties in erotic life, and varied neurotic symptoms, are manifestations of this vindictive attitude. Abraham's description of the different types and the material by which he substantiates his classification are above criticism, and later experience has largely confirmed his findings. He himself corrected his somewhat rigid differentiation of wish fulfillment and revengeful types by emphasizing the predominance of one or the other component in the same individual.

Like any pioneer's, Abraham's findings are to some extent one-sided. In my opinion he puts too much emphasis on penis envy in its normal and neurotic manifestations. He connects woman's conscious and unconscious desire to take over man's role too closely with the fantasy relating to the possession of a masculine organ.

[6] ABRAHAM, K.: Manifestations of the female castration complex. Selected papers of K. Abraham. London: Hogarth.

[7] FREUD, S.: The taboo of virginity. Collected Papers, vol. 4.

[8] OPHUIJSEN, J. H. W. VAN: Contributions to the masculinity complex of women. Internat. J. Psycho-Analysis, vol. 5, 1924.

My own later experience can be summed up in the view that woman's masculine wishes, and her difficulty in mastering them, result from multiple psychologic influences, in which penis envy does play a part but does not constitute a primary cause. Even though we assume the existence of latent masculinity in every woman, we believe that the development toward femininity proceeds by virtue of a constitutional impulse. The difficult situations that must be solved on this path may produce a disposition to a traumatic effect, but this effect takes place and hinders the development toward femininity only when the normal difficulties are accompanied by particularly aggravating elements. The girl's genital trauma, the portentous fact that at a certain stage of her development she lacks an adequate organ for the outlet of inner excitations, cannot be the result of an external experience. The narcissistic mortification, the envy aroused by the real experience of seeing the masculine organ, does leave a strong impression, but cannot be made responsible for all the positive and negative consequent manifestations in feminine development.

In our view the genital trauma has a different meaning. It is a biologically predetermined inhibition of development that paves the way to femininity and at the same time creates a traumatic disposition, just like any situation in which forces acting in opposite directions have to fight things out. We refer to the processes described in chapter vi, processes centered around the conflict between the instinctual drives and their inhibition. This phase of development and the "lack of an organ" that characterizes it create a dispositional-traumatic readiness for penis envy as well as for subsequent experiences that are also mastered in normal development.

The sight of the male sex organ can have a traumatic effect, but only provided that a long chain of earlier experiences calculated to create this effect has preceded it, and that the inhibitive process has encountered difficulties. It is no accident that penis envy is usually accompanied by intensified aggressions. These aggressions are, in our view, intensified not as a result of penis envy, but as a result of the rage and excitation accumulated in the preceding development. The motives of these emotions vary; they may, for instance, express feelings of envy that have been present before. A little girl may become very jealous of her brothers and sisters, and her little brother's "extra" organ may serve to touch off aggressive reactions. The visual experience of the anatomic difference may then endow these reactions with a particularly envious character.

The fact that the boy has an organ that can actually be grasped and thus has the possibility of transferring psychologic processes to material, real ones, creates an obscure feeling in the girl that he can manage his sadistic impulses, anxieties, and masturbatory struggles better than she can master hers. The general human tendency to project inner dangers outside oneself in order to master them more efficiently, also seems to play a part in her envious evaluation of the male organ.

The typical manifestations accompanying penis envy are always the same: (1) the girl accuses her mother (more rarely her father) of having wronged her; (2) she accuses herself of having destroyed her penis by masturbation; (3) she fears that it is concealed inside the body and she anxiously (or hopefully) expects it to grow later on.

However, because penis envy is itself an accompaniment to other processes, the predominance of one or another of its components depends on the situation as a whole. If the intensified aggressions are directed against the mother, the accusation is directed against her; if the girl expects proofs of love from her father that are not given her, or if he has taken over the punitive function, her resentment, protests, and vindictive tendencies will be directed against him.

If the girl's fantasy is preoccupied with processes taking place inside the body (for instance, if she is interested in her mother's pregnancy), her ideas with regard to the sex organ will be directed toward the inside of the body; in other words, she will develop the usually anxiety-laden fantasy that the penis is concealed inside. The reappearance of this idea in puberty often provides the motive for the obsessional wish to be operated upon. We can assume that Nancy's assertion (p. 63) that "something" remained in her body after her operation referred not only to a pregnancy fantasy but also to a still more obscure object.

A sweet little girl whose fantasies are directed toward fulfillments in the future will also expect a later fulfillment of her penis wish.

It is characteristic that girls with obsessional-neurotic dispositions tend to display aggressive reactions of penis envy, while those predisposed to hysteria tend to hope for a future growth; the displacement of wish fantasies to the future is generally a symptom of hysteria. From the presence of self-accusations it is possible not only to recognize the influence of masturbatory processes, but also to infer a later tendency to guilt reactions.

In one way or another, there is no woman in whom one could not discover some traces of the genital trauma in the form of penis envy. In some women these tendencies are not active, in others they contribute to character formation and produce neurotic symptoms.

Masculinity complex and penis envy (or wish) are not identical concepts, even though they naturally condition each other. An adult woman who out of ambition or for other reasons harbors a conscious rationalized wish for masculinity has long ago sublimated the wish for a masculine-active genital organ. Her accusations are then directed against the social order or against her own incapacity for masculine achievements. Not so with the unconscious wish for masculinity: in this case, even if it does not originate in penis envy, it is more or less accompanied by an unconscious desire for a male organ. George Sand, for instance, was always sad when she recalled the song about the laurel branches or her fall from her nurse's arms. She herself was surprised at the peculiarity of the human soul that makes it cling to such slight memories. Even in less masculine women such memories serve as centers around which the genital complex forms. The events to which they refer sometimes did not take place at all; the false memory arises from the need to give the genital trauma a realistic content.

There are also women in whom the penis wish or wish to be a man assumes a direct and primitive form. They dress like men, act like men, fight with or against men, instead of letting themselves be loved; they display their active castration desires toward the other sex in unveiled form and in their case one does not need to look long for signs of penis envy. In earlier generations they wore their hair short as a sign of their "masculine protest," bound their chests flat, and were interested only in activities that were considered unbecoming to the feminine sex. Such women have really turned away from femininity and constitute a type in which, it is possible to suspect, the wish for masculinity is constitutionally determined. Their ancient prototypes are the Amazons, and it can be seen that the nature of these women has been preserved through the centuries and that they assert their existence independently of social regimes. In our own day this form of the masculinity complex is extremely rare, for our modern girls can act and struggle in a much more rational and socially acceptable manner.

Another form of the penis wish sounds paradoxic because it remains within the feminine domain. For the most womanly thing in woman is her desire for a child. This feminine wish can, however, assume a masculine form if the woman wants to prove through her child that she can create something by her own activity and that the child is a product of her body, engendered by her alone. One fantasy, which I call "parthenogenetic," runs as follows: "I have a child born of me alone, I am its mother and father. I don't need or want a man for the begetting of this child." This fantasy usually arises in puberty. Psychoanalysis reveals that the fantasy life of such women is not filled with the motherly yearning for a child, but that they want to compensate for their bodily disadvantage by a positive achievement of their body. In this, the part played by the man is reduced to an insignificant mini mum. This masculine wish in woman manifests itself in various fantasies and actions.

Characteristically, this fantasy becomes a completely conscious wish in a certain feminine type that strongly strives for masculinity. Occasionally, although rarely, this fantasy is actually realized when the woman has a child by the first man who comes along: his part is limited to impregnating her. One woman of this type went overseas with the fully conscious intention of being impregnated by someone unknown, and she carried out her project. Another very intelligent woman had intercourse with a servant in order "to have her own, robust child." Many unmarried mothers give birth to children because of such an unconscious wish that has the effect of a compulsion.[9] These experiences have shown that residues of masculinity, or the wish for a male organ, can take a feminine form and be concealed behind the most motherly, most feminine attitude.

An interesting contribution to this fantasy is supplied by Antoinette Bourignon, a nun who lived in the seventeenth century. She outlined religious-scientific theories according to which mankind will be saved when women achieve the capacity for giving birth to children by themselves, without the assistance of men. "This state of innocence," she writes, "is not that of asexuality, but a kind of hermaphroditism" (*Cet état d'innocence n'est pas celui de l'asexualité, mais une sorte d'hermaphroditisme*). Her biographers report that this nun used to associate her intellectual-productive activity with physical pain that had the character of labor pains: "She felt great bodily suffering and violent griping pains like a woman

---

[9] DEUTSCH, H.: Psychoanalyse der weiblichen Sexualfunktionen.

in labor" (*Elle ressentit de grandes douleurs corporelles et comme de pressantes tranchées d'un enfantement*).[10]

In healthy, normal women, too, the organ trauma creates a disposition to later traumatic reactions. The old traumatic situation, in which the woman had no outlet for diverting her excitations, reappears in every case when the tension between wanting and being able to do something is increased, when the woman has to cope with difficult internal or external conflicts, or when regressive tendencies are mobilized. To these new difficulties also she reacts with anxiety and helplessness on the one hand and with intensified aggressive impulses on the other, and clearly displays residues of penis envy.

The incompletely mastered ghosts of the past appear also in all those situations in which woman fulfils her biologic tasks or prepares her body for them. Puberty, all the reproductive functions, and the climacterium are those feminine situations in which the old trauma is mobilized and, normally, mastered. Nature gives woman abundant opportunities to exorcise these ghosts in the real active experience of motherhood.

[10] Reinach, S.: Cultes, mythes et religions: une mystique au XVII. siècle. Quoted by H. Deutsch, op. cit.

CHAPTER NINE
Homosexuality

TWO groups of homosexual women can be distinguished. The first includes those individuals who display pronounced masculine traits in the choice of objects as well as in all other manifestations of life. The physical structure of women belonging to this group may also be more or less masculine. In some, the structure of the sexual organs has a hermaphroditic character, in others we are confronted with more or less prominent aberrations of the secondary sex characteristics. Such masculinization can affect either a large part of the body constitution or only isolated traits, such as the vocal cords, the hair growth, etc. Many cases are characterized only by the absence of certain feminine sex characteristics, such as breasts. Despite such obviously organic causes of their homosexuality, these women present many psychologic problems. This is not surprising, as the biologic verdict becomes definite only during puberty, while their previous development and education have followed the line of femininity.

The second group of homosexual women includes those who show no physical signs of abnormity and whose bodily constitution is completely feminine. The causes of their inversion are obviously psychogenic. In these cases too puberty is the period of sexual decision. The observation of bisexual tendencies in puberty has led to many important insights. It was found, for instance, that the homosexual object choice does not always express masculinity. The typical infatuation of this period, the young girl's ardent love for girl friends, may, despite its homosexual character, have a completely feminine content. The love can also be pronouncedly masculine and the bisexual tendencies may draw their masculine reinforcements from varied psychologic sources (fear of heterosexuality, identification with the father, brother, etc.)

Homosexuality manifested in later life is usually a continuation of these puberty tendencies and either remains within the framework of femininity or assumes a more or less masculine character. These differences may be predetermined even before puberty. But as a rule, tremendous and decisive changes take place at the time of sexual maturation. A little girl or a girl in prepuberty may express her violent protest against her femininity in the wildest kind of tomboyishness, yet may turn to the most tender femininity during puberty. Conversely, even a very feminine girl can under certain circumstances weather the storms of puberty only by turning toward masculinity and choosing a feminine love object.

The view that female homosexuality is in the overwhelming majority of cases psychologically determined, is supported by the fact that a great number of women whose sexual love objects are of the same sex do not give the impression that their physiologic characteristics have undergone changes in the direction of masculinity. Another noteworthy fact that points to complex psychologic motivation in the abnormal object choice is that many women whose entire emotional personality is masculine nevertheless choose men as their objects—often even very masculine men—and, conversely, that very feminine and passive women choose women as their love objects, sometimes exclusively. On the other hand, it seems that homosexual women with a rather marked bisexual disposition in their bodily structure usually also show definitely masculine interests, try to follow masculine professions, strongly emphasize their masculinity, and are masculine in their entire emotional life. In this case the existence of a biologic factor is assumed, manifesting itself in the sexual direction, and here homosexuality is explained by biologic processes. Isolated masculine sex characteristics can, however, easily lead to the false inference that in these cases too homosexuality corresponds to a biologic factor, whereas we are in reality confronted with a purely psychologic manifestation. This point can be illustrated by the following two examples.

I had occasion to observe an unmarried woman of about 30, who liked to wear masculine clothes, followed masculine professions, and openly admitted her homosexuality. Her bodily structure was feminine, except for her voice, which was just like a man's. Closer examination revealed that no organic abnormality was responsible for the masculine behavior. Her vocal characteristics had led her to think, even in her youth, that she should have been born a man, and that no one could love her; even as a very young girl she had been ridiculed and had turned away in discouragement from all things feminine. Depreciating and renouncing her own femininity, she had resolved to be a man; her homosexuality expressed not the existence of an organically determined urge, but an emotional need to love and at the same time to avoid her inferiority as a woman. Another instance is the case of a Polish legionnaire of the first world war, who, having been wounded, was found to be a girl, and came under my psychiatric care. This 18-year-old-girl had pronouncedly masculine secondary sex characteristics (a mustache, no breasts, etc.) and, like the girl mentioned above, she felt inferior as a woman, emphasized her masculinity, and had many fantasies about heroic deeds that would make her famous and compensate her for her lack of feminine charm. She had joined the army as a nurse; later by dint of clever stratagems, she succeeded in denying her sex and becoming a soldier. Apparently, once she had gratified her masculinity, her feminine nature asserted its right more strongly than before, for she fell in love with another soldier. Her comrades decided that she was homosexual, for she—at that time "he"—could not conceal her erotic feelings. Her heterosexual relationship, which I observed in its subsequent development, had a favorable outcome.

In these two cases—as in many others—the masculine sex characteristics exerted a strong psychologic influence without being the primary cause of sexually masculine feelings. These women protected themselves from their feminine inferiority by overemphasizing the other tendency. Others, on the contrary, negate their masculinity, even if they are urged in that direction by their biologic structure. As regards this point, the following personal observation of an androgynous woman whose homosexual tendencies had an unambiguously somatic basis, may be instructive.

She was a girl of about 25, delicately built, with very feminine features and fair complexion, but with a deep voice and hair on her face. Among her women friends, her conduct was irreproachably feminine; she dressed coquettishly, tried in every way to remove the hair on her face, and often complained bitterly about her organic constitution. She was very successful as an executive in an international organization, showed great energy in her chosen field, and all her professional behavior, despite her protests, revealed an absolutely masculine-active character. To the surprise of all the young girls around her she fell passionately in love with a somewhat older, motherly married woman who was certainly below the mental level of this extremely intelligent girl. Her passionate infatuation was centered around a fantasy that the woman she had chosen for her love object had to be rescued from her husband, who was unworthy of her. This young girl acquired colossal energy in her courtship, her rescue intentions were compulsive, and she tried to abduct her beloved by a ruse. This behavior strongly reminds us of certain types of men described by Freud.[1] One of these types indulges in a rescue fantasy: the man chooses a disreputable woman as his love object and is convinced that his beloved needs him, and that by his love he must rescue her from prostitution. Freud also describes a type of man who loves a woman only if another man, as a rule the husband, can claim her as his property.

The girl whose case we are describing fell in love in a way that represented a kind of combination of the erotic tendencies

[1] FREUD, S.: Contribution to the psychology of love. Collected Papers, vol. 4.

of these two types of men: she chose a respectable woman for her love object, but had to rescue her from her unworthy husband.

At a certain point her ardent suit became public, for the woman's husband brought the aggressive lover to court for disturbing his married life and attempting to seduce his wife to homosexual relations. The epilogue was unexpected: the case aroused the interest of a well known sexologist, who discovered that the girl in question was a real hermaphrodite; he succeeded in transforming her into a man by an operation. The success of the operation was confirmed when the woman whom the "girl" had courted divorced her husband and was married and impregnated by the newly created man. The latter had had—he declared—no idea of his peculiar structure, and had considered himself a homosexual woman. He later wrote and published a book called *The Girlhood Years of a Man.*

Freud published an essay entitled "Psychogenesis of a Case of Homosexuality in a Woman,"[2] in which he described the love history of a chaste young girl who was passionately in love with a high class prostitute and displayed the same rescue aspirations that he had described in men.

The behavior in our case reminded us to a certain extent of Freud's patient, whose manner of loving was, according to Freud, strongly masculine. He left these questions unanswered: Was the young girl he described a homosexual as a result of her constitution, or had the inversion been caused exclusively by the psychologic motives he discovered during his analysis of her?

From a psychologic point of view it would naturally be of great interest to know whether the whole development of the above mentioned girl-man had proceeded along a straight line and whether the intensification of the sexual drive in puberty had strengthened the masculine tendencies—as is the case with boys—or whether the influences of the environment and the patient's own assumption that he was a woman had manifested

[2] Internat. J. Psycho-Analysis, vol. 1, 1920.

themselves in some way in spite of his anatomic constitution. We noted that the person in question, although organically a full-fledged male, displayed many feminine characteristics in his behavior.

From the two cases previously described, we conclude that physiologic factors are not always fully and directly responsible for the woman's masculine and homosexual behavior, and that psychologic motives play a part. Conversely, from our last case, it follows that if we are confronted with an erotic behavior in a homosexual woman in which activity and aggression are predominant, we must take into consideration the physiologic causes. These may be at work even when the organic signs are less obvious than in the case of our sensational lover.

The experiments linking sexual functions to chemical hormonal factors draw our attention more and more in this direction. We no longer explain the manifestations of bisexuality by an innate, organic, and fixed fact, but by a predisposition, stimulated or inhibited by hormonal influences, that operates in one or the other direction.

During the years of puberty, the fate of the sexual drives is definitely decided, and as a rule the development of secondary sex characteristics is combined with their orientation toward the other sex. This decision depends on both biologic and psychologic influences, and it is to be expected that our knowledge of the interplay of the two factors will some day be so broadened and clarified that no discussion will be necessary as to which factor is primary and which secondary. Here our task is limited to investigating the psychologic processes attendant upon the development of female homosexuality, without regard to whether biologic factors contribute to or even determine the final result.

In any case it is certain that normally puberty includes a phase in which the sexual drive is directed more or less toward both sexes. This phase is preceded by another in which the individual's erotic interest seems to be turned to his own sex more than to the other. This condition of bisexuality or homosexuality can extend beyond puberty, the inclination toward individuals of the same sex may remain predominant or even exclude that toward individuals of the other sex. In the former case the woman chooses now one, now the other sex for erotic association; in the latter her choices become completely homosexual. Thus homosexuality, in form and content, appears as a continuation of puberty experiences, as their intensification and further elaboration.

It may be useful to cast a glance backward and recall the processes of puberty relevant to our subject. Even in pre-puberty the object that attracted the girl's greatest emotional interest was another girl, a kind of double of her own ego. This relationship gave the weak personality of the growing girl several advantages, in particular a certain protection against too strong ties with members of her family, especially against her ties with her mother; moreover, her own helpless ego was strengthened and made to feel more secure among the grownups as a result of her association with her friend. This relationship is a typical example of a narcissistic love choice, that is to say, love for a being with whom one identifies oneself and with whom self-love can be gratified. Common pursuits and learning about forbidden things endow this relationship with thrilling excitement, and the content of the common secrets gives it its sexual character.

The continuation of such a relationship in later life constitutes the most naïve and least complicated form of feminine homo-sexuality. The content of the secret changes and sexual curi-osity is turned toward other problems, depending upon the cultural level of the partners. The objects may change, but the conditions of this relationship remain the same: "my best friend" is the one to whom the most intimate secrets may be confided and from whom similar confidences can be expected; the woman allies herself with her friend against the "others," usually members of her family, she experiences her friend's successes and failures as though they were her own, etc. Through identification the woman can be elated by the successes of her alter ego and thus ease the pressure of her inferiority feelings. And she creates a little world, represented by her friend, that admires her own achievements, modest as they may be. In this exchange of comfort and admiration, this mutual adjustment of demands, and this easing of inferiority feelings by committing sins together and mutually granting absolution, there is gratification, and security; certain feminine types preserve such relationships for life. The sexual ingredient of this relationship usually remains unconscious, but the mutual tenderness often has an erotic character.

This union of two persons of the same sex can assume various forms; the mildest form is the most frequent. It does not exclude a heterosexual relationship, and such friendships usually are not given up even after the partners have married; even then the prepuberty form of the relationship is continued. It is surprising how often a well bred and discreet woman, without the slightest embarrassment and with obvious pleasure, confides the most intimate details of her married life to her woman friend. If she has nothing exciting to report, she sometimes—exactly as in puberty—provokes or invents experiences in order to enjoy whispering about these to her friend.

This most harmless form of homosexuality is an infantile trait that either affects the entire personality or represents merely a partial inhibition of growing up, without other manifestations. The other ingredients of the personality may be more mature.

The next form of homosexuality also involves love for a girl of the same age or slightly older. The two-girl relationships of later puberty are on a more adult level and more complicated than in prepuberty and early puberty; the manifestations are varied, full of conflict and ambivalence. The relationship can have the character of a completely sublimated friendship or its content may be tender-erotic and sometimes even openly sexual. This relation between two girls of the same age that is continued in later life and is often extremely passionate, usually takes place within the framework of unresolved bisexuality. The question "Am I a man or a woman"?—the irresolution that we have mentioned before—continues unconsciously later as "Do I love a man or a woman?" The antagonism of these mutually exclusive tendencies ends either in the predominance of one or in a compromise. The two components may also subsist with equal strength in one individual and in this case the conflict continues unsolved. As a result of this inner irresolution, various tendencies become mixed. The competition of antagonistic forces may lead to a settlement in favor of homosexuality or heterosexuality. The normal or the abnormal outcome represents a parallelogram of various forces; the unity is only apparent. Analytic observation shows that this unity does not express a real inner decision, a triumph of one of the two components of bisexuality, but that it contains forces that serve the other component too. If the outcome is normal, that is, heterosexuality, inhibitions or symptoms occur in which analysis discovers the repressed homosexual ingredient, just as in homosexuality it discovers heterosexual elements.

Our psychologic insight is greatly aided by the fact that many overtly homosexual women are acutely introspective; this enables them to confirm directly the laborious findings of psychoanalysis.

In other women, whose homosexuality has seemingly been successfully repressed and who manifest it only indirectly through disturbances of their heterosexual erotic life, attempts to approach the problem of homosexuality meet with a resistance that is extremely difficult to overcome. These women insist that they have never loved anyone of their own sex, that they hate their mothers, that all their lives they have avoided close association with their sisters, and that they have always been interested in men, although usually without any marked success.

Gradually one learns why this is so. To quote only one special case as an example: there is the woman who feels burning jealousy of another woman of a definite type who as if by accident appears on the scene as a rival each time she becomes seriously interested in a man, and who again and again spoils her heterosexual relation. Analysis reveals that the woman's interest in her rival antedates her interest in the man, who only serves as a diversion. Here the repressed homosexual attraction takes the form of jealousy that causes the pseudo-heterosexual interest to founder. The emergence of repressed homosexual tendencies in the form of jealousy was described by Freud.[3]

In less repressed forms, tender love is acknowledged but the sexual ingredient is denied. Homosexual love is usually more passionate and more violently bound to the object than hetero-sexual love, even if it lacks the desire for direct sexual gratifica-tion. This form of homosexuality is much more frequent among women than among men; it is less conspicuous and it never comes into conflict with the law, which, like public opinion, has more confidence in the platonic character of feminine than of masculine homosexuality. The passion develops within four walls, so to speak, and despite its violence its sexual aspect often remains permanently hidden. Woman's propensity to sub-limate her sexuality into goal-inhibited eroticism manifests itself especially in her homosexuality.

Returning to the puberty situation, we recall that in this period the homosexual tendencies are directed toward two kinds of persons: a girl of the same age or somewhat older, and a mature woman. The character of the latter varies: in some cases she is a harsh teacher, in others a gentle, highly idealized group leader. Both of these object choices have the same attraction. They are conceived as perfect beings. Other girls, however, fall in love, and passionately, too, with sexually dis-reputable women: this was the case, for instance, with the patient described by Freud. These kinds of love choice con-tinue in later life in different forms.

The degree of consciousness or unconsciousness of the homo-sexual tendency is not of decisive importance in determining its

[3] FREUD, S.: Certain neurotic mechanisms in jealousy, paranoia, and homosexuality. Collected Papers, vol. 2.

intensity or origin. Furthermore, the perversion often affects women who could easily have gratified hetorosexual wishes; however, either they did not have such wishes, or the gratification of these wishes, instead of yielding happiness, only intensified their yearning for their own sex.

We have repeatedly referred to a bisexual disposition, and from a psychologic point of view we have sufficient proof of its existence. In puberty, this disposition manifests itself with increased intensity, but it often manifests itself earlier in a naïve form. In George Sand, for instance, it asserted itself when as a young child she play-acted her bisexuality in front of a mirror. To transform the play into a serious pursuit, the constitutional bisexuality must be combined with psychologic motives that make a finally favorable outcome impossible. The goal of psychologic development is not to resolve this irresolution completely; its task is only to distribute the normal bisexual tendencies quantitatively, and in the process to turn those components that would lead to homosexuality to goals advantageous for the feminine individual and her normal sexuality. We have underlined the importance of a favorable association with a person of the same sex, especially in the early stages of puberty. This association is important, not only because it constitutes a protective shield against a regressive return to the mother, but also because the homosexual component develops more favorably than when it is repressed and absent. In such a relationship the unusable surplus of homosexual tendencies can be best disposed of. This takes place partly by their gratification, partly by sublimation, partly by the acting out of the ambivalent feelings relating to the mother, etc. Experience teaches us that a certain amount of real activity affords the best protection against excessive fantasy indulgence, and therefore also against the abnormal development of the homosexual tendencies.

Innate bisexuality as the biologic background of the triangle assumes an abnormal significance only if unfavorable influences are at work. We shall not deal here with persons in whom, as in our case of hermaphroditism, physiologic processes have caused a deviation of the sexual development. We shall devote our attention instead to the psychologic motives that we hold responsible for female homosexuality. Even in the most normal puberty, the still unconscious sexual yearnings of the girl in the psychologic triangle are seen to swing between the two poles of bisexuality, between attraction and repulsion. Prospects of wish fulfillment are the pole of attraction; frustration, anxiety, and mobilization of guilt feelings are the pole of repulsion. Owing to the complexity of all psychologic processes, attraction and repulsion are not evenly distributed; they operate in both directions, hence the constant wavering that expresses itself as the sexual irresolution described above. One of the worst possible results of this wavering is a state of constant suspension in an objectless narcissism. Many of the emotional disturbances that appear in puberty, such as insensitivity, depersonalization, feelings of estrangement, correspond to such an irresolution before a heterosexual and homosexual object choice, and result in a subsequent petrification of the emotional life. The greater the fear of the real demands made by sexual life, the stronger will be the effects of inner irresolution, the more regressive elements will enter into the emotional life, and the more features of the old tie with the parents will be taken over by the persons in the fantasy triangle. In any attempt to realize these fantasies and love wishes, the choice of the love objects will depend on the still existing and intensified tie with the parents.

The strength and continued effect of this tie will above all depend on the real events of puberty. In this life period the role of the parents is still very real and its transference to other persons occurs regularly. We recall Helen's (p. 82) and Evelyn's (p. 37) traumatic experiences. These took place entirely within the framework of the family. Thus one of the poles we mentioned above is the father or his substitute, the other the mother or her substitute. The subsequent fate of the triangle is determined by the girl's sensitivity to love frustration, her propensity for strong hate reactions and their overcompensation by love, her fears of the one or the other, the elements of eroticism in her tenderness for her parents and of guilt feelings in her hostility toward them. In other words, the sum total of these feelings will determine the effect of the attraction or repulsion of the two poles. The traumatic experiences of puberty that constitute the last factor to provoke the sexual decision as to homosexuality or heterosexuality, are particularly dependent on events within the family. For instance, the birth of a new child during the girl's puberty can have strongly traumatic effects. We have previously noted another traumatic situation, the timid withdrawal of the father from his growing daughter. The failure of the sublimated relation between the two may deeply injure the girl and cause her resentfully to turn away from her father. Various outcomes of this situation are possible: in one the girl provokes an open fight with the father by her frivolous behavior, the previously described prostitution fantasies are mobilized, and promiscuity may result. Another form of turning away from the father is a more intensive sublimation, frequently on the basis of previously shared interests, with the girl defiantly maintaining, "I don't need you any longer, for now I can do what you do." If this identification encroaches upon the sexual domain, the girl's disappointment in her father results in intensified homosexual tendencies.

Observation seems to show that an increased fear of the father during puberty can strengthen the girl's masochistic tie to him. This fear can also set off the defense mechanism described by A. Freud[4] as identification with the aggressor. The girl then need not fear her father, for she herself is as strong and masculine as he. This kind of identification, resulting from fear, is a frequent motive for homosexuality. The girl's previously harmless friendship with another girl assumes a sadomasochistic character; in other cases, the object is changed, the initiative of the choice remains with the aggressive one; the other girl's tendency to submissiveness completes the alliance.

[4] Op. cit.

Sometimes the girl's sublimated relation with her father has involved her playing the role of son. When this relation collapses, the role of son is continued with regard to a woman. In such cases, the girl not only displays all the gallantry of a boy in love with a mature woman, but she also directs her ambitions to the end of being admired by the woman, instead of by her parents.

A typical feature of overt female homosexuality is exchange of roles between the partners, even when one of them is more active and sadistic and the other more passive and masochistic. Because of their great facility in identifying themselves with love objects of the same sex, women can play the two roles. This fact is one of the most powerful motives for female homosexuality.

Frequently the homosexual relation takes place in a triangle composed exclusively of women: the homosexual woman usually remains faithful to one of her two partners, while she changes the other. Observation of several such cases has shown that the homosexual girl plays the role of the aggressive partner (usually in identification with the father) with regard to one of her friends, and that of a humble and submissive object (boy or girl) with regard to the other.

One often meets pairs of girls who call each other by masculine pet names, very often without realizing that sexual love is present in their tenderness. Such relations are not concealed, especially when they take place within the framework of common sublimations and without directly sexual activity. The prerequisite of harmony in such relationships is that they should not be disturbed by excessive sadomasochistic components, but this usually does occur.

If her friend retains her feminine character, the homosexual girl plays the two roles all the more easily: she gives herself all the masculine qualities and simultaneously enjoys the expectation, excitement, dependence, and devotion of her own passive femininity now projected in the other. In *The Transposed Heads*, Thomas Mann writes:

But after all they were not one like Siva, who is life and death, world and eternity in the Mother, but manifested as two entities here below; thus they were to each other like images. The my-feeling of each was tired of itself, and though each was aware that after all everything consists of what it has not got, yet on account of their very differences they intrigued each other

The differences and similarity, nonidentity and yet identity, the quasidouble experience of oneself, the simultaneous liberation from one part of one's ego and its preservation and security in the possession of the other, are among the attractions of the homosexual experience.

Analysis shows that ardent homosexual infatuations of young girls very often follow the same course. First there is a passionate heterosexual love fantasy that is somehow thwarted. The fantasy persists, but with two alterations: the passive expectation of being desired becomes active desiring, and the girl, instead of choosing a masculine object, herself becomes a man through identification. The pseudologic girl who writes herself passionate love letters and enjoys these as though they came from a boy in love, is not far removed psychologically from the girl who writes love letters to another girl. Every individual act of the homosexual in love expresses a nonfulfilled heterosexual hope. The more passionate the girl is in her narcissistic desire to be loved, the more ardent will be her active wooing of the "other." If her wooing is threatened with success, she retreats, for all her action is supposed to take place within the framework of a fantasy acted out. The motive for this form of erotic experience lies either in a heterosexual disappointment or, more frequently, in the fear of heterosexual realization and in the adolescent tendency to experience emotions not directly, but through identification.

In *La Vagabonde*, Colette describes this relation beautifully:

Two women embracing are a melancholy and touching picture of two weaknesses; perhaps they are taking refuge in each other's arms in order to sleep there, weep, flee from man who is often wicked, and to taste what is more desired than any pleasure, the bitter happiness of feeling similar, insignificant, forgotten.

This relation often grows very intense with regard to a sister, particularly if the two girls are very near each other in age, or have only brothers or older sisters, or are made strongly dependent upon each other as a result of marital conflicts between their parents, or by solitude. This love, which is probably accompanied by a great deal of overcompensated hatred and jealousy, often survives puberty and is so passionate that it can lead to tragic complications. I myself observed two double suicides, of pairs of sisters who were involved in overtly sexual, tragic love for each other.

Various rescue fantasies too are found in these homosexual adventures. The "other" suffers from bondage to school or family, leads a life unworthy of her, and must be freed with the help of the infatuated girl. Thus her own revolutionary tendency to liberate herself finds expression in the fantasy of rescuing her friend.

Disreputable women are often desired by young girls out of a kind of burning curiosity; in such loves, the girl's own prostitution fantasies are realized by identification with the beloved. Schoolgirls walk by houses of ill repute with anxiously pounding hearts; the attraction of the inmates, known only from a distance, can be very powerful. Naturally, such immature erotic games can become stabilized and permanent.

In studying this problem, our most striking finding has been that masculine tendencies in a woman are not always—and even not in the majority of cases—responsible for her homosexuality. One might expect that the psychologic motives leading to the formation of the masculinity complex can also supply the motive for homosexuality. But the question must be left open whether, in cases of strongly active-masculine behavior, biologic factors are not involved after all. In the large majority of cases, however, neither biologic nor psychologic masculinity is the sole motive for homosexuality, even when appearances seem to support this view.

There is a form of homosexuality in which masculinity is particularly ostentatious. We refer here to the active women who

try to seduce other women by promising them wondrous satisfactions. "Try it once with me," one such woman used to say
to her love object. "No man in the world can give you what I
can."

She insisted that she had never disappointed anyone sexually.
This woman behaved like a male, yet her goal was not really
masculine at all. She accurately directed her attentions to
those who unconsciously longed for the kind of gratification
that an active woman actually is more capable of giving than
a man. Her words "no man" unconsciously hinted at certain
practices in which the breasts play a prominent part. In this
form of homosexuality the masculine gesture is actually only a
means of wooing and a pretext, for the sexual goal that is desired completely excludes the masculine.

This type of homosexuality, in which there is no question of
wanting to be a man, seems to be more accessible to analytic
investigation, because it is often connected with neurotic disturbances, whereas the masculine forms less frequently supply
opportunity for psychiatric treatment, since most of these
women accept the fact of their inversion and do not desire to be
cured.

One woman who submitted to psychoanalytic treatment for
neurotic difficulties presented a picture of manifest yet not
practiced inversion. She was perfectly aware of the fact that
her erotic capacity and sexual fantasy were homosexual in
character; she had unquestionably been sexually aroused when
embracing or kissing certain women for whom she felt love.
Her relation to these women was monogamous and faithful, but
purely platonic, even when she knew that these women had
perverted tendencies like her own. While it is impossible to
say that she was attracted by any definite type of woman, it
was not at any rate the masculine type; our patient herself was
blonde and very feminine. She felt no hostility toward men,
had a number of male friends, and did not object to being liked
and courted by men. Out of sympathy, she married a man of
outspoken masculine appearance and had several children by

him; her feelings for them, although not excessively warm, were nevertheless motherly.

She could not state why her homosexuality had not become more active and urgent; she only knew that she had strong inhibitions against it, which she rationalized by social timidity, family obligations, and fear of psychic subjugation. She could trace her love feelings for women back to puberty, when they began in a typical adolescent way, directed toward teachers or other individuals in authority. Whether these persons were distinguished by particular severity is not certain; at any rate the patient was dominated by two feelings—a feeling of being sheltered and, on the other hand, a feeling of fear of the individual in question. She was never really in love with a man; she had first been attracted to her husband because she had found in him a particularly active and masculine personality. But she had been disappointed in him from the start, because, as she said, he had failed to come to her expectations. He lacked sexual passion; he also remained passive in situations in which she had expected him to be master.

For many years she had been suffering from depression and feelings of anxiety with a particular ideational content: she could not find the courage to assume the proper authoritative attitude toward women in her employ. As a matter of fact, she expected a great deal of her maids and was upset when they failed to meet her demands, but she was quite unable to give them orders, much less to reprimand them. In situations that required this of her, she was overcome by feelings of timidity and anxiety in the presence of the person to be reproved. With every change in the personnel of her household, and with the consequent anticipation of contact with a new woman, her anxiety and conflict were greatly intensified. In these situations, moreover, she consciously reproached her husband for his lack of zeal in protecting and supporting her. Many women, even women who are not homosexual, have such difficulties with their women servants. These difficulties always point to an unresolved conflict with the mother. This, as we shall see, was the case with our patient.

Our patient's depressions had become more and more frequent in recent years and were intimately associated with the
danger of suicide. She had already made a number of unsuccessful suicidal attempts; the last one had brought her to the
verge of death.

Even though this patient was dominated by strong sadistic
tendencies, her conscious personality was more reactive in
character. She was kind and gentle, but showed unmistakable
obsessional-neurotic traits, such as exaggerated decorum and
propriety. Her relation to her psychoanalyst was very pronounced and over a long period of time revealed nothing
except tenderness, respect, and a feeling of safety. She was
very happy and felt as if she had at last found a kind and understanding mother who could give her all that her own mother had
denied to her. Her mother had been a stern, cold person whom
the patient hated all her life. After her mother's death (which
occurred several years before the analysis began), the patient
had a severe depression, during which she made one of her
attempts at suicide.

During her treatment she had several attacks of depression.
They were always accompanied by characteristic dreams and
brought to light certain definite material. Without presenting
these dreams in detail, I may state that they contained practically everything we know about uterine symbolism; they were
dreams of dark holes and crevices into which the patient
crawled, dreams of comfortable dark places in which she felt
at home and in which she lingered with a feeling of peace and
release. These dreams appeared at a time when she was
obsessed by a conscious yearning for death. Our patient
repeatedly asserted that had it not been for her confidence in
psychoanalysis, nothing could have kept her from committing
suicide. One special dream picture kept reappearing in these
dreams: the patient saw herself as an infant swaddled with
strips of tape or bandages. With these dreams as a guide, it
was possible to revive two memories that had remained subconscious until then. One related to an incident directly following her latest attempt at suicide (with poison). She awoke

from a deep unconsciousness while still strapped to a stretcher, she saw the doctor leaning over her with a kind smile, realized that he had saved her life (this was actually the case), and thought: "This time you have saved me, but after all you can't give me any *real* help."

The other memory related to a dangerous operation that her mother had undergone. The patient remembered seeing her mother—wrapped up as she herself was to be later after her attempt at suicide—transported on a stretcher to the operating room.

Gradually there came to the surface childhood memories that gave access to the patient's hitherto repressed murderous hate toward her mother. These memories went back to the time between her fourth and sixth years when she was masturbating to an alarming extent, at least from her mother's point of view. Whether her masturbation really exceeded the normal amount we could not determine, nor could we get at the content of the fantasies that presumably had accompanied her masturbation. But it is a fact, according to the patient's statement, that the mother resorted to the following method. She tied the girl's hands and feet, strapped them with a belt to the railing of her bed, stood beside her and said: "Now play if you can!"

This aroused two reactions in the little girl: one was ungovernable rage against her mother, which was restrained by the fetters from discharge in motor activity. The other was intense sexual excitement, which she tried to satisfy by rubbing her buttocks against the bedding, regardless of her mother's presence, or perhaps in order to vent her spite against her mother.

The most dreadful element in this scene was for her the fact that her father, summoned by her mother, was a passive witness and did not offer to help his little daughter despite his tender affection for her.

After this incident our patient stopped masturbating, and with this renunciation for a long while repressed her sexuality. At the same time she repressed her hatred for her mother, to which she had in reality never given full expression.

I do not believe that the scene with her mother was traumatic in the sense of causing the patient's later homosexual attitude. Many scientific works on perversion wrongly tend to ascribe causal significance to such incidents. In our view, in this scene were concentrated all the tendencies that had a determining influence on our patient's whole sexual life. Her reproach that her mother had forbidden her to masturbate would certainly have been present even without this scene. The hate reaction against her mother, in accordance with the patient's aggressive constitution, was also to be seen in other childhood situations, as well as the reproach that her father did not protect her from her mother. But this scene brought all these tendencies to the boiling point and thus became the prototype for later events.

From this time on, all sexual excitement was bound up with the mother's prohibition and with the most intense aggressive impulses toward the mother. Our patient's entire psychic personality resisted these hate impulses, and, as a reaction to them, there awakened in her an intense sense of guilt toward her mother, which led to a transformation of the hate into masochistic love for her. This accounted for the patient's fear of "enslavement," by which she explained her failure to have homosexual love affairs. She was indeed afraid of being masochistically attached to her mother. It will also become clear why she was afraid of the women in her employ and why she chided her husband for not adequately protecting her against them. The inner associative connection between the childhood incident, her mother's dangerous operation, and her own attempts at suicide were clearly manifested in her dreams. Her feelings that the kind doctor who had saved her life was nevertheless unable to help her, gave expression to the disappointment in her father that she never overcame.

Contrary to our expectations, this overtly homosexual woman exhibited no trace of the masculinity complex. True, in puberty she had gone through a phase in which she displayed unmistakable signs of a strong propensity for activity of a masculine character. She developed interests that, especially for her generation, were fairly unusual in a girl of her class. This element of masculinity was then—and remained throughout our patient's life—brilliantly sublimated. Her identification with her father had an important relation to her intellectual interests, but played no part in her perverse inclinations.

As a result of the treatment, the patient was liberated from her anxiety and her condemnation of her disposition, which she herself had regarded as "sinful"; she was also able to overcome her grave neurosis. Her states of depression ceased completely and she became a happy person. The longing for death that had always accompanied her constant feeling of solitude and unsatisfied desire disappeared. She found happiness in a now uninhibited love relation with a woman. This relation had a form that was unmistakably connected with early childhood functions. No male-female contrast appeared in this relationship; the essential contrast was that of activity and passivity. With conscious understanding of their situation, the two women enacted a mother-child relation, in which sometimes one, sometimes the other played the mother—a play with double roles, so to speak. One had the impression that the feeling of happiness lay in the possibility of being able to play both roles. Sexual gratification sought in this homosexual love involved chiefly the mouth and the external genitals. It goes without saying that the experience fell far below what psychoanalysis demands of an adult personality; on the contrary, in such infantile substitutes for sexual gratifications analysis sees the danger of and not the cure for neurotic illness. But sometimes the therapeutic goal can be achieved only through a compromise. In this case, analytic treatment did not lead to the patient's renouncing homosexuality and turning toward men; thus its real task was not fulfilled. But it succeeded in bringing the unhappy woman who was constantly on the verge of suicide to a point where, by mastering her fear of and her hostility toward her mother, she could achieve tenderness and sexual gratification. A better solution of the fatal mother tie proved impossible.

We understood the course of the patient's development: after a phase of sexual irresolution during which she was still willing to love a man if he proved strong enough to save her from the danger represented by her mother, she gave up this hope. All men would prove as weak as her father (her husband, her smiling physician); she would have to remain in a state of murderous hatred toward her mother and punish herself for it by death. She could be happy and live only if she succeeded in being reconciled with her mother. Such reconciliation was possible only through a complicated regressive process, bringing her back to that phase of her life when her mother—as the child's first love object—was still loved, and gratified her wishes. The patient's hatred was transformed into deep longing for her mother, which found expression in death symbolism (the patient's dreams and attempts at suicide) and homosexual love. In the realization of this love, the incidents that had resulted in her hatred for her mother had to be made up for retrogressively: the mother who had forbidden sexual gratification through masturbation was required now not to forbid it, nay, to approve it by actively contributing to it. The mother's past denials of love, and her severe punishments, had to be made good by subsequent gratification, and this both in the passive experience in which the mother gave, instead of forbidding, and in the active experience in which the patient herself assumed the role of mother.

In such a relation the highest gratification of homosexuality can be attained. The often heard remark of the little child—"When you are little and I am big"—can be realized in a situation permitting the child to do everything to his mother that the mother once did to him.

The form that homosexual activity assumes in cases like that of our patient depends on the stage of development in which the relationship to the mother is determined. If the aim is to make good the genital trauma and to gratify penis envy, a phallic activity will develop and the homosexual relation will have a masculine character. If, on the other hand, the renewal of the mother-child relationship is more infantile—as was the case with

our patient—the activity will be localized in those bodily zones
that are connected with gratification of early childhood instinctual urges. The predilection for the oral zone in the sexual
activities of homosexual women is connected with this mother
relationship.

Most investigators have overlooked the frequency with which
female homosexuality assumes this form, a form we have traced
back to a repressed longing for the mother. These women
stand in a more or less consciously recognized mother-child
relationship to their homosexual love objects. To sleep together closely embraced, to suck each other's nipples, to feel
masturbatory genital and anal excitations, to practice intensive
mutual cunnilingus—such are the forms of gratification sought
by this type of homosexual.

One woman I observed in a psychoanalytic treatment divided
this double role between two types of objects. One type,
represented by an insignificant, needy young girl, would take
the part of the child; the other role would be taken by an older,
very energetic and authoritative woman with whom she herself
played the part of the helpless little girl. The latter kind of
relationship usually began when the patient, who was very
active and professionally ambitious, entered into a sublimated
relationship with another woman, remained for a short time in
a scarcely noticeable attitude of competition, and then began
to fail in her work in a clearly neurotic way, so that she would
be in a subordinate position in relation to the particular woman
in question. Thus, for example, she would begin technical
work in collaboration with an older woman; in the end she was
playing the part of a secretary, although she was perhaps the
more talented of the two. If sexual approaches were made
during their collaboration, the other woman always took the role
of the active seducer.

Here is this woman's life history. She had many sisters and
two brothers, of whom only one, by four years her elder, played
a role in her life. When she was only 9 months old, her mother
gave birth to a girl, who competed with her for the mother's

breast. For a long time she remained in a competitive relation with this sister, to whom, even in childhood, she gave precedence—obviously as a result of overcompensation. Thus as a very young child she heard that when there is such a slight difference in age and such a striking resemblance between two sisters as there was between her and this sister, only one of them could marry and have children. She thus retired from the feminine role in favor of her sister; and in adolescence, when her parents were divorced after the birth of the last child, she waived her claim to the father to the advantage of her sister and remained with her mother.

At a very early age she displayed reaction formations on the basis of aggressive tendencies that, arising before the birth of the next sister (when she was 6) were suggestive of obsessional neurosis; they did not, however, develop to any great degree. During her mother's pregnancy at that time she reproached herself bitterly for not being as kind to her mother and the expected baby as her younger sister, who, she was convinced, prayed nightly for the welfare of her mother and the baby.

Her aggressive reactions related chiefly to her pregnant mother and the unborn child. This woman's life was always under the pressure of guilt feelings, and the formation of her character resulted from her attempts to compensate by kindness her murderous hatred for her mother and the child.

During her mother's next two pregnancies—she again gave birth to girls—the same reaction occurred, and the psychic situation of the child changed only with the birth of her youngest sister, when she was 12 years old. Previously, in her earlier childhood, she had always thought of her father as a mysterious, strange, and powerful man, in whose presence one could not help feeling timid and anxious; but her attitude gradually changed, for the father had acquired a heart ailment that finally incapacitated him for work. The family was thus involved in material difficulties, and this induced in the little girl the desire to take over her father's role. She then gave free play to fantasies in which she held high positions and supported her family. As a matter of fact, by dint of hard work, she later realized these fantasies.

In spite of the identification with her father and in spite of the fact that she envied her brother's masculinity, her attitude at the time of her youngest sister's birth was completely feminine. She was now highly pleased with the role of being a "little mother," and claimed the newborn child entirely for herself. In this situation she was behaving exactly like every normal girl. Her relation to her father too was normal at that time. After she had dethroned him from his position of supreme and unapproachable power, she could overcome her intense fear and love him tenderly.

With this turning toward her father she fell into new difficulties. Her sense of guilt toward her mother was too strong to stand the additional charge that would have resulted from rivalry with her for the father's affections. And so she renounced—as she had once renounced competition with her younger sister—competition for her father's love and again, this time definitely, turned toward her mother.

This woman's homosexuality had a manifold psychologic determination. She negated—just like the other patient—her childish angry hatred for her mother and her envy of the newborn baby, by re-experiencing the old situations that obviously still survived in her emotions and, in contrast to their actual nature in the past, endowed them with a gratifying character. In her sexual experiences with women older than herself, she assumed the role of the child who re-experiences the delights of being loved by her mother and fed from her mother's breast. Her passive and submissive attitude toward these older love objects still bore the traces of her old guilt-laden relationship to her mother.

Her erotic relations with younger women gave her an opportunity to gratify other wishes. The type of relationship that she had with the young girls corresponded not only to the active part of the original mother-child relationship, in which she made a typical identification with the nourishing mother, but quite clearly made use of new elements taken from the time of her puberty, when her youngest sister was born. The young girl was always a surrogate for her youngest sister—toward whom she actually had assumed a maternal role as a lifelong sublimation—but she was unsublimatedly homosexual with her love object, another young girl of her little sister's age. In this relationship, she was at times the mother who suckles her child and at times the suckled child herself. In this sexual experience she was able to transform the hate of her mother into love, for she was given the mother's breast; at the same time, she could be the active, suckling mother and thereby transform the aggression against her mother into activity.

In these two briefly sketched case histories[5] of female homosexuality, we observe that the instinct aberration was caused not by biologic predisposition, but by childhood events. In view of the deep intimacy of the mother-child relationship, we should not be surprised to find that longing for the mother, strengthened by a sense of guilt, can dominate a woman's affective life and exert an influence on her sexual desires. In the first of our two cases, the yearning for the mother was associated with a desire for death. The transformation of this wish into sexual gratification proved our patient's salvation, a life-affirming protection against destruction.

We selected these two cases from among a large number of others. Going over the recorded experiences of specialists in the sexual field, we are struck by their strong tendency to explain inversion by purely biologic causes and to neglect deeper psychologic motives. More particularly, the motive constituted by the mother tie is seemingly overlooked by the majority of writers. For instance, one of the women whom Havelock Ellis mentions in his material, reported that she had had her first erotic experience, at the age of 16, with a woman:

I felt like an orphan child who had suddenly acquired a mother, and through her I began to feel less antagonistic to grown people and to feel the

---

[5] Cf. Deutsch, H.: On female homosexuality. Psychoanalyt. Quart., vol. 1, 1932.

first respect I had ever felt for what they said. . . . My love for her was perfectly pure, and I thought of her as simply maternal. She never roused the least feeling in me that I can think of as sexual. I liked her to touch me and she sometimes held me in her arms or let me sit on her lap. At bedtime she used to come and say good night and kiss me upon the mouth.⁶

Elsewhere this girl declared that she felt her first sexual sensations at the same age (16), in connection with her teacher. From her whole biography it is clear that she tried to eliminate the sexual ingredients from her erotic relations to women as long as she could, yet later she became overtly homosexual.

Another of Havelock Ellis' informants was stimulated to her first love feelings by a teacher:

The teacher's face seemed very beautiful, but sad, and she thought about her continually, though not coming in personal contact with her.

This girl's love was chiefly directed to women older than herself, and

The feelings evoked were feelings of pity and compassion and tenderness for a person who seemed to be very sad and very much depressed. It is this quality or combination of qualities which has always made the appeal in my own case.⁷

The first of Havelock Ellis' women had the most violent hate feelings toward her mother during her entire childhood, chiefly as a result of her resentment at being a girl. She transferred this hatred to the whole world, and she reconciled herself with mankind only through erotic love for a motherly woman. The second woman connected her love with feelings of pity and obviously subordinated it to her sense of guilt.

This deep unconscious relation to the mother is often expressed in the poems and autobiographic writings of homosexual women; their painful and tender longing for feminine love rarely assumes a masculine character.

While we ascribe a primary character to this mother tie and

⁶ Ellis, H.: Op. cit., vol. 1, pt. 4, p. 238.
⁷ Ibid., p. 227.

support the view that in a large percentage of homosexual women the urge to union with the mother is predominant, analytic experience teaches us that this primary tie must be strengthened by other elements in order to infringe so powerfully and directly upon the woman's adult life. These additional elements gain their decisive strength during puberty. In the triangular situation, the mother's attraction and the girl's eternal longing for her must prove stronger than the biologic demand of heterosexuality. The father's favorable or unfavorable influence always affects the original mother tie during puberty. His love may be rejected by the girl as a result of fear; her disappointment in him, or his failure to gratify her, may influence her need for love in favor of the earlier mother tie. Her sense of guilt, and her need to reconcile herself with her mother, strengthen the attraction of the mother's magnetic field—to use our previous analogy again.

More extensive experience has discredited the view frequently advanced by psychoanalysts that the girl's childish relation to her mother ends up in hatred and that the later attachment consists of a little remnant of love and overcompensated hate. A verse in D. H. Lawrence's novel, *Sons and Lovers*, expresses a profound truth:

> A son's my son till he takes him a wife,
> But my daughter's my daughter the whole of her life.

Only if this love is accompanied by an excess of infantile regressive elements or hate components, does danger arise of a pathologic distortion of the love for the mother into homosexuality. Otherwise it is a blessing in woman's life.

CHAPTER TEN

The Influence of the Enviornment

ADJUSTMENT to reality is the main purpose of all education, including psychoanalytic therapy. The individual's capacity for adjustment presupposes a certain degree of satisfaction with the environment, and this in turn depends on his emotional state. The bridge between the environment and the individual, from the beginning of his life, is his affective relationship to this environment. The acceptance of reality is determined by love and need of protection on the one hand and by fear of punishment and of emotional isolation on the other. The developmental history gives us an insight into the ways and means by which the individual learns to master his primitive aggressions against the environment and his fears of it through "love." The aggressive components of love are familiar to us; and jealousy, competition, and hatred for the rival accompany the human being from the cradle to the grave. The objects of these emotions change, and the field in which the emotional conflicts take place is gradually extended. The individual's relations to his cultural environment always reproduce more or less his relationship to the first little environment of his childhood, in the form of a new edition reshaped by external influences.

In our social structure built up over hundreds of years, the family constitutes the individual's first environment and prefigures his later more extensive socialization. The feelings of rivalry and competition, which are often considered the results of cultural conditions, can be seen fully blossoming within the framework of the family, in the interrelationships of its members. These feelings appear so regularly and so universally that one is justified in calling them part of man's natural disposition. They are characteristic not only of human nature; domesticated animals display them with unmistakable clarity. The best-natured dog furiously attacks his rival not only to deprive him of his bone, but also when he feels that his master is showing less tenderness toward him in favor of the rival. He may even ignore the food that is set before him— food that satisfies his instinct of self-preservation—when he sees that his rival is receiving the pleasure of being petted. In animals less degenerated as a result of domestication, a disposition to such reactions can also be noted. Close and prolonged observation of the friendly relations between cows in a pasture, for example, shows that these animals too, under certain circumstances, manifest modes of behavior that can be compared to man's. The mutual licking of the skin, for instance, serves some physiologic need, but there is no doubt that in the course of this process pleasurable sensations are developed. In connection with these, the group life of cows reveals features that remind us of human rivalry behavior.

The family atmosphere in which human children live intensifies the inclination to envious competitiveness. In order to complete adjustment to reality, the adolescent draws upon the means and forces with which nature has endowed him, but which have been molded by education so that in human society he will not be too troublesome because of excessive aggressions or too helpless because of inhibitions. Often instinctual forces overcome the influence of education; often the requirements of the given social milieu turn out to be too difficult, or the young person's ability to adjust and master his environment turns out to be inadequate. Feelings of inferiority, helplessness, and fear on the one hand, and the intensification of the aggressive forces on the other, can exceed the individual's limit of tolerance, and in that event he enters into a conflict with himself or society. Psychic conflicts that have constantly accompanied his development, and that were kept in equilibrium under certain conditions, may become intensified when confronted with the increased demands of the environment. The individual's inner harmony is destroyed and

he becomes neurotically ill, because the cultural requirements
have proved too difficult for him. The question as to whether
he is too weak or the environment too exacting, strongly
reminds us of the question as to whether the hen or the egg
comes first. The same is true of aggressions, competitiveness,
and all the human evils that are intensified by irritating elements in the living conditions. We refer here to the greater
difficulty in gratifying the various instinctual needs and the
aspirations of the ego, for instance, as a result of greater internal
or external obstacles to sublimation, etc.

Naturally each cultural milieu creates its own forms of expression for the unchanging psychic processes in man and
affects the various components of his psychic structure in a
specific manner. This leads to cultural, racial, and national
differences; these can be regarded as the façade behind which
are concealed the eternal, deep-rooted, only quantitatively
distinguishable, and variable components of the psychic life.
Cultural factors can, nevertheless, be so powerful that they
extensively modify human behavior and influence even the
deepest, biologically conditioned, instinctual manifestations;
they can impress their form on the organic constitution and
determine not only the frequency and intensity of neuroses,
but their clinical forms. Thus, the well known fact that
certain types of neuroses are prevalent in one country while
others are frequent in another, can certainly be explained by
cultural differences. Further, it has even been observed that
various periods of history have been characterized by the
prevalence of one or another psychic disease; changes in this
respect can be noted within relatively short intervals of time.
For instance, cases of dramatic, symptom-rich hysteria were
strikingly rare during the thirties; recently, before the outbreak
of the present war, they began to be more frequent.

Nor is there any doubt that competition between individuals,
and everything that this brings in its train, is more strongly
marked in an individualistic social system. It is not unreason-
able to hope that a collectivistic organization of society might

weaken the competitive spirit that has become intolerably fierce in the relations both between individuals and between individuals and society. Such an organization would transform individual competition into group competition and thus make it more bearable. Group formations certainly offer us better protection against excessive growth of individual feelings than purely individualistic organizations. A new form of society might also bring about a decrease in the number and intensity of our neuroses. At present our information from countries whose experiences could permit us to make more definite statements on this subject is still incomplete.

Nor can it be denied that in addition to using the greater submissiveness of woman—a submissiveness stemming from her passivity—in the interests of his own sexual urge, man has frequently taken social advantage of her physical weakness and lesser capacity for active struggle. The best illustration of this are the European capitalist countries where female industrial labor has been ruthlessly and aggressively exploited. The materialist doctrine holds the economic system responsible for this exploitation of woman and completely neglects her own not always conscious disposition passively to accept this system. In the course of recent years the protest against the social and political inequality of the sexes has lost much of its impetus because the demands of women gradually became a matter of course in democratic countries. Our next task is to organize social equality in such a way that the biologic and psychologic differences between the sexes are taken into account. It would be tempting to undertake a thorough cultural-historical psychoanalytic study of woman and to investigate the conditions under which the various components of her psychic life have asserted themselves. Here, however, we shall deal only with the developments that we have partly witnessed ourselves and that give us an opportunity to observe the effect of social changes on woman's psychic reactions.

When one considers the differences between the sexes in their relation to social equality, sexual problems must be dealt with first.　It is still too early to appraise the results of woman's sexual freedom and of the sanctioning of polygamy in collectivist societies, because the reports concerning these matters seem very contradictory.　We shall, however, study from the psychoanalytic point of view those reports which seem to us most relevant.

The Ways of Love, by Alexandra Kollontay, the prominent Russian political leader, examines the very core of the problem that interests us here.　Although not a great literary work, it is an important cultural and historical document, because it expresses faithfully the ideas of Russian women and young girls in the first period of the Russian revolution.　It gives us an insight into certain psychologic processes and at the same time shows what effect swift cultural changes have upon these processes.　The author held an important government position during the Russian revolutionary upheavals and thus had opportunity to study the histories of many individual women.　Even though the cases she describes are presented in fictional form, one feels that they are based on the direct experiences of a person who has tried to be objective.　What makes her book particularly valuable is that she raises present day problems without expressing any desire to solve them. She herself seems uncertain whether the conflicts she describes are merely individual feminine tragedies or the result of the social upheaval.　She neither praises nor condemns; although she has faith in the greatness and creativity of the revolution, she refrains from passing judgment on the newly emerging forms of love and life.

She depicts the life of three generations.　Her chief characters are three women who have fanatical faith in revolutionary progress and who conceive their lifework as service to their social ideals.　According to the period in which they live, they belong to different political parties with different programs and methods of organization; but all three of them ardently desire the liberation of the Russian people and their lives are full of self-sacrificing activity on behalf of this ideal. Their emotional relations with each other have nothing to do with the maelstrom of party struggles. What separates them, the field in which they are unable to see eye to eye, is eroticism, the area of life that lies outside their social tasks, the personal feminine area. Each of them defends her own approach to these problems against that of the others and tries to explain the differences between them by the difference between the generations. In the eyes of the youngest, the older is reactionary; the latter suffers from the former's moral indignation, begins to doubt herself, and asks herself in despair whether, because of her old-fashioned beliefs, she is really incapable of understanding the new morality of her daughter. She is practically defenseless against that fatal term of abuse, "bourgeois prejudices," because it confuses her and makes her wonder whether she is not after all really prejudiced.

She knows that she found herself in a similar situation with regard to her own mother, and had the same feeling that she was advanced and that the preceding generation was full of "prejudices."

We shall subject the life histories of these women to a brief psychologic analysis in the hope of gaining a better understanding of their problems than they themselves had.

First we shall try to ascertain to what extent the misunderstanding between the three generations resulted from the fact that environmental influences shaped their psychology differently.

The conflicts between them are described by one who, because she represents the intermediate generation, is pressed from two sides. Olga Sergeyevna Vaselovskaya is the daughter of Maria Stepanovna Olshevich, whose portrait she clearly draws for us. According to her description, Maria was a typical cultural worker of the nineties—a publisher of popular scientific books and a tireless leader in the field of popular education. She enjoyed great respect among the liberal political figures of her time. Although she did not participate in the underground revolutionary movement, she rendered valuable services to it. In her theoretic views she was close to the Narodniki, the revolutionary people's party of the eighties. Her whole personality was severe and awe-inspiring. She always spoke briefly and to the point and smoked cigarettes. She dressed simply and not according to the mode, yet she remained a "lady," caring for her hands, wearing a gold ring with a ruby, etc. Her appearance was quite different from that of the rather careless type of "illegal" woman revolutionaries.

Olga learns from her strict and conscientious mother that the latter in her youth was disappointed in love. This experience crystallized the firm moral code she had certainly already formed. She despises and condemns everyone who does not live according to this code and does not feel and think as she does about questions of sexual morality. A conflict arises between mother and daughter, not because of their political differences, but because of their different concepts of morality, especially with regard to their own love experiences. Maria Stepanovna has always been a progressive in her personal life; first she freed herself from her dependence upon her parents, marrying against their will, and later, when she fell in love with another man, she broke the fetters of her marriage and motherhood. During all these vicissitudes she worked indefatigably and with iron determination for the cause of popular enlightenment. While her first marriage condemned her to a certain degree of passivity, her situation changed completely in her second marriage. Sergey Ivanovich, her second husband, was a Russian intellectual, obscurely idealistic but helpless in all practical matters, who spoke with heartfelt emotion of the misery of the peasants and the necessity of working for their betterment. His and Maria's daughter, Olga, refers to her father somewhat deprecatingly as "that Chekhovian hero." This idealist fell into an absolutely passive dependence upon his energetic, active wife, became a shadowy revolutionary under her influence, went with her into exile, and helped her in her work. At the same time he deteriorated spiritually, grew fat and flabby, and took to drinking. His married life with Maria ended when his proud wife caught him *flagrante delicto* with Arisha, the milkmaid, and learned that he had impregnated her. Of course, Maria did what was commanded by her moral code: she at once left her husband, taking her little daughter, Olga, with her, and, unconcerned for her personal fate, continued working for her cause. Although she later asserted that she had loved Sergey and had remained faithful to him, she never displayed much longing for him or sentimentality about her marriage. Olga learned this story directly from her mother, whom she always respected and admired.

The Russian liberals had nothing but approval for Maria when, in order to satisfy her desire for freedom, she abruptly left her first husband and two children. After all, in doing this she expressed that liberalistic philosophy that places individual rights above the conventions of society and advocates woman's liberation from the fetters of monogamous bourgeois marriage in favor of the free erotic choice; at the same time, however, the institution of marriage is still maintained. In western Europe and North America this ideology was generally accepted at the time Maria became its pioneer in Russia. Ibsen's Nora was its literary expression. Thus, Maria Stepanovna's personal destiny to a large extent reflected the contemporary libertarian trends that she championed.

Closer psychologic analysis of Maria's personality shows that she is endowed with an energetic nature and exuberant rebellious individuality. She must translate her energy into activity, into unremitting labor in the service of society. The marriage of Ibsen's Nora founders because she believes that she has duties toward herself, and the same conviction determines the behavior of Maria Stepanovna. This kind and broad-minded woman, who displays forbearance toward every social transgression, is absolutely intolerant when a personal principle is at stake. As we follow the course of her life, we have the impression that she wants to subordinate her emotions to her ideals. We do not even know whether she experienced the human feeling of jealousy when she discovered Sergey's liaison. She probably immediately suppressed such feelings, and her moral code completely determined her behavior, fitting it to her ideal pattern. Thus, what we would term cold egoism, narcissistic self-mortification, and intolerance toward the love object in less idealistic and lofty personalities, is excused and even admired in her case.

Women like Maria Stepanovna are familiar to us, for they have appeared in different historical periods. When they do not subordinate their personal emotional life to the social revolution, they act in the same way for the sake of religion or some other conservative or revolutionary ideology. God is remote from the Russian women in Maria's circles, their religion is personal morality and the revolution; whatever the revolution demands is sacred, and individual desires must be subordinated to it.

Maria Stepanovna and women like her are never free from dogma and system even in purely personal matters. They draw the inspiration and strength to realize their system either from themselves or from the environment. Whether the system serves a conservative or revolutionary goal is a matter of secondary importance. These women are extraordinarily loyal to their ideals, even in the face of death. Their own emotional relations also represent ideals, and they remain faithful to their emotions whether they feel them or not. Maria remains faithful to her second husband, because she once professed love for him—and even then her love served an ideal of freedom. It is very difficult to decide whether such women have warm emotions at first, while later their subsequent absorption in social, religious, or other idealistic activities deprives them of much of their warmth, or whether from the very beginning they are incapable of really strong feelings and thus easily adapt their erotic demands to their ideals. The erotic atmosphere around them is usually icy, and harmony with a man is achieved only by such means as Maria used, that is, through common devotion to something impersonal.

In Maria's love relation there is one feature that we encounter very frequently. She is the type of the active, perhaps even excessively active woman who chooses as her love object a passive, usually feminine man whom she can easily turn into an instrument for her own ideas. Usually, the man is wrecked as a personality; in his subsequent "masculine protest" he begins to hate the once worshiped woman and turns with his erotic need to an inferior being who shows respect and admiration for his weak masculinity. This is what happened to the husband of Maria Stepanovna, the intolerant, active, principled revolutionary woman, who, as a psychologic type, can be encountered in various historical epochs in many milieus and social conditions. It is only the content of the principles, the façade adapted to the environment, that changes according to the milieu and the period. But she herself is always the same. Tender sympathy, loving identification with her husband, motherly warmth toward her children—qualities that, if necessary, can lead to the neglect of principles—usually are and remain alien to her. Sometimes such a woman is endowed with a degree of eroticism that brings her closer to one of the types of feminine women we have described above (p. 209); sometimes she is surrounded by a troop of children and resembles our active matriarchal type (p. 283); but most often her affectivity serves values far removed from the emotional and the personal.

We do not know why Maria developed into that type of woman or what factors contributed to her development. But much of her daughter Olga's life will be clarified for us by our knowledge of her mother.

Olga Sergeyevna has never been directly in the feminist movement. As a matter of fact Maria Stepanovna was not directly interested in the emancipation of women either. She demanded equal rights for all, and for herself as a woman too, but her social activity was in behalf of sexually undifferentiated ideals, above all in behalf of popular education. Her daughter, Olga, occupies a prominent position in the soviet republic and is an extremely efficient organizer. This

woman's new postulate is "free love." While her mother's
ideal was a freely contracted love marriage, Olga's ideal is
freedom from the conventional marriage ties. Even as a
young girl she is interested in revolutionary ideas and studies
social problems. She is influenced in this direction by the
atmosphere of her home, and in her puberty she does not
experience the usual fate of young middle class girls who
become revolutionary as a protest against their milieu. Far
from opposing Olga's revolutionary ideals, Maria Stepanovna
is proud when her 16-year-old daughter is arrested as an
underground worker. But Olga goes through a personal
revolution, in the course of which she frees herself from her
mother's influence and adopts more radical political and moral
ideas. While the mother was a Narodnik, Olga becomes a
Marxist under the influence of a Bolshevik. Against her
mother's advice and will she lives, "according to principle,"
as she says, in a free marriage with an older comrade, C., who
assumes the role of her political guide and educator.

It is not surprising that Olga loves a man much older than
herself and abandons herself to his influence. In this respect
she is like all adolescent girls, regardless of the social conditions
in which they live, although in her concept of "free love" she
expresses the new social order. It must be remembered that
after her parents had separated, Olga became a fatherless girl;
in her mother's stories and perhaps in her own memories, her
father is weak, passive, devaluated, and she chooses her love
object out of opposition to him.

After C. is deported and torn away from her, she accepts a
position as governess in the home of M., a married engineer.
She does not like him: she finds him lacking in ideas, and his
intellectual level is lower than hers, let alone C's. He is obviously happily married to a "fragile doll in lace and furs" and
has five healthy children by her. Olga is annoyed by this
atmosphere of satisfaction and family happiness. The man's
love for his pretty wife and his concern over her health in-
furiate Olga, and she delights in making the attractive matron

suffer to the point of tears by her aggressive behavior. She talks a great deal about life in exile, about the great task facing the revolutionaries, and about their sufferings for their ideals, and expresses her contempt for the satiated happiness of the bourgeoisie. Later she acknowledges that her hatred for the happily married couple was so intense and conscious that she even daydreamed of doing something that might provoke the police to invade the privacy of this peaceful family.

We are quite familiar with this type of behavior, irrespective of the social surroundings. In our democratic social order also, adolescent girls protest against the unbearable atmosphere of their homes, reproach their parents for being conservative, find their married relationship "philistine and disgusting," and express their protest in various ways, according to their cultural level. Sometimes their protest assumes a higher form and they join radical groups; in other cases, they demonstrate their liberation from the home milieu through "free love" that does not always stem from an inner need and is not always accompanied by feelings of happiness. If they do not succeed in outgrowing this adolescent attitude, it is repeated at the next opportunity in another milieu. Young girls of the poorer classes who act out their family conflicts to an excessive degree are placed in foster homes. Many case records of social agencies that concern themselves with young people remind us of Olga's experience in the engineer's home. The girls whose life histories are recorded in these offices transferred their conflicts with their parents to their foster homes, were infuriated by the harmony of the foster parents' married life, seduced their foster fathers, or, according to their disposition, falsely accused these men of trying to seduce them.

Olga falls passionately in love with the hated and despised M. and unscrupously destroys his marriage. But she herself then enters into a conflict the motives of which are unclear to her. This conflict arises from the fact that she loves—as she says—both men, M. and C., and neither can nor will give up either of them. As a Bolshevik, she despises the handsome

M., yet the slightest sign of indifference on his part causes her intense pain, and when he tries to take her, she gives herself as a matter of course.   At the same time, she thinks with the greatest tenderness and yearning of her former lover, who is now living in exile.   Her soul needs him, spiritually he is much closer to her; without him her life is cold and empty.   She turns to her mother for advice and help, and, as was to be expected, her mother demands that she separate from one or the other of the two men.   Maria's monogamous morality, entirely orientated toward love for one man, can neither understand nor approve of this conflict.   Thus Olga remains suspended in a love triangle between an "earthly" and a "heavenly" love, unable to choose between the two.   Inability to reach an emotional decision in such a conflict occurs very frequently, and we ascribe it to a neurotic character.   We are very familiar with the split between sensual and spiritual love in men, but it occurs also in women, as the case of Olga shows.

When Olga is made pregnant by M., her mother thinks that this fact should determine her daughter's decision.   But Olga reacts to her mother's advice in a manner that throws much light on her complicated situation: the more her mother takes the part of the new lover, the more Olga feels attached to the old one.   In her eyes, it is as if her mother and M. formed a liberal bourgeois alliance against the proletarian camp, to which she and C. belong.

We shall not continue our psychologic analysis of Olga's conflict.   What interests us is that she herself, out of deepest conviction, tries to give her purely erotic and psychologic problem a sociologic explanation, and regards her disagreement with her mother as the result of their belonging to different generations.   The only factor in her case that, in our opinion, can be regarded as expressing an environmental influence, is that Olga, when she wrecks a marriage and simultaneously maintains relations with two men, displays no inhibitions arising from a body of social ethics.   She has no feelings of social guilt, because her own ideal demands, conditioned by her philosophy, are in accord with the prevailing moral ideas.

She lives in a milieu that sanctions simultaneous love for several men and no longer recognizes the rights of marriage as an institution. In this respect she is in opposition to her mother and reflects a conflict between two generations. But the genesis and solution of such a conflict have nothing to do with the social milieu, either in Olga or in our neurotics. Olga's triangle collapses for psychologic reasons, because neither the bourgeois M. nor the Marxist C. wishes to share the woman he loves with another man. Both withdraw, M. into a good job, C. to the White Guards, apparently from a need for revenge, just like any reactionary bourgeois.

In later life, Olga saves the remnants of her emotional warmth from disappointment and lovelessness and, along with her consuming activity for the "cause," enjoys the personal luxury of a serene love relation. She lives in a free marriage with a certain Comrade R., who is much younger than she, sickly and passive. She herself describes him as her disciple, and everybody knows that she is far superior to him and that in all things she is the highest authority for him. She has a responsible position in an industrial organization, gives herself entirely to her work, and is just as much respected as her mother was.

She has another characteristic in common with her mother: after vain efforts to find another form of love than that her mother knows, she nevertheless, like many other women living under entirely different social conditions, ends up by completely identifying herself with her mother; she too assumes an active leading role in regard to her man. In a perhaps less trivial and more tragic form, her fate is an exact replica of her mother's—and she experiences this fate in a "misunderstanding" with the younger generation. This misunderstanding is profoundly psychologic, and once again the confused Olga and her ilk try to explain it by socio-ideologic differences. "You may scold me," she cries in despair, "if I am only backward, if the new conditions have again given birth to another, new psychology."

We might reply to this woman, so efficient and intelligent,

devoted to such a great cause and yet so confused: "No, these new conditions have only put a new wrapping around the old psychology."

Olga has a daughter, Genia, who gives us a glimpse of the "new psychology" of the third generation. After several years of separation from her child, Olga, now married, takes her daughter into her home. There is a great shortage of apartments in the new soviet land, and the mother, daughter, and stepfather, in a spirit of realistic adjustment, consider it natural to live together in one room. Genia is strong, energetic, an untiring and extremely valuable worker for the cause. Olga finds her a stimulating comrade and feels toward her not as a mother but as a friend. Then one day she discovers that Genia and Comrade R., Olga's life companion, have a sexual relationship. The theme of incest, transferred in this case to the young stepdaughter or stepfather, recurs in various cultures, in widely separated epochs, in old myths and modern dramas.

Olga's reaction to this discovery is what one would expect it to be. She is in despair, insulted, deeply hurt in her love for R., but above all horrified by her daughter's act. What seems to her most ugly and intolerable is Genia's attitude, her heartlessness and her conviction of her right to do what she has done, a right that she defends with cold intellectual arguments. She shows no sign of repentance or pity for her mother, much less love or passion that might excuse her relation with R.; nor does she manifest the slightest desire to get out of this situation. On the contrary, she accuses her mother of backwardness and lack of understanding. Genia extends the Marxist philosophy of the abolition of private property to love and argues that Comrade R. is not her mother's private possession and that he and she, Genia, have the right to give free expression to their impulses.

Genia is pregnant, and Olga has no doubt that Comrade R. is responsible for it. The young daughter, with a matter-of-factness that sounds cynical to the "reactionary" mother, declares that she does not know who the father of the child is, because she has had sexual intercourse with another man too.

Most alarming and incomprehensible to Olga is Genia's open admission that she has never loved any man. She tells her mother that she had sexual intercourse with several men as a very young girl when she went to the front carrying gifts for the soldiers. She felt no physical urge to do this, but it gave her a kind of easy, conflictless pleasure that did not place any responsibilities upon her. If she had sold herself like a prostitute or been raped, it would have been another matter. But as she acted of her own volition and these acts pleased her at the moment, the matter, in her opinion, is completely outside the field of any moral judgment. Genia advances the typical argument that we so frequently hear from modern adolescent girls: "If I were a twenty-year-old young man and had sexual intercourse with women at the front, would anyone object to it?"

Has she not the same rights as a man? Has she ever been unaware of her duty to society? Has she ever forgotten her responsibilities to the party? And is this not the only yardstick and moral criterion? With whom and with how many men she has sexual intercourse is a minor matter. True, she is pregnant and thinks it advisable not to bring children into the world in this period of struggle. The new law permits abortions. Genia feels free of guilt at the very bottom of her heart. It does not occur to her that her mother is suffering, that Andrey (Comrade R.) may become unbalanced, that a pregnancy has psychologic significance. She evaluates all human relationships from the point of view of economic property rights and considers it wrong to claim private property rights in love relationships.

Olga still tries to stress the intensity of her love and suffering as factors that justify her indignation; but for Genia neither love nor suffering, neither happiness nor repentance is involved. She has the calm conviction that she is entitled to take her pleasure whenever she pleases. She does not display

a trace of warmth, nor the most elementary consideration
for another human being. Actually the passive Andrey for
her is nothing but a male. Her liaison with him is an accidental
product of the one-room apartment, and in his weakness he
is an object of her protective care. As for her other lover,
Abrasha, she does not love him either, but he has a certain
power over her, she must obey him, she cannot do otherwise;
and his attraction for her lies in the fact that she feels she must
submit to his will!

According to Genia's own words, however, she is not as
incapable of feeling as she seems. She loves her mother after
a fashion and suffers when she discovers that Olga is so "reactionary." She also loves men in her own way: for instance,
Lenin, for whom she would even sacrifice her life. She also
loves Comrade Gerasim, the party secretary, with whom she
has no personal relations and who is her superior in party
matters. She obeys him even when he is not right. Is it not
curious that the active, cold, superior Genia speaks of love only
in relation to men who make her submit?

If we consider Genia as a product of her time, as the "new
femininity" of the early twenties, we shall discover that in
spite of appearances to the contrary she confirms a theory of
femininity that she herself would reject as extremely reactionary: the theory that the subjection of the feminine sex,
which recurs over and over again in human history, stems
from a characteristic feminine tendency to submit to the
standards and demands of the prevailing morality. In matters
of love, this energetic, clear-sighted, and revolutionary girl is,
without suspecting it, a passive object that automatically
succumbs to the influences acting upon her in the form of the
"new ideology." She submits, almost as if by a reflex, to the
suggestive power of the new, without realizing that it represents
the action of the rulers over the ruled.

It is erroneous to think that because the fetters of the
bourgeois social order have been broken, Genia is now a "free
human being" in the sexual as well as the sociopolitical sense.
She explicitly emphasizes the moral difference between her

actions and the promiscuity of a prostitute. The latter does it for the sake of money, while Genia does it only for pleasure. Thus she subjects her actions to the moral evaluation that is proper to her generation. The fact that she does not love her sexual objects and that she has no desire for love happiness does not strike her as a defect; on the contrary, she boasts with a certain pride of her promiscuous sexual life, which she regards as "freedom." She knows that she is incapable of love but she considers her enthusiasm for ideas and her work for their realization as compensating factors. The spiritualization of sexual life, certain spiritual qualities, and the individual character of the love object are not prerequisites in Genia's love relationship. Feminine eroticism, monogamous love, of which we have spoken above in the light of Genia's attitude, seem like a sort of fairy tale that arose under definite cultural conditions and that is still dependent upon them.

Yet actually Genia's type of love life is not as new to us as she and her comrades like to believe. We have observed similar behavior under quite different political and social conditions. For instance, we know frigid polygamous women who constantly change their love objects just as Genia does, and women who for definite psychologic reasons are in constant need of something new in their sexual experiences, in order to protect themselves from growing dull through habituation. Others are driven to new love experiences by the rapid dying away of their emotions, still others flee from some unconscious tie into frequently changing relationships, without ever being able to satisfy their longing. The number of motivations is large and usually they stem from deep psychic sources. This does not seem to be the case with Genia; one has the impression that her sexual life is completely separate from her soul. She resembles those women and girls whose sexual actions really have very little to do with sexuality conceived as erotic or sensual experience. Because their emotions are so little involved in sexual acts, there is no quantitative limit to their polygamy. Genia denies that in addition to the monogamy demanded by the bourgeois society that she hates, there is also a psychologically justified, free monogamy. This is because she is emotionally incapable of such relationship. She rationalizes her incapacity with the aid of a social ideology. She thinks that she follows the new commandment of sexual freedom out of revolutionary enthusiasm, and in this she is surely right to some extent. But Genia is unaware of the presence of deep-rooted personal individual causes that impel her to accept the new commandment unconditionally.

To understand Genia's individual motives we must cast a glance at her life history. The few things we know about her suffice to give us some idea of it. She was a fatherless child and from her earliest childhood she was also deprived of a tender motherly atmosphere. She lived for some time with her cold, dutiful grandmother and later, as we learn from Olga, with various "friends." These friends were certainly revolutionaries who spent all the ardor of their emotions for the cause. Which of them had the time or emotional freedom to pay attention to something so irrelevant as the emotional life of a little child? Thus this aspect of her life was doubtless neglected and she learned to love only "ideals," not living beings. She insists that she loves her mother; but hers is an infantile kind of love that gladly accepts the mother as the giver of all good things and the ideal prototype, but that is unable to take the mother's feelings and sufferings into account. Genia's protestations that she loves men reminds us strongly of the typical infatuations of narcissistic adolescent girls, who tie their longing to an object without really loving it. The duke in Maria Bashkirtseff's love fantasies (p. 97) psychologically plays the same role as Lenin or Comrade Gerasim plays for Genia. In this kind of love choice, the differences of intellectual level are not psychologically important. Yet now and then Genia displays a very feminine behavior: she has intense feelings for men only when she can subordinate herself to their superior power.

We consider Genia an emotionally disturbed personality

that succeeds in feeling superior through a socio-ideologic rationalization of her neurotic or instinctual actions. Her sexual urge is thus not freed from its fetters through the change in the cultural demands; nor is she a personality that is changed by social influences. What she represents is the effect of an ideology on predetermined, chiefly unconscious psychic processes in a personality with an immature and therefore disturbed emotional life.

However, the mobilization and strengthening of such reactions, above all Genia's liberation from guilt feelings, results from the social conditions. The shortage of apartment space, the ardent desire to do something for the cause, lack of time for emotional relationships, in brief, the emergency atmosphere of the revolution, all help to create numerous Genias. We have the impression that they can be found most frequently in certain intellectual circles; they are perhaps the product of a generation that, even in a less radical milieu, considers work, ideals, and intellectuality to be compensations for the weakness and shallowness of its emotional life.

Maria Stepanovna, Olga Sergeyevna, and Genia use their social ideology to conceal and rationalize their purely individual motives, in a manner which is often useful for the community. In Maria, a desire for individual liberation and the belief in woman's right to self-determination merge into a social ideal that takes the place of warm love emotions. Olga considers the neurotic split in her love feelings an expression of freedom and permits herself recklessly to gratify her aggression against the other woman, without experiencing social feelings of guilt because she looks upon her actions as those of a fighter for progress. Genia, the most infantile of the three, who regresses farthest into the past in her emotional life, paradoxically becomes the proponent of what is supposed to be the greatest step forward in woman's emancipation.[1]

[1] The term infantile is here used in a purely psychologic sense and does not imply any social value judgment. Under certain conditions, a type of behavior that stems from psychologically infantile sources, like rebellion against authority, may be more

The individual psychologic problems are not always so obvious as in these representatives of three generations of women. But we can say that the relation between psychologic factors and cultural or social trends may lead to developments that have the appearance of being determined exclusively by environmental influences. Sometimes the social element is used as a substitute for the repressed psychic tendencies, often even in direct opposition to them. In other cases, the ideology for which a woman fights serves as a rationalization of her own actions; often she tries frantically to adapt her mode of life to the existing social ideals without any real psychologic necessity for doing so.

In Kollontay's description of her women, there are two circumstances that must be kept in mind. In the first place, it is striking that the men to whom her heroines tie their lives are passive weaklings, subordinated and inferior to these women. Is this a mere coincidence? In the second place, the attitude of these women to motherhood is peculiar. Maria takes her little daughter away with her when she leaves her husband and does not even ask herself whether it is right or wrong to rear a child without a father. Olga vigorously rejects the idea of having an abortion, but she separates herself from her child in order to be free to work for the cause. Genia undergoes an abortion without displaying the slightest sign of the normal feminine reaction to this experience. She has no time to give birth to a child or to love it. So this is how the attitudes have been transformed in the course of three generations! Is this progress, and does this progress bring more freedom and potentialities of happiness to women—or is such freedom won at the price of inability to experience the most intense feminine happiness?

---

adapted to reality and more rational than so-called "adult" behavior that conforms to the demands of society. Immature individuals are often in the van of social development, and progress is inaugurated by the unsatisfied individual who strives for freedom. The fact that their bondage may lie in their own souls, and that they project the causes for it in the outside world, does not affect the social value of their actions.

It should be noted here that in the course of the last two decades the attitude of the Russian revolution toward marriage and maternity has undergone profound changes. For many years now, promiscuity and frequent divorces have been frowned upon in the Soviet Union. Abortions are forbidden, while the constitution and many local regulations provide for the security of mothers and children. The last decade has witnessed an ever increasing trend toward the strictest monogamy and respect for family life.

I have used Alexandra Kollontay's book as an illustration because it is particularly suitable for the presentation of our problem. The files of our social agencies contain innumerable case histories of women who have transferred their psychologic conflicts to social, environmental conditions. Often the social mask is so convincing that one tries to find a social solution of the problem involved. Satisfactory results are frequently obtained for a short time, yet the psychologic component soon proves more powerful and supplies fuel for an ever renewed conflict with the environment.

Maria, Olga, and Genia, who belong to three generations, coexist in every generation; they vary their personalities by emphasizing now one, now another psychologic ingredient, according to internal or external influences. These three types of women are perhaps not so different from one another after all. Only in their modes of solving their timeless problems do these representatives of the different generations seem to be partly influenced by the social structure.

The Russian woman has gone through the fire of revolution, has largely freed her activity from social fetters, and continues fighting at the side of her man for their common aims. The American woman has achieved her social goal through the more peaceful means of democratic progress. But the femininity of both is fighting its silent struggles on a quite different front, just like that of all women of whatever race, color, language, or culture.

We shall now turn our attention to developments that we

can observe more directly. For we too are living in a situation of social upheaval that can bring about rapid transformations of human behavior.

We recall that in the interval between the two world wars American opinion was disturbed by certain striking developments in the young people of both sexes. These related not only to the increase of the aggressive forces and the unbearable competitiveness that hardly left the last generation time to breathe. Other more regressive manifestations of this restless competitiveness disturbed us even more. In addition to the over-intensified intellectual and athletic activity that served competitive purposes, a terrifying emotional bleakness and superficiality was noted in these young people. One could not help feeling that the young men, despite their overactivity, had an increasing tendency toward passivity, while the unmistakable increase of activity in the young women, and their tendency toward masculinization, were accompanied by the same shallowness and emotional inertia that the boys displayed. While the boy's overactivity betrayed, in its overcompensating character, the passivity and emotional emptiness concealed behind it, the girl's masculinization unfortunately expressed not only her growing social emancipation, but also her impoverished emotional life, resulting from an overgrowth of her intellect. The typical process of intellectualization that we have observed as a temporary manifestation of adolescence (p. 128) was displayed by both sexes to a greater extent than before and for a long time after puberty. We have no adequate information about the causes of this behavior, but we see that this psychologic picture has been completely transformed by the war. It is true that the observations we have gathered since the outbreak of hostilities can be appraised only superficially.

In our attempts to understand the psychic transformation of people, especially youth, we must keep in mind that war is an emergency situation and like all such situations opens up all the reservoirs of fear in the human soul. The more acute and unexpected the emergency, the more profoundly does it terrify the mind, just as sudden natural phenomena, like thunder and lightning, mobilize the fears of a child. Even if fear is brilliantly mastered and the individual's reactions to the war seem rational and logical, its existence must not be overlooked.

The methods of overcoming fear are various; we must distinguish individual reactions from mass phenomena. Gradually, in the course of time, the individual modes of reaction also combine into mass phenomena. One of the methods of mastering fear that is applied in wartime to individuals and to masses, is active participation in the events. Reality compels everyone to resort, *nolens volens*, to these methods, and the young of both sexes are subject to the same compulsion. Intellectual skepticism and emotional callousness are under fire from two sides: the demands of objective reality and the subjective need actively to combat the intensified fears. This need leads to a general psychologic mobilization.

Within this framework of the general mass manifestation we shall also consider more individual phenomena. Especially in women, who are less subject to pressure from outside then men, the more individual methods of coping with the situation are noticeable. In some women, the active mastering of fear has a rather obsessional character, and in others it has a more hysterical one. In the first case, under the pressure of the inner anxiety that has been mobilized, as well as of external events, the sense of guilt is intensified, and the need to suffer and to sacrifice oneself for the general cause expresses itself in various ways—for instance, in the abandonment of previous gratifying activity and the assumption of difficult occupations directly connected with the war. Often the war sacrifice must be connected with immediate dangers, and the choice of occupation is determined by this wish. The self-denial and dependability of this feminine type are beyond all praise. Information received from the theater of war shows that this group of women who are actively participating in the war stands out favorably as compared to the others. They are particularly successful in overcoming fear through purposeful activity and in thus finding release from feelings of guilt.

The hysterical forms of mastering fear are more varied. Here too sacrifice plays an important role, but it assumes a more conscious, dazzling, ecstatic character. In very young girls this desire to sacrifice themselves implies grave sexual dangers; the fact that every young soldier must actually face death deeply stirs the heated imaginations of such girls. They feel that they must give the man, already dedicated to death in their fantasy, everything that can increase the "last joys of life." Their personal fears are intensified by the general motives for fear inherent in the war atmosphere, and in them the mastering of fear through activity extends to various fields, including sexuality. This activity usually involves a loosening of the ties with their old authorities and creates a tendency to rebellion, especially against the mother. I have observed several young girls who left their homes in a fit of rage when their mothers objected to their having interrupted their school work in order to plunge into strenuous and often not particularly important "war activity." The war gives them a well rationalized opportunity to satisfy the tendency to run away that exists in any case.

In observing feminine reactions to the war, one must distinguish between those that take place in the nondangerous hinterland and those that occur closer to the battle zone. In the first case, the war is chiefly experienced in fantasy, and unless the impact of external conditions produces an adjustment to reality, bizarre acting out often takes place, of the kind we have mentioned earlier in our discussion of puberty. Young girls of this type use the war as a rationalization and realize fantasies that otherwise would have been repressed. Fortunately, the opposite pattern of behavior can also be observed: many young girls who formerly let life pass them by, and displayed no particular interest in the community, are "awakened" through the war to purposeful activity and actually perform

valuable war work.   But even in these latter cases the limit of
real necessity is often crossed, and a gratifying and valuable
occupation is given up as soon as internal and external difficulties no longer need to be mastered.   In this situation the
freezing of workers to their jobs recently instituted by the
United States government performs a worth while educational task.

The closer the danger, the more active is woman's participation in the war, and not only as method of mastering fear.   In
all wars women awaken to activity when their children, husbands, and homes are threatened; because they often use the
same methods, we often confuse the different psychologic aims
they pursue.   Women's activity in war-stricken countries is
mobilized by the deepest motherly protective instincts; their
methods must often wear a masculine mask in order to assert
themselves.   In 1812, the Russian peasant women fought at
the side of their husbands as guerillas, often wearing men's
clothes, just as they do today.   They did not know anything
about the demands of equality, and after the war they perhaps
said once again with sadness: "He does not love me any more,
for he no longer beats me."

The psychology of women who voluntarily expose themselves
to the immediate dangers of war is different.   The wish actively to master dangers has a much more personal character;
it was there from the beginning, but here too, the closer the
danger, the more active the methods of mastering fear.   Eyewitnesses report that these actions often assume an intense,
hypomanic character.   In such cases, women are suddenly
overcome by states of anxiety and depression, especially when
there is a lull in their professional activity; this often provides a
motive for drinking and abruptly abandoning sexual inhibitions.
Rumors about the promiscuity of women working in the war
zones are doubtless exaggerated but not entirely untrue.   The
motives for this are numerous and deep-seated.   Many women
are driven to seek "experience" by their own restlessness and
fear; with others it is a frivolous, nonchalant attitude that

leads them abruptly to overcome their own sexual inhibitions. These women think that it is "part of their job" to behave like men in everything, that is to say, to drink, to be rowdy, and to have no sexual "prejudices." They remind us of Genia, who had frequent sexual intercourse with soldiers, not from sexual need, but because of her wish for equality.

In brief, the constant awareness of her active, direct participation in the war has become a psychologic necessity for the young girl as well as for the more mature woman. This participation sometimes serves simply the adaptation to reality, sometimes the sense of guilt, and sometimes the narcissistic feeling of self-importance. In young girls war activity often draws all the fantasies of puberty into its whirlpool. All the fears of this phase of feminine development—the fear of sexual experience, the fear of the approaching dangers of the reproductive function, the anguish caused by feelings of guilt and personal inadequacy—now coalesce to form one all-absorbing war fear.

The fear seizes not only them, but all human beings; some are aware of it, others disavow it. For many it is a fear of death, justified by reality, for others it is only a summons of fate, a provocation of the fear of death that always lurks in the human soul, repressed and postponed to a distant future. The intensified need for activity in all cases furthers the rational overcoming of this fear.

Along with these active methods of mastering fear, we simultaneously observe an increasing number of developments that indicate a strengthening of the regressive forces in the present emergency atmosphere. Adult women are re-experiencing adolescence in all its forms; mature mothers—especially after they are obliged to separate from their sons—fill their fantasy life with exactly the same contents as their adolescent daughters. During hours of solitude they evoke in detail the myth of the loving hero who dies a heroic death on the battlefield, and this masochistic girlish dream is completely separated from their realistic, often very absorbing everyday occupations.

This hero is now the absent son.   I know one case of a 50-year-old woman who, after her only son had joined the forces, fell ill with a grave form of agoraphobia, in which she repeated all her puberty fears.   As a young girl she had for a time suffered from a typical dread of open spaces and remained at home in order to protect herself from the realization of definite wishes.   The danger that threatened her now was that she might follow her son if she listened to her inner longing, which her adult self rejected as absurd.   For thirty-five years she had remained free from fear, even when separated from her son, and only the war tension mobilized this adolescent emotion in the aging woman

Girls and women who do not engage in this activity, either because they were always particularly passive or because they are paralyzed by the war fears, naturally fall into still greater dangers.   Either they escape to the protection of their homes, without taking part in war activities, or their participation assumes the character of complete passivity and devotion.   They especially fall into sexual dangers for which they are unable to carry the burden of responsibility.   From their ranks come many of the involuntary war mothers who are slowly becoming one of our war problems.

It is worth while to devote our special attention to war mothers as a psychologic problem.   Here, in many cases, the responsible factor is man's war psychology.   According to reports of eyewitnesses, the soldier's sexual readiness is particularly strong immediately before going into action, amidst intense preparations, or during lulls in the battle.   One observation confirmed from many sources suggests that in the face of the imminent danger of death, the need awakens in man to secure his own immortality, and in him too, quite unconsciously, the sexual act serves the reproductive function.   "Thou art me too now.   Thou art all there will be of me," says Robert Jordan in Hemingway's *For Whom the Bell Tolls*, and these symbolic words are very really experienced by many who believe themselves doomed to die.   In periods of increased tension human beings have a tendency to experience reality in a more primitive manner, that is to say, not only objectively, but also symbolically. The symbolic method of overcoming death often leads to consciously undesired but very realistic pregnancies, for girls who, because they sympathize with this unconscious desire of man, agree to his unexpressed proposal and let themselves be impregnated by the "unknown soldier." They are seduced not as a result of their own sexual excitation, but through serving the lust for life of others. This motive also plays a tremendous role in many young brides and unmarried girls who hasten to become pregnant by their husbands or lovers about to be drafted into the army. The desire to continue the relation with the departing man in this form and to secure a common future with him is certainly a factor in their behavior, but the danger of death that heightens the desire for a continuation of life is a much stronger although unconscious factor.

In the atmosphere of the war emergency, man, beset by fears of annihilation, experiences his own physical and spiritual projection into the woman through the sexual act much more strongly than at other times, and this feeling manifests itself in his unconscious urge to beget a child. Introspective men later become conscious of this urge and provide us with information about it that otherwise would come only from creative writers or the insane.

In this connection it is interesting to recall Strindberg's description of his own experiences. In a fit of morbid jealousy he was overwhelmed in a negative way by the same feeling that Hemingway's hero and our present day soldiers experience in a positive way. He believed that in his sexual experience with one whom he thought faithless he had given up a part of his soul. He was in despair because he had mixed his blood with hers and given her his own impulses; he wanted to take himself back, to reclaim that part of himself without which he could no longer live. Apparently, people who are mentally sound are under certain conditions subject to the same emotions that Strindberg experienced in insanity. In preparing themselves psycho-

logically for death they summon all the gods of life to their aid.
As for woman, the desire to continue her sexual relation with
her man in a child is always present in her, not only in wartime.
The ideas of death and of new life implicit in the act of propagation are also deeply rooted in the feminine soul. Now this
inherent disposition is accompanied by her identification with
the man—particularly when the love relation is good—and the
appeal to the gods of life manifests itself through the numerous
pregnancies that occur under the most unfavorable conditions,
against the conscious will of the woman involved.

Another frequent motive for war motherhood stems not from
woman's need for love, but from her doubts about this love.
Marriages are concluded in a hurry in order to silence these
doubts. She hopes that the expected child will strengthen a
relation that stands on insecure foundations, while her unconscious moral feeling demands that she give the man about to
face a hard and dangerous life every form of comfort and assur-
ance. The hazards of war and the importance the man acquires through them transfigure the relationship, and this,
together with pregnancy, that self-imposed proof of love,
facilitates the woman's task.

In general, all modes of reaction to the war emergency make
use of whatever means people have as individuals. Only
because the processes are identical in many individuals do they
develop into a mass phenomenon.

In this war we are learning how much woman's role in society
depends upon the environment. Women are leaving their
homes en masse; in various war services, uniformed or not, they
have been drawn into the fighting machine and their performance is good, often distinguished. But even today, after a relatively short time, a yearning for "home" is noticeable in these
women, and they keep at their jobs only so long as they are inspired by ideologic enthusiasm or are financially compelled to
work. But even if the strongly emotional motive to serve the
cause is present, women feel an increasing need for more personal, direct emotional experiences, for that life atmosphere in

which they play their passive feminine role, and in which they are more creative than in the war activities they have undertaken out of sheer necessity.

Competitiveness has not yet entirely taken hold of woman. Erotic and tender motives still dominate her, rather than aggressive ones. The ambition of women who have joined the ranks, like that of adolescent girls, takes the form of "See how well I'm doing this, love me more than the others." A humorous cartoon showing a girl in uniform pointing at her instructor and saying, "Look, isn't he (or she) cute?" expresses an actual fact in a naïve form.

Another effect of the war environment upon women might cause misgivings were it not temporary in character: the affective balance of woman's life fails when her work overtaxes her emotions. When very active, women do not seem to manage their emotional capacities correctly. They become poorer in feeling rather than richer in their direct, more personal object relations.

We must not let ourselves be blinded by the successful, useful, and "normal," that is, intensified war activity of women. We rejoice at their efficiency and capability, but we must not overlook the fact that many things that impress us as "activity" do not always stem from active forces. Along with active adjustment to reality and active work in the service of patriotic and social ideology, suggestions from the outside and autosuggestion often play a decisive role. There is a passive acceptance of the general mood. The passive and masochistic motive often concealed behind the active achievement still serves the "primeval feminine core."

There is no doubt that many women use the opportunity of being masculine, an opportunity created by the war, for the gratification of their wishes in this respect. The uniform and the coarse working overalls are a symbol of masculinity not only for women but also for men—for the latter in proportion as they feel that they are really passive and feminine, for the former in proportion to their active and masculine tendencies.

In men, this is a reaction to definite inner dangers; in many women the uniform serves a double purpose—gratification of their own masculinity complex and protection against social prejudices with regard to which they feel better equipped when they have a more masculine appearance.

Predictions, especially in periods of rapid and unexpected upheavals, usually prove false. Therefore we shall refrain from making any; we shall only weigh the possible postwar developments in the field of feminine psychology. In this we may be helped by our own personal experience in the past.

As a direct witness of European developments after the first world war, I saw the manner in which sex differences expressed themselves at that time. We shall not speak here of the increase in the passive-feminine tendencies of men. The masculinization of women was unmistakably expressed in their invasion of the masculine professions, the changes in their appearance, dress, coiffure, etc., and their energetic attempts to give their body structure a more masculine character. Reducing cures that often assumed bizarre forms and sometimes ended in death were supposed to overcome the inherent physical constitution of women. Sports activities, greater intellectualization, the one-child system so widespread in the European middle class, were the visible forms in which the turning away from femininity manifested itself. Unless our observation is erroneous, the strata of women that actively participated in the war effort were not carried away by this trend. The proletarian and petty bourgeois women, those who had really replaced men at hard work in factories, on railroads, etc., turned their jobs back to the men with a feeling of relief, and "hurried home." It also appears that in these very strata, despite the increasing misery and unemployment, the birth rate went up after the war.

In this country during the present war incomparably wider strata of women are active in occupational fields. As a result of the war the whole feminine world will become aroused to an interest in community problems and will be able to participate more fully in what has hitherto been a masculine activity. The masculinity complex will become less odious, because neurotic conflict will be replaced by a better sublimation less obstructed from without.   But the majority of women whom war has made more active than ever, will return as quickly and energetically as possible to the basically conservative because always dominant feminine experience, regardless of social and cultural upheavals.   The external forms of this experience will be adapted to the social changes and are at present unpredictable.

While we recognize the importance of social factors, we assume that certain feminine psychic manifestations are constant and are subject to cultural influences only to the extent that now one and now another of their aspects is intensified.   The primeval feminine Autonoë, the fertile Demeter, the motherless Pallas Athene, the androgynous Amazon, are all creations of mythologic fantasy; yet they seem to have really existed in all societies.   These prototypes of the feminine psyche recur constantly, always the same, yet always different, according to their culture, their race, and the degree of historical development of their society.   The façade may change, but the feminine core remains unchanged throughout all storms.

Bibliography

ABRAHAM, K.: Aüsserungsformen des weiblichen Kastrationskomplexes. Internat. Ztschr. f. Psychoanal., vol. 7, 1921. Manifestations of the female castration complex. Internat. J. Psycho-Analysis, vol. 3, 111, 1922.

ADDAMS, J.: The spirit of youth and the city streets. New York: Macmillan, 1930.

ALLENDY, R.: Sadism in woman. Psychoanalyt. Rev. 20: 437, 1933.

BACHOFEN, J. J.: Mutterrecht und Urreligion. Leipzig: Koerner.

BÁLINT, M.: A contribution to the psychology of menstruation. Psychoanalyt. Quart., vol. 6, 1937.

BASHKIRTSEFF, M.: Journal of a young artist. New York: Cassel, 1889.

BENEDEK, T., AND RUBENSTEIN, B. B.: The sexual cycle in women. Psychosom. Med. Monog., vol. 3. Washington, D. C.: National Research Council, 1942.

BENSON, S.: Junior miss. New York: Random House, 1941.

BERNFELD, S.: Die heutige Psychologie der Pubertät. Imago, vol. 13, 1927.

BLOS, P.: The adolescent personality. New York: Appleton-Century, 1941.

BONAPARTE, M.: Passivität, Masochismus und Weiblichkeit. Internat. Ztschr. f. Psychoanal., vol. 21, 1935. Passivity, masochism and femininity. Internat. J. Psycho-Analysis, vol. 16, 1935.

BORESFIELD, P.: The castration complex in women. Psychoanalyt. Rev., vol. 11, 1924.

BRIERLEY, M.: Some problems of integration in women. Internat. J. Psycho-Analysis, vol. 8, 1932.

——: Specific determinants in feminine development. Ibid., vol. 17, 1936.

BRODY, M. W.: An analysis of the psychosexual development of a female, with special reference to homosexuality. Psychoanalyt. Rev., vol. 30, 1943.

BRONNER, A. F.: Emotional problems of adolescence: The child's emotions. Chicago: Univ. Chicago Press, 1930.

BRUNSWICK, R. M.: Die Analyse eines Eifersuchtswahnes. Internat. Ztschr. f. Psychoanal., vol. 14, 1928. The analysis of a case of paranoia. J. Nerv. & Ment. Dis. 70: 1, 151, 1929.

——: The preoedipal phase of the libido development. Psychoanalyt Quart., vol. 9, 1940.

——: The accepted lie. Ibid., vol. 12, 1943.

Bühler, C.: Das Seelenleben des Jugendlichen. Jena, 1922.

Chadwick, M.: The psychological problems in menstruation. New York: Nerv. & Ment. Dis. Pub. Co., 1932.

[Chicago] Institute for Psychoanalysis: Growing up in a world at war. Chicago: Institute for Psychoanalysis, 1942.

———: Women in wartime. Chicago: Institute for Psychoanalysis, 1943.

Clothier, F.: Psychological implications of unmarried parenthood. Am. J. Orthopsychiat., vol. 13, no. 2, 1943.

Cobb, S.: Borderlines of psychiatry. Cambridge, Mass.: Harvard Univ. Press, 1943.

Colette [pseud.]: La vagabonde (ed. 42). Paris: Ollendorf, 1911.

Daly, C. D.: Der Menstruationskomplex. Imago, vol. 14, 1928. The menstruation complex in literature. Psychoanalyt. Quart., vol. 4, 1935.

Deutsch, H.: Psychoanalyse der weiblichen Sexualfunktionen. Vienna: Internat. Psychoanal. Verlag, 1925.

———: Psychologie des Weibes in den Funktionen der Fortpflanzung. Internat. Ztschr. f. Psychoanal., vol. 11, 1925. The psychology of women in relation to the functions of reproduction. Internat. J. Psycho-Analysis, vol. 6, 1925.

———: Der feminine Masochismus und seine Beziehung zur Frigidität. Internat. Ztschr. f. Psychoanal., vol. 16, 1930. The significance of masochism in the mental life of women. Internat. J. Psycho-Analysis, vol. 6, 1925.

———: Über die Weiblichkeit. Imago, vol. 19, 1933.

———: Über die weibliche Homosexualität. Internat. Ztschr. f. Psychoanal., vol. 18, 1932. On female homosexuality. Psychoanalyt. Quart., vol. 1, 1932.

———: Mütterlichkeit und Sexualität. Imago, vol. 19, 1933. Motherhood and sexuality. Psychoanalyt. Quart., vol. 2, 1933.

———: Ein Frauenschicksal: George Sand. Imago, vol. 14, 1928.

———: Über die pathologische Lüge (pseudologia phantastica). Internat. Ztschr. f. Psychoanal., vol. 8, 1922.

———: Zur Psychologie der manisch-depressiven Zustände, insbesondere der chronischen Hypomanie. Ibid., vol. 19, 1933.

———: Über bestimmte Widerstandsformen. Ibid., vol. 24, 1939. A discussion of certain forms of resistance. Internat. J. Psycho-Analysis, vol. 20, 1939.

———: Über einen Typus der Pseudoaffectivität—„als ob." Ibid., vol. 20, 1934. Some forms of emotional disturbances and their relationship to schizophrenia. Psychoanalyt. Quart., vol. 11, 1942.

Dollard, J.: Caste and class in a southern town. Publ. for Institute of Human Relations. New Haven, Conn.: Yale Univ. Press, 1937.

DOOLEY, L.: Psychoanalysis of the character and genius of Emily Brontë. Psychoanalyt. Rev., vol. 17, 1930.

EISLER, J. N.: Über hysterische Erscheinungen am Uterus. Internat. Ztschr. f. Psychoanal., vol. 9, 1923.

EISSLER, K.: On certain problems of female sexual development. Psychoanalyt. Quart., vol. 8, 1939.

ELLIS, H.: Studies in the psychology of sex. New York: Random House, 1928. Vol. 1, pt. 4; vol. 2, pt. 3.

FENICHEL, O.: Weiteres zur präoedipalen Phase der Mädchen. Internat. Ztschr. f. Psychoanal., vol. 20, 1934.

———: Zur Oekonomie der Pseudologia phantastica. Ibid., vol. 24, 1939.

FERENCZI, S.: Male and female: Psychoanalytic reflections on the "theory of genitality" and on secondary and tertiary sex differences. Psychoanalyt. Quart., vol. 5, 1936.

———: Masculine and feminine. Psychoanalyt. Rev., vol. 17, 1930.

FIGNER, V.: Nacht über Russland. Berlin: Malik, 1928.

FREISTADT-LEDERER, A. VON: In Erwartung der Menstruation. Ztschr. f. Psychoanal. Paedag., supp., Menstruation, vol. 5, 1931.

FREUD, A.: Das Ich und die Abwehrmechanismen. Vienna: Internat. Psychoanal. Verlag, 1936. The ego and the mechanisms of defense. London: Hogarth, 1937.

FREUD, S.: Drei Abhandlungen zur Sexualtheorie. Gesammelte Schriften, vol. 5. Three contributions to the theory of sex. New York: Nerv. & Ment. Pub. Co., 1910.

———: Über die Psychogenese eines Falles von weiblicher Homosexualität. Internat. Ztschr. f. Psychoanal., vol. 6, 1920; Gesammelte Schriften, vol. 5. The psychogenesis of a case of female homosexuality. Internat. J. Psycho-Analysis, vol. 1, 1920.

———: Beiträge zur Psychologie des Liebeslebens. Gesammelte Schriften, vol. 5. The taboo of virginity: Contribution to the psychology of love. Collected Papers, vol. 4.

———: Über einige neurotische Mechanismen bei Eifersucht, Paranoia und Homosexualität. Gesammelte Schriften, vol. 5. Certain neurotic mechanisms in jealousy, paranoia and homosexuality. Collected Papers, vol. 2.

———: Einige psychische Folgen des anatomischen Geschlechtsunterschiedes. Gesammelte Schriften, vol. 11. Some psychological consequences of the anatomical distinction between the sexes. Internat. J. Psycho-Analysis, vol. 8, 1927.

———: Das Ich und das Es. Gesammelte Schriften, vol. 6. The ego and the id. London: Hogarth, 1927.

———: Introductory lectures on psychoanalysis. Transl. by Joan Rivière. London: Allen & Unwin, 1929.

Freud, S.: Über die weibliche Sexualität. Gesammelte Schriften, vol. 12. Concerning the sexuality of woman. Psychoanalyt. Quart., vol. 1, 1932.

———: Psychology of women. In: New introductory lectures on psychoanalysis. New York: Norton, 1933.

———: Zur Einführung des Narzissmus. Gesammelte Schriften, vol. 6. On narcissism: An introduction. Collected Papers, vol. 4.

———: The economic problem in masochism. Collected Papers, vol. 2.

———: Motiv der Kästchenwahl. Gesammelte Schriften, vol. 10.

Friedlander, K.: Charlotte Brontë, zur Frage des masochistischen Charakters. Imago, vol. 26, 1941.

Hann-Kende, F.: Über Klitorisonanie und Penisneid. Internat. Ztschr. f. Psychoanal., vol. 19, 1933.

Hárnik, I.: Schicksale des Narzissmus bei Mann und Weib. Internat. Ztschr. f. Psychoanal., vol. 9, 1923. The various developments undergone by narcissism in men and women. Internat. J. Psycho-Analysis, vol. 5, 1924.

Hartmann, H.: Ich-Psychologie und Anpassungsproblem. Internat. Ztschr. f. Psychoanal., vol. 24, 1939.

Hayward, E. P.: Types of female castration reaction. Psychoanalyt. Quart., vol. 12, 1943.

Hendrick, I.: Work and the pleasure principle. Psychoanalyt. Quart., vol. 12, 1943.

Hitschmann, E., and Bergler, E.: Frigidity in women: Its characteristics and treatment. New York: Nerv. & Ment. Dis. Pub. Co., 1936.

Horney, K.: Zur Genese des weiblichen Kastrationskomplexes. Internat. Ztschr. f. Psychoanal., vol. 9, 1923. On the genesis of the castration complex in women. Internat. J. Psycho-Analysis, vol. 5, 1924.

———: Flucht aus der Weiblichkeit. Internat. Ztschr. f. Psychoanal., vol. 12, 1926. The flight from womanhood. Internat. J. Psycho-Analysis, vol. 7, 1926.

———: New ways in psychoanalysis. New York, Norton, 1939.

———: Die prämenstruellen Verstimmungen. Ztschr. f. Psychoanal. Paedag., vol. 5, 1931.

———: Die Angst vor der Frau. Internat. Ztschr. f. Psychoanal., vol. 18, 1932. The dread of woman. Internat. J. Psycho-Analysis, vol. 13, 1932.

———: Die Verleugnung der Vagina. Ibid., vol. 19, 1933. The denial of the vagina. Internat. J. Psycho-Analysis, vol. 14, 1933.

———: The overevaluation of love: A study of a common present-day type. Psychoanalyt. Quart., vol. 3, 1934.

———: The problem of feminine masochism. Psychoanalyt. Rev., vol. 22, 1935.

[HUG-HELLMUTH, H.]: Tagebuch eines halbwüchsigen Mädchens (ed. 2). Vienna, 1921. A young girl's diary. New York: Seltzer, 1921. (Publ. anonymously.)

JACOBSON, E.: Wege der weiblichen Über-Ich-Bildung. Internat. Ztschr. f. Psychoanal., vol. 23, 1937.

JONES, E.: Notes on Abraham, K. (see above). Internat. J. Psycho-Analysis, vol. 3, 1922.

———: The early development of female sexuality; Early female sexuality. In: Papers on psychoanalysis. London: Balliere, 1938.

KLEIN, M.: Introduction to child analysis. London: Hogarth, 1932.

———: The psychoanalysis of children. London: Hogarth, 1932.

KNIGHT, R. P.: Functional disturbances in the sexual life of women. Bull. Menninger Clin., vol. 7, 1943.

KOLLONTAY, A.: Wege der Liebe. Berlin: Malik, 1925.

LAMPL-DE GROOT, J.: Zu den Problemen der Weiblichkeit. Internat. Ztschr. f. Psychoanal., vol. 19, 1933. Problems of femininity. Psychoanalyt. Quart., vol. 2, 1933.

———: Zur Entwicklungsgeschichte des Oedipuskomplexes der Frau. Internat. Ztschr. f. Psychoanal., vol. 8, 1927. The evolution of the Oedipus complex in women. Internat. J. Psycho-Analysis, 9: 332, 1928.

LAWRENCE, D. H.: Sons and lovers. New York: Random House, 1922.

LEWIN, B. D.: Kotschmieren, Menses und weibliches Ueber-Ich. Internat. Ztschr. f. Psychoanal., vol. 16, 1930.

LORAND, S.: Contribution to the problem of vaginal orgasm. Internat. J. Psycho-Analysis, vol. 15, 1939.

MANN, T.: The transposed heads. New York: Knopf, 1941.

MEAD, M.: Sex and temperament in three primitive societies. New York: Morrow, 1935.

MEISENHEIMER, J.: Geschlecht und Geschlechter. Jena: Fischer, 1921.

MENG, H.: Über Pubertät und Pubertätsaufklärung. Ztschr. f. psychoanal. Paedag., suppl., Menstruation, vol. 5, 1931.

MENNINGER, K. A.: Psychogenic influences on the appearance of the menstrual period. Internat. J. Psycho-Analysis, vol. 22, 1941.

MICHAELIS, K.: Das Kind. Transl. from the Danish by M. Mann. Berlin: Axel Juncker.

MUELLER, J.: Ein Beitrag sur Frage der Libidoentwicklung des Mädchens in der genitalen Phase. Internat. Ztschr. f. Psychoanal., vol. 17, 1931. A contribution to the problem of libidinal development in the genital phase in girls. Internat. J. Psycho-Analysis, vol. 13, 1932.

MUELLER-BRAUNSCHWEIG, C.: Zur Genese des weiblichen Über-Ichs. Internat. Ztschr. f. Psychoanal., vol. 12, 1926. The genesis of the feminine super-ego. Internat. J. Psycho-Analysis, vol. 7, 1926.

NUNBERG, H.: Ichstärke und Ichschwäche. Internat. Ztschr. f. Psychoanal., vol. 24, 1939. Ego strength and ego weakness. Am. Imago, vol.
3, 1942.

OPHUIJSEN, J. H. W. VAN: Beiträge zum Männlichkeitskomplex der Frau.
Internat. Ztschr. f. ärztl. Psychoanal., vol. 4, 1916–18. Contributions to
the masculinity complex in women. Internat. J. Psycho-Analysis, vol.
5, 1924.

PAYNE, S. M.: Zur Auffassung der Weiblichkeit. Internat. Ztschr. f. Psychoanal., vol. 22, 1934 (transl. from lecture, Nov. 28, 1934, British Psychological Society, Medical Section).

PFEFFER, E.: Menstruation und Aufklärung. Ztschr. f. psychoanal.
Paedag., vol. 5, 1931.

PIPAL, K.: Wie es bei Hansi war. Ztschr. f. psychoanal. Paedag., vol. 5,
1931.

PLOSS-BARTELLS: Das Weib. Berlin: Neufeld, 1927.

RADO, S.: Eine ängstliche Mutter Internat. Ztschr. f. Psychoanal., vol.
13, 1927. An anxious mother: A contribution to the analysis of the ego.
Internat. J. Psycho-Analysis, vol. 9, 1928.

———: Fear of castration in women. Psychoanalyt. Quart., vol. 2, 1933.
Die Kastrationsangst des Weibes. Vienna: Internat. Psychoanal. Verlag,
1934.

———: A critical examination of the concept of bisexuality. Psychosom.
Med., vol. 2, no. 4, 1940.

RANK, B.: Zur Rolle der Frau in der Entwicklung der menschlichen Gesellschaft. Imago, vol. 10, 1924.

RANK, O.: Die "Matrone von Ephesus": Ein Deutungsversuch der Fabel
von der treulosen Witwe. Internat. Ztschr. f. ärztl. Psychoanal., vol. 1,
1913.

REICH, A.: A contribution to the psychoanalysis of extreme submissiveness
in women. Psychoanalyt. Quart., vol. 9, 1940.

REYMONT, L.: The peasants. New York: Knopf, 1924–25.

RICKMANN, J.: A psychological factor in the aetiology of descensus uteri,
laceration of the perineum and vaginismus. Internat. J. Psycho-Analysis,
vol. 7, 1926.

RINAKER, C.: A psychoanalytical note on Jane Austen. Psychoanalyt.
Quart., vol. 5, 1936.

RIVIÈRE, J.: Weiblichkeit als Maske. Internat. Ztschr. f. Psychoanal,.
vol. 15, 1929. Womanliness as a masquerade. Internat. J. Psycho-
Analysis, vol. 10, 1929.

ROTTER, L.: Zur Psychologie der weiblichen Sexualität. Internat. Ztschr.
f. Psychoanal., vol. 20, 1934.

Sachs, H.: Über einen Antrieb bei der Bildung des weiblichen Über-Ichs. Internat. Ztschr. f. Psychoanal., vol. 14, 1928. One of the motive factors in the formation of the super-ego in women. Internat. J. Psycho-Analysis, vol. 10, 1929.

Saussure, R. de: Le complexe de Jocaste. Internat. Ztschr. f. Psychoanal., vol. 6, 1920.

Schenken, C.: Menstruationsängste. Ztschr. f. psychoanal. Paedag., vol. 5, 1931.

Schmideberg, M.: Psychoanalytisches zur Menstruation. Ztschr. f. psychoanal. Paedag., vol. 5, 1931.

Searl, M. N.: A note on the relation between physical and psychical differences in boys and girls. Internat. J. Psycho-Analysis, vol. 19, 1938.

Seifulina, L.: Verinea. Berlin: Malik, 1925.

Spielrein, S.: Zwei Menseszräume. Internat. Ztschr. f. ärztl. Psychoanal., vol. 2, 1914.

Thompson, C.: The rôle of women in this culture. J. Biol. & Path. Interpersonal Relations, vol. 4, no. 1, 1941.

Tolstoi, L.: War and peace. Transl. by Louise and Aylmer Maude. New York: Simon & Schuster, 1942.

Vorwahl, H.: Erwartung und Eintreffen der Menstruation im Seelenleben der Mädchen. Ztschr. f. psychoanal. Paedag., vol. 5, 1931.

Werfel, F.: The Song of Bernadette. New York: Viking, 1942.

Williams, F. F.: Adolescence. New York: Farrar & Rinehart, 1930.

Winterstein, A.: Die Pubertätsriten der Mädchen und ihre Spuren im Märchen. Imago, vol. 14, 1928.

Wittels, F.: Mona Lisa und weibliche Schönheit: Eine Studie über Bisexualität. Imago, vol. 20, 1934. Mona Lisa and feminine beauty: A study in bisexuality. Internat. J. Psycho-Analysis, vol. 15, 1934.

———: Der psychologische Inhalt von Männlich und Weiblich. Imago, vol. 20, 1934.

———: A type of woman with a three-fold love life. Internat. J. Psycho-Analysis, vol. 16, 1935. Frauen mit dreigeteiltem Liebesleben. Internat. Ztschr. f. Psychoanal., vol. 22, 1936.

———: Die libidinöse Struktur des kriminellen Psychopathen. Ibid., vol. 23, 1937.

Zachry, C. B.: Emotion and conduct in adolescence. New York: Appleton-Century, 1940.

Zeromski, S.: Wierna rzeka (Faithful river). London: Kolib, 1940.

Index